"After counseling troubled teens and hurting parents for 25 years, I can say with m...
youth cult...
more of too...
addicted to...
thorough, ...
definitely a...

...t of
...mps

"The ...
organizatio...
today unde...
understand...
Having bee...
crying neec...
should have...
contempora...
—**B**...

"If you...
victory in th...
lasting, life-...
patience, ar...
discernmen...
tool for you....
life and wall...

"This fi...
Family is wi...
every day for the lives of our kids. This book will help you as a parent to become aware of what the enemy is doing in the music culture, and what you can do to guide and protect your kids from his lies. My thanks to the authors for creating a resource that I can use with my own teenagers."

— **Dawson McAllister**, host of the nationally syndicated teen call-in show, *Dawson McAllister Live*

Faith ✳ Hope ✳ Love

FROM THE LIBRARY OF

MARK & TERRI JAGOW

©CREATIVE GRAPHICS, EUGENE, OR 1-800-368-3671

"What I most appreciate about *Chart Watch* is that it does not give a wholesale condemnation of any particular type of music. Bob Smithouser and Bob Waliszewski give us a balanced, serious, relevant approach to the field of pop music. This is an area of constant change and cause of concern for parents of teenagers. *Chart Watch* is a tool parents will find helpful as they seek to guide their children in their love and appreciation of music."

—**Duffy Robbins**, Chairman, Department
of Youth Ministry, Eastern College

"*Chart Watch* is in the tradition of clear-sighted helpfulness that has always characterized Focus on the Family. As parents, we know that the music our children listen to shapes their souls for better or worse, and we can see it happening. But to be credible in our guidance, we must know the music in a way that our children will respect. This is the crucial accomplishment of *Chart Watch*—it helps equip us to approach our children in love and wisdom with the guidance they need and will respect amidst all the passions this topic provokes."

—**Dr. Alan L. Keyes**, educator, radio host, author, and former
candidate for the 1996 Republican Presidential nomination

Chart WATCH

Chart WATCH

From the editors of
Focus on the Family's

PLUGGED IN™

Bob Smithouser and Bob Waliszewski

Tyndale House Publishers, Wheaton, Illinois

CHART WATCH
Copyright © 1998 by Focus on the Family. All rights reserved.

Library of Congress Cataloging-in-Publication Data
Smithouser, Bob.
    Chart watch: more than 400 album reviews, and practical ways to help families make sound music choices / by Bob Smithouser and Bob Waliszewski.
    p.   cm.
    Includes index.
    ISBN 1-56179-628-X
    1. Rock music—Reviews. 2. Rock music—Discography. 3. Rock music—Moral and ethical aspects. I. Waliszewski, Bob. II. Title.
    ML156.9.S65 1998
    781.66—dc21   98-11829
                                                                        CIP

    MN

A Focus on the Family book.
Published by Tyndale House Publishers, Wheaton, Illinois.

Cover Design: Bradley Lind/H. Vincent Yorke
Cover Photos: ©1997 PhotoDisc, Inc.
Printed in the United States of America
98 99 00 01 02/10 9 8 7 6 5 4 3 2 1

*This book is lovingly dedicated to our wives, Leesa and Julie;
our children, Kelsey, Trevor, and Shelby; and above all, our
Lord Jesus Christ—the creator of music and the author of Truth.*

Contents

Acknowledgments xi

Foreword by Michael W. Smith xiii

Introduction:
   Our Approach to Music—and How You Can Best
      Use This Book 1

PART ONE

   Keys to Lyrical Literacy and Discernment

Chapter 1:
   Why We Can't Ignore What Music Is Saying 9

Chapter 2:
   The Need for Biblical Discernment 19

Chapter 3:
   Philosophical Hurdles Facing Today's Teens 27

Chapter 4:
   How to Make Discernment a Family Affair 37

PART TWO

   CD Reviews 51

Conclusion:
   You Can Impact the Music Industry 331

Artist Index 339

Album Index 343

Acknowledgments

On a park bench in downtown Colorado Springs—over a few New York-style hot dogs—we first presented the concept for this book to Focus on the Family Publishing's Al Janssen and Larry Weeden. More than skilled professionals, these men are dear colleagues who guided and encouraged us throughout the process. Thanks also to our editors Keith Wall and Betsy Holt for their trust, honesty, and insight, and to the folks at Tyndale for their commitment to this special partnership.

Creating a reference volume like this is actually more a "calling" than a labor of love. Long hours under headphones. Late nights studying liner notes and magazine articles. We couldn't have done it without the support of our families and others who either inspired or assisted directly in this work. We deeply appreciate the passion for families and teens upheld daily by Dr. James Dobson, H.B. London, Charlie Jarvis, and the rest of Focus's leadership. Thanks to our music monitoring mentor Bob DeMoss. Steven Isaac, Patti Gorrill, Cari Stone, and Julie Abel deserve credit for helping us track down lyric sheets, artist bios, and other elusive facts and figures. We'd also like to recognize Jim Cail for graciously scanning the CD covers, as well as for making every issue of *Plugged In* look *terrific!*

Last, and most important, praise and thanks to Almighty God for putting the burden for this project on our hearts and refusing to take it away despite seemingly insurmountable detours and delays. Lord, it's a privilege to look back and see Your hand at work. Thank You for letting us take part in this unique ministry of strengthening homes. May You receive all glory for whatever good comes from it.

Foreword

by Michael W. Smith

When I was approached to write the Foreword for this book, I was honored. As a father and musician who creates, performs, and produces music for the whole family, I understand the need for a music guide like this. As many of you know, I've toured the world as a recording artist, not only in church settings but at mainstream venues as well—and I know the impact that one song can make on someone's life. Music is a powerful outlet of expression and should not be taken lightly. The authors, Bob Smithouser and Bob Waliszewski, have created *Chart Watch* as a tool for parents to understand this truth and teach it to their children.

I love all kinds of music. But I realize I have a responsibility as an artist to present quality, uplifting music—both in its performance and writing, as well as in the lifestyle it promotes. As a father, I try to guide my children to listen to music that helps them express themselves *and* builds upon the moral values that my wife, Debbie, and I work to establish in our home.

I encourage you to listen to music as a family and help each other appreciate its beauty. But be wise in your selections. Teach your children to make good choices and help them find appropriate music that will put into words the situations they are facing. Yet also recognize that kids need music with which they can just have fun. So how can you equip your children with both entertaining and morally uplifting music? The gospel music industry can be a great resource for your family. It includes Christian artists who represent virtually every music style—from country to alternative to pop music.

You can find these artists at most music stores and in Christian bookstores nationwide.

From one parent to another, I encourage you to take the time to become familiar with this book. Bob S. and Bob W. have laid out this resource in an easy, understandable manner so you can walk through the lingo of the music business. Using *Chart Watch* as a guide to finding quality music, make sure to help your children find alternatives that meet your standards and theirs. May this book give you the tools you need to discern what music you and your child can live with—and which albums your family is better off without.

Introduction

Our Approach to Music—
and How You Can Best Use This Book

One of the greatest challenges as parents is helping our children achieve balance. We want them to enjoy their younger years, but we need to protect them from things that would undermine their physical and spiritual growth. It's a daily tightrope walk. For example, we want to provide a tasty diet, but also a nutritious one. We want them to wear attractive, comfortable clothes, but also modest attire that speaks well of who's *in* it. And when it comes to music, we want their listening to be fun, but *without* lyrics that promote violence, immoral sex, drugs, obscene language, or skewed theology. That's where *Chart Watch* comes in. This book will arm you with the information you need to successfully navigate the minefield of popular music in your home.

Over the past five years, Focus on the Family's Youth Culture Department has scoured the sales charts and pored over industry trade publications. We've kept a finger on the pulse of teens' musical tastes, dissected the hottest discs and processed that data into the 400-plus capsulized album reviews you now hold in your hand. Each entry includes a brief biographical sketch of the artist and a breakdown of the music's pro-social and objectionable content. Why so much detail? We've learned it's one thing to tell a child the CD they're interested in is either okay or off-limits; it's another to be able to articulate *why*. Armed with specifics, you now have an objective mediator in discussions about popular music.

But we didn't stop there. You've probably heard the saying, "If you give a man a fish, you give him a meal. But if you *teach* him to fish, you feed him for a lifetime." We want to teach parents *and*

1

young people how to fish. In the chapters that follow, you'll learn biblical principles of discernment that will help you raise your children to think critically about music for years to come.

<h2 style="text-align:center">BEFORE YOU BEGIN</h2>

Today's music frequently contains lewd sexual references or obscenities. While we tried to avoid being unduly explicit, at times it was necessary to reprint these specifics (toned down whenever possible) so that you would have an accurate reflection of the artist's lyrics. We apologize in advance for their offensiveness. Just remember that anything you see once in print, your children will be hearing—repeatedly and uncensored—if the music falls into their hands.

In addition, several music industry terms will pop up now and then that may or may not be familiar to you. When we refer to a record going "gold," that means it has sold 500,000 copies. A "platinum" disc has sold one million copies. Any time we mention an album or hit single's chart position, it is based on information published by the industry authority, *Billboard* magazine. If we cite a chart position without specifying *which* chart it came from (for example, R&B or country), you can assume the ranking is from the "big one"—the *pop* chart. Should we speak of an album's "lyric sheet" or "liner notes," we're talking about the thin booklet that accompanies a CD, which can include lyrics and information about (or statements by) the performers. By the way, you've probably already noticed that we use a number of terms interchangeably to describe a full-length recording (album, record, disc, CD, or project). That said, the rest is fairly self-explanatory.

To this point, we've attempted to give you a sense of what *Chart Watch* has in store for you. But it's also worth noting what this book is *not:*

◆ First and foremost, you'll discover that our purpose is *not* to judge music based on style. Other books—which often vehemently disagree with each other—have been written about the relative value of certain musical genres. That's another issue entirely, one we believe takes a back seat to the indisputable *lyrical* messages of the songs themselves.

◆ We don't operate under the assumption that anything produced outside of the Christian community is devoid of value. This book seeks to celebrate truth and condemn evil wherever it turns up. Whether or not an artist is a believer doesn't change the lyrical merit of a song about the love between a husband and wife, the importance of parenthood, chastity, honesty, sobriety, or personal sacrifice.

◆ We intentionally avoided using an oversimplified rating system (between one and four stars) or a grading scale (from F to A+) to brand each album. That would in many ways defeat the purpose of this book. Some parents might otherwise do themselves and their children a disservice by concluding, for example, that anything rated a B or higher is acceptable. Not necessarily. It is in examining the *evidence*—not a grade—that we gain understanding. Families should weigh all of the information provided against their biblically based family standard before passing final judgment on an album.

◆ We realize that a book like this could be used as a "hit list" by parents eager to raid their children's CD collections and purge them of any offensive material. If you're standing there with a Hefty bag in one hand and a sledgehammer in the other, hold on a minute. This text is no more a hit list for problematic CDs than it is a buyer's guide for the good stuff. Sure, we express some strong opinions about the material being marketed to our children, but the reviews are not a "license to kill." They are provided to assist you as you set standards for acceptable music in your home. That's why we've included discussion chapters about the inherent power of music, applying scriptural principles to song lyrics, establishing and upholding a "family standard," philosophical hurdles facing young people, and questions parents can ask to inspire critical thinking.

◆ You won't find reviews of any "best of" or "greatest hits" collections in this reference guide. Though some have charted very well, they feature material that has already appeared on previous albums—songs we most likely analyzed when they were *first* released by the artist. With all of the discs demanding our attention, we felt it best to try and avoid that kind of redundancy.

◆ At the conclusion of these secular reviews, we occasionally recommend similar-sounding alternatives from the world of Contemporary Christian Music (CCM). You might ask, "Why not include a chart at the back of the book featuring CCM comparisons to secular soundalikes?" Entire books have been published for that purpose alone. But as the recipients of thousands of letters from young people (in response to a column in Focus on the Family's teen magazines, *Brio* and *Breakaway*), we have become painfully aware that any CCM "substitute" offered had better be a stylistic bull's-eye. No one is more critical of well-intentioned near-misses than young music fans, and many mainstream artists just don't have dead ringers in the Christian arena. Every once in a while, we go out on a limb to make a comparison, but it would be misleading to try and match every secular artist with a CCM alternative.

We pray that, through this book, we can partner with you as you gently shape your child's character. There's no easy formula, no cute acrostic. If a foolproof, four-step program existed, we'd share it with you. However, through years of counseling parents by phone, reading their letters, and speaking to them at conferences, we've come to the following conclusions:

1. *Legalism* usually breeds rebellion as youngsters bide their time, waiting for the day they can sample the entertainment industry's forbidden fruit.

2. *Permissiveness* often leads to indecent exposure as children wander, aimlessly and wide-eyed, through the culture's musical enticements.

3. *Teaching discernment* encourages balance, leads to critical thinking based on clearly defined boundaries, bonds families, and gives children life skills they'll carry with them well into adulthood. Effectively dealing with the issue of setting and reinforcing musical standards takes lots of love, patience, communication, and prayer. But it *is* possible. And the rewards are great!

Part One

KEYS TO LYRICAL LITERACY AND DISCERNMENT

Chapter 1

◆ ◆ ◆ ◆ ◆ ◆ ◆ ◆ ◆

Why We Can't Ignore
What Music Is Saying

It's been more than 40 years since Elvis Presley recorded his first hit single, "Heartbreak Hotel." *Oh, how things have changed.* The psychedelic '60s. Polyester disco. Punk rock. Death metal. Seattle grunge. Gangsta rap. Ska. Since the King of Rock 'n' Roll shook the world with his pelvis, popular music has experienced quite an evolution—not just musically, but *lyrically.*

We recently got a call from a father struggling to understand the stuff his son was listening to. Having paid little attention to contemporary music since his own youth, this poor dad was floored by the sexual lyrics blaring through his teen's headphones. The tunes he described were nothing short of audio pornography. Sometimes it's hard to believe that our culture has allowed its music to reach the level of Nine Inch Nails frontman Trent Reznor screaming, *"I want to f— you like an animal."* But one thing's for sure—it didn't happen overnight. A brief look at some hit song titles from past decades reveals a telling chronology of moral erosion in pop music's romantic relationships:

◆ 1964—The Beatles sing "I Want to Hold Your Hand."
◆ 1967—The Rolling Stones make a much bolder overture with "Let's Spend the Night Together."

9

◆ 1972—The Raspberries encourage the object of their affection to "Go All the Way."

◆ 1975—Metaphorically speaking, Jethro Tull looks forward to a "Bungle in the Jungle."

◆ 1981—Even more to the point, Olivia Newton-John beckons a lover to get "Physical."

◆ 1987—Inhibitions and euphemisms disappear with George Michael's brazen declaration, "I Want Your Sex."

◆ 1991—Color Me Badd crudely and unflinchingly declares, "I Wanna Sex You Up."

◆ 1994—Exactly 30 years after The Beatles first proposed hand-holding, rapper R. Kelly scores a best-selling single with the sexually descriptive ode to intercourse, "Bump & Grind."

So much for modesty and self-control in courtship. Clearly, popular music has been at the center of a downward spiral—morally speaking—since the British Invasion. Other unhealthy agendas nothwithstanding, the music industry seems preoccupied with eroticism. If only we could return to the innocent days when it was a thrill just to hold someone's hand. Sadly, our culture has fueled and encouraged this decades-long musical decline . . . which is now being passed down as an inheritance to our children.

THE POWER OF MUSIC

Have you ever gotten a tune stuck in your head? All you need to hear are a few bars and it starts involuntarily buzzing around in there . . . *for hours.* It could be a commercial jingle or a Top-40 hit. Maybe you heard it in a shopping mall or a restaurant. We wander through a supermarket and find ourselves humming the last song we heard on the radio before getting out of the car. We carry a hymn from the morning worship service with us long into Sunday afternoon. We toss and turn in bed, trying to expunge an uninvited television theme song. And it's not just the music. The lyrics rattle around in there, too—some of which may be rather disturbing when we stop to think about them. The point is that music tends to travel with us. Good or bad, it rarely goes in one ear and out the other.

When I (Smithouser) was growing up in New Jersey, "bumper-hitching" was an ill-advised winter pastime of kids in my neighborhood. If you've never heard of it, bumper-hitching occurs on snow-packed roads when young daredevils grab the rear bumpers of slow-moving vehicles and slide along behind them. Similarly, catchy melodies have a way of grabbing hold of our subconscious and hitching a ride. They can sneak up behind us and hook on without much warning. Think back to a hit record from your own high school days. In fact, pick one you haven't heard for a few years (maybe Rod Stewart's "Maggie May" or Elton John's "Crocodile Rock"). It may come as a surprise how many of the lyrics you can recite verbatim.

I knew a guy in college who *constantly* drummed along with the music in his head. One day, a missionary girl from India was visiting our fellowship group and saw him pounding out an unheard rhythm. She remarked in broken English, "He has radio in his head." We laughed at her observation, but she was *right!* To varying degrees, we all do. And it's up to us to be the "program directors," shaking loose the negative messages that want to hitch a ride and consciously tuning in more edifying options.

Moreover, once a song gets inside of us, there's no telling when or where it may pop up. A youth pastor friend of mine told me about a time when he found himself sitting on the church platform in full view of the congregation when Eric Clapton's hit "Cocaine" invaded his attitude of worship. That tune—along with its troubling pro-drug message—was a flashback to musical choices he'd made during his youth.

Young people need to understand the pervasiveness of music, especially since today's recording industry produces, packages, and promotes some of the most destructive content ever. Much of it would have been considered pornographic a generation ago. Now it's winning Grammys. We need to challenge young people to be more mindful of the tunes they carry in their heads.

You'd Be Surprised What Gets Trapped in There

Music often tries to sell us products, services, or ideas. When NBC aired the *Seinfeld* series finale in May 1998, the network charged sponsors $2 million for just 30 seconds of TV commercial time. In some cases, advertisers used their half-minute to hook viewers with a catchy jingle. Why? Because they know it works. Music has a way of driving a message home. Want proof? Can you repeat the slogans "Like a good neighbor, State Farm is there" or "Oscar Meyer has a way with B-O-L-O-G-N-A" without hearing music? If you're like most people, the melodies come pretty easily.

Try singing the TV theme songs from *The Brady Bunch, Laverne & Shirley,* or *Gilligan's Island.* Chances are, those little ditties are also filed away, just waiting for a game of Trivial Pursuit. While exercises like these can playfully betray the human mind's capacity to retain harmless minutiae, they also reveal our ability to store *other* musically driven messages, some of which can manifest themselves in dangerous ways.

Can Music *Really* Influence Behavior?

Just recently, we heard the wonderful story of how a popular song persuaded a high school senior *not* to abort her baby. Despite being in her second trimester, Jill (not her real name) was convinced that a baby would hinder her future, so she stubbornly set out to end her pregnancy. She arrived at the doctor's office and was lying on the operating table when the Ben Folds Five song "Brick" came over the room's sound system. "Basically, the girl in the song is a high schooler going to get an abortion, and it's told from the boyfriend's perspective," the group's lead singer told *Teen People* [4/98]. Hearing "Brick" inspired Jill to get up from the table and leave the clinic. This song spoke to a teen's heart and impacted her behavior. It saved a life. Yet for every story like Jill's, there are many more without the happy ending.

A quiet Louisiana night in early May 1996. Two-thirty in the morning. While the rest of the world lay sleeping, 16-year-old Clay Logan stood in his bedroom listening to "The End," a song by the rock band The Doors. He waited patiently for his lyrical cue from lead singer Jim Morrison. Then it came. To wake his sleeping family, Logan cranked the volume. *"The killer awoke before dawn,"* the stereo blared. *"He put his boots on and came to a door and he looked inside."* The boy's parents, James and Connie, rose slowly, wiping the sleep from their eyes. The music continued, *"'Father?' 'Yes, son?' 'I want to kill you. Mother, I want to . . . kill, kill, kill, kill, kill, kill . . .'"* At that point, James and Connie were fully awake. The couple started down the hall to find out what was going on. That's where Clay met them, brandishing a handgun. He fired several times, killing his mother and wounding his father before James managed to wrestle the gun away from his son.

Clay Logan had talked about wanting to kill his parents on several occasions. No one took him seriously. Charles Ewing, a law and psychology teacher interviewed by the *Baton Rouge Advocate*, said such talk suggests that this type of crime is premeditated, but also stated, "The homicidal act, when it comes, appears to be a spontaneous, impulse act." Did hateful rock music cause Clay Logan to attack his parents? Probably not. But listening to "The End" certainly contributed to the "spontaneous, impulse act." Additional reports indicate that the 16-year-old made a steady diet of nihilistic fare. Photos of rock stars found in his room included one of the late Kurt Cobain. Spray-painted on the walls were lyrics by Marilyn Manson, whose band has sold T-shirts sporting the words "Kill Your Mom and Dad." Despite such evidence, there are still those who would foolishly assert that Clay Logan's media choices had nothing to do with the dark path he took that fateful night.

We only wish this were an isolated incident. Here are a few other fairly recent examples of life imitating art:

◆ Lyrics by the death-metal band Slayer have been connected to the 1995 rape, torture, and satanic sacrifice of 15-year-old Elyse Marie Pahler, whose body was discovered not far from her San Luis Obispo, California, home. A Christian, the virginal Elyse was selected and stalked by three teenage boys who wanted to commit the "ultimate sin against God" and earn their "ticket to hell." The youths convicted of this heinous crime had formed a rock group called Hatred. According to authorities, it was modeled after Slayer, a popular band whose perverse songs carry titles such as "Spill the Blood," "Necrophiliac," and "Kill Again." *Los Angeles Times* writer Chris Willman said of Slayer, "Nearly all [songs] deal with homicide, a fiery afterlife in hell, or a combination of the two." He went on to conclude that the band "aggressively mythologizes mass murderers." [1/17/91]

◆ "Hate is what I feel for you/I want you to know that I want you dead." Those lyrics from Silverchair's *Frogstomp* album have been put on trial along with two teens, Nicholas McDonald and Brian Bassett, accused of murdering Bassett's parents and five-year-old brother after Bassett reportedly gained inspiration from the song "Israel's Son." According to a spokesperson for the Australian grunge band, "The song seeks to criticize violence and war by portraying them in all their horror." That may be what Silverchair had intended, but Bassett apparently received a very different message.

◆ On September 7, 1994, officer William Robertson and his partner were responding to a call for police assistance when tragedy struck. As they pulled their van into a Milwaukee neighborhood looking for the alleged disturbance, one of the two teens who had placed the call signaled the other from a corner telephone booth. The trap was sprung. Using a high-powered rifle, a young sniper fixed the crosshairs of his telescopic sight on his prey, then fired. Robertson slumped dead in his seat. After an intense investigation, homicide detectives found that the murderers hadn't targeted Robertson specifically. The bored teens, who claimed

to be taking cues from rapper Tupac Shakur's album
2Pacalypse Now, simply wanted to kill a police officer for
amusement.

These are just a few tragic stories pulled from today's headlines. We could share many others, but it's not our intention to dis-
turb or depress you. We simply want to give you a glimpse of the
fallout we see regularly when families ignore the incredible power
of music to shape a person's sense of right and wrong. Admittedly,
these are *extreme* examples of how lyrics can impact attitudes and
behavior, but such tragedies prove that "harmless entertainment"
can be anything but harmless.

You're probably thinking, "My child would never go so far as to
commit murder." Few would. But how many teens will draw upon
the counsel of an erotic lyric in that moment when they're tempted
by a member of the opposite sex? How many will experiment with
drugs simply because a popular musician makes them sound appealing? There are many voices preaching to young people today. How
much impact they have on our children depends on our ability to run
interference as we protect and nurture emerging value systems.

WHAT *ELSE* IS THE INDUSTRY SAYING?

Someone once quipped, "'Tis better to remain silent and be thought
a fool than to open your mouth and remove all doubt." Musicians
have a penchant for waiving their right to remain silent, and what
comes out can be quite revealing. Audio snapshots. Unguarded
moments. We've gathered a number of priceless statements from
pop icons that say a lot about the music industry and the people in
it. What follows are high-profile examples of what Jesus alluded to
in Matthew 12:34 when He said, "Out of the overflow of the heart
the mouth speaks":

◆ "Our generation loves our pain, and if you dare f—ing take
it away from us, we're going to kill you. We like our pain.

And we're packaging it, and we're selling it." —*Popular folk-rocker* **Tori Amos** *[Rolling Stone, 11/17/94]*

◆ "We're more popular than Jesus Christ now. . . . Some of the pop stars I like are more important to me than God. . . . I would hope we mean more to people than putting money in a church basket and saying 10 Hail Marys on a Sunday." —*British rocker Noel Gallagher of the band* **Oasis** *[Newsweek, 7/21/97]*

◆ "Music is such a powerful medium now. The kids don't even know who the president is, but they know what's on MTV. I think if anyone like Hitler or Mussolini were alive now, they would have to be rock stars." *[Purr, Issue #5]* "If somebody kills themselves because of our music, then that's one less stupid person in the world." *[Rip, 2/95]* —*Gothic death-metal rocker* **Marilyn Manson**

◆ "Rock and roll should be about rebellion. It should p— your parents off, and it should offer some element of taboo. It should be dangerous." —*Nihilistic rock star Trent Reznor of the disturbing alternative/industrial act* **Nine Inch Nails** *[Rolling Stone, 3/6/97]*

◆ "My wish above all wishes about drugs is that we legalize them and grow them with love and understanding. . . . When I do really bad drugs, I'll get . . . mischievous spirits encouraging me to do things like set fires or, um, you know, kill." —*Perry Farrell, the lead singer with* **Porno for Pyros** *and cofounder of the hedonistic rock festival Lollapalooza [Details, 9/96]*

◆ "I think the Devil has gotten a bad rap. The Devil is the fallen angel, the one who was willing to embrace his dark side, whereas all the other angels were in total denial. The Devil is more like us—we're all the Devil and we're all

God." —*Folk-rocker* **Sarah McLachlan** *who, in the same interview, said it is her policy to act on various perverse sexual impulses [Details, 1/98]*

◆ "The older generation always complains that hard rockers are an angry, unstable bunch prone to violent, antisocial and frequently self-destructive behavior. In the case of most good, loud bands, they're right." —Rolling Stone *beat writer* **Jon Wiederhorn** *[Rolling Stone, 11/30/95]*

◆ "The best education [kids] could get is coming to a concert like this. There's a time in your life where everyone's got to tell someone to f—- off, so you might as well show someone how to do it." —*Punk band* **Green Day**'s *bitter lead singer, Billie Joe Armstrong [Entertainment Weekly, 12/23/94]*

◆ "[Troubled fans] write letters and come to the shows . . . hoping we can fix everything for them. But we can't. What they don't understand is that you can't save somebody from drowning if you're treading water yourself." —*Eddie Vedder, lead singer with the multimillion-selling alternative rock band* **Pearl Jam** *[Associated Press, 5/2/94]*

◆ "I remember looking at the outline of dead bodies and pictures of Charles Manson in my mom's copy of *Helter Skelter*, and I thought it was the greatest thing I'd ever seen. I was in kindergarten. Other kids loved baseball." —*Rob Zombie, lead singer with the heavy metal band* **White Zombie** *[USA Today, 6/28/95]*

◆ "Parents are easy to p—- off, so that's always fun to do. And we [recorded *Smash*] to p—- off conservative Jerry Falwell America." —*Dexter Holland, of the successful punk-rock band* **The Offspring** *[Rip, 10/94]*

Chapter 2

●●●●●●●●●

The Need for Biblical Discernment

O nce we acknowledge the power of music—and the willingness of some people to abuse it at our children's expense—we are faced with the issue of what to *do* about it. How do we help young music fans recognize the need for discernment? How do we equip our kids with the tools they need to make smart choices? We start with an understanding of how the messages carried within music fortify one of two forces engaged in spiritual conflict.

A BATTLE FOR DOMINANCE

A few years ago, I (Smithouser) satisfied an unfulfilled childhood urge by adopting a pair of baby iguanas. Liberty and Justice were about the same age and size when they arrived at their new home and, like any good father of two, I did my best to treat them equally. They scampered around the same 55-gallon aquarium. They drank from the same water dish. They soaked in warmth from the same hot rock and heat lamp. A Vita-lite shone on both. In short, my leathery pals shared an identical environment. There was just one noticeable difference in their lifestyles: diet.

While Liberty consumed fruit, vegetables, and various forms of protein, Justice was a very picky eater with a meager appetite.

Consequently, Liberty grew bigger and stronger—a richly colored, muscular animal. But lacking proper nutrition, Justice became more lethargic. She got thinner and assumed a paler shade of green. He matured. She wilted like a flower deprived of sunlight. From that point on, if Liberty wanted to bask on the hot rock, he commandeered it. If he chose to drink, she had to get out of his way. It was only a matter of time before Justice's poor diet (aggravated by Liberty's bullying) led to her death, leaving one healthy iguana to rule the aquarium.

This tale of two lizards serves as an illustration of the inner conflict facing Christians. Within each of us dwells two natures: the *flesh* and the *spirit* (John 3:6, Galatians 5:16-17, Ephesians 2:1-3). They share the same environment. Same body. Identical eyes, ears, and other senses. And like reptilian roommates, these two human natures, by definition, become territorial. Even adversarial. Each wants to rule the "aquarium" of our hearts and minds. The one that eats best will be the one that thrives. But keep in mind that the dietary preferences of the spirit and flesh are quite different from one another.

The spirit is nourished by Bible study, prayer, Christian fellowship, and serving others. According to Galatians 5:22-23, this holy regimen results in love, joy, peace, patience, kindness, goodness, faithfulness, gentleness, and self-control. It is to that end that God calls His children to engage in Spirit-led (Spirit-fed) living (John 6:63, Romans 13:14, Ephesians 4:22-24, Hebrews 5:14). However, the flesh has an appetite for junk food: music filled with profanity and graphic violence; songs celebrating rebellion, drug use, casual sex, or skewed theology. All believers have both natures at war within them, fighting for control. As one prospers and grows to dominance, the other nature, deprived of the food that fuels its development, withers.

The apostle Paul knew this internal struggle well (Romans 7:14-25), yet many teens don't understand its impact on daily decision making and overall spiritual health. Of those who do, a large percentage are tempted to compromise, confident that they're strong enough to resist the enemy's snares. We know this because hundreds of churched young people tell us so in letters we receive. "I just listen to the beat," they say, "not the lyrics." (If we were to offer one of those same teens $20 to rattle off the words to a song he supposedly pays no attention to, then how much would he remember?) As Paul warns in 1 Corinthians 10:12, such self-confidence can be a dangerous deception.

Which hungry nature are the teens in your life feeding? Which will dominate the "aquarium" of their hearts and minds? We must continue to teach youngsters to think critically and *Christianly* about music. In the daily battle between flesh and spirit, it's winner take all.

KEYS TO STARTING A HEALTHIER MUSIC DIET

Upon recognizing the wisdom of feeding the spiritual nature, children must then have the *discipline* to make that happen (James 1:22-25). Old habits die hard. And the flesh seems committed to refusing spiritual nourishment. That's why parents need to develop and nurture *new* habits in young music fans eager to go the distance for God.

Early in 1998, the Olympic torch burned bright over Nagano, Japan. Skilled athletes competed for the spoils of national pride and medals of untold personal value. For some athletes representing the United States, the road to the winter games ran through Colorado Springs, Colorado. That's where the U.S. Olympic Training Center is located—and where we were reminded of the importance of implementing a healthy music diet.

Judy Nelson serves as nutrition coordinator with the Olympic Training Center's sports medicine division. We talked about her role of providing dietary guidance to athletes. As we did, the apostle Paul's comparison of Christians to sportsmen in 1 Corinthians 9:24-27 took on new meaning. In part, that Scripture states, "Do you not know that in a race all the runners run, but only one gets the prize? Run in such a way as to get the prize. Everyone who competes in the games goes into strict training. They do it to get a crown that will not last; but we do it to get a crown that will last forever." Indeed, Christ's followers should stay in good spiritual shape.

Remember the old saying, "You are what you eat"? It can be expanded to include the music we consume. The parallels really are amazing. The more Judy described her relationship with aspiring Olympians, the more she unknowingly offered a prescription for adults who want to help young people develop a healthy media diet.

1. *Even good kids need coaching.* "You'd think that, being Olympic athletes, they'd eat what's good for them, but that's not always the case," Judy admitted. Does this sound familiar? Just as a body driven by an Olympic dream can be seduced by a Quarter Pounder with cheese, *good* kids from *solid* Christian homes and *dynamic* youth groups will be tempted to entertain themselves with tunes that are little more than audio junk food. It happens all the time. That's why parents need to guide even the most serious young Christians toward edifying choices.

2. *Reach, don't preach.* Judy has also learned that, in her profession, "preaching" nutrition doesn't work. Instead of giving athletes a rigid list of dietary do's and don'ts, she earns their respect by addressing each on his or her own level. They discuss personal needs and goals, and how the proper diet can help accomplish them. In the same way, a heavy-handed attempt at controlling children's music choices often breeds frustration. That's because presenting adolescents with a "hit list" of forbidden fare doesn't build critical-thinking skills or involve them in godly decision making. What does? Taking time to engage teens in dialogue about lyrical content and biblical standards in terms they understand.

3. *Maintain a healthy relationship.* Judy mingles with the athletes, building a rapport that earns her the *right* to give advice. Too many parents believe they have a license to lecture youngsters simply because they've been around the track a few more times. A close day-to-day relationship is vital to our effectiveness as counselors.

4. *Adapt diets to individuals.* Judy also recognizes that an athlete's age has significant impact on his or her diet. So it is with popular music. For example, even when using Philippians 4:8 and

Psalm 101:3 to establish a family standard for what plays on the family stereo, what might be acceptable listening for a teen may *not* be suitable for an eight-year-old sibling. Keep in mind that there are, of course, poisons that should not be consumed by *anyone.*

5. *Help children "dine out" wisely.* "[The athletes] eat best when they're here at the training center," Judy shared, "but if they're away at school or somewhere else, they can get into bad habits." Likewise, it's easy to control children's music diet at home or in church. But what about when they're at a friend's house? What happens when they go away to college? Adults teaching children to discern using biblical principles are the ones who truly shape their characters and equip them to run the marathon of a holy life.

6. *Accept your own limitations.* Finally, Judy Nelson realizes all she can do is offer prospective Olympians her wealth of dietary wisdom. She can't feed them. And though we hate to admit it, we can't indefinitely control the music diets of the young people we love. After we've done our prayerful best to give them healthy guidelines, it's up to *them* to bring home the gold.

LIMITING SPIRITUAL CASUALTIES IN THE CIVIL WAR OF VALUES

As Dr. James Dobson so aptly stated in his book *Children at Risk,* we are presently engaged in a "civil war of values." Music is one weapon in the enemy's arsenal, and it is racking up young casualties. Consider Elliot from Minnesota. In response to a commentary denouncing Tupac Shakur's disturbing lyrics and lifestyle, this teen sent us a letter adamantly expressing his displeasure. A staunch Tupac fan, Elliot felt we had been unfair by focusing on the album's raunchy, cop-killing, pro-drug lyrics (about 98 percent of Shakur's *Me Against the World* CD). He cited the disc's lone positive message, a song called "Dear Mama," in order to defend the gangsta rapper's entire body of work!

Casualty number two: A Michigan father wrapped up a stack of his 14-year-old's CDs and sent them our way. All but one bore an explicit lyrics sticker. The accompanying letter exposed this dad's intense pain as he wrote of their estranged relationship. He said, "My son is hooked on this degrading, offensive music. . . . After 14 years of Christian schooling, church, and Sunday school, he is rejecting Jesus and Christianity." He closed by pleading, "Please get the word out to parents before their children fall for this God-insulting music."

Letters like these underscore the importance of equipping our children with the tools to make wise decisions *for themselves* about music. And some do a good job. A mom from California explained that, during a visit to the mall, her 13-year-old daughter asked for permission to buy Alanis Morissette's CD, *Jagged Little Pill.* "Remembering the [artist's] name from your *Plugged In* newsletter," she said, "I told her to wait until I could read the review. When I saw the corrupt messages included in Morissette's music, I encouraged my daughter to read the review as well. Not only did she choose to pass on buying the CD, but she also made copies of the *Plugged In* story for three friends."

Unfortunately, when it comes to determining what's "in bounds" and what's "out of bounds," many families are in a quandary. As a matter of principle, some parents reject virtually *everything* released in the mainstream. They believe it's the "safe" route. Meanwhile, the child is telling himself, "Just wait till I move out someday; I'll listen to whatever I want." Other parents search for a happy medium, but find it frustrating trying to determine where to draw the line—with their kids equally confused. What then is a workable approach that allows youngsters the freedom to be "entertained" without the harmful side effects?

For the most part, young people who successfully navigate the land mines of today's entertainment are the ones whose parents take an active part in teaching and modeling wise choices. Just as we taught our children elementary skills, such as tying shoes and riding a bike, we must encourage them to ask this question when selecting music: "Would Jesus listen to this?" No matter what your child's age, it's not too late to introduce this litmus test. We've even seen it bear fruit in toughened adults.

Meanwhile, it is essential that you and your spouse model wise choices yourselves. Teens can smell hypocrisy a mile away. Nothing lasting can be accomplished if the sum total of "teaching" discernment is for Dad to say, "No watching MTV in this house!" as he parks in front of *Baywatch*. Or for Mom to lay down the law about modern music while neglecting to switch off the car radio when it starts blasting Billy Joel's "Only the Good Die Young." Musical discernment isn't just taught; it's *caught*.

Chapter 3

Philosophical Hurdles Facing Today's Teens

We've already established the inherent power of music, exposed some of the industry's immoral pied pipers, and alluded to the way inflammatory lyrics can fuel inner conflict. We've talked about developing healthy "music diets," and suggested some ways you can lay a solid foundation for teaching discernment in your home. So, are you motivated to lovingly engage your kids on this issue? Are you now encouraged that you can fine-tune their thinking and inspire them to cut the chaff out of their music libraries? Good! But before you get started, allow us to prepare you for a few philosophical curves you're likely to encounter on the road to discernment—especially if you're dealing with adolescents.

CONFUSING "TRUTH" AND "REALITY"

Can you articulate the difference between "reality" and "truth"? Think about it for a minute. "Reality" reflects the varying conditions and circumstances that characterize our world. "Truth," on the other hand, is objective, eternal, and absolute. For the Christian, it begins and ends with the Word of God. Why the pop quiz? Our ability to make that distinction—and teach it to our teens—is vital if we expect youngsters to develop critical thinking skills and make God-honoring entertainment choices.

Of the hundreds of letters we receive from churched teens about media issues, the most disturbing ones reveal spiritual confusion and a stubborn lack of discernment. Specifically, if we object to an album that romanticizes sin, we're told to lighten up because the artist is singing about "real life." It's sad, but many adolescents judge entertainment's appropriateness based on the changing reality of the world around them—*not* on the unchanging truth of God's Word.

Once, when we questioned some of the themes running through popular music, a girl named Sarah wrote, "Music and spiritual beliefs are two different things. Sex, drugs, alcohol—those things are all found in more places than in music. It is *reality*." She didn't try to refute our evidence; she simply deemed it irrelevant.

When we disapproved of an openly homosexual band promoting the gay lifestyle from stage, Kristen said, "I think you need to face *reality*. I don't mind homosexuality. You need to realize that you can't turn your back on *reality*."

Elsewhere, Matt objected to our disdain over obscenities and the glorification of alcohol in pop tunes. "In case you haven't noticed, there's a *real world* out there," he chided. "A little profanity and alcohol won't send you to hell in a handbasket." Maybe not, but compromise in the realm of entertainment is often symptomatic of a heart prone to waffle in other areas as well.

Several of our young critics have even stood up for MTV and its promotion of condoms and the safe-sex message. A girl named Ellen told us to "check back into *reality*." Another young man defended the network by saying, "I think that MTV is getting teenagers ready for the *real world*." If worldliness is what young people aspire to, he's right. But God calls us to embrace a higher standard. Holiness. Purity. Christlikeness. After all, if floating along on the cultural course of least resistance were acceptable, Jesus—the Truth—would have had no reason to rescue us from the worldly status quo.

Truth can set us free (John 8:32), sanctify us (John 17:17-19), and purify us (1 Peter 1:22). "Reality" cannot. Truth, as found throughout Scripture, gives us a reliable set of unwavering parameters to live by. Reality is affected by time and manipulated by the agendas of man.

Every month, we field questions like, "I know Pantera uses the f-word, and sings about drugs and suicide, but is it okay for a Christian to listen?" The answer should be obvious. Yet for many young adults, it isn't. Let's change that. Let's give young people an eternal perspective that elevates truth above trends. If we indiscriminately absorb "reality-based" lyrics, our attitudes and actions will reflect the world around us. If we dwell on truth, we will live truth. But to make that choice, teens must first understand the difference. A study of John 10:10, Romans 12:2, 2 Timothy 3:1-9 and 4:3-4, and 3 John 4 is a great place to begin.

DISTINGUISHING BETWEEN "TOLERANCE" AND "COMPROMISE"

Respecting others and embracing the many facets of humankind is, at its roots, a virtue. It engenders racial harmony. It enables men and women to appreciate one another's uniqueness. It even allows punk rockers and country music fans to peacefully coexist. But that virtue can become a liability for teens unable to distinguish between *diversity* and *perversity*.

When we suggested to teens that a concert featuring an openly gay band spewing pro-homosexual lyrics isn't exactly appropriate for Christian teens, we didn't figure it would generate much controversy. We were wrong.

"Please quit looking at gay bands as a bad thing," Leah scolded. "You are creating homophobia. Having many friends who are homosexuals, I love and respect them."

Amid a flurry of PC buzzwords, Becky said, "There is nothing wrong with opening with a gay band. It's great that they are open about their sexual preference. Being gay does not make them different in a bad way, or bad people. Maybe we need more gay bands to be open so then there won't be as much homophobia. I think we need to keep an open mind and respect others' preferences and style and even learn a little from them."

A girl named Vickey stated, "I am really upset about your comment on homosexuality. You make it sound like it's a horrible thing. I thought that if you believed in Christ, you were supposed to love your neighbor and not judge people."

Similarly, Gretchen counseled, "As Christians, we should accept people as creations of the heavenly Father, regardless of race, socio-economic class, or sexual orientation." Yet another parroted, "I think you should remember the verse about not judging others."

Students of Scripture realize that judgment has already been passed on those who persist in immorality. The same Bible that promises eternal life promises judgment (Exodus 32:34, Romans 6:23). Jesus—not tolerance—will rescue them. By pointing this out to people lost in sin, whatever that sin may be, we can help them avoid a fate similar to the one mentioned in Genesis 19:23-29.

Speaking the truth in love—now that's real love. It's how Christ dealt with the woman caught in adultery (John 8:1-11). He forgave her and told her to leave her life of sin. He didn't say, "I'm okay, you're okay. It's just an alternative lifestyle." But many teens ignore God's desire for us to lovingly confront sin. They instead pride themselves on being "open-minded," "tolerant," and "respectful" of immorality. This raises the question, "How long will it take some youngsters to go from *respecting* sin to *experimenting* with it?"

Sometimes, disoriented drowning victims will actually fight the person trying to save them. After reading these bitter responses to our cautionary column, we know how the lifeguard feels! You may encounter similar resistance in your home. If so, you're not alone. We live in an ocean of immorality, harmful trends, and flawed ideologies. And a lot of adolescents—even those from good Christian families—are sinking fast without realizing it.

"Tolerance" and "love" are two very different things—a truth young people must grasp. We're called to love all men in the name of Jesus, not ignore their debauchery in the name of diversity. Love the sinner; hate the sin (Psalm 97:10). That means showing compassion to the lost without sanctioning their depravity—or cheering wildly as they perform from stage. Matthew 5:13-16 and 2 Samuel 12 are also good places to start a family discussion about the need to take a loving stand for what's right.

AN UNWILLINGNESS TO DRAW THE LINE

We've already alluded to the fact that some teens have a hard time drawing the line and taking a stand. These days, it's chic to be "open-minded" and "tolerant" of different points of view, no matter how immoral or ungodly. A 1994 Barna Research Group/Josh McDowell Ministries survey of 3,795 *evangelical churched youth* revealed that, during a three-month period, the following was true:

◆ 66 percent lied to a parent, teacher, or other adult
◆ 59 percent lied to their peers
◆ 45 percent watched MTV once a week
◆ 36 percent cheated on an exam
◆ 23 percent smoked a cigarette or used some other tobacco product
◆ 20 percent tried to physically hurt someone
◆ 12 percent got drunk
◆ 8 percent used illegal, nonprescription drugs

This study also revealed that, at some point in their lives, 55 percent of the teens surveyed had engaged in sexual intercourse or behavior. Perhaps this is merely symptomatic of a much deeper problem. Only 29 percent disagreed with the statement, "When it comes to matters of morals and ethics, truth means different things to different people. No one can be absolutely positive they have the truth." More than half agreed that "everything in life is negotiable" (55 percent), didn't think humans are capable of "grasping the meaning of truth" (56 percent), and didn't acknowledge any objective standard of truth (57 percent). That's sad. It's also scary. When even "Christian" teens don't accept the Bible as an absolute, unwavering, and objective standard of truth, it makes our job much harder as we try and teach them to resist the undertow of moral relativism.

But truth and error do exist. And teens must learn to draw a line between them. Paul's letter to the Thessalonians makes a sharp distinction between good and evil, and demands that we do the same: "Test everything. Hold on to the good. Avoid every kind of evil" (1 Thessalonians 5:21-22). Why? Just like the fleshly and spiritual natures, good and evil can't live in harmony together.

When we put something to the test and distinguish between right and wrong, inevitably someone who disagrees with our evaluation will quote Matthew 7:1: "Do not judge, or you too will be judged." Ever been there? It's important to remember that, in this verse, Jesus was warning against judging others' thoughts, motives, and the *hidden* things of the heart that only God can see. It *doesn't* mean we should ignore sin (or sinful lyrics) and refuse to practice discernment. Christian teens tell us things like, "I know this band sings about getting high and having sex, but I'm going to keep listening because I don't think God wants me to be judgmental." Wrong! That's exactly what God wants. In cases like this—when evidence is clear—we're commanded to judge between right and wrong, truth and error, good and evil.

Similarly, 2 John 10-11 warns, "If anyone comes to you and does not bring [God's] teaching, do not take him into your house or welcome him. Anyone who welcomes him shares in his wicked work." John had harsh words for "deceivers" who would attempt to undermine the truth of Scripture. He cautioned his readers not to even *invite them home*. There are lots of deceivers in the music industry today. And even Christians are carelessly inviting them into their homes. They purchase CDs glamorizing premarital sex and play them on the family stereo. They welcome violent music videos into their living rooms and load cassettes splattered with obscenities into their portable tape players.

We don't want to imply that every artist lands at either a "black" or "white" extreme on the spectrum of lyrical acceptibility. And while some *issues* are black and white, the way they're handled in a given song may *not* be. There are definitely "gray areas" that must be traversed carefully and with prayer. Still, that doesn't excuse us from setting boundaries. We have to take the aforementioned scriptures seriously and draw a line. True discernment is impossible if teens refuse to do so.

AN EAGERNESS TO EMBRACE *ANY* ARTIST WHO THANKS GOD

"I wanna first give thanks to God, who made all this s—— possible," writes Ricardo "Kurupt" Brown in the liner notes of *Dogg Food*, the number-one debut album from rappers Tha Dogg Pound. His partner, Delmar "Daz" Arnaud, adds, "I'd like to thank the Lord Jesus Christ, King of my Life." In the case of *Dogg Food*, Jesus basically gets credit for helping the duo pen such lyrics as, "I'm in the mood for murder" and "Show me your [whore] and I'll be f——ing that b—ch till midnight."

Sadly, Tha Dogg Pound is not alone among popular musicians who misuse the Lord's name in an attempt to justify offensive messages. From liner notes to awards shows, it has become increasingly trendy in the music industry for artists to pay lip service to God while ignoring His command "to live a holy life" (1 Thessalonians 4:7). Unfortunately, many teens latch onto these spiritual claims as confirmation that the artist's music is acceptable—regardless of its lyrical content.

On the liner notes of Stone Temple Pilots's *Core* CD, the alternative rock band states, "[We] would like to thank: God, Jesus Christ. . . ." That same disc includes "Sex-Type Thing," a song defending rape.

Numerous R&B artists, from R. Kelly to Puff Daddy (both of whom made God central to their statements at the 1998 Grammy Awards), also mix spirituality and sexuality. For example, Adina Howard thanks God in the liner notes of *Do You Wanna Ride?*, yet sees nothing inconsistent about featuring tunes on the project such as "Horny for Your Love" and "You Got Me Humpin'." Likewise, Usher says in the notes of his *My Way* disc, "First and foremost, I would like to thank my Lord and Savior Jesus Christ for allowing me to successfully complete my second album." What's on it? Perverse sexuality, infidelity, and the glorification of cocaine.

Regrettably, the media has yet to recognize that Jesus and perverted, explicit sexuality don't mix. *USA Today* [9/18/95] acknowledged Jodeci's "spirituality," in part because "the group thanks God in album credits and believes it has a responsibility to help others." But somehow the newspaper failed to see any hypocrisy between the hip-hop group's overtly sexual messages (doin' some "freaky s——," "feeling so horny," "humpin'") and the tribute to Christ printed in the liner notes. Even the Christian community has bought into the group's double standard. According to Jodeci's publicity material, when the quartet returns home, "the church musicians know it's their day off" because the foursome "can be found singing their hearts out, giving thanks to God for his blessing and all their success."

Female rappers Salt-N-Pepa, on their *Very Necessary* CD, credit "my Lord and Savior Jesus for life, health, strength, and guidance." In the case of Salt-N-Pepa, that "guidance" evidently led to the violent "Heaven or Hell" ("Ask me any questions and my Smith and Wesson will answer") and "None of Your Business," a tune defending prostitution as a viable career. The latter song is quick to accuse potential critics of playing God ("The moral of this story is who are you to judge? There's only one true Judge and that's God. So chill and let my Father do his job"). Such attempts to fend off criticism are common. As a result, fans are faced with a decision: Do I judge the music, or do I "chill" and leave it up to God? In an effort to avoid "judging," even some Christians have been tempted to ignore the Lord's command of 1 Corinthians 5:11, which states, "But now I am writing you that you must not associate with anyone who calls himself a brother but is sexually immoral." Therefore, we need to help young music fans sort through two-faced liner notes and hypocritical displays of "reverence."

GOOD NEWS: MANY TEENS ARE
HEARING AND EMBRACING TRUTH!

Based on what you've read in this chapter so far, you could easily conclude that teens carry entirely too much philosophical baggage to ever embrace biblical truth. Is this generation hopeless? *Absolutely not!* In fact, we've been told that our biblical analysis of secular music in Focus on the Family's magazine for teen guys, *Breakaway,* is one of the publication's most popular features. Those young men long to hear what we have to say. Even if they disagree with us, they're interested in knowing what adults think of their music and are willing to listen because we've taken the time to thoughtfully *enter their world.* Too many kids glean their values from the latest bands by default. The lyrics have the last word because no one bothers to challenge them. If you are willing to use the material in this book to tenderly enter your child's world, you may be surprised at how receptive he or she is to the discernment message.

A young *Brio* magazine reader named Julie wrote to us recently and said, "Thanks to your reviews, I'm now undergoing major music reconstruction. You've given me that extra push to dump some really misdirected bands." Refreshing! What's even more reassuring is that Julie isn't the only young Christian choosing to practice discernment in this media-soaked culture.

Cori took issue with a Christian singer lending her voice to "a movie that was nothing but trash." Cori went on to ask, "How can she stand against sexual immorality, drinking, and cussing, and then go and sing a song for a movie that promotes that kind of thing?" A valid question.

Sure, many of the teens who write us dig in their heels in defense of explicit musicians and MTV. But the sound judgment demonstrated by Julie, Cori, and others offers hope. It proves that pockets of wisdom do exist among adolescents. Many young people are asking tough questions and challenging the notion that pop culture has the answers . . . even if they can't possibly dodge every offensive message aimed squarely at their innocence.

A few years back, my wife and I (Smithouser) bought a golden retriever puppy. For the record, Scout is a bright, generally well-behaved dog perpetually eager to please us. But on one cold winter day, our furry friend came bounding toward the door after playing outside, her once-silky paws now wet, gray, and matted with dirt. I was just about to scold her when I quickly scanned the backyard. Months of melted snow had saturated the ground, creating a muddy mess from one end of the property to the other. The poor animal couldn't help but get some mud on her paws. Instead of reprimanding her, I gave Scout a big hug and thanked her for not *rolling* in it!

The music industry is a muddy mess. And these days, even good-hearted, compliant, spiritually discerning teens trying hard to navigate that lyrical landscape will wind up with some dirt on their paws. It's inevitable. While turning a radio dial, they stumble upon a raucus ode to sexual freedom. They hear music full of angst and hopelessness in the mall or on the school bus. While at a burger joint, they're assaulted by Top-40 tunes promoting immodesty and materialism. Dirt. Mud. Slime.

Though we wish our kids could take a more sanitized route, most teens trot through some muck on their way to wisdom. Julie and Cori did. The key is that they found their way back to the house. While this is certainly not an excuse for teens to dabble in dirt, if you see only traces of mildly problematic music coming through the door with your child, don't overreact. If anything, give them credit for not *rolling* in it. Keep in mind that there's a big difference between Garth Brooks and Korn. Being soiled by a little Boyz II Men shouldn't set off the same alarm as would a romp through some Snoop Doggy Dogg. But in any case, a calm, level-headed reaction will win you points while paving the way for more productive, ongoing communication.

Chapter 4

How to Make Discernment
a Family Affair

A s you've probably noticed, teaching discernment in the realm of popular music is a process. To this point, you've acknowledged the cultural problem, examined it, and decided to do something about it in your home. Now it's time to consider a family standard by which all things are measured and to nurture the parent-child communication that makes discernment possible.

ESTABLISHING A FAMILY STANDARD

Since it's unrealistic to declare music entirely off-limits, each family must decide where to draw the line based on a study of Scripture, fervent prayer, and an understanding of each child's maturity, critical thinking skills, and commitment to holiness. We've worked with enough parents over the years to know that thoughtful Christian adults differ *substantially* on this issue. Some have zealously outlawed secular music in their homes, confident that God has led them to that decision. Others let their children listen to almost *anything*, provided they talk about it first. Between those extremes lies a broad range of possible approaches, one of which will be the right fit for your family.

Once you and your spouse have prayerfully settled on an appropriate balance between *shielding* your children from mainstream

37

music and *discussing* it with them, articulate that decision in writing. Develop the equivalent of a "family constitution" as it relates to music habits in the home. Take your time. Ponder the specifics for several days and give the Lord a chance to speak to you about the matter. It will help you work through those "gray areas." It's also important that you and your spouse be of like mind as you lovingly lay down the law (after all, it will be up to both of you to enforce it). Use the previous chapters in this book to help your children see the need for discernment. Then stick to your guns. Make it clear that all members of the family are subject to the newly established boundaries. (Note: This can be an especially daunting task if your spouse doesn't share your vision for musical purity, or you are a single parent whose child spends time with a permissive ex-spouse. In such cases, ask that your rules be respected, pray for everyone involved, and take comfort in the knowledge that you're doing the best *you* can.)

If you have small children yet to request their first CD, consider yourself blessed. Your job will be easier. They can *develop* their music habits in accordance with your constitution. On the other hand, if your children have already become fans of questionable content, you face an entirely different challenge. You can start operating under the new standard "from this day forward," but you and your spouse must determine how to deal with the garbage already piled up in your child's music collection. Here are some possible scenarios:

◆ After discovering the need for discernment, your teen may feel supernaturally convicted, and *voluntarily* purge the junk from his CD library.

◆ You can humbly accept responsibility for taking too long to "set the boundaries" and agree to replace the offensive discs with ones that meet the family standard. Since you're picking up the tab, you may even want to limit "substitutes" to edifying projects by popular *Christian* artists.

◆ A local pawn shop or used CD store might pay two or three bucks apiece for the discs you're anxious to get rid of. Since you probably don't want to put those recordings back into circulation, you can agree to purchase them from your child at the same rate and *then* break out the sledgehammer and the Hefty bag. (Hey, they're *yours* now. You can do anything you want with them!)

◆ If you have one or two "out-of-bounds" albums still in good condition, you can try returning them to the store that sold them to your child. Some retailers will refund the purchase price—or offer store credit—to a parent who returns a disc because of its offensive content.

After the family has waded through everyone's music, measured the lyrics against the family standard and weeded out everything that flunked the test, you're ready to start fresh. Be diligent. Hold firm to the new guidelines. From now on, if your youngster asks to purchase a CD, you can confidently say, "Sure, but when you bring it home, we'll review the lyrics together, and if it doesn't meet the family standard, I take the CD and you're out the money." No more excuses. The constitution is in writing and they can read it for themselves. Rest assured, if your children know it's *their* $13 on the line, they'll be much more selective about which artists they invite home.

WHEN YOU CAN'T TUNE IT OUT, TRY TEACHING

Articulating a family standard is a vital step in the discernment process. But even after we've done that, our children can *still* get blindsided by garbage: An offensive commercial on an otherwise positive TV show. An obscene bumper sticker. An unsavory T-shirt. If you're like me (Waliszewski), you want to scream, "Close your ears, kids! Shut your eyes!" My family is careful when it comes to the messages we consume, but there are still those inescapable situations when we're assaulted by something that doesn't meet our family standard. And usually those moments happen just too quickly to avoid. So what should we do?

Recently my (Waliszewski) wife Leesa, our two children (Kelsey, 10, and Trevor, 7), and I got away for a few days of snow skiing. After an afternoon of schussing, falling, and sunburning, we headed to a nearby pizza parlor. As our meal arrived, someone dropped a pocketful of quarters in the jukebox. The first song that blared through the establishment was "Smells Like Teen Spirit" by Nirvana. I remember looking across the table at Leesa, who rolled her eyes as if to say, "What's this trash we're stuck listening to?" We felt stymied. Nirvana is not welcome in our home. But what were we to do now that we were being "force-fed" Kurt Cobain and his nihilistic ramblings? My instincts wanted to yell, "Okay, kids, grab the pizza and let's head to the car *right now!*" I resisted the urge. There had to be a better solution. Indeed, there was. I turned the incident into a "teachable moment" by pointing out why the evening's dinner music failed to meet our family standard. Now, I don't want you to think we have this down to a science. We don't. But we've begun using such moments to reinforce the principles of discernment we regularly talk about and model at home. And I know it's sinking in.

I was keenly reminded of that just a few weeks later. Kelsey and I were in the car together. I'd been channel surfing and was tuned in to a country station. I'm usually good about changing the dial when I need to, but I got distracted. "Daddy," Kelsey asked, "is that a good song?" It wasn't. I turned the radio off, a bit embarrassed, but well-pleased that Kelsey had recognized it on her own.

A similar teachable moment occurred when I met Leesa and the kids for lunch. Seated catty-corner to us was a mother and her teenage boys. I couldn't help noticing that one of the boys wore a T-shirt emblazoned with KORN in big letters across the front. Later, the teens took off, leaving Mom (and her VISA) to cover the bill. I walked over to the woman and quietly inquired, "Do you mind if I ask you a question?" She didn't. "I was just wondering how you handle the fact that one of your sons wears a T-shirt promoting a band whose lead singer fantasizes about brutally killing his stepmother?" With a shocked expression, she gaped at me and replied, "I had *no* idea."

I don't know what became of mother and teen, but I imagine they had a heart-to-heart talk later that day. At least I hope they did. When I got back to my table, I told my family what I'd done and why. Later, I asked Trevor what he'd learned. "It was bad music," he said. Kelsey agreed, stating, "The teenager knew about the music, but the mom didn't."

"What is bad music?" I asked.

"Music about killing people," my daughter replied. I've heard her on another occasion say, "music with bad words." Later in life, my children and I will talk about other problematic elements—sexual issues for one. But for now, "killing people" and "bad words" are things they understand.

Bob Hartman, one of the founding members of the popular Christian rock band Petra, had this to say in an interview printed in the *St. Louis Metro Voice* [7/97]: "[Teenagers] have a choice of a lot of music. If we think we can totally shelter them from the world, we are sadly mistaken. . . . Responsible parents should teach their children to be discerning and understand when philosophies contradict Christian truth. Once young people are out from under their parents' control, they are going to have to make choices themselves and will need the tools to be discerning. Whether or not they have those tools depends on whether parents take the time to help them analyze music from a Christian worldview."

He's absolutely right. I'm pleased that my children are developing discernment and making it personal. One thing's for sure, there will be plenty of teachable moments in the days and years to come.

"BUT I'M AFRAID I'VE *MISSED* THOSE MOMENTS!"

In Proverbs 22:6, King Solomon advised, "Train a child in the way he should go, and when he is old he will not turn from it." Sound advice. Of course, Solomon didn't have to contend with MTV, but the principle still holds true today as we try to teach discernment to youngsters bombarded by the media.

For some parents, the promise of Proverbs 22:6 inspires expectant optimism. The children are still young. Mom and Dad do their best to make biblically based entertainment choices and monitor what's going into Junior's system. When the family listens to music together, *communication* becomes *education*. As certain CD purchase requests are denied, a rational explanation usually does the trick. No shouting matches. No slamming doors. And, ultimately, hope results from the foundation being laid.

There are, however, many loving mothers and fathers for whom Proverbs 22:6 is like a pebble in their shoe—a painful reminder that, for whatever reason, they missed that "window of opportunity." The children are older. They've developed some unhealthy habits in selecting music and resist—or rebel against—parental guidance. Storms of conflict rage in the home. And rescue seems hopeless. Even in caring Christian families, this dilemma is surprisingly common.

If you can identify with that disappointment, it may be worth revisiting the 1969 movie *Marooned*. In the film, three astronauts face certain death when a malfunction leaves them stranded in space. Ground control scrambles to organize a rescue mission. The crew's oxygen is running low. It's a race against time. Then, just as the countdown for the rescue craft nears blast-off, a violent storm covers the cape, making it impossible to launch. All appears lost until scientists realize that the eye of the storm is due to pass directly over the launch site, and if their timing is perfect, it could provide the opening they need. Sure enough, the rocket blasts through the hole to rendezvous with the crippled craft, just in the nick of time.

Obviously, the ideal time to attempt a rescue is *before* a storm hits. Solomon understood that. For many adults, however, the need to help young people be more discerning about the voices of the culture isn't acknowledged until dark clouds have already begun rolling in. Does that sound familiar? Don't lose hope. While it's preferable to "train a child in the way he should go," a new window of opportunity could arrive in the midst of present conflict . . . *the eye of the storm.* Make no mistake; there's no foolproof formula for renewal. Each situation is different. But with prayer, love, and sensitivity, it's *never* too late to reverse patterns of poor decision making.

We were in Nashville several years ago and visited with country singer Ricky Skaggs. He's a brother in the Lord and a dedicated family man. Even *he* has struggled with setting standards for media consumption in his home. Ricky admitted, "We came in real late on our teenagers, especially with my oldest son." Music was just part of the problem. His son struggled—as many teens do—with an overall spirit of rebellion. But in time, that spirit softened. "He had come to the end of his rope," Ricky explained. "He said, 'Dad, I don't like the life I've been living. I want to change. I want to get myself right with God, with you, and with my friends.' We only have a certain degree of openness with our children unless they open the door all the way. We've got to love our kids where they are, no matter what they do. That's what brought the prodigal back."

Ricky Skaggs's testimony stands as a shining example of hope for frustrated parents of adolescents. By praying and keeping the lines of communication open, we can set the stage for change, a rescue of sorts. Is there a storm raging in your home over popular music? Be encouraged. Your next window of opportunity could come right in the *middle* of it.

KEYS TO EFFECTIVE COMMUNICATION

We've talked at length about the need for parent-child communication on the road to discernment. Perhaps that's the biggest obstacle you're facing right now. Your teen won't open up to you. Discussions have a way of turning into arguments. You may even feel like you're not on the same team. It may be a phase, or maybe there's so much hostility built up between you that conducting a civil conversation seems an impossible task. Sensitivity to these key elements of interaction will help you build stronger relationships in the home:

◆ *Be a good listener.* Many times, parents *think* they're listening when, to some extent, they're busy making assumptions or thinking about the response they're going to give. Don't prejudge albums or artists. Make sure you hear your child out before coming to any conclusions. Put down the newspaper. Turn off the TV. Stay focused and be a fact collector. Ask questions before rendering an opinion. This requires a significant investment of time and energy. By the way, listening is *not* the same as agreeing. It is a demonstration of respect for another person's feelings and ideas, not an endorsement of them.

◆ *Carry on a conversation, not an argument.* There's a difference between conversing and arguing. A conversation involves speaking, listening, and thinking. An argument is mostly speaking (with the volume turned way up). If a conversation turns into an argument, end it. Separate. Agree to revisit the issue when you both cool down and feel you can return to a civil discussion of the facts. If we want our kids to be, as James 1:19 states, "quick to listen, slow to speak and slow to become angry," we need to set the example.

◆ *Avoid sarcasm.* By definition, sarcasm is caustic. Sarcasm can provoke hurt feelings, and words uttered in a "humorous moment" can continue to cause pain later. Parents who communicate by issuing a steady flow of sarcasm can expect casualties. We're not suggesting a moratorium on playful sarcasm, but there should be boundaries. Also, we tend to reap what we sow, and we may not like it. When sarcasm comes back at us from our teens, we often accuse them of being disrespectful. It never hurts to say what we mean and mean what we say, regardless of the topic being discussed.

◆ *Refrain from using silence as a weapon.* Silence is itself a powerful form of communication. It's easy to think of silence as being neutral. But the absence of a positive message can sometimes be as damaging as the presence of a negative one. Children will always assign meaning to silence. Coupled with their own insecurities, it can suggest: "She's mad at me," "What did I do wrong?" or "He doesn't really care about me at all." If you must be silent, try to offer at least a few words of explanation—if only to put your children's minds at ease. Some parents use silence to "send a message" to their kids. They punish with silence and withdraw affection in order to stir specific responses. It is very likely young people *won't* get the intended message, and even more likely that their response will compound the problem. We should be honest about our motives and resist the temptation to hide behind silence.

◆ *Refuse to be patronizing.* If we "talk down" to our children, making them feel stupid or childish, they will resent it. Condescension often triggers defensiveness and anger. We should give kids whatever credit we can for being mature and able to use common sense, because in most cases they tend to live up to—or *down* to—our expectations of them.

◆ *Deal constructively with anger.* Usually, anger results from some combination of hurt feelings, disappointment, and anxiety. Discuss the deeper issue, which may be an unmet need or an unfulfilled expectation. It often helps to find the "what if" phrases lurking in a teen's thinking ("What if I can't . . ." or "What if my friends think . . ."). Never attack one another's character. Anger can be verbally expressed with respect when it's aimed at specific *behavior* or the *issue* in question. "We need to honor God in our home" will get you further than "Are you *blind?* Can't you see the *foolishness* of the choices you've made?" Also, don't let anger serve as a smoke screen. Teens and adults often use anger to derail a conversation. It can be a diversionary tactic for turning attention away from one's own negative actions. Stay focused on the core issue.

◆ *Choose battles carefully.* As children move into the teen years, "rules" should slowly give way to "advice," even with music. This transition will usually be slower than the teen wants and faster than the parent wants. Still, it needs to take place. It may be time to rethink the old rules. Determine which battles are really worth fighting and which issues are important enough to risk damaging the relationship. Some absolutes *are* worth that conflict, but they are few and should be chosen carefully. Once you are confident about which rules to keep intact, clearly communicate your position on those key issues and don't waffle when challenged. All other areas are now open for negotiation in a whole new context.

DISCUSSION STARTERS

By now, you've probably visited the reference section of this book to investigate a CD or two that you found lying around the house. You've read about the artists. You've boned up on their lyrics and philosophical agendas. And maybe you've been encouraged by your child's edifying preferences. Or perhaps you've met with a shock, and while you feel the need to sit down with your child and discuss what you've read, there's just enough emotional tension running through you to make it difficult to determine how to start a level-headed discussion. If you identify more closely with the *second* scenario, one thing becomes clear: You're perfectly normal. Relax. Take a deep breath and let it out slowly. Here are some questions that may help you engage your young music fan and crack open the door to discernment. (Caution: Don't let yourself get upset if your queries are met by shrugging shoulders, grunts, and "I dunno"s. All are part of a dialect commonly employed by the species known as "teenager."):

◆ What is it about music in general that attracts you? Why do you like *this* particular style more than other types of music?

◆ Why do you listen to this particular artist? (If it's simply because *friends* do, ask, "Why do your friends listen to it?")

◆ How does this music make you *feel?*

◆ Do the themes on this CD reflect reality? Do they reflect *truth?*

◆ How do these songs compare with the values you've been taught here at home or in church?

◆ Do you think these lyrics have *any* effect on how close you feel to your family, friends, or God? Why or why not?

◆ Would you feel comfortable if Jesus sat here listening to this music with you? (See Matthew 28:20.) Do you think He'd care? What do you think He'd say about these lyrics?

◆ Does your *music* have an opinion of *God?* What is it?

◆ What would happen if you imitated the lifestyles and choices of the characters in these songs?

◆ Is there a kind of music you think is inappropriate to listen to? Where would you draw the line?

◆ How does it make you feel to know that, by purchasing a CD, you are supporting the morals and ideas that it's promoting?

◆ What do you think this song is saying? Do you agree or disagree with it?

◆ Do you think some people might take this song *literally?* What could that lead to?

◆ Do you think our "family standard" for music is unfair? Why or why not? (If necessary, lovingly use biblical principles to defend your constitution.)

Make Learning Fun

Some children may find "discernment lessons" more enjoyable if parents make a game of them. Recently, I (Smithouser) was inspired to create a musical discernment game that my wife, daughter and I can play on long car trips. It's a variation on tic-tac-toe. I hope it will, at the very least, provide a starting point for brainstorming some fun ideas of your own.

Begin by drawing a large square on a piece of paper. Divide it into nine *equal* squares so it looks like a boxed-in tic-tac-toe grid. Label each box with a thought commonly expressed in popular song lyrics. These statements can be positive or negative, though negatives should be general and not explicit (examples: use of the term "making love," a line about smoking cigarettes, singer mentions drinking beer, etc.). Once you've designed the "game card," give a copy to each player and turn on the car radio. We recommend an oldies station—especially for preteens—since pop songs from the 1960s tend to avoid explicit content.

The game has now begun. Listen carefully to what the songs are saying and get ready to mark off boxes as their contents are reflected in the lyrics. When an item pops up, the person who calls it out first gets credit for it. Take a brief time-out each time an item is identified, but let the song continue playing as it may reveal more about that item's context. Ask, "Is that a positive or negative idea? Why?" Discuss it together. What is the song's overall message? How does that relate to other conversations you've had about this subject? Proceed with the game once you've dealt with the issue to your satisfaction. The game ends when someone has marked off three in a row—vertically, horizontally, or diagonally.

If you're uncomfortable with the unpredictability of mainstream radio, you can always pop a tape into your car's cassette player instead. The same rules apply. You can even use Christian music to help children pick out *spiritual* concepts. Of course, how you approach the game will have a lot to do with your child's maturity and your family standard. The key is getting children to look past the melody or the beat and into a tune's *message*. Clearly, teaching discernment doesn't have to be dry and confrontational. And while families may approach this task from very different perspectives, the important thing is that children walk away richer for the experience. You're only limited by your own creativity!

RELATED SCRIPTURE READINGS

No discussion of music in a Christian home would be complete without the wisdom of Scripture. As you talk about discernment as a family, be ready to examine these passages. Be creative. You may want to walk through them systematically as part of your family devotional time. You could share a verse each night at the dinner table. In any case, parents taking a stand against immoral lyrics can rest assured that God's Word backs them up.

The War Within Us

John 3:1-21	◆ Jesus talks about flesh and spirit
Romans 7:14-25	◆ Paul admits his own struggles
Romans 8:1-17	◆ Jesus: Cure for the sinful nature
Galatians 5:16-25	◆ Keys to living by the Spirit
Ephesians 2:1-5	◆ The sinful nature brings death
Ephesians 4:17-24	◆ Out with the old, in with the new

Avoiding Indecent Exposure

Exodus 20:1-21	◆ God's original Top-10 list
Psalm 11:4-7	◆ The dangers of loving violence
Psalm 101	◆ David's pledge of purity
Philippians 4:4-8	◆ Your heart's best defense
Colossians 2:8	◆ Watch out for deceivers!
Colossians 3:1-10	◆ Trading junk for jewels
1 Thessalonians 5:21-22	◆ Test everything
1 Timothy 4:7-16	◆ A call to young Christians
2 Timothy 4:3-4	◆ Don't waffle on the truth

Preparing a Defense

Psalm 119:9-16	◆ Armed with God's resources
Matthew 6:22-23	◆ Protecting the eyes
Romans 12:1-2	◆ Don't be conformed; be transformed
1 Corinthians 9:24-27	◆ Training to win
2 Corinthians 10:3-5	◆ Taking thoughts prisoner

Ephesians 6:10-18	◆ The full armor of God
1 Thessalonians 4:3-8	◆ Control your passions
1 Peter 1:13-16	◆ Follow the Commander
2 Peter 1:3-11	◆ Everything we need for life and godliness

The Value of Wisdom

Genesis 41:15-40	◆ Joseph interprets dreams
1 Kings 3:7-12	◆ Solomon asks for discernment
Proverbs 3:21-26	◆ Benefits of discernment
Ecclesiastes 9:13-18	◆ A tale of wisdom as strength
Matthew 5:13-16	◆ Salt and light to the world
John 10:1-18	◆ Knowing the Shepherd's voice
Philippians 1:9-11	◆ The apostle's prayer for you

Part Two

CD REVIEWS

WARNING:

In an attempt to fully educate parents and teens about the messages communicated by the artists featured in this book, many of the following reviews contain direct quotes from lyrics. Though we have attempted to sanitize vulgar references by abbreviating them, some material may be offensive due to its graphic nature.

Aaliyah

◆ ◆ ◆ ◆ ◆ ◆ ◆ ◆ ◆ ◆ ◆ ◆ ◆ ◆ ◆ ◆ ◆

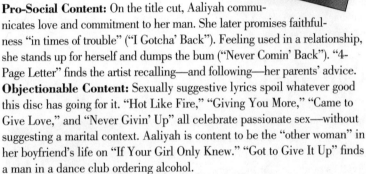

New York-born Aaliyah began performing at a young age. By the time she was 11, she was singing onstage in Las Vegas as part of a five-night stand with Gladys Knight's troupe.

Title: *One in a Million* (1997)
Label: Atlantic
Genre: R&B
Pro-Social Content: On the title cut, Aaliyah communicates love and commitment to her man. She later promises faithfulness "in times of trouble" ("I Gotcha' Back"). Feeling used in a relationship, she stands up for herself and dumps the bum ("Never Comin' Back"). "4-Page Letter" finds the artist recalling—and following—her parents' advice.
Objectionable Content: Sexually suggestive lyrics spoil whatever good this disc has going for it. "Hot Like Fire," "Giving You More," "Came to Give Love," and "Never Givin' Up" all celebrate passionate sex—without suggesting a marital context. Aaliyah is content to be the "other woman" in her boyfriend's life on "If Your Girl Only Knew." "Got to Give It Up" finds a man in a dance club ordering alcohol.
Summary/Advisory: This teenage former wife of salacious rapper R. Kelly does have some positive things to say. Unfortunately, they get lost amid the hormones. While she may employ more subtlety than her ex-husband, Aaliyah is still much too steamy for young R&B fans.

Abdul, Paula

◆ ◆ ◆ ◆ ◆ ◆ ◆ ◆ ◆ ◆ ◆ ◆ ◆ ◆ ◆ ◆ ◆

Paula Abdul was born to parents of Brazilian and French-Canadian descent. She began performing at age seven and has choreographed several music videos and television award shows. A former Los Angeles Lakers cheerleader, Abdul has sold more than 11 million albums.

Title: *Head Over Heels* (1995)
Label: Virgin

Genre: Pop/Dance/R&B

Pro-Social Content: "My Love Is for Real" repents of romantic mistakes, pledging to set things right, as do "Missing You" and "Cry for Me." Other tracks ("Ain't Never Gonna Give You Up," "If I Were Your Girl") promise relational loyalty.

Objectionable Content: How much of "Get Your Groove On" talks about dirty dancing and how much refers to sex is anyone's guess. Either way, it's trouble. The pulsating "Sexy Thoughts" and "Crazy Cool" also glorify breathless ecstasy with no mention of marriage. "Ho-Down," a song about taking revenge on a gossip, mentions a backseat sexual encounter.

Summary/Advisory: Abdul avoids *explicit* content, but relies heavily on sensual, suggestive lyrics. It had been four years since her last album. As a comeback attempt, *Head Over Heels* trips over its own feet, stumbling into erotic preoccupations.

Above the Law

◆ ◆ ◆ ◆ ◆ ◆ ◆ ◆ ◆ ◆ ◆ ◆ ◆ ◆ ◆ ◆ ◆ ◆ ◆

The rap group includes Don "Cold 187um" Hutchison, Go Mack, Total K-oss, and KM.G. Eric "Eazy E" Wright and Dr. Dre have both served as producers for these gangsta rappers.

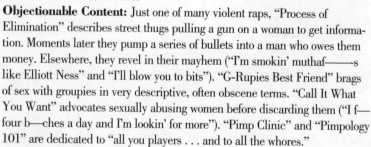

Title: *Black Mafia Life* (1993)
Label: Ruthless
Genre: Gangsta rap
Pro-Social Content: None

Objectionable Content: Just one of many violent raps, "Process of Elimination" describes street thugs pulling a gun on a woman to get information. Moments later they pump a series of bullets into a man who owes them money. Elsewhere, they revel in their mayhem ("I'm smokin' muthaf——s like Elliott Ness" and "I'll blow you to bits"). "G-Rupies Best Friend" brags of sex with groupies in very descriptive, often obscene terms. "Call It What You Want" advocates sexually abusing women before discarding them ("I f— four b—ches a day and I'm lookin' for more"). "Pimp Clinic" and "Pimpology 101" are dedicated to "all you players . . . and to all the whores."

Summary/Advisory: No good will ever come from exposure to this hateful, hedonistic trash. *Black Mafia Life* includes a much-deserved explicit lyrics advisory.

Ace of Base

◆ ◆ ◆ ◆ ◆ ◆ ◆ ◆ ◆ ◆ ◆ ◆ ◆ ◆ ◆ ◆ ◆ ◆

Ace of Base, a quartet that hails from Sweden, consists of Jonas "Joker" Berggren, Ulf "Buddha" Ekberg, Jenny, and Linn. Their first CD sold a combined total of 17 million units worldwide, making Ace of Base the biggest-selling debut group of 1994. The act was also voted Best New Artist/Group by the American Music Awards, *Billboard* Music Awards, and World Music Awards.

Title: *The Bridge* (1995)
Label: EMI
Genre: Pop
Pro-Social Content: "Beautiful Life" is a joyful admonition to hang tough when times get hard. The singer refuses to compromise who she is on "Never Gonna Say I'm Sorry" and reverently alludes to God on various tracks. "Ravine" is a metaphor for her struggle with pride, which she credits the Lord with healing. Prayers for a better world ("Nothing to cry for/No one to die for") provide material for "Perfect World." "Experience Pearls" believes Romans 8:28—that good things can come from bad situations.
Objectionable Content: One otherwise positive song ("My Deja Vu") includes the line "I wanna see you dancing naked." Another uses a mild profanity (a—).
Summary/Advisory: The Swedish foursome Ace of Base trades on electrified grooves and generally upbeat lyrics. Optimism. Humility. Willingness to serve others. With the noted exceptions, *The Bridge* is a fine effort.

Title: *The Sign* (1993)
Label: Arista
Genre: Dance pop
Pro-Social Content: "All That She Wants" warns a young man about a woman out for a one-night stand ("She's a hunter, you're the fox . . . beware of that flashing in her eyes"). Two songs ("Don't Turn Around" and the number-one single, "The Sign") demonstrate strength in the wake of romantic rejection. "Happy Nation" promotes brotherhood. Selfless love for a partner drives "Voulez-vous Danser."

Objectionable Content: Contradicting the sentiment in "Voulez-vous Danser," "Living in Danger" encourages egocentric living. "Dancer in a Daydream" tantalizingly propositions a prospective sexual partner ("I want to be your lover, but you're so shy . . . join me in my jungle wet and wild").
Summary/Advisory: Musically upbeat and enjoyable, *The Sign*'s fresh dance-club sound would really swing if it weren't weighed down by mixed messages.

Aerosmith

◆ ◆ ◆ ◆ ◆ ◆ ◆ ◆ ◆ ◆ ◆ ◆ ◆ ◆ ◆ ◆ ◆ ◆ ◆ ◆

Aerosmith is Steven Tyler (father of Gen-X actress Liv), Joe Perry, Brad Whitford, Tom Hamilton, and Joey Kramer. This group—known in part for its members' much-publicized battles with drug and alcohol abuse—has released a dozen albums since 1973. The band has also appeared on NBC's *Saturday Night Live* and in the film *Wayne's World 2*.

Title: *Nine Lives* (1997)
Label: Columbia
Genre: Rock
Pro-Social Content: "Fallen Angels" appears to mourn children who "vanish out of sight." One line on "Kiss Your Past Goodbye" urges a woman to put hurtful memories behind her.
Objectionable Content: Sex with a Hindu priestess is lead singer Steven Tyler's objective on "Taste of India." Drug slang—aggravated by the artist admitting that he's "feeling suicidal"—mars "Crash." Tyler claims to use Prozac as a "fixer" and have "a needle in [his] arm" ("The Farm"). He blurts the f-word on "Attitude Adjustment" and the Top-40 hit "Falling in Love (Is Hard on the Knees)." Sly sexual references throughout this disc ("puss and booty," "pink as the bing on your cherry") underscore the erotic irresponsibility of tracks such as "Pink" and "Hole in My Soul." Furthermore, the liner notes contain disturbing illustrations.
Summary/Advisory: After 24 years and 12 albums to date, these long-time advocates of sex, drugs, and rock 'n' roll still haven't grown up. And they haven't fizzled out; this disc debuted at number one. Finicky teens asking for *Nine Lives* should check out several cuts from Whitecross's *Flytrap* instead.

Title: *Get a Grip* (1993)
Label: Geffen
Genre: Hard rock
Pro-Social Content: A line on the Top-20 hit "Livin' on the Edge" condemns racial prejudice. "Amazing" refers to life as a journey and describes a sort of conversion experience ("With the blink of an eye, you finally see the light . . . I'm sayin' a prayer for the desperate hearts tonight").
Objectionable Content: Aerosmith glorifies alcohol and drug use throughout, denouncing crack only because the "buzz" doesn't last long enough ("Fever"). Expressing animosity for the upper class, "Eat the Rich" serves up the affluent on a hostile platter (though wealth obtained by screaming to guitar riffs must be acceptable). Cheap, quick sex without marital boundaries is encouraged on the despair-driven "Shut Up and Dance." "Flesh" is a celebration of raging hormones ("since Eve did Adam . . . everybody gotta have flesh"), while "Fever" reduces women to objects of lust ("I'd rather be O.D.in' on the crack of her a—").
Summary/Advisory: This adrenalized number-1 debut is album number 17 in the band's long history. Mixed messages peppered with obscenity make this one seem at home on the group's hedonistic résumé. But it has no place in discerning homes.

Alice in Chains

◆ ◆ ◆ ◆ ◆ ◆ ◆ ◆ ◆ ◆ ◆ ◆ ◆ ◆ ◆ ◆ ◆

Alice in Chains has had two albums debut at number 1 (*Jar of Flies, Alice in Chains*). This Seattle-based band was once known as a metal band but is now associated with the alternative scene.

Title: *Alice in Chains* (1995)
Label: Columbia
Genre: Alternative
Pro-Social Content: For the most part, just isolated lines. "Again" refuses to repeat past mistakes. "Shame on You" speaks of correcting bad habits and strives for inner peace.
Objectionable Content: Several tracks use the f-word to punctuate strains of hopelessness and despair. With a vengeance, "Grind" and "Sludge Factory" take pleasure in the pain of others. The latter encourages listeners to "repay all who caused strife." Other songs glorify

drug use. "God Am" is a bitter, blasphemous "prayer" that blames the Almighty for the world's problems.

Summary/Advisory: Dark. Brooding. Cold. *Rolling Stone* [11/30/95] said the band is "like a slashed wrist—stark, bloody, and dramatic, but more indicative of a cry for help than a true desire to spiral into the void." Surely, their well-chronicled drug use isn't helping. Teens should steer clear of *Alice*.

Title: *Jar of Flies* (1994)
Label: Columbia
Genre: Alternative/Grunge rock
Pro-Social Content: "No Excuses" expresses commitment to a friend. Soul searching leads the band to observe that "arrogance is potent" ("Rotten Apple") and a heart can become hard ("I Stay Away").
Objectionable Content: Such philosophical ramblings mean nothing if they don't point to solutions. Wallowing in misery, "Nutshell" even contemplates suicide ("I fight this battle all alone, no one to cry to, no place to call home . . . I'd feel better dead"). "Don't Follow" glorifies alcohol use—this from a group proudly outspoken about its abuse of illegal substances. With the exception of the melodic "Whale and Wasp," *Jar of Flies*'s dark, eerie music and haunting lyrics seem determined to create a sense of despair in the listener.
Summary/Advisory: This seven-track, extended play collection comes from an act that has described itself as "Satan's penis incarnated into a band" [*Rip*, 12/93]. This vivid self-portrait alone should give discerning parents more than enough reason to keep *Flies* out of the house.

Title: *Dirt* (1992)
Label: Columbia
Genre: Alternative metal
Pro-Social Content: Quite a bit of soul-searching is evident. On "Them Bones," "Sickman," and "Down in a Hole," the group explores themes of man's mortality and the "dirty and diseased" condition of the soul. "God Smack" opposes drug use ("Can't get high/Or you will die"). "Rooster" is a tribute to guitarist Jerry Cantrell's father, a Vietnam veteran.
Objectionable Content: "Junkhead" and "Hate to Feel" undeniably set forth the mindset of the drug user. "Dirt" graphically conveys suicidal leanings ("I want to taste dirty stinging pistol/In my mouth, on my tongue/I want you to scrape me from the walls"). In interviews, the group argues that it attempts to examine these life choices. But some young fans may take

lyrics out of context and act on the wrong cue. There's also a heavy dose of profanity on this unstickered album.

Summary/Advisory: Yet another Seattle alternative metal band, Alice in Chains has made inroads with solid musicianship and thoughtful but dark lyrics. However, if placed in the wrong hands, *Dirt* could inspire drug use or even suicide.

All-4-One

◆ ◆ ◆ ◆ ◆ ◆ ◆ ◆ ◆ ◆ ◆ ◆ ◆ ◆ ◆ ◆ ◆ ◆ ◆ ◆

The voices of Tony Borowiak, Jamie Jones, Alfred Nevarez, and Delicious provide All-4-One's trademark four-part harmony. The single "I Swear" (also a country smash for John Michael Montgomery) was 1994's biggest-selling single and became the third most successful single of the rock era. Their self-titled debut album has sold more than 5 million copies and the band has garnered a Grammy award.

Title: *And the Music Speaks* (1995)
Label: Atlantic
Genre: Doo-wop/Hip-hop
Pro-Social Content: Both "I'm Sorry" and "Here for You" admit mistakes, seek forgiveness, and desire reconciliation. True love and long-term commitment take the fore on "I Can Love You Like That," "Giving You My Heart Forever," and "These Arms." A woman's love makes life's hues more vivid on "Colors of Love." Best of all, the project concludes with "We Dedicate," a rendition of "Jesus Loves Me" that exalts Christ and credits Him with specific blessings.

Objectionable Content: Though not explicit (like the quartet's previous disc), isolated lines request sexual intimacy ("makin' love").

Summary/Advisory: Beyond its smooth R&B harmonies, *And the Music Speaks* actually has something of value to say—a step up from the guys' double-minded debut. Still room for improvement, but a decent overall effort.

Title: *All-4-One* (1994)
Label: Atlantic
Genre: Doo-wop/Hip-hop

Pro-Social Content: These young men use pleasant R&B harmonies to convey lasting romantic commitment ("I Swear," "So in Love," "A Better Man"). Other lyrically buoyant love songs ("Something About You," "Without You") are harmless fun.

Objectionable Content: Several tunes solicit sex in explicit terms. "Skillz" cheapens a woman to the sum of her anatomical parts ("Little rump shaker . . . workin' booty left to right"). "The Bomb" boldly states, "You want to sex me/girl why don't you let me . . . let's get it on"). On "Breathless," the boys strive to make a woman moan in ecstasy. The propositions on "Down to the Last Drop" and "Here If You're Ready" are more subtle but not any more suitable.

Summary/Advisory: The album starts promisingly, but it's all-4-nothing. The few offensive tracks are reason enough to avoid it.

Amos, Tori

◆ ◆ ◆ ◆ ◆ ◆ ◆ ◆ ◆ ◆ ◆ ◆ ◆ ◆ ◆ ◆ ◆ ◆ ◆ ◆

Born in North Carolina, this daughter of a Methodist preacher could play the piano by the age of three and was composing musical scores by the age of four. Her first two albums sold more than 2 million copies each.

Title: *From the Choirgirl Hotel* (1998)
Label: Atlantic
Genre: Pop/Folk/Contemporary classical
Pro-Social Content: None
Objectionable Content: Theologically confused, Amos speaks of black magic ("Jackie's Strength"), Eastern mysticism ("Cruel"), past lives on other planets ("Black-Dove January"), and a female god who plays poker with the fates of men ("Liquid Diamonds"). This tormented artist's career-long disdain for Christianity resurfaces on "Spark," which ruminates, "If the Divine master plan is perfection, maybe next I'll give Judas a try." Sexual references mar "Raspberry Swirl" ("If you want inside her . . .") and "Jackie's Strength" ("My bridesmaids getting laid"). "Playboy Mommy" appears to involve a wartime prostitute asking her dead daughter to be more accepting of her lifestyle. The hopelessness of "Iieeee" is aggravated by amoral references to illegal drugs on both "Jackie's Strength" and "She's Your Cocaine." The f-word shows up on "Northern Lad."

Summary/Advisory: While more subdued than her last disc, Amos's *Choirgirl* is no less tormented. Emptiness and pain. Irresponsible sexuality. Theological bilge. In short, skip it.

Title: *Boys for Pele* (1996)
Label: Atlantic
Genre: Rock/Folk/Contemporary classical
Pro-Social Content: What little may exist lies veiled in lyrical obscurity.
Objectionable Content: Bitter spiritual confusion and a distaste for Christianity appear on several cuts, including "Muhammad My Friend" ("It was a girl back in Bethlehem/And on that fateful day when she was crucified/She wore Shiseido Red and we drank tea"). "Father Lucifer" flippantly asks the devil, "How's your Jesus Christ been hanging?" Amid orgasmic breathiness, Amos repeatedly blurts "Starf——er just like my daddy" on "Professional Widow," a song that may allude to heroin use. "Blood Roses" is darkly erotic while "Doughnut Song" expresses hatred.
Summary/Advisory: Amos claims her songs reflect the breakdown of patriarchy and the idea of women rising to claim their own power. Maybe, but when she's not spouting obscenities, blaspheming God, or bashing men, she whines despairingly and enigmatically with ridiculous lines like, "If I lose my Cracker Jacks at the tidal wave, I got a place in the Pope's rubber robe." Huh? One of the CD photos shows this disturbed artist breast-feeding a pig. A weird, acerbic, and *pointless* effort.

Apple, Fiona

◆ ◆ ◆ ◆ ◆ ◆ ◆ ◆ ◆ ◆ ◆ ◆ ◆ ◆ ◆ ◆ ◆ ◆ ◆ ◆

Fiona Apple was a teenager when her debut album, *Tidal,* was released in July 1996. She has been featured in the *New York Times, Rolling Stone,* and *Time,* hosted MTV's *120 Minutes,* performed on *Saturday Night Live,* and won a Grammy in 1998 for "Criminal" (Best Female Rock Performance).

Title: *Tidal* (1997)
Label: Sony
Genre: Rock/Folk
Pro-Social Content: While not perky and musically upbeat, many of these burdened, introspective tracks convey some optimism in the

midst of relational soul searching ("The First Taste," "Slow Like Honey," "Pale September," "The Child Is Gone"). On "Criminal," the singer deeply regrets emotional game-playing that hurt a young man ("It's a sad, sad world when a girl will break a boy just because she can"). Though Apple confesses that she's unsure what to believe in, "Never Is a Promise" does value honesty and courage.

Objectionable Content: "Shadowboxer" and "Pale September" fail to establish a marital context for intimate relationships. An uncommonly bitter "Sleep to Dream" finds the artist telling a lover, "You say love is a hell you cannot bear/And I say gimme mine back and then go there for all I care" before announcing that she intends to live wildly.

Summary/Advisory: Laid-back, coffee-house vocals add a pleading depth to Fiona Apple's painfully honest lyrics. Her record label says her music "haunts as it inspires." Sadly, the overall impression is more confessional than inspirational. The fruit from Apple's tree isn't rotten, but it is bruised—and could be much sweeter.

Aqua

◆ ◆ ◆ ◆ ◆ ◆ ◆ ◆ ◆ ◆ ◆ ◆ ◆ ◆ ◆ ◆ ◆ ◆ ◆ ◆

Danish-Norwegian Aqua is composed of Soren Raasted, Claus Norreen, Rene Dif, and the only female in the group, Lene Nystrom. The band's first single, "Roses Are Red," was released in September 1996 and went straight to the charts, where it stayed for several months. After "Barbie Doll" achieved popularity, the band had a run-in with Mattel because the toy manufacturer felt that the song portrayed their product in a negative light.

Title: *Aquarium* (1997)
Label: MCA
Genre: Pop/Dance
Pro-Social Content: Bouncy tunes deal with various dimensions of romance, including sweet affection ("Roses Are Red," "Good Morning Sunshine"), a frustrated woman's inability to contact her man ("Calling You"), the end to a summer of love ("Doctor Jones"), a "tough-love" confrontation ("Be a Man"), and regrets over unfaithfulness with a desire for reconciliation ("Turn Back Time").

Objectionable Content: Just like Robin Hood, "My Oh My" wishes to dishonestly redistribute wealth. Tequila flows during an all-night party where a sexual conquest is brewing ("Heat of the Night"). In fact, sexual suggestiveness and innuendo mar several tunes. On "Barbie Doll," the plastic female invites Ken to undress her and "kiss me here, touch me there, hanky panky." The singer uses candy store lingo to convey sexual desires ("Lollipop").

Summary/Advisory: Elements of Abba, Ace of Base, and Madonna can be heard floating through Aqua's upbeat musical *Aquarium*. Too bad its thumping dance grooves are swimming with lyrics that play to hormonal urges.

Babyface

◆ ◆ ◆ ◆ ◆ ◆ ◆ ◆ ◆ ◆ ◆ ◆ ◆ ◆ ◆ ◆ ◆ ◆ ◆ ◆

Songwriter/producer Kenny "Babyface" Edwards is one of the most influential men in the music business today. He has racked up more than 100 Top-10 hits on the R&B and pop charts, amassing sales of 70 million albums and 20 million singles. Although the lion's share of these projects were recorded by others (Toni Braxton, Boyz II Men, TLC), Babyface has himself sold more than 5 million albums in the United States.

Title: *The Day* (1996)
Label: Epic
Genre: R&B
Pro-Social Content: Smooth, at times poetic love songs thank God for a committed partner ("Every Time I Close My Eyes"), pledge devotion ("I Said I Love You"), and express a man's desire to work tirelessly at a relationship ("Seven Seas"). On the title track, Babyface rejoices in the prospect of becoming a father, referring to the baby as a "blessing straight from God." "How Come, How Long" decries domestic violence. "Simple Days" recalls a time when men kept their word and friends remained faithful.

Objectionable Content: The artist crudely asks his lover, "Why must you always think I wanna get in your pants?" ("Talk to Me"). The answer *may* be found in his many titillating comments and sexual come-ons (on "This Is for the Lover in You," "When Your Body Gets Weak," "All Day Thinkin'").

Summary/Advisory: As a songwriter and producer, Babyface has developed a reputation for creating Top-10 pop and R&B hits. Quite a few reflect the same erotic preoccupation that spoils this collection of otherwise positive themes. Encourage young fans of the genre not to seize *The Day.*

Backstreet Boys

◆ ◆

Backstreet Boys consists of five members: Kevin Richardson, Brian Littrell, A.J. McLean, Howie Dorough, and Nick Carter. Their self-titled debut album went multiplatinum, while the single, "Quit Playing Games (With My Heart)," sold more than a million copies.

Title: *Backstreet Boys* (1997)
Label: Jive
Genre: R&B/Pop
Pro-Social Content: Sounding remarkably similar to '80s grooves by Kool & The Gang, "As Long As You Love Me" boasts unconditional love. Similarly, "All I Have to Give," "I'll Never Break Your Heart," and "Anywhere for You" express a willingness to do whatever it takes to forge a strong relationship. Other songs seek to restore one. On the hit single "Quit Playing Games (With My Heart)," the singer longs to return to days before insensitivity and manipulation threatened to destroy the friendship. "Darlin'" sees the solution to romantic trials in honest communication.

Objectionable Content: Though the song "Get Down" actually speaks of dancing, that term is also slang for sex. Innuendo peppers "If You Want It to Be Good Girl (Get Yourself a Bad Boy)," a Prince/Michael Jackson hybrid with lines such as, "There's a thing your mama shouldn't know/There's a thing I really wanna show you." A disappointing final cut.
Summary/Advisory: The liner notes include Philippians 4:3. And lyrically, these guys have some positive things to say. With the noted exceptions, their debut disc shows promise.

Badu, Erykah

◆ ◆ ◆ ◆ ◆ ◆ ◆ ◆ ◆ ◆ ◆ ◆ ◆ ◆ ◆ ◆ ◆ ◆ ◆

Born Erykah Wright, her adopted last name is an Islamic designation that means "giver of light." Her *Baduizm* disc debuted at number two, the highest chart position to date for a first release from a female singer. It also captured Grammys for Best R&B Album and Best Female R&B Vocal Performance (for "On & On") in 1998.

Title: *Baduizm* (1997)
Label: Universal
Genre: R&B/Jazz
Pro-Social Content: The artist resists another person's attempts to "rearrange" and "control" her ("Certainly") and remembers with affection her grandmother's sound advice about life ("Appletree"). On "Drama," Badu tells anxious listeners, "Lift up your hearts to God/Lift up your souls/Teach your children wisdom." The hit single "On & On" denounces intellectuals who fail to acknowledge God.
Objectionable Content: "On & On" also includes the f-word, an inappropriate use of God's name, and other profanities. "Otherside of the Game" finds a woman excusing her man's dishonest business dealings because "it pays the bills." On "4-Leaf Clover," Badu embraces various superstitions ("Touch a four-leaf clover . . . hold onto your rabbit's foot"). She subtly applauds the offensive rap group Wu-Tang Clan ("Afro").
Summary/Advisory: Smooth instrumentals and sweet, passionate vocals make it easy to like Badu's sound. But any upbeat musings here are poisoned by coarse vocabulary and waffling morals. Best to avoid this inconsistent effort.

Baker, Anita

◆ ◆ ◆ ◆ ◆ ◆ ◆ ◆ ◆ ◆ ◆ ◆ ◆ ◆ ◆ ◆ ◆ ◆

Anita Baker was born in Memphis, Tennessee, and raised in Detroit, Michigan, before serving as the lead singer with the soul group Chapter 8 from 1976 to 1984. Her first solo hit, "Sweet Love," achieved Top-10 status.

Title: *Rhythm of Love* (1994)
Label: Elektra
Genre: R&B/Jazz/Pop
Pro-Social Content: For the most part, these sweet love songs stay on the straight and narrow, stressing vocal passion and emotional transparency. On "You Belong to Me," Baker reminds her man that true love is *exclusive* love. "I Apologize" expresses regret for words spoken in anger. Several cuts examine the long-term benefits of romantic commitment ("Sometimes I Wonder Why," "Baby," "It's Been You").
Objectionable Content: Nothing explicit. Baker tells a friend that she has imagined "cav[ing] in to sweet surrender" with him in "a love dream so tender" ("It's Been You").
Summary/Advisory: With the above exception, fans of mellow R&B sounds will find these original ballads and remakes of adult contemporary classics ("My Funny Valentine," "You Belong to Me," and "Look of Love") a winning combination.

Beastie Boys

◆ ◆ ◆ ◆ ◆ ◆ ◆ ◆ ◆ ◆ ◆ ◆ ◆ ◆ ◆ ◆ ◆ ◆ ◆ ◆

Originally called the Young Aborigines, Beastie Boys is Michael Diamond, Adam Horovitz, and Adam Yauch. The boys have entertained in various musical capacities, including movie roles, soundtracks, and a tour with the NYC Tibetan Freedom Concert in November 1997.

Title: *Ill Communication* (1994)
Label: Capitol
Genre: Rap
Pro-Social Content: Environmental conciousness and a kudo to Martin Luther King's pacifism are central to "The Update." "Sure Shot" takes issue with common rap terms degrading women (hypocritical, considering the group's past efforts).
Objectionable Content: Although "Get It Together" puts down crack use, the group pleads for the legalization of marijuana on "B-Boys Makin' with the Freak Freak." Profanity

appears throughout this stickered project with an emphasis on the f-word and the boys' descriptions of their genitalia. Pro basketball star Bill Laimbeer is the target of significant verbal abuse on "Tough Guy." "Bodhisattva Vow" promotes reincarnation and other Buddhist teachings. "Get It Together" is one long sexual come-on.

Summary/Advisory: Lyrics such as, "I'm all about screwin'" and "I'm workin' on rhymes . . . a little something stupid for the twisted and sick" provide insight into this band's agenda. What's really twisted and sick is that *Ill* debuted as the best-selling pop and number-2 R&B disc. Steer clear.

Beatles, The

◆ ◆

The Beatles were formed in Liverpool, England, in the late 1950s. Besides the familiar John Lennon, Paul McCartney, and George Harrison, the group originally included Stu Sutcliffe (bass) and Pete Best (drums). Ringo Starr replaced Best in 1962. The 1996 singles "Free As a Bird" and "Real Love" gave the Beatles their 21st and 22nd gold singles, the most for any group in history. The band, which starred in films such as *Help!* and *A Hard Day's Night,* has sold more than 100 million albums.

Title: *Anthology 3* (1996)
Label: Capitol
Genre: Classic rock
Pro-Social Content: Love songs such as "I Will," "For You Blue," "Something," "Honey Pie," and "Step Inside Love" bask in the warm fuzzies of committed relationships. "All Things Must Pass" recognizes the temporal nature of life. The truth of 2 Corinthians 9:6 is expressed in romantic terms on "The End" ("In the end, the love you take is equal to the love you make"). A Bible aids in the revival of vengeful "Rocky Raccoon." "Goodnight" is a tender lullaby written by John Lennon for his young son.
Objectionable Content: Veiled drug references include "I need a fix," "I roll a stoney," "he shoots Coca Cola," and "JoJo left his home . . . for some California grass." "Polythene Pam" and "Get Back" allude to sexually ambiguous individuals. A family conducts a midnight seance on "Cry Baby

Cry." Several cuts recommend alcohol, and a mass-murderer is treated comically on "Maxwell's Silver Hammer." "Why Don't We Do It in the Road" is a sexual proposition, and "I've Got a Feeling" states, "everybody had a wet dream."

Summary/Advisory: True to the standard set by Anthologies 1 and 2, this final chapter in the Beatles trilogy also debuted at number 1. This double-disc collection of previously unreleased masters is a muffled blend of innocence and depravity.

Title: *Anthology 2* (1996)
Label: Capitol
Genre: Classic rock
Pro-Social Content: Nearly a dozen songs espouse upbeat sentiments about love and romance, even in cases where a relationship is struggling. "Help" and "Got to Get You into My Life" confess the need to rely on others for support. Other tunes value people over material possessions ("And Your Bird Can Sing," "If You've Got Trouble"). Fly-on-the-wall songs such as "Penny Lane" and "Being for the Benefit of Mr. Kite" honor the daily activities of common people.
Objectionable Content: Most notably a smattering of Eastern religious influences and subtle drug references. Alcohol is consumed on "Norwegian Wood" and "Rock and Roll Music." "I Am the Walrus" pokes fun at a "pornographic princess." One profanity pops up.
Summary/Advisory: This double-disc (128 minutes of music) scored a number-1 debut. Not as solid as *Anthology 1,* but this second of three compilations avoids the blatant promotion of vice so common in today's music. More good stuff than problems. Still, use discretion.

Title: *Anthology 1* (1995)
Label: Capitol
Genre: Classic rock
Pro-Social Content: *Anthology 1* celebrates the innocence of the Fab Four's early years. Ballads like "Love Me Do," "She Loves You," "Till There Was You," "All My Loving," "And I Love Her," "From Me to You," "Eight Days a Week," and others address the range of warm fuzzies associated with falling in love, giving one's heart away, and the hurt resulting from lost or unrequited love.
Objectionable Content: "Money (That's What I Want)" values cold hard cash over a loving relationship. An interview clip refers to a specific alcoholic concoction as a Beatle favorite. That's all—in two hours of content.

Summary/Advisory: This unique double disc (a 60-track collection of tunes, interview clips, and outtakes) spent its first month at number 1. For fans of John, Paul, George, and Ringo (and music history buffs), it's the passport for a wonderful nostalgia trip. Now that the Beatles are being embraced by young music fans again, *Anthology 1* may also help bridge a generation gap in many homes. However, it may lead teens to sample subsequent *Anthology* discs covering the more "psychedelic" stages of the band's career. Use discernment. (SEE ALSO: McCartney, Paul)

Beck

◆ ◆ ◆ ◆ ◆ ◆ ◆ ◆ ◆ ◆ ◆ ◆ ◆ ◆ ◆ ◆ ◆ ◆

Born Beck Hansen near Kansas City, he is a singer, songwriter, and guitarist. Beck has recorded such songs as "MTV Makes Me Want to Smoke Crack."

Title: *Odelay* (1996)
Label: DGC/Bong Load
Genre: Folk rock/Pop/Rap
Pro-Social Content: Fragmented ideas could be interpreted as positive, but this entire project reflects a disjointed stream of consciousness.

Objectionable Content: General themes are hard to make out, but isolated lines prove problematic. Vague contexts notwithstanding, the word *suicide* appears on "Hotwax," "High 5," and "Novacane." The artist alludes to bisexuality on "Where It's At." "Devil's Haircut" refers to "discount orgies" amid expressions of hopelessness. Several profanities find their way onto "High 5."
Summary/Advisory: Feedback. Distortion. An effects-laden background track including what sounds like a dentist's drill. That's the "music." Lyrically, one man's nonsense is another man's offbeat street poetry. And while Beck Hansen has toned down the offensive material of his last effort, *Odelay* fails to clear the hurdle of acceptability.

Title: *Mellow Gold* (1994)
Label: Geffen
Genre: Folk/Rap
Pro-Social Content: None
Objectionable Content: Labeled with an advisory sticker, *Mellow Gold*

weaves together lyrics that range from pointless ("spray paint the vegeta-bles, dog food stalls, beefcake panty hose") to negative ("I'm a loser, baby, so why don't you kill me?" on the hit single, "Loser") to downright explicit ("You lousy puke," "Make me feel like an a—hole"). Song titles include "F—in' with My Head." In addition to vile language, numerous angry tunes advocate gun-toting violence, drug and alcohol use, and consorting with the devil.

Summary/Advisory: At the time of this album's release, Beck told *Rolling Stone*, "The whole concept of *Mellow Gold* is that it's like a satanic K-Tel record found in a trash dumpster." They should have left it there. This worthless disc spews refuse from start to finish.

Bell Biv DeVoe

◆ ◆ ◆ ◆ ◆ ◆ ◆ ◆ ◆ ◆ ◆ ◆ ◆ ◆ ◆ ◆ ◆ ◆ ◆

Ricky Bell, Michael Bivins, and Ronnie DeVoe formed this hip-hop trio in 1989. They found immediate success with their first single, "Poison," which debuted on the charts at number 3. Their second album, *Hootie Mack*, peaked at number 19 in 1993.

Title: *Hootie Mack* (1993)
Label: MCA
Genre: Rap/Hip-hop
Pro-Social Content: The father of an illegitimate child steps forth to take responsibility on "The Situation." "Show Me the Way" is an anti-crack song, but the message loses its meaning beside tunes promoting marijuana use ("Nickel," "Hootie Mack").

Objectionable Content: "Lost in the Moment" and "Something in Your Eyes" epitomize an animalistic lack of self-control ("I'll take you to the peak and make you wanna scream"). Raunchy tunes, including "Ghetto Booty," demean women by portraying them as sex objects. On "From the Back," DeVoe describes sodomizing his "ho" (whore).

Summary/Advisory: *Hootie Mack* is saturated with profanity and sexual street slang. The few marginally positive elements on the disc in no way warrant wading through the rest of it.

Ben Folds Five

◆ ◆ ◆ ◆ ◆ ◆ ◆ ◆ ◆ ◆ ◆ ◆ ◆ ◆ ◆ ◆ ◆ ◆ ◆

Don't be fooled by the band's name; Ben Folds Five is actually a *threesome*—Ben Folds, Robert Sledge, and Darren Jesse. The members joined forces in 1994 in Chapel Hill, North Carolina, and went on to perform at the Lollapalooza and H.O.R.D.E. tours, and recorded the album *Whatever and Ever Amen*, which went gold.

Title: *Whatever and Ever Amen* (1997)
Label: Sony
Genre: Pop/Rock
Pro-Social Content: Though not written to convey a pro-life message, the Top-20 single "Brick" does so when it details the emotional and relational struggles the singer and his girlfriend encountered when she chose to abort their baby.
Objectionable Content: Lots of hostility. Lacking more intelligent forms of expression, this angry trio spews the f-word and various other profanities ("you b—ch," "bulls—," "p—ed," "kiss my a—") in the heat of malicious rage. A vengeful individual lashes out at his grade-school nemeses ("One Angry Dwarf and Two Hundred Solemn Faces"). On "Song for the Dumped," he verbally attacks a girl who just broke up with him. Two songs give an approving nod to marijuana use. One of them, "Battle of Who Could Care Less," is an anthem celebrating apathy and boredom. Depressing stuff.
Summary/Advisory: Fine musicianship aside, *Whatever and Ever Amen* is a disturbingly acerbic album. These guys need to lighten up and count their blessings—and quit dragging teens into their bleak, cynical world.

Better Than Ezra

◆ ◆ ◆ ◆ ◆ ◆ ◆ ◆ ◆ ◆ ◆ ◆ ◆ ◆ ◆ ◆ ◆ ◆ ◆

Better Than Ezra is a trio made up of Kevin Griffin, Tom Drummond, and Cary Bonnecaze. Their debut album, *Deluxe*, has sold more than a million copies.

Title: *Deluxe* (1995)
Label: Elektra
Genre: Rock/Alternative

Pro-Social Content: "Rosealia" points out the destructive nature of jealousy, stating that it "can rip your heart out" and "turn a hand into a fist." The artist wants to avoid messing up yet another relationship on "Killer Inside." Much of the album consists of neutral content ("Southern Girl," "This Time of Year," "Cry in the Sun," "Coyote").

Objectionable Content: "Summerhouse" implies that some murders may be justified. Similarly, on "Porcelain," the singer fantasizes about killing a lover who caused him emotional pain ("I wish I could kill you, savor the sight . . . That I was the last one you ever loved"). The hedonistic "Teenager" tells young people "if it feels good, do it" and "wrap yourself in black" in response to parental oppression. An untitled track refers to gays-for-hire as "streetside Jesus."

Summary/Advisory: Kevin Griffin's lead vocals sound a lot like Garth Brooks with a slight rock inflection. Very pleasant to listen to. But several warped tunes spoil an otherwise interesting effort. Teens can do better than Ezra.

Black, Clint

◆ ◆

This country singer was born in Long Branch, N.J., and grew up in Texas. He won the Country Music Association's Horizon Award for promising new talent (1989) and captured Male Vocalist of the Year honors one year later. In 1991, he joined the Grand Ole Opry and married actress Lisa Hartman. Black had a brief cameo as a riverboat gambler in the 1994 movie *Maverick*, the soundtrack for which featured his hit "Good Run of Bad Luck."

Title: *No Time to Kill* (1993)
Label: RCA
Genre: Country
Pro-Social Content: On the title song, Black counts his days as precious gifts to be respected and values each moment as an opportunity. "Half the Man" credits his wife with being "half the man that I am" and talks of his dependence on her for support. "I'll Take Texas" is a bouncy

tribute to the Lone Star state. The ability of a song to put a spring in our step is the focus of "State of Mind."

Objectionable Content: None

Summary/Advisory: Clint turns a phrase as he borrows from the title of his first album, *Killin' Time*. He also turns a corner. *No Time to Kill* demonstrates lyrical maturity. Instead of "drinkin' [him]self blind," Black avoids any endorsement of alcohol use or abuse. And, although a few songs mourn romances beyond repair, all of the relationships are wholesome. For young fans of hot fiddles and pedal steel guitar, a solid pick!

Blackstreet

◆ ◆ ◆ ◆ ◆ ◆ ◆ ◆ ◆ ◆ ◆ ◆ ◆ ◆ ◆ ◆ ◆ ◆ ◆

Blackstreet is headed up by Teddy "Street" Riley. The group also features Chauncey "Black" Hannibal, Mark L. Middleton, and Eric "E" Williams. Their million-selling *Another Level* peaked at number 1 on the R&B chart, number 3 on the pop chart.

Title: *Another Level* (1996)
Label: Interscope
Genre: R&B
Pro-Social Content: "The Lord Is Real" honors God for His saving grace, guidance, and friendship. The artists' mothers impart positive (at times Christian) advice to their sons on "Motherlude." Several love songs

express long-term commitment while bracing for bumps in the road ahead ("Let's Stay in Love," "I Can't Get You out of My Mind"). A remake of the Beatles's hit "Can't Buy Me Love" prizes relationships above cold, hard cash.

Objectionable Content: A pair of mild profanities mar "I Can't Get You out of My Mind," which finds a man defending past involvements with other women. The boys are in a perpetual sexual lather on "Good Lovin'," "Fix," and "I'll Give It to You." Meanwhile, the Grammy-winning Top-10 single "No Diggity" appears to pay tribute to a prostitute.

Summary/Advisory: Good rhythms, and the cuts directing listeners to God merit praise. If only the lyrics didn't descend to another level inhabited by shallow seduction and hormonal prowling. Detour around Blackstreet.

Blessid Union of Souls

◆ ◆

Blessid Union of Souls consists of Eliot Sloan, Jeff Pence, Charly Roth, and Eddie Hedges. Their first album, *Home,* went gold and yielded three hit singles.

Title: *Blessid Union of Souls* (1997)
Label: EMI
Genre: Rock/Acoustic rock
Pro-Social Content: This project specializes in songs about friendship, commitment, and relational reconciliation. A man is instructed to support the woman in his life by embracing her in times of need ("Hold Her Closer"). On

"Scenes from a Coffee House," loving friends are perfectly content to share platonic companionship. The idea that "love is the reason that we live" inspires a man to avoid taking advantage of the impressionable woman he cares for ("Jelly"). Sharing another's life through good and bad, and wishing him or her the best, is a recurring theme ("Peace and Love," "I Wanna Be There," "My Friend," "It's Your Day").
Objectionable Content: One mild profanity on "I Wanna Be There."
Summary/Advisory: Eliot Sloan—whose lead vocals sound at times like Michael W. Smith—has said that his group's popularity is due mostly to its "positive lyrical vibe." Not too shabby musically, either. With one minor exception, a terrific follow-up to the band's equally upbeat *Home.*

Title: *Home* (1995)
Label: EMI
Genre: Rock/Acoustic rock
Pro-Social Content: Love is the remedy for cultural ills (drug abuse, greed, violence) according to the Top-10 single "I Believe." One line from that hit, "All we do is eliminate our future with the things we do today," points out that actions have consequences. A man shows an apprehensive love-interest patience and understanding ("Let Me Be the One"). "End of the World" reminds us that life goes on after a romance goes sour. "Home" points to heaven as a refuge of peace and togetherness. The artist pays tribute to—and prays for—his grandmother ("Nora") and looks forward to seeing her "on the other side." "Heaven" boldly addresses God's existence,

man's eternal nature, and the need to pray for one's enemies.

Objectionable Content: An isolated line mentions fathering two children out of wedlock.

Summary/Advisory: Overall, an excellent release, both musically and lyrically. A solid, stylish alternative to bands like Counting Crows.

Blige, Mary J.

◆ ◆ ◆ ◆ ◆ ◆ ◆ ◆ ◆ ◆ ◆ ◆ ◆ ◆ ◆ ◆ ◆ ◆ ◆

Hailing from the projects of Yonkers, N.Y., Mary J. Blige (nicknamed the "Queen of Hip-hop Soul" by her fans) is a major player in the world of R&B music. Her rookie effort earned double platinum honors (more than 2 million sold), while her second album exceeded the achievements of her debut.

Title: *Share My World* (1997)
Label: MCA
Genre: R&B

Pro-Social Content: Romantic commitment and relational optimism characterize "Keep Your Head," "Our Love," and the title track. On "Everything," the artist praises a man for consistently chasing away her blues. Elsewhere, Blige seeks to overcome "all the negativity" in the world and experience peace. "Thank You Lord" praises God for her success.

Objectionable Content: The carnal often drowns out the spiritual. Songs such as "It's On," "Seven Days," and "Missing You" either reflect upon or fantasize about sexual encounters—not explicit, but not appropriate either. Profanities mar "Not Gon' Cry" and "Love Is All We Need."

Summary/Advisory: Blige's reputation is built on smooth R&B grooves and silky, Motown-inflected vocals. Lyrically, her *World* is a diverse place. Despite some romantic and spiritual messages, this disc suffers from mild profanity, simmering sexuality, and questionable content from guest rappers.

Title: *My Life* (1994)
Label: Uptown/MCA
Genre: R&B/Hip-hop

Pro-Social Content: "My Life" is a testimony of sorts, crediting "the man up above" with the ability to give us peace of mind when we're feeling down. "Be Happy" seeks "a sign from the sweet Lord above" concerning a romance. Most songs reflect a spirit of love and devotion ("I'm the Only Woman," "I Never Wanna Live Without You," "You Gotta Believe") and a desire for reconciliation ("I'm Goin' Down," "Mary's Joint," "Don't Go"). "I Love You" demonstrates the principle of "tough love."

Objectionable Content: The project opens with a phone conversation punctuated by profanity and racial slang. "Mary Jane" beckons a lover into the bedroom. Two other songs briefly allude to sexual activity.

Summary/Advisory: Smooth vocals and (for the most part) solid lyrics make Mary J. one of R&B's most promising artists. But she seems o-Blige-d to toss in a steamy tune or two, turning a positive disc into a mixed bag.

Blind Melon

◆ ◆

Blind Melon was formed in 1989 by guitarist Roger Stevens and bassist Brad Smith. In a conversation with *Rip* magazine [9/95], the band's lead vocalist Shannon Hoon referred to his history of drug use by saying, "I would be lying if I said that I didn't learn a lot of things being high on various amounts of whatever it was that was in front of me. . . . I take it past  the point of mental stimulation, turning it into physical anni-hilation." Prophetic. A month after that interview appeared, Hoon died of an accidental overdose, bringing an end to this commercially successful alternative rock group.

Title: *Blind Melon* (1993)
Label: Capitol
Genre: Rock
Pro-Social Content: "Change" suggests that a person can overcome circumstances through change. Although hopeful (compared to the rest of this record), it fails to mention biblical specifics.
Objectionable Content: Recreational drug use is promoted on several tunes ("I'm feeling better when I'm high"), and two tracks blatantly reject Christians and their faith ("Holyman" and "Soak the Skin"). "I Wonder" and "Time" talk about enduring a dark, bleak, living hell here on earth. All

things considered (including lines about excretory functions), this album paints a generally dismal picture of life.

Summary/Advisory: Heavy MTV exposure vaulted this band to stardom. But Melon's message is just another loud diatribe about the miseries of human existence, avoiding reality with drugs, and a denial of spiritual truth.

Blues Traveler

◆ ◆ ◆ ◆ ◆ ◆ ◆ ◆ ◆ ◆ ◆ ◆ ◆ ◆ ◆ ◆ ◆ ◆ ◆

Blues Traveler consists of John Popper, Chan Kinchla, Brendan Hill, and Bobby Sheehan. Frontman John Popper has been called the "Hendrix of the harmonica" and is the man primarily responsible for organizing the annual H.O.R.D.E. (Horizons of Rock Developing Everywhere) festival, a neo-hippy rock bacchanalia. The band appeared in the 1998 movie *Blues Brothers 2000*.

Title: *Straight on Till Morning* (1997)
Label: A&M
Genre: Rock/Blues
Pro-Social Content: "Justify the Thrill" condemns racially motivated violence. Lead singer John Popper vulnerably discloses his deep love for a woman who inspires him ("Yours"), gets nostalgic about a romance ("Canadian Rose"), and underscores the brevity of life, urging listeners to leave their mark ("Great Big World").
Objectionable Content: Vulgarities and profanities mar "Most Precarious" and "May My Way," while the f-word appears on "Business As Usual." The perplexing "Psycho Joe" is a song about a killer facing execution on which the artist adopts the voice of social con-science, but he treads a thin line between absurd, tongue-in-cheek com-mentary and a frighteningly nonchalant attitude toward our treatment of violent criminals.
Summary/Advisory: Stylistically akin to the Allman Brothers (with hints of Jimmy Buffett), the passionate guitar- and harmonica-driven sound of Blues Traveler could find parents and teens humming along together. However, *Straight on Till Morning* falls short due to its volatile vocabulary and philosophical ambiguity. The band's *Four* is better.

Title: *Four* (1994)
Label: A&M
Genre: Rock
Pro-Social Content: "Just Wait" counsels a struggling soul with expressions of love and encouragement ("There's no such thing as a failure who keeps trying"). "Run-Around" projects hope in the midst of a broken relationship. The singer pledges support to his sibling on "Brother John." Clouds have silver linings on "Stand," where trials are treated as opportunities for growth ("Every challenge could have paradise behind it"). "Price to Pay" paints a vivid picture of the emotional consequences associated with one-night stands.
Objectionable Content: Two mild expletives appear on "Freedom," which selfishly expresses a desire to take unfair advantage of others.
Summary/Advisory: Cover art of a cat smoking what looks like a marijuana joint will raise more eyebrows than the album's content. In "classic rock" style, *Four* delivers its messages with a sense of strength and optimism. Not perfect, but predominantly positive.

Bolton, Michael

◆ ◆

Michael Bolton continues to earn his status as one of the industry's most successful singer/songwriters. He is an accomplished vocalist and musician with an impressive array of musical experiences and awards to his credit. He has also collaborated with artists ranging from Cher to Luciano Pavarotti—and assists numerous charitable and humanitarian foundations.

Title: *The One Thing* (1993)
Label: Columbia
Genre: Adult contemporary
Pro-Social Content: Eight of the 10 tracks on this hot album express uncompromising romantic commitment. Even the Top-15 single "I Said I Loved You . . . But I Lied" defies its title by stating, "I lied 'cause this is more than love I feel inside." He expresses his devotion to a future partner on "Completely." "Ain't Got Nothing If You Ain't Got Love" claims "fortune and fame [are] just things that ya leave behind," a sentiment Bolton models through his foundation, which supports children and women at risk

and provides access to education for underprivileged young people. That theme also permeates the lyrics to "In the Arms of Love," which would sound equally at home if played on a Christian radio station.

Objectionable Content: None

Summary/Advisory: Bolton's passionate vocals and belief in enduring romantic love make *The One Thing* an uplifting effort from start to finish.

Title: *Timeless (The Classics)* (1992)
Label: Columbia
Genre: Soul/Pop/Adult contemporary
Pro-Social Content: Only the bluesy "Since I Fell for You" and memorable Beatles lament "Yesterday" dim the album's otherwise sunny outlook on love ("To Love Somebody," "You Send Me," "Bring It on Home to Me"). Via a remake of the Four Tops's number-1 hit from 1966, "Reach out I'll Be There," Bolton commits to support, love, and shelter a floundering, disillusioned woman. Music soothes the savage beast via Dobie Gray's classic, "Drift Away." Bolton closes with Irving Berlin's seasonal favorite, "White Christmas."

Objectionable Content: None

Summary/Advisory: Bolton's soulful voice is adored by fans, tolerated by casual channel surfers, and maligned by critics. Say what you want—he keeps it clean. *Timeless (The Classics)* is an album of lushly arranged rhythm and blues, pop standards, and Motown favorites likely to endear him to many teens as well as parents.

Bon Jovi

◆ ◆ ◆ ◆ ◆ ◆ ◆ ◆ ◆ ◆ ◆ ◆ ◆ ◆ ◆ ◆ ◆ ◆ ◆

Led by Jon Bon Jovi (actual name: Bongiovi), this edgy New Jersey arena-rock band also features Richie Sambora, Dave Bryan, Alec John Such, and Tico Torres. In recent years, Jon has launched a career in motion pictures, appearing in the films *Moonlight and Valentino*, *The Leading Man*, *Little City*, *Row Your Boat*, *No Looking Back*, and *Homegrown*.

Title: *Keep the Faith* (1992)
Label: Warner Bros.

Genre: Pop/Metal/Rock

Pro-Social Content: "Keep the Faith" seeks to achieve peace with estranged parents. "I Believe" preaches self-reliance in a world of commercially peddled ideologies, though it fails to distinguish between secular worldviews and Christianity.

Objectionable Content: Drinking makes unwelcome appearances on "Dry County," "I Want You," and "Bed of Roses" (where Bon Jovi is "wasted and wounded . . . a bottle of vodka . . . still lodged" in his head). "Gonna Sleep When I'm Dead" assumes you can show up for the "party" in heaven after living a morally reckless life "built for speed" here on earth.

Summary/Advisory: Bon Jovi's attempt to infuse this album with religious imagery actually presents themes closer to the principles of secularism and hedonism. The imagery borders on blasphemy in the sexually charged "Bed of Roses" ("Close as the Holy Ghost is/Lay you down on a bed of roses"). The record title suggests religious convictions that fail to surface while offering a self-serving "salvation" teens can do without.

Bone Thugs N Harmony

◆ ◆

This Cleveland-based group is made up of five members who go by the names Layzie Bone, Krayzie Bone, Bizzy Bone, Wish Bone, and Flesh 'N Bone. Band members claim they "keep it real" because they actually lived the gangsta lifestyle—selling drugs and committing crimes. All band members are in their teens or early 20s.

Title: *The Art of War* (1997)

Label: Ruthless

Genre: Gangsta rap

Pro-Social Content: The rappers tell young fans not to follow their example on "If I Could Teach the World." "Mo' Thug-Family Tree" says "Thank you, Jesus Christ, for giving up your life"; however . . .

Objectionable Content: . . . the track goes on to boast, "Weed and party all the time . . . keep on thuggin'; that's how we make our livin'." Amid a shower of f-words and other obscenities, the artist makes violent threats ("put him in a coffin . . . left his guts in my truck," "you gonna

be bloody red," "it's time for warfare," "flippin' off police," "we sendin' 'em home in a body bag") and associates drugs and alcohol with urban machismo ("We buck with justice, smoke blunts," "So get high and analyze your crime"). "Body Rott" talks of communicating with the dead and cursing the living via a Ouija board.

Summary/Advisory: Two positives on a 28-track collection is a pitiful ratio. And in context, even those sentiments ring hollow, as do the guys' claims of "Doin' our best to serve God." *The Art of War* is nothing more than two hours of vicious, confused ramblings.

Title: *E. 1999 Eternal* (1995)
Label: Ruthless
Genre: Gangsta rap
Pro-Social Content: None
Objectionable Content: A Ouija board is used to tell the rappers' futures ("Mr. Ouija 2"), apply a curse ("No Shorts, No Losses"), and urge a gun-toting gangsta to kill someone ("Mo' Murda"). Six other obscenity-strewn tracks promote marijuana use. Still, the act's violent soul dominates this disc. "Crept and We Came" boasts about "pulling the trigger to blow out your brains." Cop killing appears on "Shotz to Tha Double Glock" and "Die Die Die." Bill collectors had better watch their backs as well ("Mr. Bill Collector"). Ugly, hateful stuff.
Summary/Advisory: Violence. Drugs. Dabbling in the occult. This chart-topping pop and R&B effort is a shamefully consistent follow-up to the group's 3 million-selling debut. Teens should turn a deaf ear to this trash.

Title: *Creepin On Ah Come Up* (1994)
Label: Ruthless
Genre: Gangsta rap
Pro-Social Content: None
Objectionable Content: The Thugs consult a Ouija board to ask, "Will I die by murder?" on "Mr. Ouija." Start to finish, "muthaf———" and other obscenities attempt to demonstrate streetwise prowess, but instead magnify thinly veiled ignorance. The orgiastic "Moe Cheese" is nothing more than instrumentals and sound effects from sex in session. Drinking and drugs get a plug on "Thuggish Ruggish Bone," which also encourages violence. Many references to gangsta warfare include sexualized brutality against women ("Foe Tha Love of $"), cop killing ("No Surrender"), and armed robbery (the title track).
Summary/Advisory: Bad to the bone, this nauseating extended play disc (stickered for explicit lyrics) is hateful refuse from beginning to end.

Boston

◆ ◆ ◆ ◆ ◆ ◆ ◆ ◆ ◆ ◆ ◆ ◆ ◆ ◆ ◆ ◆ ◆ ◆ ◆

Not just another band out of Boston, this multi-platinum group from Beantown has charted two number-1 albums, *Don't Look Back* (1978) and *Third Stage* (1986). The band started out as the quintet of Tom Scholz, Brad Delp, Barry Goudreau, Fran Sheehan, and Sib Hashian. By 1986, the group consisted solely of Scholz and Delp.

Title: *Walk On* (1994)
Label: MCA
Genre: Rock
Pro-Social Content: "We Can Make It" seeks to resolve a troubled relationship (although it plays like a love song, the liner notes qualify it as being "from a father to his son"). The title cut honors people who choose to stand for what's right, maintaining a positive attitude in the face of opposition. "Livin' for You" speaks of prayer in a positive context, denounces lying, and views true love as meeting the needs of others.
Objectionable Content: Sexual concessions are called for on "Surrender to Me," which describes a lover as "still kind of sleazy" and "good at teasing." On "Livin' for You," the singer describes a woman as his "religion."
Summary/Advisory: Adults will remember this classic rock band for tunes like "More Than a Feeling" and "Don't Look Back." After an eight-year absence, Boston returned with this disc that took four years to complete. But lyrical inconsistency spoils an otherwise fine effort.

Boyz II Men

◆ ◆ ◆ ◆ ◆ ◆ ◆ ◆ ◆ ◆ ◆ ◆ ◆ ◆ ◆ ◆ ◆ ◆ ◆

Boyz II Men is comprised of Michael McCary, Wanya Morris, Shawn Stockman, and Nathan Morris. Their debut album sold more than 7 million copies, winning in excess of 15 different awards. In 1993, they broke Elvis's long-standing record of 13 weeks at number one with "End of the Road." They beat their own record in 1994 when "I'll Make Love to You" stayed on top for 14 consecutive weeks.

Title: *Evolution* (1997)
Label: Motown
Genre: R&B/Hip-hop
Pro-Social Content: The reverent and prayerful "Dear God" values eternal things over the worldly and thanks the Father for His love, grace, and the atoning death of Christ—outstanding! "Can't Let Her Go" expresses romantic commitment ("She knows I'm never leavin'"). "Never" and "Baby C'mon" encourage a woman to remain upbeat in the wake of heartbreak. The Boyz pay tribute to their mothers for years of love, faithfulness, and moral guidance ("A Song for Mama").

Objectionable Content: "Girl in the Life Magazine" confuses infatuation with true love. The singer reminisces about coed skinny-dipping (the number-1 hit "4 Seasons of Loneliness") and offers to dry off and lotion down his partner after a bath ("Human II").

Summary/Advisory: Impressive, impassioned harmonies. Smooth instrumentation. Best of all, the Boyz have experienced a positive lyrical evolution. While not perfect, these messages are a vast improvement over the blatant sexual come-ons on their last album.

Title: *II* (1994)
Label: Motown
Genre: Hip-hop/Doo-wop/Soul
Pro-Social Content: A repentant man desires a closer, healthier relationship with his lady on "Water Runs Dry" (promising better, more loving communication) and "On Bended Knee" (humbly accepting blame for the couple's strife). "Trying Times" and "Thank You" express appreciation for a lover's long-term faithfulness. The Boyz also celebrate friendship by "Vibin'."

Objectionable Content: "I'll Make Love to You" is one long sexual come-on ("Throw your clothes on the floor/I'm gonna take my clothes off, too"). Similarly, "50 Candles" describes a feverish sexual encounter in progress.

Summary/Advisory: It's no wonder Boyz II Men is such a popular group. This talented urban quartet blends upbeat melodies with smooth vocal harmonies. But like All-4-One (peers with a similar sound), the Boyz can't seem to resist including a song or two in which raging hormones take center stage, thus spoiling an otherwise enjoyable effort.

Brandt, Paul

◆ ◆ ◆ ◆ ◆ ◆ ◆ ◆ ◆ ◆ ◆ ◆ ◆ ◆ ◆ ◆ ◆ ◆ ◆

A native Canadian, Paul Brandt was born and raised in Calgary, Alberta. *Calm Before the Storm* earned its place among the nation's Top 15 country albums.

Title: *Calm Before the Storm* (1996)
Label: Reprise
Genre: Country

Pro-Social Content: Lifelong love and commitment take the fore on "Take It from Me" and "I Do." With pedal-steel regrets, "I Meant to Do That" enumerates acts of kindness that, left undone, can lead to relational failure. Inner beauty outweighs cosmetic attraction when the artist looks "On the Inside" of a woman. An impressive departure from typical honky tonk fare, "12-Step Recovery" *doesn't* include getting drunk among its recommendations for rebounding from a broken heart. A man refuses to serve as a romantic stepping-stone for a wandering woman on "Pass Me By (If You're Only Passing Through)"—a remake of Ronnie Milsap's remake of the old Johnny Rodriguez classic.

Objectionable Content: Minor. Several cuts take place in a bar, but with just one passing reference to alcohol.

Summary/Advisory: Rich vocals and wholesome lyrics elevate this Canadian baritone above the Nashville norm. *Calm Before the Storm's* blend of uptempo tunes and thoughtful ballads gives discerning country music fans reason to kick up their heels.

Brandy

◆ ◆ ◆ ◆ ◆ ◆ ◆ ◆ ◆ ◆ ◆ ◆ ◆ ◆ ◆ ◆ ◆ ◆ ◆

At the tender age of 15, Brandy Norwood became one of the top recording artists for Atlantic records. Her self-titled debut sold more than 3 million copies, and she was nominated for Best New Artist of the Year. She also starred in her own nationally televised sitcom, *Moesha*.

Title: *Brandy* (1994)
Label: Atlantic
Genre: R&B

Pro-Social Content: Both of the hit singles ("Baby" and "I Wanna Be Down") pledge devotion to a romantic partner, while "Best Friend" thanks a friend for caring, promising to do likewise. Other themes include humbly battling for restoration in fractured relationships ("As Long As You're Here") and keeping romantic disappointments in perspective ("Brokenhearted").

Brandy refuses to be distracted from pursuing her dreams or made to conform on "Movin' On" ("Trying to keep my mind pointed to a higher plane . . . I don't want to stand with the crowd"). "Give Me You" appears to credit God with being a faithful friend.

Objectionable Content: None

Summary/Advisory: Unlike all-girl acts with a similar sound, Brandy's urban rhythms don't emphasize breathless sexual encounters. *Brandy* is a lyrically refreshing debut. Still, this teen appears in the Hollywood slasher sequel to *I Know What You Did Last Summer*, which could signal a shift toward questionable fare.

Braxton, Toni

◆ ◆ ◆ ◆ ◆ ◆ ◆ ◆ ◆ ◆ ◆ ◆ ◆ ◆ ◆ ◆ ◆ ◆ ◆ ◆

Since releasing her self-titled debut in July 1993, Braxton has sold more than 15 million albums worldwide. She has won three Grammy awards, three American Music awards and two Soul Train awards. On January 23, 1998, Braxton filed for bankruptcy after debts and an unprofitable European concert tour left her owing $2.8 million.

Title: *Secrets* (1996)
Label: LaFace
Genre: R&B/Pop/Soul

Pro-Social Content: On "Why Should I Care," the artist practices "tough love" with a dishonest man. A number of lyrics find Braxton sifting through the pieces of a broken heart. She also seeks an understanding, faithful, sensitive guy "that knows right from wrong" and will "keep his loving at home" ("Find Me a Man").

Objectionable Content: "Talking in His Sleep" misrepresents adultery as a "petty crime of sexual indiscretion." Racy and imprudent, the hit single "You're Making Me High" envisions a sexual encounter ("I can imagine you touching my private parts . . . all I want is moonlights, with you there inside me"). She also propositions a man by using sexually suggestive lingo ("Come on Over Here"). A mild profanity is uttered twice.

Summary/Advisory: Lilting vocals and silky smooth rhythms would signal that these songs are radio-friendly. But a closer listen reveals inconsistent messages on *Secrets*. Psssst! Skip it.

Title: *Toni Braxton* (1993)
Label: LaFace
Genre: Pop/Hip-hop
Pro-Social Content: Braxton expresses appreciation to the man in her life on "How Many Ways" and acknowledges that relationships require effort on "You Mean the World to Me" ("Now it's gonna take some workin' . . . tell me you'll always be true").

Objectionable Content: Premarital sex is indirectly condoned on "Love Affair" when she rejects sex with another out of devotion to a boyfriend. Such lyrical ambiguity invades several cuts, leaving the listener to fill in the relational context ("Breathe Again," "Spending My Time with You"). A preoccupation with unfaithful lovers and dysfunctional attitudes also mars this effort. Braxton complains that her lover has been "hittin' every girl in town" ("Seven Whole Days") and even sleeping with her best friend ("Best Friend").

Summary/Advisory: A talented woman. But dynamic vocals can't save this disappointing debut mired in mixed messages.

Brooks, Garth

◆ ◆ ◆ ◆ ◆ ◆ ◆ ◆ ◆ ◆ ◆ ◆ ◆ ◆ ◆ ◆ ◆ ◆ ◆ ◆

Garth Brooks released his first album, *Garth Brooks*, in 1989. In 1994 alone, his list of tangible accolades included the American Music Awards' Best Country Male Vocalist, Academy of Country Music's Entertainer of the Year and *Billboard*'s No. 1 Country Male Artist. Brooks is now the only male artist in Recording Industry Association of America history to have two solo albums top the 10 million-unit sales mark and is surpassed only by The Beatles in total album sales.

Title: *Sevens* (1997)
Genre: Country
Pro-Social Content: The artist pays tribute to the inspirational love of a woman ("You Move Me") and the beauty, work ethic, and mothering skills of either his woman or his truck ("Cowboy Cadillac"). During a Christmas truce, WWII enemies sing "Silent Night" together from their trenches on "Belleau Wood." The cautionary "She's Gonna Make It" describes the emotional fallout from divorce. With a "no guts, no glory" attitude, Brooks applauds those who risk failure in life and love ("How You Ever Gonna Know"). "Fit for a King" honors a homeless former alcoholic who shares the gospel on a street corner.
Objectionable Content: "Two Pina Coladas" finds the singer seeking solace in alcohol, while "Longneck Bottle" sends mixed messages about drinking. A man and woman—both otherwise married—express feelings for each other ("In Another's Eyes").
Summary/Advisory: With these exceptions, *Sevens* delivers more inspiring messages than we've heard on a single Garth Brooks's disc in long time. In its first two weeks, this number-1 chartbuster sold a record 1.5 million copies, catapulting Brooks ahead of Elvis Presley in total career album sales.

Title: *Fresh Horses* (1995)
Label: Capitol
Genre: Country
Pro-Social Content: Motivated by love for mankind and a disgust for worldly cynicism, "The Change" expresses the desire to rescue one lost soul even though a thousand more may perish ("It's not the world that I am changing/I do this so the world will know that it will not change me"). Likewise, "Ireland" is the poetic diary of a soldier prepared to die for his country.
Objectionable Content: "That Ol' Wind" implies that intimate relations between strangers can produce genuine love. A veiled reference to sex appears on "It's Midnight Cinderella." "Rollin'" describes a sexual proposition from a wild woman and mentions "getting naked." On the number-1 country hit "She's Every Woman," the artist explains that he has had numerous lovers—and fantasized about others.
Summary/Advisory: As musically enjoyable as Brooks's earlier efforts, *Fresh Horses* is just as lyrically inconsistent. Too bad there aren't more tunes like "The Change," which proves Garth is at his best when he doesn't "party on." Find the single. Skip the disc.

Title: *In Pieces* (1993)
Genre: Country

Label: Liberty
Pro-Social Content: Branders—and their spiritual roots—are honored in "The Cowboy Song."
Objectionable Content: On "The Night I Called the Old Man Out," a boy respects his father's authority only after Dad bloodies him in a fistfight. Also, "love" can be found in a one-night stand ("Callin' Baton Rouge"), an adulterous affair ("The Night Will Only Know"), and rebellious teen sex in the back of a pickup truck ("Ain't Going Down"). Alcohol flows on several tracks, including "American Honky-Tonk Bar Association," which replaces church and family with the local tavern.
Summary/Advisory: This disc soared to the top of the pop and country charts. And it's musically enjoyable. Too bad the family-friendly values Garth conveyed on earlier albums are falling *In Pieces.*

Brooks & Dunn

◆ ◆ ◆ ◆ ◆ ◆ ◆ ◆ ◆ ◆ ◆ ◆ ◆ ◆ ◆ ◆ ◆ ◆

High-energy singing and country songwriting by partners Kix Brooks and Ronnie Dunn have propelled this twosome to numerous number-1 singles, sold-out concerts, and platinum albums. This Grammy-award winning duo secured the top spot on the country chart with *Borderline,* and even more recently released a greatest hits collection.

Title: *Borderline* (1996)
Label: Arista
Genre: Country
Pro-Social Content: A love song praises Maria for easing the singer's mind and setting his soul free ("My Maria"). "I Am That Man" pledges a love that's "true and strong" to a romantically with-drawn woman, while "My Love Will Follow You" refuses to give up on one who has abandoned the relationship. "Why Would I Say Goodbye" 'fesses up to stubborn pride and seeks a female's forgiveness.
Objectionable Content: Typical of this duo's lyrics, whiskey flows liberally. "Redneck Rhythm and Blues" lives for the work whistle and a trip to the local "waterin' hole." If a love goes bad, the boys recommend beer and booze to ease the pain ("More Than a Margarita," "One Heartache at a Time," "Tequila Town"). A married couple looks forward to some wild partying (the woman in a "low-cut dress") on "Mama Don't Get Dressed Up for Nothing."

Summary/Advisory: Stylistically, it's Jimmy Buffett in cowboy boots—no big departure for Kix Brooks and Ronnie Dunn. Too bad an unhealthy preoccupation with alcohol puts a burr in the saddle of this number-1 country disc. Many fine Christian artists with a similar country flavor point teens to *Jesus* for comfort . . . *not* to a bottle.

Title: *Hard Workin' Man* (1993)
Label: Arista
Genre: Country
Pro-Social Content: On "She Used to Be Mine," Dunn accepts responsibility for a failed relationship and makes his pain an example of the consequence of not treating a woman well.
Objectionable Content: Several of these tunes, including "Heartbroke Out of My Mind" and "Mexican Minute," mention drinking as a way to escape reality or kill pain. On the title cut, a week's pay is spent to secure the company of a "weekend beauty." Elsewhere, Brooks desires a woman who "acts like Madonna, but she listens to Merle [Haggard]" ("Rock My World Little Country Girl"). Not a single mention of solid, meaningful relationships.
Summary/Advisory: This popular country duo promotes a wild, often irresponsible lifestyle that includes plenty of alcohol and barroom flirtation. With all the positive country acts charting these days, teens can afford to "boot scoot" past this one.

Brown, Foxy

◆ ◆ ◆ ◆ ◆ ◆ ◆ ◆ ◆ ◆ ◆ ◆ ◆ ◆ ◆ ◆ ◆

Teenager Foxy Brown (17 when she recorded *Ill Na Na*) has accumulated a staggering 3.5 million *singles* sold. Her music career was launched after she helped record a track for L.L. Cool J's *Mr. Smith* album.

Title: *Ill Na Na* (1996)
Label: Def Jam/PolyGram
Genre: Gangsta rap
Pro-Social Content: None
Objectionable Content: The disc begins with the statement, "The following previews have been approved for all audiences by the committee for audio-visual sound." Nothing could be further from the truth.

Obscenities, explicit sex, and references to gangsta violence abound. Brown describes a lifestyle of drugs, guns, and cop killing on "(Holy Matrimony) Letter to the Firm." The vengeful "Intro" ends with a gunshot. Violence is also glamorized on "The Chase," "The Promise," and "Interlude . . . The Set Up." "No One's" applauds high-stakes gambling and smoking marijuana. Sexual bragging using raw language ("Fox Boogie") and a lewd mention of Pee Wee Herman masturbating ("Ill Na Na") epitomize the sleaze.

Summary/Advisory: What makes this audio porn even more revolting is that it was recorded by a 17-year-old girl. Teens' requests for the trashy tunes of Foxy Brown deserve the reply, "*Ill?* No, no!"

Browne, Jackson

◆ ◆ ◆ ◆ ◆ ◆ ◆ ◆ ◆ ◆ ◆ ◆ ◆ ◆ ◆ ◆ ◆ ◆ ◆

Jackson Browne's career as a singer-songwriter has spanned more than a quarter century. His songs have been recorded by artists such as Linda Ronstadt, The Byrds, The Eagles, and The Nitty Gritty Dirt Band.

Title: *I'm Alive* (1993)
Genre: Acoustic rock
Pro-Social Content: On "Sky Blue and Black" and "I'll Do Anything," the artist expresses his love and devotion to a woman. A line from the latter states, "I make your happiness my responsibility." The object of his affection dominates his thoughts on "Everywhere I Go." Marital reconciliation is the focus of "Too Many Angels" ("I want to watch the children as they run; I want this darkness gone"). Other songs involve facing lost love with a spirit of optimism and perseverance ("I'm Alive," "Take This Rain").

Objectionable Content: "My Problem Is You" abdicates behavioral responsibility, stating, "For some kinds of pleasure there are no defenses."

Summary/Advisory: Adults may remember Browne from 1978 when he was "Running on Empty." Whether or not he can stage a comeback remains to be seen. Overall, *I'm Alive* is a solid effort, weaving together pro-social poetry and acoustic guitar melodies.

Bush

◆ ◆ ◆ ◆ ◆ ◆ ◆ ◆ ◆ ◆ ◆ ◆ ◆ ◆ ◆ ◆ ◆ ◆ ◆ ◆

Composed of Gavin Rossdale, Dave Parsons, Nigel Pulsford, and Robin Goodridge, the band began in 1992 by playing in Europe. *Razorblade Suitcase* debuted at number 1 on *Billboard*'s pop album chart.

Title: *Razorblade Suitcase* (1996)
Label: Trauma
Genre: Alternative
Pro-Social Content: Isolated lines—plucked from thematic disarray—express love for another ("Swallowed") and some optimism ("Distant Voices," "Communicator"); however . . .
Objectionable Content: . . . hopelessness prevails. Lacking any genuine answers to life's

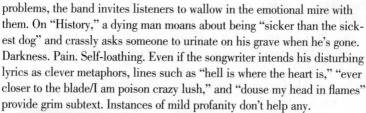

problems, the band invites listeners to wallow in the emotional mire with them. On "History," a dying man moans about being "sicker than the sickest dog" and crassly asks someone to urinate on his grave when he's gone. Darkness. Pain. Self-loathing. Even if the songwriter intends his disturbing lyrics as clever metaphors, lines such as "hell is where the heart is," "ever closer to the blade/I am poison crazy lush," and "douse my head in flames" provide grim subtext. Instances of mild profanity don't help any.
Summary/Advisory: The overwhelming nihilism on *Razorblade Suitcase* gives parents ample reason to send this band packing. Young fans of the genre should give the Christian group Plankeye a listen instead.

Title: *Sixteen Stone* (1995)
Label: Trauma
Genre: Alternative
Pro-Social Content: Isolated lines express love.
Objectionable Content: An MTV buzz bin favorite, "Everything Zen" links rage and erotica by repeating, "There's no sex in your violence." The singer also refers to his "a—hole brother" in the midst of pessimistic soul searching. Various tracks portray life as miserable and meaningless ("Machinehead," "Bomb"). "Swim" sinks like a stone because of sexual references ("We're naked again . . . I wanna fit inside you"). Contextual ambiguity on tunes dealing with death could send dangerous messages. "Bomb" shouts "Blow me away, see if I care . . . kill a man, kill a girl."

"Swim" repeats, "I wanna die." On the macho, gun-toting "Testosterone," the artist calls himself a whore "big into war."
Summary/Advisory: Some might call this "Nirvana-esque poetry." Nihilistic noise is more like it. Don't let Bush take root in your home; deep-six requests for *Sixteen Stone.*

Butthole Surfers

◆ ◆

King Coffey, Gibby Haynes, and Paul Leary make up the trio called Butthole Surfers. Founded in 1981 by Leary and Haynes, the band has 13 albums to its credit. Capitol Records released an alternative cover for *Electriclarryland* since four retail outlets—including Wal-Mart—said they found the original cover art (a pencil jammed into the bloodied ear of a cartoon character) objectionable.

Title: *Electriclarryland* (1996)
Label: Capitol
Genre: Punk rock
Pro-Social Content: No praiseworthy themes in this 51-minute stream of consciousness.
Objectionable Content: "My Brother's Wife" appears to be about a man lusting after his sister-in-law. "Birds" can't soar above its own dismal outlook on life, convinced that "you'll always end up on the floor wasted." After describing a possible gender-bending sixsome, the monotone vocalist bemoans that a man was shot in the leg instead of in the head ("Pepper"). "The Lord Is a Monkey" refers to God as a primate and goes on to tell of a woman with "dope up her a—" who castrated a man and sewed his testicles to his head. Disgusting. But how much more should we expect from a band whose cover art features a rendering of a pencil penetrating a human ear?
Summary/Advisory: Psychotic musings or drug-induced absurdity? Hard to say for sure. One interviewer described this cryptic novelty act as "one of the most depraved, tasteless, and thoroughly naughty bands ever." That, along with the group's sick moniker, says it all. Don't let teens visit *Electriclarryland.*

Cake

◆ ◆ ◆ ◆ ◆ ◆ ◆ ◆ ◆ ◆ ◆ ◆ ◆ ◆ ◆ ◆ ◆ ◆ ◆ ◆

The Sacramento-based Cake formed in September 1991. Band members include John McCrea, Greg Brown, Victor Damiani, Todd Roper, and Vince di Fiore. Their first album, *Motorcade of Generosity*, received critical acclaim from underground sources.

Title: *Fashion Nugget* (1997)
Label: Capricorn
Genre: Rock/Rap/Novelty
Pro-Social Content: "Perhaps, Perhaps, Perhaps" and "Open Book" articulate the need for communication in relationships.
Objectionable Content: Marred by an unclear context, a woman with "healthy breasts" is described as bouncing on a man's "Italian Leather Sofa." "Nugget" angrily (and repeatedly) exclaims, "Shut the f—- up!" The f-word also appears on the otherwise upbeat "I Will Survive." Uncouth imagery lands "Race Car Ya-Yas" in the pits—visions of cars in which "large, fuzzy dice still hang proudly like testicles from rearview mirrors."
Summary/Advisory: Put diverse musical genres in a big blender, hit mix, and you end up with Cake, an interesting combination of stylistic ingredients. But lyrically, this is no "family" recipe. Lightweight pro-social messages and neutral nonsense songs are no match for the band's coarse language and sexual innuendo.

Campbell, Tevin

◆ ◆ ◆ ◆ ◆ ◆ ◆ ◆ ◆ ◆ ◆ ◆ ◆ ◆ ◆ ◆ ◆ ◆ ◆ ◆

Tevin Campbell has been singing since he was four years old. He has collaborated with a variety of artists, including Quincy Jones, Puffy Combs, and Keith Crouch.

Title: *I'm Ready* (1993)
Label: Qwest/Warner Bros.
Genre: Hip-hop/Pop
Pro-Social Content: "Always in My Heart" pledges loving devotion. Working through relational trials is the focus of both the title track and

"Can We Talk." "Infant Child" states that God is always faithful to His children.

Objectionable Content: On "Shhh," a woman's erotic breathing provides background for teens having sex on a kitchen table. "The Halls of Desire" opens a series of doors (each a metaphor for a step toward intercourse), justifying the behavior by saying, "If you go [in], you'll come out with a smile and that's reason enough." Instead of offering positive solutions, rebellion is the recommended response to racial injustice on "Uncle Sam" and "Paris 1798430," which blame America for the struggles facing young blacks.

Summary/Advisory: Smooth vocals and a catchy style, but lyrically confused. Despite several positive facets, this effort is no gem.

Candlebox

◆ ◆

This hard-rock band, consisting of Kevin Martin, Peter Klett, Bardi Martin, and Scott Mercado, has toured with Metallica and Rush, and was a part of Woodstock II in 1994.

Title: *Candlebox* (1993)
Label: Maverick/Sire/Warner Bros.
Genre: Hard rock
Pro-Social Content: A sense of optimism permeates "Change." "He Calls Home" identifies with the troubled existence of the homeless. Amid raw language, the singer rejects drugs on "You" while pledging loyalty to a friend.

Objectionable Content: The dismal "Don't You" propagates hopelessness. Despite romantic sentiments early, "Blossom" deteriorates into hateful domination ("You will feel the hate I breed/You're under me/You will feel the pain I want to bring"). Also, obscenities (including the f-word) punctuate lyrics on numerous tracks—even songs with reasonably praiseworthy themes.

Summary/Advisory: This debut disc has a few redeeming elements, but the band's explicit, gratuitous use of profanity far overshadows them. Snuff out requests for *Candlebox*.

Cardigans, The

◆ ◆ ◆ ◆ ◆ ◆ ◆ ◆ ◆ ◆ ◆ ◆ ◆ ◆ ◆ ◆ ◆ ◆

The Cardigans formed in October 1992 in
Jonkoping, Sweden. The band includes Peter
Svensson, Magnus Sveningsson, Nina Persson,
Bengt Lagerberg, and Lasse Johansson.

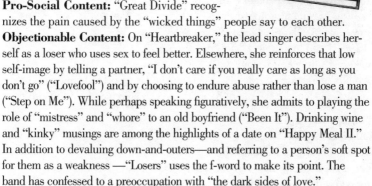

Title: *First Band on the Moon* (1997)
Label: Mercury
Genre: Pop
Pro-Social Content: "Great Divide" recog-
nizes the pain caused by the "wicked things" people say to each other.
Objectionable Content: On "Heartbreaker," the lead singer describes herself as a loser who uses sex to feel better. Elsewhere, she reinforces that low
self-image by telling a partner, "I don't care if you really care as long as you
don't go" ("Lovefool") and by choosing to endure abuse rather than lose a man
("Step on Me"). While perhaps speaking figuratively, she admits to playing the
role of "mistress" and "whore" to an old boyfriend ("Been It"). Drinking wine
and "kinky" musings are among the highlights of a date on "Happy Meal II."
In addition to devaluing down-and-outers—and referring to a person's soft spot
for them as a weakness —"Losers" uses the f-word to make its point. The
band has confessed to a preoccupation with "the dark sides of love."
Summary/Advisory: The Cardigans specialize in bouncy pop melodies
(sung by Nina Persson) with stylistic throwbacks to the early '70s. But that
sonic perfume does little more than aromatize songs about relational dysfunction and misery.

Carey, Mariah

◆ ◆ ◆ ◆ ◆ ◆ ◆ ◆ ◆ ◆ ◆ ◆ ◆ ◆ ◆ ◆ ◆ ◆

Mariah's life has always been deeply rooted in music due to the influence of
her mother, a jazz vocalist and opera singer. She first appeared on radio
playlists in 1990 with her hit single "Vision of Love." Mariah Carey was the
first artist to have her first five singles all go to number 1.

Title: *Butterfly* (1997)
Label: Columbia
Genre: Pop/R&B

Pro-Social Content: Carey mourns a loss of innocence on "Close My Eyes." "Breakdown" and "Butterfly" depict a woman's internal struggles as she emotionally jockeys for position in romantic relationships. "Whenever You Call" pledges lasting devotion to the man in her life.

Objectionable Content: More than usual for this artist. She longs to get "between the sheets" with an unattainable man, choosing to drown her sorrows in alcohol ("Babydoll"). While more subtle, "Honey" and "My All" crave sexual intimacy. Carey recalls a night of champagne and forbidden desire during which she "threw caution to the wind" ("The Roof") and an Independence Day highlighted by casual sexual fireworks ("Fourth of July").

Summary/Advisory: *Entertainment Weekly* [9/19/97] said this project "aims to present its maker as a fully grown woman dipping into a new, sexually liberated lifestyle." It succeeds. And Carey is taking millions of young fans along for the romp. Avoid the moth-eaten morals of *Butterfly*.

Title: *Daydream* (1995)
Label: Columbia
Genre: Pop/Adult contemporary
Pro-Social Content: "One Sweet Day" looks forward to a heavenly reunion with a friend and credits God with hearing prayer. The source is uncertain, but "I Am Free" thanks someone for redemptive love. Carey cries out in humility for a relationship to be restored (a remake of Journey's 1981 hit, "Open Arms"). She expresses a love that is longsuffering on "Always Be My Baby" and "Forever."

Objectionable Content: Nothing explicit. On "Melt Away" Mariah says, "When you talk to me in that sensual tone . . . I lose my self-control." A similar line appears on "Long Ago."

Summary/Advisory: *Daydream*'s pretty, lilting melodies don't break any new ground, but will surely satisfy fans of Carey's earlier work. The disc is mostly positive, but an even better option would be the singer's Christ-centered 1994 holiday release, *Merry Christmas*.

Title: *Merry Christmas* (1994)
Label: Columbia
Genre: Pop/Seasonal
Pro-Social Content: From a soulful rendition of "Silent Night" to the

rousing urban-gospel favorite "Jesus, Oh What a Wonderful Child," reverent yuletide melodies comprise the heart and soul of this disc. Other familiar carols include "Hark! The Herald Angels Sing," "Joy to the World," and "O Holy Night." Carey co-wrote "Jesus Born on This Day," which states, "He is our light and salvation . . . He is the King of all nations/Behold the Lamb of God has come . . . He is our Lord and Savior." The freshly penned "Miss You Most" and "All I Want for Chistmas Is You" make the point that a commercialized holiday can't take the place of being close to loved ones.

Objectionable Content: Some families may object to Carey's "snow-bunny" liner photos.

Summary/Advisory: It's rare that a mainstream Christmas album captures the true meaning of the season. This one does, beautifully. *Merry Christmas* delivers wholesome lyrics and fun, upbeat melodies perfectly suited to Carey's trademark, four-octave vocal calisthenics. It's one gift worth unwrapping early . . . and playing all year 'round!

Title: *Music Box* (1993)
Label: Columbia
Genre: Pop/Soul
Pro-Social Content: "I've Been Thinking About You" describes falling in love with a long-time platonic friend. The title track thanks a lover for his faithful support in hard times ("When I am low, you wash away my tears and take me through the loneliness and emptiness"). Carey seeks and pledges lasting devotion to her man on "All I've Ever Wanted" and "Never Forget You."

Objectionable Content: Some lyrical ambiguity leaves it up to the listener to determine the relational context of several love songs.

Summary/Advisory: Carey's soulful vocals are the best in the business. Happily for listeners, she uses them to enhance predominantly positive messages on *Music Box*.

Carlisle, Bob

◆ ◆ ◆ ◆ ◆ ◆ ◆ ◆ ◆ ◆ ◆ ◆ ◆ ◆ ◆ ◆ ◆ ◆ ◆

This singer/songwriter grew up in Santa Ana, California, and played in a variety of bands—Good News, Psalm 150, and Allies—before going solo in 1993. A gospel artist, Carlisle shocked the pop music industry with the overwhelming mainstream acceptance of his song "Butterfly Kisses" nearly a year after it was originally released. It won a 1998 Grammy for Best Country Song and earned his *Shades of Grace* album multiplatinum status.

Title: *Butterfly Kisses: Shades of Grace* (1996)
Label: Diadem
Genre: Adult contemporary/Gospel
Pro-Social Content: The surprise smash "Butterfly Kisses" is a dad's reflection on his daughter's metamorphosis into a bride waiting for him to escort her down the aisle. "On My Knees" points to Jesus as the loving Savior born to bear the world's sins. Other songs exalt honesty and integrity ("Man of His Word"), the love of a woman ("You Must Have Been an Angel"), and God's call for us to administer His grace to hurting people ("I'm Gonna Be Ready"). Carlisle asks the pointed question, "When Jesus calls, what will you say?" on "I'm Gonna Be Ready." A strongly evangelical effort.
Objectionable Content: None
Summary/Advisory: Few artists convey meekness and humility with as much raw vocal power as Bob Carlisle. On the strength of "Butterfly Kisses," this multimillion-selling album spent several weeks atop *Billboard*'s pop chart. Impressive. Some might even call it a miracle. *Butterfly Kisses: Shades of Grace* is truly a crossover hit that takes the *cross* over.

Carpenter, Mary Chapin

◆ ◆

Carpenter was a world traveler long before embarking on a music career that has earned her numerous Wammies, Grammys, and awards from the Country Music Association and the Academy of Country Music. She has lived in New Jersey, Tokyo, and Washington, D.C., and graduated from Brown University in Providence, Rhode Island. While honing her writing skills, Carpenter took a job in 1983 with an R.J. Reynolds philanthropic organization involved in human rights issues in Central America and South Africa.

Title: *Stones in the Road* (1994)
Label: Columbia
Genre: Country

Pro-Social Content: "Why Walk When You Can Fly" takes a realistic, optimistic, and self-less view of life ("Why take when you could be giving?"). MCC wants to let go of the past and forge a new relational future with her man on "House of Cards." Hope amid brokenness is central to several songs. The sad ballad "John Doe No. 24" relates the true story of a mentally

ill, deaf, and blind man who died alone after being institutionalized most of his life—a moving testimony to the value of every human life.

Objectionable Content: In isolated lines, she calls love "genuine voodoo" (the hit single "Shut Up and Kiss Me") and utters, "We kiss your a—" ("Stones in the Road").

Summary/Advisory: MCC communicates the emotional turmoil of romance with honesty and a sense of hope. Her poetic lyrics avoid superficiality but can sometimes get a little too colorful (as noted above). Otherwise, a solid effort.

Carter, Deana

◆ ◆ ◆ ◆ ◆ ◆ ◆ ◆ ◆ ◆ ◆ ◆ ◆ ◆ ◆ ◆ ◆ ◆

Deana Carter was born in Nashville, Tennessee, on January 4, 1966. Her father is legendary guitarist Fred Carter Jr. Deana contributed a country/pop version of "Once Upon a December" to the soundtrack of 20th Century Fox's animated feature, *Anastasia*.

Title: *Did I Shave My Legs for This?* (1996)
Label: Capitol
Genre: Country
Pro-Social Content: Carter reminisces nostalgically about young love via fond recollections of sharing an ice cream cone ("If This Is Love"), singing and dancing spontaneously ("We Danced Anyway"), and receiving a boy's ring ("Before We Ever Heard Goodbye"). Good, clean fun. She demonstrates self-respect by questioning her suitor's intentions on "Count Me In." The tender "That's How You Know It's Love" identifies a solid relationship as one in which sacrifice and selflessness reign supreme ("If you get out in the drivin' rain, stand in the eye of the hurricane, and never think twice . . . That's how you know it's meant to be").

Objectionable Content: "Strawberry Wine" *may* allude to a girl losing her virginity on a hot summer night, though it could also be perceived simply as the innocent remembrance of a first kiss.

Summary/Advisory: As a child in a musical home, Carter says she faced a choice at family reunions: "You either found a harmony part or washed dishes. I chose the harmony part." Except for the ambiguity of the number-1 country single "Strawberry Wine," her aversion to dishwashing has paid off for more than 3 million discerning country music fans.

Chapman, Tracy

◆ ◆

Chapman's self-titled debut album sold more than 10 million copies worldwide. She received three Grammy awards in 1989. Her album *New Beginning* went platinum.

Title: *New Beginning* (1995)
Label: Elektra
Genre: Rock/Folk
Pro-Social Content: Several ballads explore loving relationships. "The Promise" assures a partner that, should reconciliation be desired, the door is always open. To deepen intimacy, she reveals her own history of ups and downs on "At This Point in My Life." Chapman also urges a friend to testify against social injustices ("Tell It Like It Is") and tells of a man whose unwise decisions proved fatal ("Cold Feet"). Elsewhere, she denounces divisiveness, war, and lack of communication.

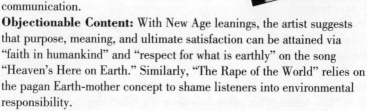

Objectionable Content: With New Age leanings, the artist suggests that purpose, meaning, and ultimate satisfaction can be attained via "faith in humankind" and "respect for what is earthly" on the song "Heaven's Here on Earth." Similarly, "The Rape of the World" relies on the pagan Earth-mother concept to shame listeners into environmental responsibility.

Summary/Advisory: *New Beginning* glides along on pleasant acoustic rhythms and earnest vocals. Too bad faulty theology mars this otherwise worthwhile, socially conscious collection.

Chemical Brothers, The

◆ ◆ ◆ ◆ ◆ ◆ ◆ ◆ ◆ ◆ ◆ ◆ ◆ ◆ ◆ ◆ ◆ ◆ ◆

The Chemical Brothers is London-based duo Tom Rowlands and Ed Simons. The pair have been an explosive force in techno music—and a rave staple—since 1994. Their song "Block Rockin' Beats" won a 1998 Grammy for Best Rock Instrumental Performance.

Title: *Dig Your Own Hole* (1997)
Label: Astralwerks
Genre: Electronica/Trip-hop
Pro-Social Content: None
Objectionable Content: A woman wakes up in the company of a stranger, the implication being that they've had sex ("Sunday morning I'm waking up/Can't even focus on a coffee cup/Don't even know whose bed I'm in"). A lover is

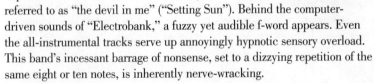

referred to as "the devil in me" ("Setting Sun"). Behind the computer-driven sounds of "Electrobank," a fuzzy yet audible f-word appears. Even the all-instrumental tracks serve up annoyingly hypnotic sensory overload. This band's incessant barrage of nonsense, set to a dizzying repetition of the same eight or ten notes, is inherently nerve-wracking.
Summary/Advisory: Explosive musical chemistry. It's a shame the unrelenting, intoxicating dance beats don't subside long enough for young listeners to clear their heads. Lyrics offer more tangible evidence that The Chemical Brothers are experimenting with unstable elements.

Chumbawamba

◆ ◆ ◆ ◆ ◆ ◆ ◆ ◆ ◆ ◆ ◆ ◆ ◆ ◆ ◆ ◆ ◆ ◆ ◆

The members of this Leeds, England, band (Lou Watts, Danbert Nobacon, Paul Greco, Jude Abbott, Alice Nutter, Dunstan Bruce, Harry Hamer, and Neil Ferguson) spent the 1980s living together communally. Now, with the success of *Tubthumper,* they've got a platinum record to hang on their collective wall.

Title: *Tubthumper* (1997)
Label: Republic/Universal
Genre: Dance/Techno pop

Pro-Social Content: Isolated lines here and there. "Amnesia" indicates that what we sow we will reap. "One by One" suggests that some principles are worth dying for. The persevering singer on "Tubthumping" repeats, "I get knocked down, but I get up again."

Objectionable Content: Just as some individual lyrics warrant praise, others deserve a thumping. "I'd rather take drugs than have sex" is a line heard on "I Want More." "Amnesia" describes the dismantling of a human head. "Outsider" could be interpreted as saying that breaking the law is a good way for teens to have fun. Life is portrayed as miserable, bleak, and pointless ("Creepy Crawling," "Good Ship Lifestyle"). "Mary Mary" includes backward masking of someone reciting "Hail Marys," but worse yet is the enraged confession of a rebellious girl who boasts of drug use, immodesty, and selling her soul "for sex and gin." Alcohol flows on the Top-10 single, "Tubthumping."

Summary/Advisory: While musically intriguing, Chumbawamba communicates little of value. In fact, this British band has a reputation for promoting anarchy, bashing religion, and crusading for a radical gay agenda. Some of that misguided passion shows on this disc.

Clapton, Eric

◆ ◆

In the late 1960s, one of the most prominent pieces of graffiti seen in London and New York was "Clapton is God." Thirty years later, his fame continues. A former member of the rock bands The Roosters, Cream, Derek and the Dominoes, The Yardbirds, Blind Faith, and John Lennon's Plastic Ono Band, Eric Clapton is a well-traveled double-inductee to the Rock 'n' Roll Hall of Fame. His '90s hit singles "Tears in Heaven" and "Change the World" have earned enough awards to cover most mantels.

Title: *Pilgrim* (1998)
Label: Reprise
Genre: Blues/Rock
Pro-Social Content: Several songs indicate that Clapton longs for spiritual understanding. The grieving artist looks heavenward for solace on "Broken Hearted," "My Father's Eyes," and "River of Tears." He reveals

inner pain, raising a flurry of questions on both the title track and "Inside of Me." "You Were There" thanks God for sticking around through sinful years and personal tragedy. The closing down of a three-ring traveling show serves as a metaphor for the untimely death of Clapton's young son ("Circus"). A remake of Bob Dylan's "Born in Time" finds a man in love rejoicing over his woman's return.

Objectionable Content: The disc falters when the singer threatens his ex with a shotgun on "Sick and Tired" ("I may have to blow your brains out, baby/Then you won't bother me no more").

Summary/Advisory: With the noted exception, *Pilgrim* chronicles a hopeful leg of this vulnerable dad's journey out of sorrow. His creative lamentations echo pain, but Clapton now seems to be looking in the right place for answers. Let's pray that he finds them.

Title: *From the Cradle* (1994)
Label: Reprise
Genre: Blues
Pro-Social Content: By definition, "the blues" focus on life's hard times. But, despite a lack of emotional uplift, Clapton's earnest poetry avoids promoting drugs, alcohol, or suicide as solutions to Bayou angst. "Sinner's Prayer" asks for the Lord's mercy. Most of these songs are simply innocuous expressions of inner turmoil.

Objectionable Content: "Hoochie Coochie Man" speaks of voodoo prophecy and fortune-telling. On "Five Years Ago," Clapton views his future wife as a meal ticket ("Next woman I marry, she gonna work, bring me the gold").

Summary/Advisory: In typical Clapton style, *Cradle* rocks with 60 minutes of dizzying blues guitar licks, wailing harmonica, and a backbeat begging for empathy. But skillful instrumentals can't compensate for the disc's lyrical emptiness. Although it avoids steering listeners toward destructive pseudo-solutions (with the noted exceptions), it wallows in self-pity, failing to offer any hope.

Title: *Unplugged* (1992)
Label: Reprise
Genre: Blues/Rock
Pro-Social Content: Faith, dreams, and love are central to "Running on

Faith." Clapton offers "consolation" to a woman let down by her man ("Layla"). The tender, Grammy-dominating "Tears in Heaven" was inspired by his four-year-old son's tragic death. On it, Clapton wonders if his boy would recognize him in the afterlife, reminding himself that "there'll be no more tears in heaven." On "Lonely Stranger," a forthright wanderer warns someone not to grow too attached. This live acoustic project also features a half-dozen rather neutral blues standards.

Objectionable Content: The artist longs for the days when he bought his friends "bootleg whiskey, champagne, and wine" ("Nobody Knows You When You're Down and Out"). Though vague, "Alberta" seems to describe a woman of loose morals. "Old Love" alludes to past intimacies with a lover who's no longer around.

Summary/Advisory: In a musical era dominated by artists trading on hype and shock value, these back-to-basics blues provide a refreshing escape. The disc's few caveats are minor. But while Clapton's blues aren't nearly as bitter and nihilistic as those of his moaning young contemporaries in the alternative genre, his lyrics could stand an injection of optimism.

Cohn, Marc

◆ ◆ ◆ ◆ ◆ ◆ ◆ ◆ ◆ ◆ ◆ ◆ ◆ ◆ ◆ ◆ ◆ ◆ ◆

Born in Cleveland, Ohio, Cohn began playing the piano and guitar at an early age. He joined his first band at age 16 and played in various acts and clubs on both coasts before releasing his self-titled debut album in 1991. Cohn earned a Grammy for Best New Artist that year.

Title: *The Rainy Season* (1993)
Label: Atlantic
Genre: Folk/Rock
Pro-Social Content: "Rest for the Weary" reinforces the supportive value of family ("my mother stood beside him") and talks of a place that sounds a lot like heaven. Cohn desires that kind of marital commitment himself on "Walk Through the World." He acknowledges how a newborn can rule the lives of its parents on "Baby King." A beautiful poem set to music rounds out the disc as "The Things

We've Handed Down" lets us eavesdrop on a hopeful father affectionately welcoming his unborn child into the generational flow.

Objectionable Content: None

Summary/Advisory: Cohn sticks to overwhelmingly positive themes that affirm healthy human relationships. Overall, a terrific selection, both musically and lyrically.

Cole, Natalie

◆ ◆ ◆ ◆ ◆ ◆ ◆ ◆ ◆ ◆ ◆ ◆ ◆ ◆ ◆ ◆ ◆

The daughter of music giant Nat "King" Cole, Natalie has carved out her own niche as a talented solo artist. She made her professional debut at age 11 and won a Grammy in 1975 for Best New Artist. She has since amassed a string of gold and platinum records.

Title: *Take a Look* (1993)
Label: Elektra
Genre: Adult contemporary
Pro-Social Content: Lovely, time-honored ballads, including "I Wish You Love," "As Time Goes By," and "Cry Me a River" harken back to a time when the recording industry valued romance over sex. That nostalgia is refreshing. Several songs offer hope in dealing with unrequited love. The title cut decries hatred and the present cultural chaos ("Lord, what's happening to this human race?").

Objectionable Content: Nothing explicit, but "Lovers" leaves the relational context open for interpretation when it recommends "makin' love, really gettin' it on."

Summary/Advisory: Teens fond of Harry Connick Jr. will enjoy this romantic time warp as well. The 18-track follow-up to Cole's Grammy-winning *Unforgettable* blends classic ballads with smooth jazz, scat, and melodies from the big-band era, resulting in a playful potpourri of adult contemporary tunes. Delightful vocal work. With the one exception noted above, *Take a Look* is worth a listen—a predominantly positive pick.

Cole, Paula

◆ ◆ ◆ ◆ ◆ ◆ ◆ ◆ ◆ ◆ ◆ ◆ ◆ ◆ ◆ ◆ ◆ ◆ ◆

A native of Rockport, Massachusetts, Paula Cole attended Berklee College of Music in Boston where she studied jazz singing and improvisation. In 1996, she participated in the Lilith music festival and found herself nominated for an industry-best seven Grammys in 1998 (she took home one statuette for Best New Artist).

Title: *This Fire* (1996)
Label: Warner Bros.
Genre: Folk/Alternative
Pro-Social Content: On the hummably upbeat "I Don't Want to Wait," the artist asks for prayer and peace on earth.
Objectionable Content: Vivid images of Cole's sexual fantasies (from bondage to posing as a dippy centerfold) dominate the lusty "Feelin' Love." Elsewhere, public immodesty passes for freedom, and the artist recalls "sex-starved teachers trying to touch my a—" ("Tiger"). An undercurrent of angst and hostility flows through "Mississippi" and the obscenity-laced "Throwing Stones" ("So call me a b—ch in heat and I'll call you a muthaf———."). Lots of pain. Other cuts give a nod to reincarnation ("Hush Hush Hush") and, depending on the interpretation, drug use ("Carmen").
Summary/Advisory: Lyrically vague at times, *This Fire* leaves listeners to ponder the smoldering ashes of frustration and bitterness. Not bad artistically, but virtually devoid of hope and rife with problematic elements. Fans of Paula Cole's style would do better with Rebecca St. James's edifying release, *God.*

Collective Soul

◆ ◆ ◆ ◆ ◆ ◆ ◆ ◆ ◆ ◆ ◆ ◆ ◆ ◆ ◆ ◆ ◆ ◆ ◆

Collective Soul is made up of Ed and Dean Roland, Ross Childress, Will Turpin, and Shane Evans. The group's first single, "Shine," earned Recording Industry Association of America gold and was named *Billboard*'s number 1 Hot Album Rock Track of 1994.

Title: *Disciplined Breakdown* (1997)
Label: Atlantic
Genre: Rock
Pro-Social Content: While not thematically "Christian," the band frequently
makes use of biblical imagery and vocabulary in optimistic songs such as "Precious
Declaration" ("I was blind, but now I
see/Salvation has discovered me"). Lyrics
elevate faith, peace, forgiveness, truth, calm,

and love while rebuking selfishness, despair, fear, greed, pride, and aimless
meandering through life. "Giving" and "Everything" sound very much like
prayers for noble character traits. "Blame" offers redemption to someone
"tasting sin and swallowing pain." Written in memory of a deceased friend,
"Maybe" speaks of the joy of heaven and the sorrow experienced by those
on earth following a loss.
Objectionable Content: The title cut relates a man's tortured slide toward
a welcome collapse.
Summary/Advisory: One band member said, "These songs allow themselves to be read in many different contexts." With the noted exception, they
should uplift Christian teens hearing them through the filter of biblical truth.

Title: *Collective Soul* (1995)
Label: Atlantic
Genre: Rock
Pro-Social Content: A girl seeks the answers to life's questions from her
mother on "When the Water Falls." The "goods" desired on "Collection of
Goods" include peace, hope, love, and caring. According to "Simple," the
remedy for a troubled mind is to "let love seek and let love find . . . let love
lead and let love flow."
Objectionable Content: "Where the River Flows" has pantheistic leanings. A line on "Untitled" lacks faith in preachers. On "December," the
artist admits to being "Lost as you swear I am." Also, "Bleed" takes a pessimistic view of life.
Summary/Advisory: After displaying near-biblical spirituality on their
first disc, *Hints, Allegations & Things Left Unsaid*, Collective Soul felt
uncomfortable with the "gospel" image and sought to shed it this time out.
They have. For the most part, these lyrics lack the hope and uplift of *Hints*.
A real disappointment.

Title: *Hints, Allegations & Things Left Unsaid* (1994)
Label: Atlantic
Genre: Rock/Alternative
Pro-Social Content: "Reach" is a reverent prayer for direction and purpose in life, pleading for love, guidance, and salvation. Likewise, "Goodnight, Good Guy" intercedes on behalf of another ("I pray the Lord to keep [and] hold you tight"), and "Shine" urges, "Oh, heaven let your light shine down." Perseverance in hard times is the focus of "Sister Don't Cry." "Breath" encourages the sowing and reaping of love. The lyricist speaks from God's perspective on "All" ("Come lay your troubles down to rest . . . my kingdom is all yours to receive"). With "Love Lifted Me" and "Heaven's Already Here," Collective Soul offers hope and encouragement—a refreshing change amid a musical style known for promoting despair.
Objectionable Content: None
Summary/Advisory: According to *Hints*, even amid the pain of broken and hurting relationships, there is reason to remain optimistic. Add theologically sound references to God and youngsters have a solid mainstream alternative to bands like The Offspring or Bush.

Collins, Phil

◆ ◆

Born in London, this pop vocalist/multi-instrumentalist/composer began his entertainment career as a child actor. In 1970, he joined the band Genesis as its drummer, becoming the lead singer in 1975. His first solo album was released in 1981, and Collins went on to star in the 1988 feature film *Buster*.

Title: *Both Sides* (1993)
Label: Atlantic
Genre: Adult contemporary
Pro-Social Content: The title track points to communication as a crucial step toward better understanding one another and healing society's ills. "We Wait and We Wonder" goes even further, asking "how this happened, killing the old, the innocent, the young." "We're Sons of Our Fathers" addresses our declining society and questions rebellious youth ("Our sons and daughters seem to be beyond our control/Their smile is fading fast/They're losing their

soul"). Other songs reflect on how past decisions have life-altering implications. He pledges his love on "There's a Place for Us."

Objectionable Content: "Please Come Out Tonight" asks a lover to spend the night.

Summary/Advisory: A mostly solid pick from a thoughtful solo artist who seeks to uplift the human spirit.

Colvin, Shawn

◆ ◆ ◆ ◆ ◆ ◆ ◆ ◆ ◆ ◆ ◆ ◆ ◆ ◆ ◆ ◆ ◆ ◆ ◆ ◆

Shawn Colvin signed with Columbia Records in 1989 and performed background vocals on albums by Suzanne Vega and Mary Chapin Carpenter before making her mark. *A Few Small Repairs* is her most successful disc to date, selling approximately one million copies. Colvin, the 1998 Grammy winner for Record of the Year *and* Song of the Year ("Sunny Came Home"), was born in South Dakota.

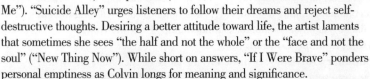

Title: *A Few Small Repairs* (1996)
Label: Columbia
Genre: Folk/Adult contemporary
Pro-Social Content: Songs express love ("You and the Mona Lisa") and optimism ("Nothin' on Me"). "Suicide Alley" urges listeners to follow their dreams and reject self-destructive thoughts. Desiring a better attitude toward life, the artist laments that sometimes she sees "the half and not the whole" or the "face and not the soul" ("New Thing Now"). While short on answers, "If I Were Brave" ponders personal emptiness as Colvin longs for meaning and significance.

Objectionable Content: On the award-winning single "Sunny Came Home," a woman seeks fiery revenge on her persecutors. Profanity appears on several tracks, including the brashly rebellious "Trouble." The artist credits drunkenness with giving her "heart" and a creative spark ("The Facts Jimmy"). Though probably intended as sarcastic hyperbole, "I Want It Back" excuses character flaws in a celebrity ("You mighta killed, you might be cruel/You might be stupid, but we love you/You're in the paper").

Summary/Advisory: This critically acclaimed disc erects some positive sentiments on a crumbling foundation of questionable themes—not up to code for young fans. That's too bad. Some lyrical tinkering might have fixed *A Few Small Repairs*.

Connick Jr., Harry

◆ ◆ ◆ ◆ ◆ ◆ ◆ ◆ ◆ ◆ ◆ ◆ ◆ ◆ ◆ ◆ ◆ ◆ ◆ ◆

Harry Connick Jr. made his musical debut with a New Orleans jazz band while working clubs in the French Quarter and studying piano with Ellis Marsalis and James Booker—all before the age of 10. In 1989, his work on the soundtrack for the Billy Crystal/Meg Ryan film *When Harry Met Sally* led to his first multiplatinum album. Connick has also acted in films, including *Memphis Belle*, *Independence Day*, *Hope Floats* and the violent thriller *Copycat* (as a serial killer).

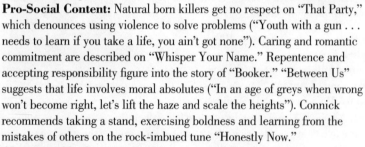

Title: *She* (1994)
Label: Columbia
Genre: Jazz/Pop
Pro-Social Content: Natural born killers get no respect on "That Party," which denounces using violence to solve problems ("Youth with a gun . . . needs to learn if you take a life, you ain't got none"). Caring and romantic commitment are described on "Whisper Your Name." Repentence and accepting responsibility figure into the story of "Booker." "Between Us" suggests that life involves moral absolutes ("In an age of greys when wrong won't become right, let's lift the haze and scale the heights"). Connick recommends taking a stand, exercising boldness and learning from the mistakes of others on the rock-imbued tune "Honestly Now."
Objectionable Content: None
Summary/Advisory: Stylistically, a change of pace from the crooner's Sinatra-esque jazz repertoire. But despite the infusion of pop/rock elements, Connick's lyrics continue to reflect wholesome ideals.

Title: *25* (1992)
Label: Columbia
Genre: Jazz/Pop
Pro-Social Content: "Stardust," "On the Street Where You Live," and "This Time the Dream's on Me" all promote a positive view of romance.
Objectionable Content: None
Summary/Advisory: Connick, minus the big band, showcases his solo piano artistry and vocals on this companion to the concurrently released *11*, an album preserving his prodigy at that age. Especially noteworthy is the

passion and polish of Hoagy Carmichael's classic "Stardust," masterfully played by Ellis Marsalis. Also not to be missed are "On the Street Where You Live," Duke Ellington's "Caravan," and the intimate three-piece rendition of Johnny Mercer's "On The Atchison, Topeka and The Santa Fe." A jazzy change of pace!

Coolio

◆ ◆

Coolio, a native of Compton, California, saw his career take off in 1994 with the release of the party anthem "Fantastic Voyage," which went platinum and became a Top-10 hit. He has been nominated for a Grammy, an MTV Video Award, and several *Billboard* video and music awards. The single "Gangsta's Paradise," from the *Dangerous Minds* motion picture soundtrack, sold 1.5 million copies, becoming the best-selling song of 1995.

Title: *Gangsta's Paradise* (1995)
Label: Tommy Boy
Genre: Gangsta rap/Hip-hop
Pro-Social Content: On "Smilin'," the man who fathered a child during a one-night stand takes responsibility for his actions. Coolio apologizes for referring to women as "b—ches and hos" on "For My Sistas."
Objectionable Content: These same two disrespectful expressions show up elsewhere on the disc ("Is This Me?" and "Recoup This"). And the language gets worse. Frequent use of the f-word. Crude sexual slang. "Too Hot" promotes the safe-sex myth and rejects abstinence as impractical ("Kids ain't checkin' for abstis—t/So put a condom in their hand"). Cheap sex is the rapper's goal on "Cruisin'" and "Sumpin'." "A Thing Goin' On" listens in on two infidels sharing sex, "weed," and wine. Numerous cuts glorify gangsta violence, including "Recoup This," a spoken piece in which an artist shoots his agent and secretary over money. 1995's best-selling single, "Gangsta's Paradise," makes violent threats. "Revolution" supports the rioting in L.A. and boasts, "In my mutherf—in' *self* I trust!"

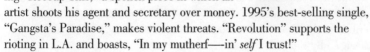

Summary/Advisory: Pointless trash exploiting urban decay. Lewd and irresponsible. Avoid it.

Title: *It Takes a Thief* (1994)
Label: Tommy Boy
Genre: Gangsta rap
Pro-Social Content: None
Objectionable Content: Coolio sums up his philosophy of life with, "I do what I do to survive . . . that's why I pack a .45. Life is a b—ch and then you die." He condones street violence and murder on numerous cuts, including the shooting of police on "Bring Back Somethin' Fo Da Hood" ("Black cop, white cop [gunshot] f—- the color of his skin; make sure he's shot [gunshot]"). Lewd sexual references abound as well, often employing the f-word and referring to women as "b—ches" and "hos." He even tells a man to shoot a prostitute on "Ugly B—ches." Of the disc's 61 minutes, what isn't sexual or violent promotes drug use. "Ghetto Cartoon" even defames beloved animated characters in gangsta style.
Summary/Advisory: Stickered for explicit content, *Thief* will steal teens' innocence given half a chance. Lock it up and lose the key.

Cooper, Alice

◆ ◆ ◆ ◆ ◆ ◆ ◆ ◆ ◆ ◆ ◆ ◆ ◆ ◆ ◆ ◆ ◆ ◆ ◆ ◆

The son of a minister, Vincent Furnier was born in Detroit, Michigan. When he turned 18, he left home to start a rock group, which led him to change his name to Alice Cooper in 1966. Disturbing behavior on stage and a satanic pose earned him a reputation for inspiring teen rebellion. Cooper has appeared in at least four films, including *Prince of Darkness* and *Wayne's World*.

Title: *The Last Temptation* (1994)
Label: Epic
Genre: Rock
Pro-Social Content: Teens are encouraged to identify evil in the form of drugs ("Bad Place Alone") and sex ("You're My Temptation"), and resist its seductive tendrils. "Lullaby" examines the consequences of sin. "Unholy War" reveals the nature of spiritual battle. Grace and redemption take the fore on "It's Me" and "Cleansed By Fire."
Objectionable Content: None, though some lines could be misunderstood apart from the disc's overall theme.

Summary/Advisory: This concept album is best reviewed as the sum of its musical parts. Ten songs combine to spin the tale of a sideshow devil trying to lure a bored teen into sex, drugs, and crime. The macabre makeup may remain, but this '70s shock-rocker has changed his tune. *Temptation* is a spiritually charged rock-opera climaxing with a Christ-centered victory over Satan ("What about truth/What about life/What about glory/What about Christ/What about peace/What about love/What about faith in God above"). A positive shock from AC.

Counting Crows
◆ ◆

Members of Counting Crows include Adam Duritz, David Bryson, Charlie Gillingham, Matt Malley, Dan Vickrey, and Ben Mize. They won an MTV Video Award in 1994 and have been nominated for other honors. *Recovering the Satellites* debuted at number 1 with 161,000 units sold the first week.

Title: *Recovering the Satellites* (1996)
Label: Geffen
Genre: Alternative
Pro-Social Content: A line on "Miller's Angels" acknowledges "God's unwavering love." "A Long December" looks somewhat optimistically toward future days ("Maybe this year will be better than the last").
Objectionable Content: Several tracks imply that life is dark and depressing ("Daylight Fading," "Have You Seen Me Lately," and the title cut). The artist cries, "I will wrap myself in pain" on "Goodnight Elisabeth." A few harsh profanities—including the f-word—punctuate these lyrics. Album art includes a pencil sketch of a man extending his middle finger. The self-destructive woman described on "Another Horsedreamer's Blues" seeks a cure for loneliness in pills and gambling.
Summary/Advisory: A gloomy undercurrent runs through this project. Not much *explicit* trouble, but negativity suffocates the disc's very few bright spots. Don't let *Satellites* transmit into your home. The CCM band Satellite Soul is a solid Christian alternative for fans of this musical style.

Title: *August & Everything After* (1994)
Label: Geffen
Genre: Rock
Pro-Social Content: A handful of potentially positive tunes deal with relationships, but context and true intent are cloaked in a lyrical haze.
Objectionable Content: The artist and "Mr. Jones" fantasize aloud about beautiful women and fame while they pass around a bottle of booze. "Rain King" espouses a misguided theology involving "a sea of pens and feathers . . . faith and sex and God in the belly of a black-winged bird." "Perfect Blue Buildings" paints life as meaningless. A depressed, suicidal woman "parks her car . . . takes her clothes off, says she's close to understanding Jesus" on "Round Here."
Summary/Advisory: The band's obscure, symbolic poetry (delivered with gritty Bruce Springsteen- and U2-style vocals) leaves a lot to the listener's imagination. But taken at face value, certain problematic lyrics would indicate that the Crows are for the birds.

Cranberries, The

◆ ◆ ◆ ◆ ◆ ◆ ◆ ◆ ◆ ◆ ◆ ◆ ◆ ◆ ◆ ◆ ◆ ◆ ◆ ◆

Once called Cranberry Saw Us (a play on the Thanksgiving dinner staple), this Irish band recruited lead singer Dolores O'Riordan in 1990 and was soon signed to a record deal by Island. In 1994, O'Riordan married Don Burton, a former stage manager for Duran Duran, who became the manager of The Cranberries.

Title: *To the Faithful Departed* (1996)
Label: Island
Genre: Alternative
Pro-Social Content: "Salvation" is an anti-drug anthem advising "all the kids with heroin eyes, don't do it." Two cuts ("Warchild" and "Bosnia") condemn war, reminding listeners of the pain suffered by innocent children. Though it

ends with a triumphant chant and simulated gunshots, "I Just Shot John Lennon" clearly opposes violence, pointing to the ex-Beatle's 1980 murder as "a sad and sorry and sickening sight." One of several sincere love songs, "Not Hollywood" distinguishes between true love and the kind portrayed on the silver screen. "Joe" is a tribute to the lead singer's grandfather.

Objectionable Content: Minor. "I'm Still Remembering" paints an overly sympathetic picture of nihilistic suicide victim Kurt Cobain. A mild profanity appears on "Free to Decide."

Summary/Advisory: The Cranberries's first two albums have sold a combined total of 10 million copies. One reason is the way Dolores O'Riordan weaves her Irish rock roots into passionate, at times tortured vocals that cry out for justice. This new effort is *Faithful* to that tradition—socially conscious and mostly optimistic.

Title: *No Need to Argue* (1994)
Label: Island
Genre: Irish alternative rock
Pro-Social Content: With passionate protest, "Zombie" reflects on the innocent casualties of war. On "Ode to My Family," the singer pays tribute to caring parents and, in spite of her fame, humbly refuses to bask in celebrity. She also asks for prayer ("Empty") and thanks her husband for words of encouragement ("Dreaming My Dreams"), pledging commitment to him in the process. "The Icicle Melts" decries child abuse.

Objectionable Content: On "Ridiculous Thoughts," the singer second-guesses her decision to be honest. The word *damn* pops up twice on "Ode to My Family."

Summary/Advisory: Despite being driven by passionate, tortured vocals, *No Need to Argue* is surprisingly optimistic—even on tunes describing failed relationships. For fans of socially conscious alternative rock, The Cranberries are, for the most part, a worthwhile side dish.

Title: *Everybody Else Is Doing It, So Why Can't We?* (1993)
Label: Island
Genre: Alternative
Pro-Social Content: On "Pretty," the lead singer reinforces someone's innate value by repeating the lyric "You're so pretty the way you are." She also practices "tough love" whenever the man in her life demonstrates a lack of respect or faithfulness ("Linger," "Wanted," "Put Me Down," "Still Can't . . ."). "Sunday" examines the shortcomings of one-sided love. These tunes are honest, if not terribly optimistic, about the trials some relationships endure.

Objectionable Content: Several songs present dysfunctional relationships without offering positive alternatives. Depending on how it's taken, the album's title could inspire young people to experiment with risky behavior.

Summary/Advisory: The Cranberries rely on a brooding, at times eerie, musical style typical of their Irish rock roots. Lyrically, the band does an admirable job of defining social ills. Unfortunately, *Everybody Else Is Doing It, So Why Can't We?* falls short of providing hopeful solutions.

Crash Test Dummies

◆ ◆

Crash Test Dummies is a five-person band from Winnipeg, Manitoba. Members include Brad Roberts, Ellen Reid, Dan Roberts, Ben Darvill, and Michel Dorge. The band won Canada's 1991 Juno award for Group of the Year and has been nominated for three Grammy awards.

Title: *A Worm's Life* (1996)
Label: Arista
Genre: Rock
Pro-Social Content: The lead singer endeavors not to hate those who've wronged him on "My Enemies." He looks for good amid repulsiveness ("All of This Ugly") and warns us not to stick a fork in a plugged-in toaster or lick cold metal things ("There Are Many Dangers").

Objectionable Content: CTD's nonsensical poetry has its problems. Though not blasphemous, "An Old Scab" and "Overachievers" could be interpreted as making light of prayer. There's also a metaphorical reference to sex and an immodest testimony regarding the use of a bidet.

Summary/Advisory: The operative word is *weird.* Again, the Dummies use cryptic silliness as bait to hook music buyers in a sea of musical soundalikes. *A Worm's Life* avoids patently offensive content, but rampant ambiguity and a few questionable lines may inspire families to fish elsewhere.

Title: *God Shuffled His Feet* (1994)
Label: Arista
Genre: Pop/Rock
Pro-Social Content: None, though several nonsensical songs avoid offensive themes.

Objectionable Content: A wave of sexual double entendres floods "Swimming in Your Ocean." "In the Days of the Caveman" includes Darwinist philosophies ("See in the shape of my body leftover parts from the apes and monkeys"). Tequila and swimsuit magazines are recommended as positive distractions on "I Think I'll Disappear Now." The title track is disturbing in its irreverence for God, His nature, and biblical concepts, while the hit single "Mmm Mmm Mmm Mmm" shows disrespect for churchgoers. Other songs speak positively of alcohol, medieval potions, and psychic phenomena.

Summary/Advisory: With a Jethro Tull-minus-the-flute style and lyrics often bordering on utter nonsense, Crash Test Dummies has found a niche with an audience tired of the downer music of various alternative bands. This group has a more upbeat tone, though it comes off sounding like the same tune played 12 different ways. These guys don't take themselves too seriously. But herein lies the problem: The band doesn't take its lyrics seriously either, offering several less-than-wholesome messages. Crash Test Dummies are an accident waiting to happen.

Creed

◆ ◆ ◆ ◆ ◆ ◆ ◆ ◆ ◆ ◆ ◆ ◆ ◆ ◆ ◆ ◆ ◆ ◆ ◆

Creed is Scott Stapp, Brian Marshall, Scott Phillips, and Mark Tremonti. Stapp and Tremonti initially shared their mutual desire to be part of a rock band while classmates at an Orlando, Florida, high school. Years later, a chance meeting reunited the pair, and with the addition of Florida natives Phillips and Marshall, Creed was born in 1995.

Title: *My Own Prison* (1997)
Label: Wind-up
Genre: Alternative
Pro-Social Content: The band empathizes with a girl forced to grow up in a dysfunctional family ("Sister") and longs for racial equality and brotherhood among mankind ("One"). The social commentary "In America" looks askance at abortion, hypocrisy, the worship of money, and promiscuity. Otherwise fatalistic, "My Own Prison" acknowledges Christ's sacrifical death as the pathway to eternal life.

Objectionable Content: Bitter disillusionment is manifested in numerous lyrics confessing misery ("Torn"), anger ("One"), and hopelessness ("Illusion"). "Pity for a Dime" finds lead vocalist Scott Stapp wallowing in self-doubt and denial, confessing a loss of faith. "Ode" expresses self-destructive nihilism. There's also a profane use of God's name on "What's This Life For."

Summary/Advisory: Lots of searching, but positive statements are well overshadowed by an outright rejection of biblical truth. Stapp says, "If it weren't for music, I might have ended up some crazed street preacher. Rock-n-roll is my religion." Not exactly the narrow path. Keep teens out of *Prison.*

Crow, Sheryl

◆ ◆ ◆ ◆ ◆ ◆ ◆ ◆ ◆ ◆ ◆ ◆ ◆ ◆ ◆ ◆ ◆ ◆ ◆ ◆

Sheryl Crow began piano lessons at age five, could play songs by ear at age six and composed her first song at the age of 13. Before beginning her solo singing career, her songs were recorded by artists such as Eric Clapton and Wynonna Judd. Crow was nominated for five Grammys in 1995, winning three. Her *Tuesday Night Music Club* CD has sold more than 6 million copies.

Title: *Sheryl Crow* (1996)
Label: A&M
Genre: Rock/Pop
Pro-Social Content: An honorable priest offers "a little grace" to a down-and-out woman on "Sweet Rosalyn." Other tunes mourn the carnage of war ("Redemption Days") and the epidemic street violence that continues to claim young lives ("Love Is a Good Thing"). Crow regrets a European fling on "The Book" ("Sometimes we come to learn by mistake that the love you once made can't be undone").

Objectionable Content: "Home" finds the artist longing to awake in the embrace of a stranger. Similarly, "Ordinary Morning" describes the dawn following a one-night stand. "Maybe Angels" refers to "holy rollers" who "don't know nothin' 'bout saving me." Crow admits "I still get stoned" on her ode to selfishness, "If It Makes You Happy." Abortion is portrayed as a woman's way to "take care of her own body" ("Hard to Make a Stand"). Other tracks allude to Ouija boards and booze.

Summary/Advisory: The Grammy winner's follow-up to her 6-million-selling *Tuesday Night Music Club* is nothing to crow about. Problems outweigh praises. Despite a social consciousness, this project's approach to religion and sexual ethics is inconsistent at best.

Title: *Tuesday Night Music Club* (1994)
Label: A&M
Genre: Rock/Pop/Funk
Pro-Social Content: Newlyweds face common struggles but remain committed on "No One Said It Would Be Easy." "Can't Cry Anymore" expresses concern for a brother with "real problems," including heroin use.
Objectionable Content: Getting "a good beer buzz in the morning" is endorsed on the irresponsible anthem "All I Wanna Do." Recreational drug and alcohol use also appear on "Leaving Las Vegas," "Run, Baby, Run," and "The Na-Na Song." The latter spews crude, nonsensical references to male genitalia. Other cuts recommend relational dishonesty and commitmentless sex.
Summary/Advisory: This salacious disc took six months to become an overnight sensation. The Grammy-winning single "All I Wanna Do" may have a catchy chorus, but teens are just as likely to catch hold of Crow's disturbing worldview. One to avoid.

Cypress Hill

◆ ◆ ◆ ◆ ◆ ◆ ◆ ◆ ◆ ◆ ◆ ◆ ◆ ◆ ◆ ◆ ◆ ◆ ◆ ◆

Cypress Hill is made up of DJ Muggs, B-Real, and Sen Dog. Their *Black Sunday* album debuted at number 1, registering (at that time) the highest first-week take of any rap album in the brief history of SoundScan.

Title: *III (Temples of Boom)* (1995)
Label: Ruffhouse/Columbia
Genre: Gangsta rap
Pro-Social Content: None
Objectionable Content: Riddled with profanity, this disc obsesses over drug use, employing street slang for marijuana (chronic, Mauiwowie, indo, Afrigani, baca lua lua, spliff, hemp, weed, blunt, bud, joint). "Boom Diddy Bye Bye" features racial violence ("As I pull the trigger on my

nine/Say goodnight ni——r!"). The artist also claims to be "a natural born cop killer" on "Stoned Raiders." Other cuts demean women as sex objects to be abused, with explicit language adding insult to injury ("Illusions," "No Rest for the Wicked," "Boom Biddy Bye Bye").

Summary/Advisory: This band is the first to be named official spokesmen for the National Organization to Reform Marijuana Laws. *III (Temples of Boom)* reflects that zeal, along with a general maliciousness toward others. A nasty effort from beginning to end.

Title: *Black Sunday* (1993)
Label: Ruffhouse/Columbia
Genre: Rap
Pro-Social Content: None
Objectionable Content: Song titles such as "Hits from the Bong," "I Wanna Get High," and "Legalize It" provide some indication of the group's pro-drug agenda. Lines from these cuts include, "I smoke s—— straight off the roach clip," "Inhale, exhale/Just got an ounce in the mail/I like the blunt," and "I take hits from the bong . . . I love you Mary Jane [slang for marijuana]." A deplorable twisting of Scripture finds Genesis 1:12 being used to justify recreational drug use ("Legalize It"). The artist gets violently protective of his stash on "A to the K," "What Go Around Come Around Kid," and "Insane in the Brain." Gunplay and murder even include a cop-killing ("When the S—— Goes Down"). Profanities and obscenities inhabit numerous tracks, while a vulgar sexual epithet characterizes the trouble with "Lil Putos."

Summary/Advisory: This disc has the distinction of being the first rap album to spend multiple weeks at number one on the pop chart. Its appeal? An evangelistic zeal for drugs and the glorification of gangsta violence.

Cyrus, Billy Ray

◆ ◆ ◆ ◆ ◆ ◆ ◆ ◆ ◆ ◆ ◆ ◆ ◆ ◆ ◆ ◆ ◆ ◆

A native of Flatwoods, Kentucky, Billy Ray Cyrus burst onto the country scene with the hit "Achy Breaky Heart" in 1992. That platinum smash earned him a Country Music Association Award for Single of the Year and inspired a phenomenally popular line dance.

Title: *It Won't Be the Last* (1993)

Label: Mercury
Genre: Country/Pop
Pro-Social Content: "In the Heart of a Woman" implies that relationships take work and urges a man to express his love to his lady and "give her room to grow, treat her tender." He explores the dreams upon which people rely to cope with despair on "Dreamin' in Color, Livin' in Black and White."
Objectionable Content: Conversation is deemed essential to ignite a passionate rendezvous on "Talk Some." "Words by Heart" recalls adolescent sex ("that night on my bed") and drowns the blues with a beer.
Summary/Advisory: With his Lil' Abner, beefcake image, Cyrus has won numerous fans and achieved surprising success on the pop charts. This album trades mostly on songs mourning lost love. Not very inspirational. Neither are his casual attitudes toward sex and alcohol. In spite of some redeeming elements, better options exist.

Danzig

◆ ◆ ◆ ◆ ◆ ◆ ◆ ◆ ◆ ◆ ◆ ◆ ◆ ◆ ◆ ◆ ◆ ◆ ◆

This death metal band's single, "Mother," reached the Top 100. Members are Glenn Danzig, John Christ, Eerie Von, and Chuck Biscuits (who replaced Joey Castillo in 1994). The CD cover for *Thrall-demonsweatlive* has been purposely omitted due to extremely graphic imagery.

Title: *Thrall-demonsweatlive* (1993)
Label: Def American
Genre: Death metal
Pro-Social Content: None
Objectionable Content: Like many of the band's patently evil tunes, "Snakes of Christ" blasphemes Jesus and promotes demonology. On "Mother," Glenn Danzig jeers at caring parents, issuing them a sinister warning to guard their children from his influence. He admits the source of his inspiration ("Faces of a million hells rage inside these veins," "My middle name is Misery/Said I'm evil child and don't you mess around with me," "If you're looking for trouble, just stare in this face"). Dark and satanic.
Summary/Advisory: Even MTV refused to air Danzig's video featuring hardcore sadomasochism and two leashed amputees in leather. Deuteronomy 18:10-11 says, "Let no one be found among you who . . . practices . . . sorcery, interprets omens, engages in witchcraft, or casts spells." Such individuals also have no place in teens' music libraries.

Dave Matthews Band

◆ ◆

This quintet includes Dave Matthews, Boyd Tinsley, LeRoi Moore, Stefan Lessard, and Carter Beauford. *Under the Table and Dreaming* went quadruple platinum and earned two Grammys. *Crash* and *Before These Crowded Streets* debuted at numbers 2 and 1, respectively. In a sexually explicit conversation with *Details* magazine [6/98], Matthews was quoted as saying, "If there's the often-imagined bearded God in the sky who made us in His image, He's an incredibly cruel bastard."

Title: *Before These Crowded Streets* (1998)
Label: RCA
Genre: Rock
Pro-Social Content: "The Last Stop" questions the wisdom of seeking peace through war, hatred, dishonesty, and bloodshed. The singer examines people's pain when they're forced to readjust in the wake of life's disappointments ("The Dreaming Tree"). Abandoning worries and learning to relax is the lesson of "Pantala Naga Pampa." "Pig" clings to the "light of love" for hope. A man regrets making a mistake and seeks help during his recovery from it ("The Stone").
Objectionable Content: Lines promoting drunkenness undo "Crush" and the crude, sexually charged "Rapunzel." "Stay (Wasting Time)" finds the artist tasting his lover's perspiration. Self-reliance gives way to bitterness and animosity on "Don't Drink the Water" ("I live with my hatred, I live with my jealousy . . . I don't need anybody but me . . . I will bury you").
Summary/Advisory: This album debuted at number 1. Once again, jazzy, funk-infused rock is confounded by lyrical obscurity. Some positives do exist, but teens who walk through *Crowded Streets* will encounter enough trouble that it's worth rerouting them.

Title: *Crash* (1996)
Label: RCA
Genre: Rock
Pro-Social Content: A groveling man asks forgiveness for an unnamed

mistake ("Let You Down"). On "Two Step," he thanks a romantic partner for enhancing his journey through life. "#41" prescribes prayer, vulnerability, and communication to soothe relational ills; "Drive In Drive Out" adds a sense of humor to the mix. Fear and greed are deemed divisive ("Cry Freedom"), and the simple life is preferred to fame and fortune ("Proudest Monkey").

Objectionable Content: The voyeuristic "Crash Into Me" paints the artist as a lustful Peeping Tom. "Say Goodbye" is no better; it's a sexual come-on to a woman involved with another man ("Tomorrow go back to your man . . . Tonight let's go all the way"). Various excesses (including alcohol) are described on "Too Much," but the singer seems resigned to the habits. Luke 12:19 is distorted to justify a wild beach party featuring nudity and tequila.

Summary/Advisory: Stylish acoustic guitar work. A jazzy folk-rock sound. The disc soars when it stays focused on positive themes, but reckless partying, alcohol, and casual sex ultimately cause it to *Crash*.

Title: *Under the Table and Dreaming* (1994)
Label: RCA
Genre: Rock
Pro-Social Content: "Satellite" ponders the phenomenon of instant media and cultural voyeurism ("Someone's secrets you've seen . . . Satellite dish in my yard, tell me more"). A friend is invited to share her troubles on the optimistic "The Best of What's Around."

Objectionable Content: Life reflects little meaning or purpose on "Dancing Nancies." "Ant's Marching" is equally pessimistic as it explores relational miscommunication. As a "remedy [for] feelin' low," Matthews says, "I take a drink, sit back, relax, smoke my mind make me feel better for a small time" ("Jimi Thing"). Although the artist wishes he didn't drink and smoke, life's trials leave him with a death wish and a drug habit on "Rhyme & Reason," making it hard to tell if the tune is condemning or promoting substance abuse.

Summary/Advisory: Sharp instrumental work. It's a shame Matthews's artsy blues rock, cryptic lyrics, and tortured vocals dwell mostly on dark themes. Teens should keep *Under the Table* out of the stereo.

Depeche Mode

◆ ◆ ◆ ◆ ◆ ◆ ◆ ◆ ◆ ◆ ◆ ◆ ◆ ◆ ◆ ◆ ◆ ◆ ◆

The group's name is French for "fast fashion." Depeche Mode originated in Basildon, England, and began with David Gahan, Martin Gore, Vince Clarke, and Andy Fletcher. Clarke was replaced in 1982 by Alan Wilder when he left to form the band Yaz, and later, Erasure.

Title: *Songs of Faith and Devotion* (1993)
Label: Sire/Reprise
Genre: Alternative/Dance/Pop
Pro-Social Content: "Get Right With Me" conveys faith in mankind and a measure of hope ("Friends, if you've lost your way you will find it again someday"), while asking people to be real, humble, and sincere.

Objectionable Content: Sadistic selfishness is characteristic of "Judas" ("suffer some misery if you want my love . . . risk your health for me") and "Mercy in You," which celebrates an abusive relationship ("I suffer from greed, longing to feed on the mercy in you"). "One Caress" includes the theologically absurd statement, "I have to believe that sin can make me a better man." "Walking in My Shoes" makes excuses for an amoral lifestyle and, as on "Condemnation," the singer has no use for repentance or absolution.

Summary/Advisory: The project's title is misleading. Teens looking to Depeche Mode will find no faith and very little devotion worth imitating.

Des'ree

◆ ◆ ◆ ◆ ◆ ◆ ◆ ◆ ◆ ◆ ◆ ◆ ◆ ◆ ◆ ◆ ◆ ◆ ◆

Des'ree was born in London, England. Her Epic debut was released in 1992. Two years later, *I Ain't Movin'* slowly sold more than 500,000 copies and spent more than six months on the charts.

Title: *I Ain't Movin'* (1994)
Label: Epic
Genre: R&B-tinged pop/Adult contemporary
Pro-Social Content: Delightful celebrations of life abound. Des'ree exalts virtues such as honesty, bravery, and steadfastness ("I Ain't Movin'"), truth

and justice ("Herald the Day"), caring, sharing, and loving ("Living in the City") and heeding parental wisdom ("You Gotta Be"). "Little Child" laments world hunger, recommending prayer as a remedy. "Trip on Love" applauds parental affection. Though vague, "Love Is Here" may point to God as the author of love.

Objectionable Content: Just a line in "Strong Enough" ("Never criticize, keep an open mind") that could lead to moral compromise.

Summary/Advisory: A pleasant, soulful collection that's lyrically encouraging. If this disc truly represents Des'ree's artistic stand, let's hope she really *ain't* movin'.

Diamond Rio

◆ ◆ ◆ ◆ ◆ ◆ ◆ ◆ ◆ ◆ ◆ ◆ ◆ ◆ ◆ ◆ ◆ ◆ ◆ ◆

This six-man band is made up of Marty Roe, Jimmy Olander, Gene Johnson, Dan Truman, Dana Williams, and Brian Prout. Each of Diamond Rio's first eight singles spent exactly 20 weeks on the country chart.

Title: *Love a Little Stronger* (1994)
Label: Arista
Genre: Country
Pro-Social Content: Two cuts acknowledge the need to work at strengthening romantic bonds ("Finish What We Started," "Love a Little Stronger"). A son reflects on his father's thankless profession on "Kentucky Mine." "Down by the River" upholds the institution of marriage as desirable, however . . .

Objectionable Content: In the same song, the engaged couple has an impromptu lovemaking session on the bank to celebrate the occasion. Also, the blue-collar ballad of "Bubba Hyde" esteems a man for his reputation as a Friday night party animal ("a honky-tonkin' fool till closing time").

Summary/Advisory: This band of professing Christians should've known better than to spoil an otherwise fine effort with a few unsavory themes. It may be the first time a lump of coal has come from a Diamond.

Diffie, Joe

◆ ◆ ◆ ◆ ◆ ◆ ◆ ◆ ◆ ◆ ◆ ◆ ◆ ◆ ◆ ◆ ◆ ◆ ◆

In 1990, Diffie was the first country singer to be
accorded a number-1 hit his first time around
with "Home." The Oklahoman joined the Grand
Ole Opry in 1993, had several number-1
singles, and won *Billboard*'s Top Singles
Artist award.

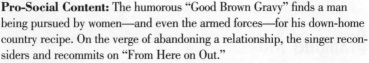

Title: *Third Rock from the Sun* (1994)
Label: Epic
Genre: Country
Pro-Social Content: The humorous "Good Brown Gravy" finds a man
being pursued by women—and even the armed forces—for his down-home
country recipe. On the verge of abandoning a relationship, the singer recon-
siders and recommits on "From Here on Out."
Objectionable Content: "Wild Blue Yonder" seeks solace in a bottle of
whiskey. Though admittedly cynical, a common guy longs to be "a one-man
woman juggling act" on "I'd Like to Have a Problem Like That." "So Help
Me Girl" alludes to physical intimacy without a clear relational context.
Elsewhere, a lovesick man beats up another of the girl's suitors ("Junior's in
Love").
Summary/Advisory: Much of Diffie's latest effort treads on neutral
ground. Still, *Third Rock* relies on a honky-tonk mentality that occasionally
sends it rolling off course.

Dion, Celine

◆ ◆ ◆ ◆ ◆ ◆ ◆ ◆ ◆ ◆ ◆ ◆ ◆ ◆ ◆ ◆ ◆ ◆ ◆

The youngest of 14 children from a highly musical family in Quebec, Celine
Dion gave her first public performance of traditional French-Canadian
songs at age five. Since the release of her landmark album *The Colour of My
Love* in 1993, Celine has sold more than 20 million albums around the
world. She has earned Grammy, Juno, Felix, and World Music awards.

Title: *Let's Talk About Love* (1997)
Label: Sony
Genre: Pop/Adult contemporary

Pro-Social Content: Songs celebrate love in various forms: its fundamental role in life ("Where Is Love"); its ability to inspire eternal romantic devotion ("To Love You More," "Immortality," "Miles to Go Before I Sleep," and the theme from *Titanic*, "My Heart Will Go On"); the love that binds humanity ("Let's Talk About Love"); a near-spiritual faith in a partner ("Just a Little Bit of Love"); and the affection of a good man ("The Reason"). "Treat Her Like a Lady" scolds men who selfishly use women. The artist grapples with whether or not to express her fondness for a man ("Tell Him"), and remains optimistic in the wake of a breakup ("Love Is on the Way").

Objectionable Content: One mild profanity appears in "Why Oh Why"'s printed lyrics, but it's *not* in the song.

Summary/Advisory: These 15 new songs showcase the same powerful vocals and positive messages Celine's fans have come to expect. The only surprises are good ones—guest appearances by Luciano Pavarotti, Carole King, Barbra Streisand, and the Bee Gees. Solid!

Title: *Falling Into You* (1996)
Label: Epic
Genre: Pop/Adult contemporary
Pro-Social Content: "Call the Man," which praises a nameless individual capable of calming the chaos and confusion in life with "love beyond repair," could easily be interpreted as a song about Jesus. Pledges of devotion and romantic commitment dominate this project ("Make You Happy," "If That's What It Takes," "Declaration of Love," the number-1 hit "Because You Loved Me," and "River Deep, Mountain High," a remake of the 1971 Supremes/Four Tops collaboration). Each conveys a spirit of faithfulness and fidelity. Life's trials pale in comparison to the thought of losing her partner on "I Don't Know." "I Love You" regrets not expressing feelings of affection sooner.

Objectionable Content: Casual references to sex outside of marriage mar two otherwise acceptable songs.

Summary/Advisory: These caveats aside, *Falling* stands tall, delivering passionate melodies with dynamite messages of hope and love. Accused of being a goody-goody, Dion told *Entertainment Weekly* [3/29/96], "I'm not afraid to be nice." Good to hear!

Title: *The Colour of My Love* (1993)
Label: 550 Music
Genre: Adult contemporary
Pro-Social Content: Like many of her songs, the poetic title track paints a picture of "devoted love until we die." "When I Fall in Love" wholeheartedly reserves that deepest emotion for one special person. On "Real Emotion," she tells her man to skip the material gifts in favor of "something from the heart."
Objectionable Content: The number-1 pop hit "The Power of Love" appears to relate a first-time sexual encounter ruled by the passion of the moment. A girl rejects the wisdom of her parents on "Everybody's Talkin' My Baby Down." "Love Doesn't Ask Why" jettisons absolute values when making moral decisions ("Don't ask me if this feelin's right or wrong . . . there's no plan, it's not in our hands").
Summary/Advisory: Great music and powerful vocals, but *Colour* lacks lyrical consistency. Not explicit, but disappointing nonetheless. *Falling Into You* and *Let's Talk About Love* are better picks.

Dogg Pound, Tha

◆ ◆ ◆ ◆ ◆ ◆ ◆ ◆ ◆ ◆ ◆ ◆ ◆ ◆ ◆ ◆ ◆ ◆ ◆

Rappers Delmar "Daz" Arnaud and Ricardo "Kurupt" Brown, better known as Tha Dogg Pound, broke into the music business working with their gangsta mentors Dr. Dre and Snoop Doggy Dogg. A prerelease controversy surrounding *Dogg Food* (one of the industry's largest street-date violations on record) helped push Time Warner to divest itself of this project and its Interscope Records subsidiary.

Title: *Dogg Food* (1995)
Label: Death Row/Interscope
Genre: Gangsta rap
Pro-Social Content: On "Reality," the artist pledges that, no matter how tough life gets, he won't pursue the cowardly cop-out of suicide.
Objectionable Content: Violent threats on "Dogg Pound Gangstaz" ("I came to violate you, desecrate you") and "Ridin', Slippin', Slidin'" ("I'm in the mood for murder") are just the tip of the iceberg. Six tracks glorify drugs and alcohol—from gin and cognac to marijuana and cocaine. Extreme sexual

perversion features lewd descriptions of oral sex ("Let's Play House," "If We All F——"), anal sex ("Respect"), casual sex with multiple partners ("Some Bomb Azz P——y," "New York, New York," "One By One," "If We All F——"), and gay intercourse ("Dogg Pound Gangstaz," "Smooth"). This rap duo suggests that promiscuous women "might as well get paid" by becoming prostitutes ("Big Pimpin 2"). They bark obscenities throughout.

Summary/Advisory: Kurupt boasted to *Rolling Stone* [11/2/95], "Just call us the profanity kings. The second they stop our music is the second they have to stop pornography." A line from "A Doggz Day Afternoon" sums up this disc when it says, "I got a sadistic mind, I find I'm mentally sick." Avoid this mangy pair's misogynistic drool.

Dr. Dre

◆ ◆ ◆ ◆ ◆ ◆ ◆ ◆ ◆ ◆ ◆ ◆ ◆ ◆ ◆ ◆ ◆ ◆ ◆ ◆

Raised in Compton, California, as Andre Young, the man known as Dr. Dre co-founded the rap groups N.W.A. and World Class Wreckin' Cru. In 1992, he started the nefarious label Death Row Records. *The Chronic* sold more than 3 million units.

Title: *The Chronic* (1993)
Label: Interscope
Genre: Rap
Pro-Social Content: None
Objectionable Content: Nearly every song describes murder or violence, usually with "AKs," "Uzis," "hollow points," and such typified in titles like "A Nigga Witta Gun" and "Rat-Tat-Tat-Tat." "Deez Nuuts" and "The Doctor's Office" graphically boast of sexual exploits. "The Day the Niggaz Took Over" condones looting and arson in the L.A. riots. The title track (a dramatized drug party), "The $20 Sack Pyramid," and other songs openly promote the use of "the chronic". . . that's street shorthand for marijuana.

Summary/Advisory: This time as a solo artist, Dre once again wracks record stores with the advocation of crime, drug use, explicit sex, and graphic violence (a chronic problem!). The *Denver Post* [4/4/95] printed the following Dr. Dre quote: "America loves violence. America is obsessed with murder. I think murder sells a lot more than sex. They say sex sells. I think murder sells." He's doing his best to prove it. Another socially irresponsible record.

Dylan, Bob

◆ ◆

The artist responsible for six platinum LPs and more than twice as many gold albums, Bob Dylan (born Robert Allen Zimmerman) is a veteran singer, songwriter, guitarist, and harmonica player. He landed his first record deal in 1961 and is credited with developing the style known today as "folk-rock." Dylan—who borrowed his stage name from poet Dylan Thomas—was a member of the Traveling Wilburys (along with Roy Orbison, George Harrison, Tom Petty, and ELO's Jeff Lynne). He was welcomed into the Rock 'n' Roll Hall of Fame in 1988 and given Grammy's Lifetime Achievement Award in 1991.

Title: *Time Out of Mind* (1997)
Label: Columbia
Genre: Blues/Folk
Pro-Social Content: Reeling from the pain of romantic strife, Dylan states, "I know God is my shield and He won't lead me astray" ("'Til I Fell in Love with You"). On "Dirt Road Blues," he uses a spiritual salvation metaphor to describe how he'd feel if his woman would return. Two of the disc's numerous blues tracks ("Cold Irons Bound," "Not Dark Yet") convey optimism. The artist commits to stand by his partner through life's trying times on "To Make You Feel My Love" (a Dylan original that was a modest hit for Billy Joel in 1997 and a bigger hit for Garth Brooks in 1998).
Objectionable Content: "Million Miles" appears to contain sexual over-tones. A man with no conscience finds alcohol appealing ("Highlands"). The jilted singer isn't sure if he would "kiss or kill" his ex if she were "Standing in the Doorway."
Summary/Advisory: Lots of relational introspection from this master of melancholy. Musically, he's still sharp (the disc won a Grammy in 1998). However, *Time*'s truly positive sentiments don't create a lasting impression, leaving listeners to meander through the mournful middle ground of Dylan's pained poetry.

Title: *Good as I Been to You* (1992)
Label: Columbia
Genre: Folk

Pro-Social Content: The artist longs for "Hard Times" to leave him alone. "Jim Jones" yearns for freedom after being sentenced to life on a slave ship.

Objectionable Content: A scoundrel named "Blackjack Davey" steals a 16-year-old bride who eagerly declares, "I'll forsake my house and home/And I'll forsake my baby/I'll forsake my husband, too/For the love of Blackjack Davey." "Little Maggie" turns to alcohol as a temporary solution to her relational troubles. Two men violently beat a pair of army recruiters after being verbally threatened ("Arthur McBride"). On "Frankie and Albert," a man's two-timing leads his woman to shoot him dead in a fit of passion (after she goes drinking at the corner saloon). The singer—relegated to a chain gang—appears to be threatening the woman in his life on "You're Gonna Quit Me" ("Day you quit me, baby/That's the day you die").

Summary/Advisory: The legendary Dylan draws only on himself, his guitar, and a set of biographical folk tunes. Many of these poetic story songs share interesting snapshots from diverse lives. Unfortunately, most of Dylan's characters lack noble qualities.

Eazy-E

◆ ◆ ◆ ◆ ◆ ◆ ◆ ◆ ◆ ◆ ◆ ◆ ◆ ◆ ◆ ◆ ◆ ◆

Gangsta rapper Eric Wright was known by the music world and his fans as Eazy-E. An admitted drug dealer, he used his ill-gotten gain to start Ruthless Records in 1988. Wright was an original member of the hard-core gangsta rap group N.W.A. (which stands for Niggaz With Attitude). He recorded nine albums and fathered seven children by six different women before dying of AIDS in 1995.

Title: *It's On (Dr. Dre) 187UmKilla* (1993)
Label: Ruthless
Genre: Gangsta rap
Pro-Social Content: None
Objectionable Content: Repeated uses of the f-word pepper this distasteful collection. Tracks glorify violence toward women ("Boyz N Tha Hood"), misogyny with oral and anal sex ("Gimme That Nutt," "Still a

Nigga"), drug and alcohol abuse ("Down 2 Tha Last Roach"), and the idea that disputes find their solutions at the end of a gun. One of those feuds is with Snoop Doggy Dogg and ex-partner Dr. Dre on "Real MuthaPhukkin' G's." Eazy-E refers to them as "f—in' actors, pranksters, studio gangstas." "Any Last Werdz" boasts of committing a drive-by murder. He even perverts the Green Acres theme by substituting sexually explicit lyrics.

Summary/Advisory: Avoid this lewd, hateful rubbish at all costs.

Enigma
◆ ◆ ◆ ◆ ◆ ◆ ◆ ◆ ◆ ◆ ◆ ◆ ◆ ◆ ◆ ◆ ◆ ◆ ◆ ◆

Michael Cretu is the producer, composer, songwriter, and instrumentalist for Enigma, a New Age band from Germany. His wife, Sandra, provides the vocals.

Title: *The Cross of Changes* (1994)
Label: Charisma
Genre: Synthesized rock/New Age
Pro-Social Content: Isolated lines, such as "Don't play games with the ones you love" and "For the ones who abuse his name, there'll be no escape on judgment day" have merit. But the overall context doesn't support them.

Objectionable Content: New Age philosophies denying the Jesus of Scripture appear in the liner notes. In fact, "Second Chapter" espouses reincarnation ("It takes many lives till we succeed, to clear the debts of many, many hundred years"). The band blames Christianity for destroying the polytheistic purity of some cultures on "Silent Warrior" ("White men won in the name of God with the cross as an alibi"). Lyrical confusion also equates love and hate on "I Love You . . . I'll Kill You."

Summary/Advisory: Teens looking for spiritual meaning in life could be led astray by the evangelistic efforts of Enigma. It's best if they don't take up *The Cross of Changes.*

Enya

◆ ◆ ◆ ◆ ◆ ◆ ◆ ◆ ◆ ◆ ◆ ◆ ◆ ◆ ◆ ◆ ◆ ◆ ◆

Enya was born Eithne Ni Bhraonain in Donegal, Ireland. *The Memory of Trees* is Enya's third major solo album and her first since *Shepherd Moons*, a project that earned the artist a 1992 Grammy award and exceeded sales of 9 million units worldwide.

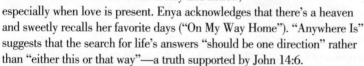

Title: *The Memory of Trees* (1995)
Label: Reprise
Genre: New Age/Adult contemporary
Pro-Social Content: "Hope Has a Place"
assures listeners that life is not dreary and hollow,
especially when love is present. Enya acknowledges that there's a heaven and sweetly recalls her favorite days ("On My Way Home"). "Anywhere Is" suggests that the search for life's answers "should be one direction" rather than "either this or that way"—a truth supported by John 14:6.
Objectionable Content: When Enya wonders if the "stars sign the life that is to be mine," it seems like a reference to astrological predestination. Equally ambiguous, "China Roses" speaks of being led by the moon.
Summary/Advisory: Enya's rich instrumentation and soothing vocals make for enjoyable background listening. Even so, this gifted artist's spiritual references, as vague as they are, may be too equivocal for many families (the album's unconventional sound sent it to number 1 on the New Age album chart). The Celtic band Iona provides a solid Christian alternative in the same musical vein.

Estefan, Gloria

◆ ◆ ◆ ◆ ◆ ◆ ◆ ◆ ◆ ◆ ◆ ◆ ◆ ◆ ◆ ◆ ◆ ◆ ◆

Estefan was born in Havana, Cuba. At the tender age of 16 months, her family fled to Miami, Florida. She grew into a powerful songstress whose three albums in the 1980s (with Miami Sound Machine) all went platinum. On March 20, 1990, Estefan suffered a broken vertebra in a serious bus accident, but after surgery and therapy she has made a miraculous recovery. Estefan has sold more than 18 million albums—recording her lyrics in both English and Spanish.

Title: *Destiny* (1996)
Label: Epic
Genre: Pop/Latin
Pro-Social Content: On "Along Came You,"
Estefan expresses love to her young daughter,
elevating motherhood as her "one true purpose."
The artist's amorous praise extends to her hus-
band on the title cut. She also pledges commit-

ment through relational trials ("I'm Not Giving You Up") and a willingness
to "go the distance" to fulfill a promise ("Reach"). The soul-searching "Path
of the Right Love" may refer to God in its plea to "reach out for love" and
share kindness with the hurting masses. In an industry downright phobic
about differentiating behavior as "right" and "wrong," Estefan does just that
with "Higher," a song that promotes getting ahead in life without lying,
cheating, or stealing. The fun "You'll Be Mine (Party Time)" rejoices in life
and love, never in sexual carousing or drunken shenanigans.
Objectionable Content: None
Summary/Advisory: This former lead singer for Miami Sound Machine
had a difficult childhood and was nearly killed in a bus accident in
1990. Is she bitter? Not in the least. Her wholesome, upbeat, and
unapologetic celebration of life puts whining Gen-Xers to shame. A
terrific pop effort.

Etheridge, Melissa

◆ ◆ ◆ ◆ ◆ ◆ ◆ ◆ ◆ ◆ ◆ ◆ ◆ ◆ ◆ ◆ ◆ ◆ ◆

Melissa Etheridge hails from America's heartland, where she grew up in
middle-class Leavenworth, Kansas. After moving to L.A., she was signed by
Island records and released her first album in 1988. Total album sales
exceed 10 million units.

Title: *Yes I Am* (1993)
Label: Island
Genre: Rock
Pro-Social Content: Not much. One song
expresses relational commitment ("I'm the only
one who'll walk across the fire for you").
Objectionable Content: "Silent Legacy"
considers prayer worthless. Right and wrong

are irrelevant in the quest for a man's love ("I could dance with the devil on a Saturday night . . . smoke, drink, swear"). Several cuts also appear to be anti-parent ("Come to My Window," "Silent Legacy"). A woman caves in to sexual temptation on "Resist." "All American Girl" encourages perseverance during a trial, but with no solutions (amid despair and alienation, it could also be suggesting abortion for a young mother-to-be).
Summary/Advisory: Earthy vocals carry worldly messages. Here, soul-searching usually leads to hedonistic nihilism. Skip it.

Everclear

◆ ◆

This Portland, Oregon-based alternative rock trio is made up of Art Alexakis, Craig Montoya, and Greg Eklund. Capitol records signed Everclear in 1994, leading to the million-selling *Sparkle and Fade*.

Title: *Sparkle and Fade* (1996)
Label: Capitol
Genre: Alternative
Pro-Social Content: "Pale Green Stars" relates the emotional pain of a child watching her parents fight and her dad walk out.
Objectionable Content: Though drugs nearly destroyed frontman Art Alexakis, the band has no trouble glorifying their use to teens ("Heroin Girl," "Chemical Smile"). On "Summerland," the singer takes a fatalistic view of life, wishing to escape into "cheap red wine." Similarly, an alcoholic stupor is preferred to reality on "The Twistinside" ("Everyday in the afternoon, I like to let the arms of a bar wrap around me tight . . . cross-eyed and smiling as I watch the world go twisting by"). On a more vengeful note, "You Make Me Feel Like a Whore" longs for the day when the artist can make a so-called friend burn with self-loathing.
Summary/Advisory: The best way to wrap up an analysis of *Sparkle and Fade* is with the band's description of itself: "Everclear is . . . like 180-proof alcohol. It's another name for moonshine, basically. It looks like water, but it's pure evil. It's a lot like us." Teens should steer clear.

Ewing, Skip

◆ ◆ ◆ ◆ ◆ ◆ ◆ ◆ ◆ ◆ ◆ ◆ ◆ ◆ ◆ ◆ ◆ ◆ ◆

Skip Ewing's music received attention on a broad scale in 1988 with the hit singles "I Don't Have Far to Fall" and "Burnin' a Hole in My Heart." Besides being known as an entertainer, Ewing is recognized as a songwriter. More than 100 of his songs have been recorded by other musicians. "Love Me" (a hit for Collin Raye) was nominated for Single of the Year and Song of the Year in 1991 by the Country Music Association.

Title: *Until I Found You* (1997)
Label: Word Nashville
Genre: Country
Pro-Social Content: Once again, Ewing specializes in jubilant celebrations of romantic love ("All That Matters to Me," "The Answer to My Prayer," "Until I Found You"). "Make Time" recognizes the frenzied pace of life that must be overcome to achieve a solid marriage. The bouncy "Mary Go Round" recalls how a couple met at a county fair, courted, and grew a family together. A man confusing "the wrong and the right" digs himself a deeper and deeper hole in life, and the artist uses the story as a warning to the rest of us ("The Hole"). Other tracks point out that love takes work ("A Sliver of the Moon," "I Got a Job to Do") and imply that it's well worth the effort.
Objectionable Content: "Some Fools" wallows in the misery of lost love.
Summary/Advisory: *Until I Found You* features breezy country melodies and heartfelt ballads that, with one minor exception, add up to a great disc for young fans of the genre.

Fagen, Donald

◆ ◆ ◆ ◆ ◆ ◆ ◆ ◆ ◆ ◆ ◆ ◆ ◆ ◆ ◆ ◆ ◆ ◆ ◆

Donald Fagen was born in Passaic, New Jersey. He and Walter Becker released their first album under the name Steely Dan in 1972. The duo's first five discs went gold; their last three went platinum. Steely Dan disbanded in 1981, and Fagen embarked on a solo career.

Title: *Kamakiriad* (1993)

Label: Reprise
Genre: Progressive rock/Jazz
Pro-Social Content: Positive references to
fatherhood and family are heard on "Trans-
Island Highway" and "Tomorrow's Girls."
Objectionable Content: Apart from one
veiled reference to implicit sex on "Florida
Room" ("but in her Florida room there's a
hurricane"), nothing on this record merits parental
concern.

Summary/Advisory: The signature vocal sound Fagen popularized with
Steely Dan is the centerpiece of this enjoyable album. There's no heavy social
agenda, no obscenities or explicit sex. Just a custom-tooled, steam-powered
Kamakiri roadster that drives the listener on a fun, relaxed journey through
eight upbeat, instrumentally dynamic tracks. Overall, a positive pick.

Foo Fighters

◆ ◆ ◆ ◆ ◆ ◆ ◆ ◆ ◆ ◆ ◆ ◆ ◆ ◆ ◆ ◆ ◆ ◆ ◆ ◆

Foo Fighters is made up of Dave Grohl (formerly of Nirvana), William
Goldsmith, Nate Mendel, and Pat Smear. The band's name is taken from a
term used to describe strange aerial phenomena reported by U.S. Air Force
pilots during World War II.

Title: *The Colour and the Shape* (1997)
Label: Capitol
Genre: Alternative/Rock
Pro-Social Content: The singer is happy to be
reunited with a love ("Up in Arms"). He longs
for relational healing on "See You," telling the
one-time object of his frustration, "I'm done
resenting you."

Objectionable Content: More problems here than on the band's last
project. Harsh profanities (including the f-word) make an occasionally
angry album seem that much nastier. "Hey, Johnny Park!" includes the
selfish sentiment, "Now that I've found my reward, I'd throw it away long
before I'd share a piece of mine with you." Whining self-destructiveness
and misery dominate "My Poor Brain." On "Everlong," the artist is invited
to "waste away" with a woman of questionable sanity. Though vague,

"Monkey Wrench" could be interpreted as the frustrations of a teen whose parents refuse to accept his homosexuality.

Summary/Advisory: Fronted by Dave Grohl, this band has gotten darker and more profane since its last release. Parents may wish to redirect teens to CCM alternatives Plankeye and Grammatrain.

Title: *Foo Fighters* (1995)
Label: Roswell/Capitol
Genre: Alternative

Pro-Social Content: Apparently in response to Kurt Cobain's suicide, the song "I'll Stick Around" determines to learn from another's pain and unwise actions ("I had no other hand in your ever-desperate plan . . . I'll stick around and learn from all that came from it"). Otherwise, mostly vague lyrics and veiled meanings.

Objectionable Content: Profanity ("pi—ed," "sh—") appears on several tracks.

Summary/Advisory: All of these songs were written by Dave Grohl, who used to be the drummer for grunge pioneers Nirvana. With *Foo Fighters*, Grohl moves toward neutral ground, trading deeply depressing themes for perplexing, ambiguous messages. Even so, the occasional crudities are crystal clear. Fans of this hard-edged musical style would be better off listening to Plankeye, Grammatrain, or Poor Old Lu. (SEE ALSO: Nirvana)

Foxworthy, Jeff

◆ ◆ ◆ ◆ ◆ ◆ ◆ ◆ ◆ ◆ ◆ ◆ ◆ ◆ ◆ ◆ ◆ ◆ ◆

Comedian Jeff Foxworthy is one of only two artists to sell more than a million copies of a spoken word album since Eddie Murphy managed the feat in 1984. Foxworthy has appeared on the *Tonight Show* and two Showtime specials and has been nominated for two Cable ACE awards. He also starred in his own sitcom, *The Jeff Foxworthy Show*, on ABC.

Title: *Games Rednecks Play* (1995)
Label: Warner Bros.
Genre: Comedy

Pro-Social Content: Lots of laughs from neutral material, including family-oriented humor ("You learn a lot from your kids. Just a few days ago I learned you can get three boxes of raisins into the cassette player of a Jeep"). Foxworthy also claims, "I love being a parent."

Objectionable Content: Affectionate slams on Southerners aside, he jokes about sex, mooning, drunkenness, leering at the Victoria's Secret catalog, and using pornography at a fertility clinic. Mild profanity. Anatomical references. Biological functions.

Summary/Advisory: Twang, timing, and an intimate knowledge of his targets make this talented jester fresh and funny. But while not nearly as explicit as the average comedy album, *Rednecks* still wanders off the straight and narrow onto some questionable backroads. Teens should try the Christian humor of Mark Lowry instead.

Franklin, Kirk

◆ ◆ ◆ ◆ ◆ ◆ ◆ ◆ ◆ ◆ ◆ ◆ ◆ ◆ ◆ ◆ ◆ ◆ ◆

(SEE: Kirk Franklin and the Family)

Fugees

◆ ◆ ◆ ◆ ◆ ◆ ◆ ◆ ◆ ◆ ◆ ◆ ◆ ◆ ◆ ◆ ◆ ◆ ◆

This New Jersey-based band is made up of Wyclef "Clef" Jean, Prakazrel "Pras" Michel, and Lauryn "L" Hill. *The Score* peaked at number 1 on both the R&B and pop charts, selling more than 5 million copies. In early 1998, Fugees cavorted with Big Bird and Snuffleupagus as part of the *Sesame Street* special, "Elmopalooza."

Title: *The Score* (1996)
Label: Columbia/Ruffhouse
Genre: Hip-hop/Gangsta rap
Pro-Social Content: None
Objectionable Content: A near-constant stream of profanity flows through more than 73 minutes of audio sludge. Glorifications of violence include bragging about a robbery ("Ready or Not"), hateful threats against police ("Red Intro"), gang shootings ("The Score"), planning an assassination ("Zealots"),

and much more. The artist invites Newt Gingrich to engage in oral sex ("The Beast") and decries black-on-black violence by stating, "Only problem we have is killing the people who don't look like us who oppress us/S——, you wanna impress me? Shoot the muthaf—— who turned off my lights/Shoot somebody who makin' my bills high." Other tracks recommend smoking marijuana, downing whiskey sours, and drinking moonshine. The trio's theology is a disturbing blend of Rastafarianism, voodoo, and a warped view of Christianity. The title cut finds a man in a bar boasting of a sexual conquest. **Summary/Advisory:** Its rasta-reggae flavor is all that sets this effort apart from run-of-the-mill gangsta trash. Incessant profanity. Drugs. Alcohol. Murder. Take the parental advisory seriously and point teens away from *The Score*.

Galactic Cowboys

◆ ◆ ◆ ◆ ◆ ◆ ◆ ◆ ◆ ◆ ◆ ◆ ◆ ◆ ◆ ◆ ◆ ◆ ◆ ◆

This band is Ben Huggins, Wally Farkas, Monty Colvin, and Alan Doss. Having called it quits after 1993's *Space in Your Face*, Galactic Cowboys was resurrected by Metal Blade CEO Brian Slagel.

Title: *Machine Fish* (1996)
Label: Metal Blade
Genre: Rock/Heavy metal
Pro-Social Content: Facing the unknown with confidence is the subject of "Fear Not." The singer cries out to God for help in overcoming anxiety ("Stress") and assails worldly solutions to life's problems that ignore the Almighty ("Idle Minds"). "9th of June" exposes as charlatans those who set specific dates for Christ's return. Reminiscent of Romans 7:14-22, "The Struggle" describes the inner battle waged within a person contemplating a decision between right and wrong. "Psychotic Companion" takes a swipe at Psychic Friends and other telephone astrologers. On "Easy to Love," a man praises someone special "sent down from above." The Cowboys seize pride and ego by the throat on "Pattin' Yourself on the Back."
Objectionable Content: None
Summary/Advisory: Solid messages throughout. While this mainstream band's raw sound may rage too wildly at times to meet some families' standards, households already fluent in the language of heavy metal will find *Machine Fish* to be a light in a very dark genre.

Title: *Space in Your Face* (1993)
Label: Geffen
Genre: Alternative
Pro-Social Content: Pro-life sentiments permeate "If I Were a Killer," which points an accusing finger at the Supreme Court, abortion doctors, and bleeding-heart liberals quick to excuse criminal violence. "Blind" considers the value of repentance, avoiding evil, and seeking wisdom. The band measures its own puny trials against the challenges facing others on "No Problems" ("I saw a man with no legs . . . I've got no reason to complain"). "Do What I Do" attempts to keep criticism in proper perspective while pressing on toward a goal.
Objectionable Content: None
Summary/Advisory: Although cryptic at times, the Cowboys communicate positive philosophies to fans of a musical genre overcome with nihilism. A positive secular alternative to Metallica and other bands with a heavy sound.

Garbage

◆ ◆ ◆ ◆ ◆ ◆ ◆ ◆ ◆ ◆ ◆ ◆ ◆ ◆ ◆ ◆ ◆ ◆ ◆ ◆

Garbage consists of Shirley Manson, Steve Marker, Duke Erikson, and Butch Vig. The bandmates (sans Manson) came together in 1993. Manson was later recruited by the other three who saw her performing with her former band, Angelfish, on MTV's *120 Minutes*.

Title: *Garbage* (1995)
Label: Almo Sounds
Genre: Alternative/Pop
Pro-Social Content: "Fix Me Now" admits that where there is shadow, there is light.
Objectionable Content: The disturbing "As Heaven Is Wide" concludes that the only relief from a troubled conscience is total *separation* from God. The singer plots vindictive revenge against a lover on "Vow" ("I've come to cut you up . . . and break your soul apart"). Similarly, she acts out relational frustration by burning down that person's house on "Not My Idea." Advice given on the appropriately

titled "Stupid Girl" includes denouncing faith and love. A crude sexual proposition ("Supervixen") seems to offer the only comfort from life's darkness, misery, and pain—which is exalted on "Only Happy When It Rains" ("I feel good when things are going wrong . . . I'm riding high on deep depression"). Hopelessness abounds.

Summary/Advisory: Artists today have turned moping into an art form. Lead singer Shirley Manson says her band's members share "a certain melancholy and an interest in the perverse." It shows. Usually, trash takes a few days to stink up the house, but don't wait that long to put *Garbage* out at the curb. Teens intrigued by Manson's vocal style should pick up a copy of *God* by Rebecca St. James instead.

Geto Boys

◆ ◆ ◆ ◆ ◆ ◆ ◆ ◆ ◆ ◆ ◆ ◆ ◆ ◆ ◆ ◆ ◆ ◆

Bushwick Bill, Willie D, and Scarface make up the Geto Boys. Their 1996 release, *The Resurrection,* debuted at number 1 on the R&B chart and number 6 on the pop chart. The group changed its name from Ghetto Boys to Geto Boys in 1990.

Title: *The Resurrection* (1996)
Label: Rap-A-Lot/NooTrybe
Genre: Gangsta rap
Pro-Social Content: None
Objectionable Content: Tunes glorify alcohol ("Blind Leading the Blind"), marijuana ("Geto Boys and Girls"), and crack cocaine ("First Light of the Day"). The f-word gets frequent play, and women are called "hos," "tramps," and "sluts." "Point of No Return" makes vicious threats against Bob Dole and the late J. Edgar Hoover, while "Open Minded" promotes cop-killing. Suicide gets an approving nod on "I Just Wanna Die." Other cuts urge listeners to live for the moment, recommending brutal violence as a solution to life's problems.

Summary/Advisory: While they wouldn't want their own kids listening to their tapes, the Geto Boys are happy to sell them to ours. Willie D told *USA Today,* "I'd love to stick the tape in and say, 'Listen to what Daddy did.' But then Hugh Hefner can't show off his magazines to kids either. . . . For me, it's a business. I say it to get paid." Don't contribute to his hypocrisy; avoid buying this trash. (SEE ALSO: Willie D)

Gibson, Debbie

◆ ◆

This native of Long Island, New York, saw her first two pop albums (1987's *Out of the Blue* and 1989's *Electric Youth*) go multiplatinum. In 1991, Gibson appeared as Eponine in the Broadway production of *Les Miserables.*

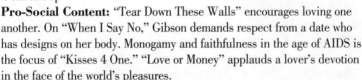

Title: *Body Mind Soul* (1993)
Label: Atlantic
Genre: Pop

Pro-Social Content: "Tear Down These Walls" encourages loving one another. On "When I Say No," Gibson demands respect from a date who has designs on her body. Monogamy and faithfulness in the age of AIDS is the focus of "Kisses 4 One." "Love or Money" applauds a lover's devotion in the face of the world's pleasures.

Objectionable Content: "Shock Your Mama" is trouble. Although Gibson claims it was never meant to be taken seriously, it suggests a wild sexual ride ("Though I'm all good news in my Sunday shoes, I'm gonna wear you out on Saturday night"). "Losin' Myself" involves total surrender to a lover. On "Little Birdie" she is so deeply in love she "can't tell wrong from right" and eventually gives in ("baby, what the h——?").

Summary/Advisory: These messages are a surprise in light of Gibson's outspoken stand for virginity. Here she seems willing to send mixed signals to young fans. Passion runs through all of the themes on this album. Unfortunately, they're not consistently positive.

Gill, Vince

◆ ◆

Every one of native Oklahoman Vince Gill's six albums has sold a million copies or more. His many awards include eight Grammys and more than a dozen nods from the Country Music Association. Gill was a member of Pure Prairie League, the Cherry Bombs, and The New Nashville Cats before going solo. This CMA Male Vocalist of the Year (1991–93) has performed hit duets with the likes of Reba McEntire, Rosanne Cash, Patty Loveless, and next-door neighbor Amy Grant.

Title: *When Love Finds You* (1994)
Label: MCA
Genre: Country
Pro-Social Content: Wishful thinking on "If
I Had My Way" pictures a world of love with no
hunger or war (background vocals by Amy
Grant). "Real Lady's Man" warns a friend of the
consequences of affairs ("For the softness of a
stranger I threw good love away/Friend, there

ain't no higher price to pay"). Gill pays tribute to a person who has died
("Go Rest High on That Mountain"), crooning "go to heaven shoutin' love
for the Father and the Son." Deep commitment on "If There's Anything I
Can Do" is enhanced by the assurance that things will get better in God's
"much bigger plan."
Objectionable Content: "What the Cowgirls Do" includes partying,
where they "chugalug longnecks till their money's all gone." True love is
confused with impulsive, fiery passion on "Maybe Tonight."
Summary/Advisory: A few disturbing themes cloud an otherwise outstanding effort—an unfortunate trend for this talented artist.

Title: *I Still Believe in You* (1992)
Label: MCA
Genre: Country
Pro-Social Content: "Pretty Words" warns women about the consequences
of one-night stands. "No Future in the Past" is a no-booze blues tune focused
on recovering from a failed romance. Working through tough times, communicating and preserving relationships are the themes of "Don't Let Our Love
Start Slippin' Away." "I Still Believe in You" is an apology from Vince to his
wife for not making their relationship his first priority ("Everybody wants a
little piece of my time, but still I put you at the end of the line").
Objectionable Content: A carousing husband tries his wife's patience
and ignores her preaching on "One More Last Chance." "Under These
Conditions" sends mixed messages about fidelity. Though the parties
involved resist cheating on their spouses, they clearly want to. Potential
consequences deter them rather than moral conviction.
Summary/Advisory: Great vocal work. If only Gill's thoughtful melodies
and heartfelt stories of love lost weren't clouded by these less honorable
messages. The title track was voted Country Song of the Year for 1992 and
earned Gill a Grammy for Best Male Country Vocal Performance.

Gin Blossoms

◆ ◆

Congratulations I'm Sorry became a Top-10 album for this Arizona-based quintet consisting of Robin Williams, Jesse Valenzuela, Scott Johnson, Bill Leen, and Philip Rhodes. The group's previous guitarist, Doug Hopkins, committed suicide in 1993.

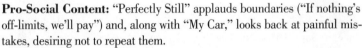

Title: *Congratulations I'm Sorry* (1996)
Label: A&M
Genre: Rock
Pro-Social Content: "Perfectly Still" applauds boundaries ("If nothing's off-limits, we'll pay") and, along with "My Car," looks back at painful mistakes, desiring not to repeat them.
Objectionable Content: Mild profanity mars the bouncy yet ultimately defeatist "Follow You Down," which concludes, "What the h——, we've already been forever d—ned." Similarly, the singer confesses, "I'm high and I'm hopeless" on "Competition Smile." Teens could get the impression that morality is relative from "I Can't Figure You Out." Several tracks give an approving nod to cigarette smoking. An indiscretion is swept under the rug on "Whitewash" as the artist chooses to forget that the sin ever happened rather than atone for it.
Summary/Advisory: While not patently offensive, *Congratulations I'm Sorry* has several tracks that spoil an otherwise enjoyable effort. Too bad, because the Blossoms's country-infused, traditional rock melodies have the potential to unite parents and teens willing to meet in the middle, musically speaking. Maybe next time.

Ginuwine

◆ ◆

The artist who calls himself Ginuwine is a native of Washington, D.C. His CD *The Bachelor* has sold more than a million copies.

Title: *The Bachelor* (1997)
Label: Epic
Genre: R&B

Pro-Social Content: The best of this disc is neutral. Two songs explore the pain of unfaithfulness and romantic breakups.

Objectionable Content: One sexual come-on after another. "Pony" features innuendo (with a western theme) as it describes intercourse. This rutting artist propositions a woman he doesn't even know ("Tell Me Do You Wanna") and expects sex in return for having spent some money on a date ("I'll Do Anything/I'm Sorry"). A female rapper asks for anal sex on "Holler." Ginuwine, in an endorsement of the gangsta lifestyle, states, "Only real G's roll with me" ("When Doves Cry"). Alcohol use—and possibly drug use—infects several cuts.

Summary/Advisory: At times, he sounds a little like Michael Jackson, Prince, or Boyz II Men. But layering velvety vocals atop these lyrics is like reupholstering an electric chair. This may be an 18-track CD, but Ginuwine has a one-track mind . . . sex. Fans of this musical genre should give Christian artists Troy Johnson and Take 6 a spin.

God's Property from Kirk Franklin's Nu Nation

◆ ◆ ◆ ◆ ◆ ◆ ◆ ◆ ◆ ◆ ◆ ◆ ◆ ◆ ◆ ◆ ◆ ◆ ◆ ◆

Gospel superstar Kirk Franklin leads this Dallas-based, 50-voice mass choir in jazz, gospel, and pop tunes. A strongly evangelistic effort, *God's Property* hit number 3 on the pop chart and sold more than 2 million copies.

Title: *God's Property* (1997)
Label: B-Rite Music
Genre: Gospel/R&B
Pro-Social Content: Seventy-two minutes of jubilant, God-honoring praise. Vibrant explosions of spiritual ecstasy characterize "Stomp" and "It's Rainin'." "More Than I Can Bear," "He Will Take the Pain Away," and

"My Life Is in Your Hands" express trust in the Lord as a faithful Friend waiting to guide us through life's storms. Other songs ponder God's devout affection for His children ("Love"), thank Christ for going to the cross ("So Good"), and revel in the change Jesus can make in a person's life ("You Are the Only One," "Sweet Spirit"). On "Faith," Franklin reminds listeners that, with God, they can accomplish the impossible and see the invisible.

Objectionable Content: None

Summary/Advisory: Kirk Franklin's earlier projects featured the Family. Here, he's supported by God's Property—with the same edifying result. Passionate, choir-backed gospel soul and in-your-face R&B grooves drive home the joy of knowing Jesus. A terrific mainstream hit!

Goo Goo Dolls

◆ ◆ ◆ ◆ ◆ ◆ ◆ ◆ ◆ ◆ ◆ ◆ ◆ ◆ ◆ ◆ ◆ ◆ ◆

Goo Goo Dolls got its start in Buffalo, New York, in 1986. The band has opened for Soul Asylum and appeared on *Late Night with Conan O'Brien. A Boy Named Goo* sold more than 2 million copies.

Title: *A Boy Named Goo* (1995)
Label: Metal Blade/Warner Bros.
Genre: Alternative
Pro-Social Content: The Top-10 radio single "Name" offers sanctuary to a hurting soul. That's about it.
Objectionable Content: Alcohol is equated with fun times on "Eyes Wide Open." The artist also wants to "even the score" with a woman who has caused him pain ("Slave Girl") and complains that life is empty, bleak, and meaningless ("Flat Top," "Ain't That Unusual," "Only One"). The f-word is thrown in for emphasis on "Only One."

Summary/Advisory: Misery loves company. And like many of this pessimistic band's "glass-is-half-empty" peers, the Goo Goo Dolls would love to drag young fans into their dismal world devoid of hope.

Grant, Amy

◆ ◆ ◆ ◆ ◆ ◆ ◆ ◆ ◆ ◆ ◆ ◆ ◆ ◆ ◆ ◆ ◆ ◆ ◆

Amy Grant's career has spanned more than two decades. Along the way, she's garnered five Grammy and 22 Dove awards, produced five long-form videos and sold more than 20 million albums. She is married to Christian recording artist and TNN talk-show host Gary Chapman.

Title: *Behind the Eyes* (1997)
Label: Myrrh
Genre: Pop
Pro-Social Content: "Takes a Little Time" urges listeners tossed about by life's storms to hang in there. Answers to the "why" questions lie "Somewhere Down the Road," where mighty arms (God?) wait to embrace weary travelers. "Nobody Home" mourns the death of a small town full of childhood memories. Despite the prospect of being separated by years and miles, Amy pledges devotion to a companion on "I Will Be Your Friend." The title track longs for a day when the commonality of people's fears, pain, and disappointments would unite them. Remedies for relational difficulties include love ("Every Road") and a spontaneous excursion ("Leave It All Behind").
Objectionable Content: None
Summary/Advisory: By now, most long-time Amy Grant fans have resigned themselves to the fact that her CCM days are over. Any holdouts will be convinced with one look into her *Eyes*. But while this Top-10 disc doesn't address God, the artist's upbeat views of life make it a solid mainstream effort.

Title: *House of Love* (1994)
Label: A&M
Genre: Pop
Pro-Social Content: Bouncy melodies and socially conscious ballads applaud timeless, unconditional romantic love ("Say You'll Be Mine," "Whatever It Takes," "Our Love," and "Oh How the Years Go By"). "Helping Hand" encourages brotherly kindness and a servant's heart. Hope for future generations and a celebration of life are the focus of "Children of the World." The environmentally sensitive "Big Yellow Taxi" says to enjoy life's gifts before they're gone.

Objectionable Content: "Say You'll Be Mine" longs breathlessly for a physical relationship ("Every time I close my eyes I dream about hugging you, holding you, kissing you boy"). "Lucky One" also seems preoccupied with intimacy.

Summary/Advisory: As mainstream pop albums go, a pretty wholesome pick. But Grant fans expecting a return to Christ-centered content will be disappointed in *House*'s foundation.

Green Day

◆ ◆ ◆ ◆ ◆ ◆ ◆ ◆ ◆ ◆ ◆ ◆ ◆ ◆ ◆ ◆ ◆ ◆ ◆ ◆

The punk band consists of Billie Joe Armstrong, Mike Dirnt, and Tre Cool. Their amazingly popular *Dookie* disc sold more than 10 million copies. Since then, Green Day's stardom has fizzled with each successive release. *Insomniac* (1995) debuted at number 2, selling 2 million units. After lingering nearly four months on the charts, *Nimrod* (1997) failed to sell even 500,000 during that stretch. In a *Rolling Stone* interview [1/26/95], Dirnt advocated drug use, stating, "To me, everybody should drop acid at least once."

Title: *Insomniac* (1995)
Label: Reprise
Genre: Punk rock
Pro-Social Content: "Westbound Sign" questions the wisdom of a girl's decision to seek fame and fortune far from home.
Objectionable Content: The f-word peppers this 33-minute ode to self-loathing and despair. "Armatage Shanks" states, "I must insist on being a pessimist." The artist also confesses to being "limp with hate" ("Panic Song") and in a "rotting existence" ("Stuart and the Ave"). Cocaine and amphetamine use is applauded on "Geek Stink Breath." "Tight Wad Hill" is the story of a thrill-seeking drug addict. Elsewhere, the singer selfishly waits for his parents to die in order to collect his inheritance ("Brat").

Summary/Advisory: This follow-up to the band's 10 million-selling debut album, *Dookie*, landed at number 1 its first week on the charts. Anyone this introspective and devoid of peace is destined to *become* an insomniac. On "Geek Stink Breath," Billie Joe Armstrong sings, "I'm on a mission/I made my decision to lead a path of self-destruction." Pray that teens don't follow him.

Title: *Dookie* (1994)
Label: Reprise
Genre: Punk rock
Pro-Social Content: None
Objectionable Content: Dark tracks painted with large brush strokes of apathy, hopelessness, boredom, and despair dominate this disc ("Pulling Teeth," "Longview," "Burnout"). Other obscenity-laced themes include self-diagnosed insanity ("Basket Case," "Having a Blast"), retreating into pornography and illicit sex ("Longview," "Basket Case," "F.O.D."), and self-loathing ("Sassafrass Roots"). Musical and visual images of drug use also appear. On "Chump" and "Having a Blast," the singer hatefully blames others for his woeful plight, even to the point of murdering them ("I'm taking all you down with me . . . no one is getting out alive").
Summary/Advisory: The band's appearance at Woodstock '94 seemed to temporarily boost Green Day's popularity. Too bad. *Dookie* (slang for excrement) is, itself, nihilistic waste.

Hammer

◆ ◆ ◆ ◆ ◆ ◆ ◆ ◆ ◆ ◆ ◆ ◆ ◆ ◆ ◆ ◆ ◆ ◆ ◆ ◆

Formerly known as M.C. Hammer, this early '90s rapper/producer was founder and leader of The Posse, an eight-member group of dancers, DJs, and singers. Famous for his hit singles "U Can't Touch This" and "2 Legit 2 Quit," Hammer's total album sales exceed 16 million.

Title: *The Funky Headhunter* (1994)
Label: Giant
Genre: Rap
Pro-Social Content: None
Objectionable Content: Violent threats abound. Boastful of his earlier successes and bitter toward his critics, Hammer states "these are the days of the payback." "Pumps and a Bump" includes lewd lines like "should I get it in . . . 'cause I'm comin' quick . . . slip out your clothes and take a tip." He brags about the ease of "scoring" sexually on "Don't Fight the Feelin'." "Help Lord" wallows in ghetto despair ("no love, no hope, no life").

Summary/Advisory: In the past, Hammer hit the nail on the head with predominantly positive messages. Not this time. *Headhunter* is a radical departure—without his usual social conscience.

Hanson

◆ ◆ ◆ ◆ ◆ ◆ ◆ ◆ ◆ ◆ ◆ ◆ ◆ ◆ ◆ ◆ ◆ ◆

Hanson consists of three young brothers: Isaac, Taylor, and Zachary. The home-schooled trio relies on a squeaky-clean pop image and a dedicated fan base of preadolescents. *Middle of Nowhere* has sold more than 4 million copies.

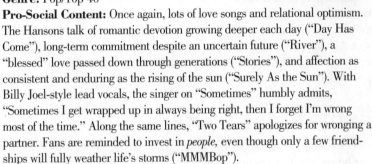

Title: *3 Car Garage* (1998)
Label: Mercury
Genre: Pop/Top 40
Pro-Social Content: Once again, lots of love songs and relational optimism. The Hansons talk of romantic devotion growing deeper each day ("Day Has Come"), long-term commitment despite an uncertain future ("River"), a "blessed" love passed down through generations ("Stories"), and affection as consistent and enduring as the rising of the sun ("Surely As the Sun"). With Billy Joel-style lead vocals, the singer on "Sometimes" humbly admits, "Sometimes I get wrapped up in always being right, then I forget I'm wrong most of the time." Along the same lines, "Two Tears" apologizes for wronging a partner. Fans are reminded to invest in *people*, even though only a few friendships will fully weather life's storms ("MMMBop").
Objectionable Content: "With You in Your Dreams" could be misinterpreted as sanctioning teens sleeping together ("If I'm gone when you wake up, please don't cry").
Summary/Advisory: As a follow-up to their surprise smash *Middle of Nowhere*, the brothers dust off some previously recorded demos for the equally retro *3 Car Garage*. "We were short on money which meant we were short on studio time," the boys explain in the liner notes. "So with a one, two, three, go approach we started recording, allowing four hours per song. . . . These are the original mixes of the songs we did in a garage somewhere in Tulsa." Production is a little raw, but fans may enjoy that earthy sincerity. The disc includes three repeats from their first release ("MMMBop," "With You in Your Dreams," and "Thinking of You"), but the rest is fresh and consistently upbeat. With the noted lyrical vagueness, Hanson's latest is worth a listen.

Title: *Middle of Nowhere* (1997)
Label: Mercury
Genre: Pop/Rock
Pro-Social Content: "I Will Come to You" pledges love and faithfulness "when the night is dark and stormy." The young Hanson brothers treasure enduring friendships in an unstable world on the number-1 smash "MMMBop," imploring listeners to invest in people who really care. Innocent love songs ("Thinking of You," "A Minute Without You") are jubilant and hopeful. Similarly upbeat tracks call for trust ("Speechless") and cooperation ("Where's the Love") in relationships. On "Weird," the boys encourage their painfully self-aware peers that everyone feels strange and out of place sometimes. Told from their grandmother's perspective, "With You in Your Dreams" reminds us that relatives who have died will live on in our memories, however . . .
Objectionable Content: The line "If I'm gone when you wake up, please don't cry" could be perceived as promoting teens sleeping together.
Summary/Advisory: Bouncy retro fun. Young fans will identify with the brothers (ages 16, 14, and 11 when this album was released) and their unhardened view of the world. Meanwhile, the band's sound will resonate with parents—a nostalgic blend of The Jackson 5 and any number of pop acts from the early '70s. Adults may question whether boys this age should be meditating on romance, but the messages are solid.

Hootie & the Blowfish

◆ ◆ ◆ ◆ ◆ ◆ ◆ ◆ ◆ ◆ ◆ ◆ ◆ ◆ ◆ ◆ ◆ ◆ ◆

This South Carolina-based band is composed of Darius Rucker, Mark Bryan, Dean Felber, and Jim "Soni" Sonefeld. Their debut album is ranked as one of the Top-15 best-selling CDs of *all time*—more than 14 million of them ushered across electronic scanners. The follow-up, *Fairweather Johnson*, debuted at number 1.

Title: *Fairweather Johnson* (1996)
Label: Atlantic
Genre: Rock
Pro-Social Content: "Honeyscrew" asks what seem to be sincere questions about the existence of God. An elderly black man shares feelings about heaven, racism, and fighting for a country that would not let him vote, and thanks God for the love of a good woman on "Old Man & Me." Several cuts value friendship during lonely or trying times ("So Strange," "The Earth

Stopped Cold at Dawn"). Other apparently positive
thoughts get lost in a haze of lyrical obscurity.
Objectionable Content: A drunk man heads
to a bar on "Fool," though to his credit he realizes the need to "grow up." Mentions of dishonesty plague at least six songs.
Summary/Advisory: This disc is the follow-up
to *Cracked Rear View*. Hootie's press bio says

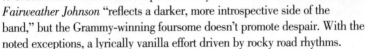

Fairweather Johnson "reflects a darker, more introspective side of the
band," but the Grammy-winning foursome doesn't promote despair. With the
noted exceptions, a lyrically vanilla effort driven by rocky road rhythms.

Title: *Cracked Rear View* (1994)
Label: Atlantic
Genre: Rock
Pro-Social Content: The hopeful "Drowning" calls for healing amid racial
hatred. "I'm Going Home" conveys the emotional struggle of a young boy
coping with the death of his mother, whom he calls his "best friend." Painful
farewells occur in various romantic contexts as well, but usually displaying
tenderness and affection for the other person rather than anger or despair
("Goodbye," "Hannah Jane," "Look Away"). With a passion found throughout
this disc, "Not Even the Trees" ponders life without a love who has passed on.
Objectionable Content: Drug and alcohol use show up on "Let Her Cry."
Unfortunately, one profanity taints "Drowning"'s anti-racism message.
Summary/Advisory: These few yet significant caveats spoil an otherwise
fine effort by a hot debut act. Gritty vocals bring to mind Bruce Springsteen.
In the future, maybe Hootie will reflect and avoid mirroring the few mis-
takes of *Cracked Rear View*.

Hornsby, Bruce

◆ ◆ ◆ ◆ ◆ ◆ ◆ ◆ ◆ ◆ ◆ ◆ ◆ ◆ ◆ ◆ ◆ ◆ ◆

Bruce Hornsby is a singer, songwriter, and pianist
who formed the band The Range in 1984. In
1986, he and his crew recorded *The Way It Is*, an
album that helped win them the Best New Artist
Grammy.

Title: *Harbor Lights* (1993)
Label: RCA

Genre: Progressive rock/Jazz

Pro-Social Content: "Field of Gray" expresses love and commitment to a friend struggling to survive in the cold, cruel world ("In my own small way, I will try to help you through"). A similar sentiment motivates "China Doll" ("I've got something for you, a few good words . . . to ease your worried mind").

Objectionable Content: "What a Time" approves of the chaos resulting from a power outage ("Everybody was fazing, hazing, oh what a time, it was time to be amazing, time to lose all reason or rhyme").

Summary/Advisory: Lyrically, Hornsby's themes zero in on life and the diverse characters who make it interesting. But it's the instrumentation that takes center stage, resulting in an aesthetically pleasing disc. With only minor exceptions, an acceptable pick.

House of Pain

◆ ◆ ◆ ◆ ◆ ◆ ◆ ◆ ◆ ◆ ◆ ◆ ◆ ◆ ◆ ◆ ◆ ◆ ◆

Consisting of Erik Shrody, Daniel O'Connor, and Leor DiMant, these Irish-American rappers made a splash with their first hit single, "Jump Around." The trio broke up in 1996.

Title: *House of Pain* (1992)
Label: Tommy Boy
Genre: Rap
Pro-Social Content: The anti-abortion stance of "All My Love" ("I can drill and not have to kill/An unborn child") makes the group one of the pro-life movement's strangest, most unsavory bedfellows.

Objectionable Content: Fully two-thirds of the album's tracks boast of "puffin' blunts," "smokin' a fat bud" or "hash," "roll[in'] spliffs" or "drink[in'] a case o' brew." The House likewise gloats about "smackin'" women ("Jump Around," "Danny Boy, Danny Boy"), filling punks "full of lead" ("Put Your Head Out"), and masturbating with a microphone ("Feel It").

Summary/Advisory: It's time to condemn this *House*. House of Pain joins Dr. Dre, Cypress Hill, Diamond, the Psychotic Neurotics, and others in a resurgence toward advocating the legalization and use of marijuana. Graphic violence and lewd sex compound the album's troubling content. Definitely one to avoid.

Houston, Whitney

◆ ◆ ◆ ◆ ◆ ◆ ◆ ◆ ◆ ◆ ◆ ◆ ◆ ◆ ◆ ◆ ◆ ◆ ◆ ◆

A product of Newark, New Jersey, Whitney Houston sang with a gospel troupe at age 11 before earning backup jobs with Chaka Khan and Lou Rawls. After a brief yet successful modeling career, the singer began recording her own records, which have sold a combined total of more than 42 million copies. She has starred in the feature films *The Bodyguard*, *Waiting to Exhale*, and *The Preacher's Wife*. Houston married rapper Bobby Brown and is a cousin of pop star and "psychic friend" Dionne Warwick.

Title: *The Preacher's Wife* (1996)
Label: Arista
Genre: Gospel/Adult contemporary
Pro-Social Content: The hit single "I Believe in You and Me" is a tender melody that pledges lifelong love to a romantic part-ner. Aerobically upbeat, "Step by Step" embraces the challenges of living day by day. Whitney Houston exuberantly cap-tures the joy of meeting a special someone on "My Heart Is Calling." "You Were Loved" reminds listeners to share their feelings with loved ones. The rest of this project is charged with a dynamic spiritual energy. Heartfelt gospel tunes extol God's faithfulness ("Hold On, Help Is on the Way," "The Lord Is My Shepherd," "I Go to the Rock," "Somebody Bigger Than You and I"). They also acknowledge Christ as King ("Who Would Imagine a King," "Joy to the World," "Joy").
Objectionable Content: None
Summary/Advisory: Perfect. This Top-3 pop disc showcases the talents of Whitney Houston on all but one song. Her brilliant vocals, backed by a soulful gospel choir, drive home edifying lyrics. *The Preacher's Wife* is a heaven-sent winner from start to finish! [This album review also appears in the "Soundtrack" section.]

Title: *The Bodyguard* (1992)
Label: Arista
Genre: R&B/Pop
Pro-Social Content: Houston's multimillion-selling remake of Dolly Parton's "I Will Always Love You" pledges lasting devotion. Her single

"Run to You" is also a positive tune about supportive romance, as are Joe Cocker's "Trust in Me" and Lisa Stansfield's "Someday (I'm Coming Back)." S.O.U.L. System's breezy rap, "It's Gonna Be a Lovely Day" and Curtis Stiger's rendition of "(What's So Funny 'Bout) Peace, Love and Understanding" are similarly upbeat. Houston delivers a lovely, biblically faithful version of "Jesus Loves Me."

Objectionable Content: "Queen of the Night" takes an aggressive sexual posture, as does Houston's hit "I'm Every Woman" (though to a lesser degree).

Summary/Advisory: One of the best selling albums of all time, *The Bodyguard* has moved more than 15 million copies since its release. Lots to like here. With the noted exceptions, this motion picture soundtrack poses little threat to teens' value systems. [This album review also appears in the "Soundtrack" section.]

Howard, Adina

◆ ◆ ◆ ◆ ◆ ◆ ◆ ◆ ◆ ◆ ◆ ◆ ◆ ◆ ◆ ◆ ◆ ◆ ◆ ◆

A native of Grand Rapids, Michigan, Adina Howard released her debut disc, *Do You Wanna Ride?* in 1995 at the age of 24. It went gold and birthed the million-selling hit single, "Freak Like Me."

Title: *Do You Wanna Ride?* (1995)
Label: EastWest
Genre: R&B/Hip-hop
Pro-Social Content: None
Objectionable Content: Explicit sexual references abound—and that's just the songs' *titles!* Lines such as "We can pump, pump, pump all through the night" ("Freak Like Me") and "I'll be your Miss Bump-N-Grind/I just wanna do you

tonight" ("Do You Wanna Ride?") pretty much tell this artist's story. On "My Up and Down," Howard takes pride in the fact that another woman's boyfriend repeatedly visits her for sexual favors ("If your girlfriend would do the freaky things I do for you . . ."). "You Got Me Humpin'" promotes unfaithfulness and oral sex. An insatiable woman pleads for sex on "Horny for Your Love" ("Seems I never get enough . . . Come and heal me with your touch"). Meanwhile, Howard gives an approving nod to marijuana with "You Can Be My N-gga," which speaks of "smoking blunts on the regular."

Summary/Advisory: This raunchy Top-40 effort features slick production and smooth vocals, but is lyrically *depraved.* Nearly every track sounds like an encounter-group confession of sexual addiction—though Howard has no desire to amend her ways. Caution teens not to accept a *Ride* from this hormonally obsessed singer.

H-Town

◆ ◆ ◆ ◆ ◆ ◆ ◆ ◆ ◆ ◆ ◆ ◆ ◆ ◆ ◆ ◆ ◆ ◆ ◆

This R&B vocal trio from Houston, Texas, is comprised of brothers Shazam and John "Dino" Commer with Darryl "GI" Jackson.

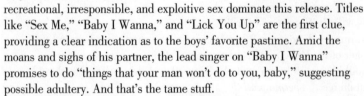

Title: *Fever for da Flavor* (1993)
Label: Luke
Genre: Hip-hop/Pop
Pro-Social Content: None
Objectionable Content: Lots. Various forms of
recreational, irresponsible, and exploitive sex dominate this release. Titles like "Sex Me," "Baby I Wanna," and "Lick You Up" are the first clue, providing a clear indication as to the boys' favorite pastime. Amid the moans and sighs of his partner, the lead singer on "Baby I Wanna" promises to do "things that your man won't do to you, baby," suggesting possible adultery. And that's the tame stuff.
Summary/Advisory: Sex, sex, and more sex. This trio of Luther Campbell (2 Live Crew) disciples not only records on his label but also furthers his lewd sexual agenda. *Fever for da Flavor* is one long, hormone-induced come-on. Teens are advised to skip Town.

Ice Cube

◆ ◆ ◆ ◆ ◆ ◆ ◆ ◆ ◆ ◆ ◆ ◆ ◆ ◆ ◆ ◆ ◆ ◆ ◆

The Los Angeles-born Ice Cube's given name is actually O'Shea Jackson. Before striking out on his own, he rapped with N.W.A., Dr. Dre, and Eazy-E. Since the release of *The Predator*, Ice Cube has transitioned into a motion picture career, appearing in such films as *Boyz N The Hood, Trespass,* and *Anaconda.*

Title: *The Predator* (1992)

Label: Priority
Genre: Rap
Pro-Social Content: On "It Was a Good Day," Cube is thankful for a day without killing. He criticizes the indignities of prison ("First Day of School") and de facto segregation ("Integration").
Objectionable Content: Ice Cube threatens violence (including shootings, bombings, and forced anal and oral sex) against targets including Los Angeles police chief Willie Williams ("Wicked"), former chief Daryl Gates ("We Had to Tear This Mothaf—-a Up"), the jury that found L.A. police officers not guilty in the Rodney King beating ("Now I Gotta Wet 'Cha"), the officers themselves ("We Had to Tear This Mothaf—-a Up"), the editor of *Billboard* magazine ("The Predator"), and even the anti-gang Guardian Angels ("Dirty Mack"). Cube, formally of the rap group N.W.A., approves of looting ("We Had to Tear This Mothaf—-a Up"), kidnapping prostitutes ("Say Hi to the Bad Guy"), and has no problem with sexual promiscuity, which he describes in graphic terms ("Dirty Mack," "It Was a Good Day").
Summary/Advisory: While it may be important to understand the anger of Ice Cube and his peers, this violent, near-paranoid attitude should be soundly rejected. A vile number-1 debut disc that should be put on ice . . . *permanently!*

Imbruglia, Natalie
◆ ◆

This singer from Australia first caught the eye of her countrymen as a soap opera actress before moving to London to pursue an acting/singing career. Her travels led her to Los Angeles in 1996 where she landed a record deal. Her first hit, "Torn," went platinum in England and earned her a guest appearance on NBC's *Saturday Night Live*.

Title: *Left of the Middle* (1997)
Label: RCA
Genre: Pop/Rock/Adult contemporary

Pro-Social Content: The artist espouses a code of ethics that includes a wariness of romantic propositions and the decision not to get ahead in life at the expense of others ("Intuition"). "Don't You Think?" condemns shallow self-absorption in a hurting world, while "Impressed" rejects silicon-enhanced beauty, fame, and wealth. Imbruglia grows impatient with one-sided relationships on "Leave Me Alone" and "Big Mistake." The hit single "Torn" finds the singer longing for her man's warm, sensitive, dignified side.

Objectionable Content: "Torn" *also* finds her consulting a fortune-teller for wisdom. Lyrical ambiguity makes "Pigeons and Crumbs" seem hopeless at times and *may* allude to a one-night stand. Lovers on "Wishing I Was There" appear to be unmarried.

Summary/Advisory: This talented artist from Down Under has zero tolerance for selfishness, phoniness, and hypocrisy. Her boldness is refreshing. Aside from its lone fortune-teller reference, *Left of the Middle's* caveats are few—and equivocal at that. Not perfect, but a good debut.

Indigo Girls

◆ ◆ ◆ ◆ ◆ ◆ ◆ ◆ ◆ ◆ ◆ ◆ ◆ ◆ ◆ ◆ ◆ ◆ ◆

This duo consists of Amy Ray and Emily Saliers. Their self-titled album, released in 1989, went gold and won a Grammy. The duo has received four subsequent Grammy nominations.

Title: *Shaming of the Sun* (1997)
Label: Epic
Genre: Rock
Pro-Social Content: A line on "Leeds" sympa-thizes with the victims of racially motivated church burnings.

Objectionable Content: The band's pro-lesbian agenda blatantly manifests itself in the lyrics. "It's Alright" addresses anti-gay big-otry and calls for tolerance. "Don't Give That Girl a Gun" describes a strained romance between two females. On "Burn All the Letters," the singer relates an affair she had with a married woman. One song actually uses religious lingo to recount lesbian passion: "I'm speaking in tongues handling you/I got religion" ("Shed Your Skin"). Reminiscence of a female houseguest causes the singer to recall "the sweat of our sadness and the twist of the sheets"

("Caramia"). She also admits to being "halfway drunk" on "Leeds." There's one use of the f-word ("Shame on You").

Summary/Advisory: Homosexual propaganda abounds. Even love songs not expressly about gay relationships will be interpreted that way in light of *Sun's* greater context. In an age of sexual confusion among teens, this disc can only do more damage.

Jackson, Alan

◆ ◆

Jackson has won numerous country music awards, including Entertainer of the Year, Male Vocalist of the Year, and several Album of the Year and Single of the Year honors. The Ford truck pitchman has produced more than *two dozen* number-1 singles.

Title: *Everything I Love* (1996)
Label: Arista
Genre: Country
Pro-Social Content: Jackson promises to keep loving his wife forever— or at least until we're able to drive "Buicks to the Moon." A man serving a jail sentence implores his son to learn from his mistakes and avoid alcohol ("Walk on the Rocks"). "Who's Cheatin' Who," a remake of Charly McClain's number-1 hit from 1981, considers the consequences of adultery.

Objectionable Content: The subtle anti-booze message of "Walk on the Rocks" is blitzed by recollections of a drunken romp with a naked woman on "Must've Had a Ball." Television and beer add up to an evening's entertainment on the number-1 country single "Little Bitty," while the artist expresses a passion for cigarettes and Jack Daniels on the title track. Elsewhere, Jackson eagerly anticipates a woman's emotional pain ("It's Time You Learned About Good-bye") and succumbs to a cheatin' heart ("Between the Devil and Me"). Disappointing.

Summary/Advisory: A few positive themes, but they're drowned out by tunes reveling in sin and selfishness. Consider CCM artist Ken Holloway instead.

Title: *Who I Am* (1994)
Label: Arista
Genre: Country
Pro-Social Content: Some great tunes about the importance of family.
"You Can't Give Up On Love" reminds spouses that "every day can't be a
honeymoon" and takes a sober look at the fallout from divorce. "Livin' on
Love" prefers the affection of a new spouse to materialistic trappings.
Jackson deems life on the road unfulfilling apart from his wife and daugh-
ters waiting at home on "Job Description." "Song for the Life" takes pride
in drinking less and enjoying life's simple pleasures more.
Objectionable Content: Several tracks glorify irresponsible living, from
rowdiness and alcohol use ("All-American Country Boy," "Who I Am") to
drunken lust ("I Don't Even Know Your Name") and venting frustration by
damaging property ("Hole in the Wall").
Summary/Advisory: The good is very good. Unfortunately, mixed messages on *Who I Am* leave young fans to wonder who Jackson *really* is—and
which behavior is worth imitating.

Title: *A Lot About Livin' (And a Little 'Bout Love)* (1992)
Label: Arista
Genre: Country
Pro-Social Content: "Tonight I Climbed the Wall" breaks down barriers
of miscommunication. "Who Says You Can't Have It All" cleverly tours a
"fool's Taj Mahal" built without love. In the hit "She's Got the Rhythm
(And I Got the Blues)," Jackson appreciates the "ball and chain" of com-
mitment with the hindsight of "having lost the prize."
Objectionable Content: While "I Don't Need the Booze (To Get a
Buzz On)" does take a worthwhile poke at alcohol abuse, it also degrades
sex to the level of a "buzz" and finds Jackson admitting he's still apt to
"wear a [Pabst] Blue Ribbon smile." "Chattahootchie" celebrates Friday-
night drinking binges that result in a "pyramid of cans," while the artist
recalls propositioning a girl for a sexual romp in the backseat of his
Chevy.
Summary/Advisory: Jackson, author of the huge hit "Don't Rock the
Jukebox," follows suit with an unsophisticated but effective set of country
songs in the Opry tradition. References to sex outside of marriage and alcohol use mar an otherwise acceptable effort.

Jackson, Janet

◆ ◆ ◆ ◆ ◆ ◆ ◆ ◆ ◆ ◆ ◆ ◆ ◆ ◆ ◆ ◆ ◆ ◆ ◆

Through 1997, this songstress/actress (Janet starred in the film *Poetic Justice* with Tupac Shakur) won eight American Music Awards, two Grammys, seven MTV Video Music Awards, and five Soul Train Music Awards. *Control* (1986) sold 5 million units, while *Rhythm Nation 1814* (1989) and *janet* (1993) each sold 6 million.

Title: *The Velvet Rope* (1997)
Label: Virgin
Genre: Pop/R&B
Pro-Social Content: Janet tells her belea-guered brother Michael to ignore the public's opinion of him ("You"). Elsewhere, isolated lines condemn hatred ("The Velvet Rope") and encourage spiritual renewal ("Special").
Objectionable Content: "Free Xone" argues on behalf of homosexual and bisexual relationships. A remake of Rod Stewart's 1976 hit "Tonight's the Night" finds the artist making sexual advances to both a "boy" and a "girl." Amid orgasmic groaning, Janet depicts someone masturbating during a telephone conversation with a friend ("Speaker Phone"). She expresses an insatiable desire for sex that is kinky ("Rope Burn"), rough ("My Need"), and casual ("Go Deep"). She chastises an abusive lover by spewing expletives and talking about oral sex ("What About"). Profanities and obscenities pop up frequently.
Summary/Advisory: Janet Jackson has come a long way since 1977 when she appeared as sweet young Penny on the TV sitcom *Good Times*. In fact, Janet's idea of "good times" has become truly perverse over the past 20 years. Her twisted *Velvet Rope* is proof positive.

Title: *janet* (1993)
Label: Virgin
Genre: Pop/Dance/R&B
Pro-Social Content: Janet celebrates her African-American heritage and pays tribute to the musical history of Harlem on "Funky Big Band."
Objectionable Content: "Throb" relies on sexual sighs and groans as it builds to an orgasmic "oh, sh——." Although not as blunt, the rest of the album echoes that sensual sentiment. "If" alludes to oral sex and features

suggestive lines such as "imagine my body undressed . . . you on the rise as you're touching my thighs." Trashing self-control, "Any Time, Any Place" depicts public sex ("I don't wanna stop just because people are watchin' us").

Summary/Advisory: A radical departure from her last album, *janet* could be the project that redefines Jackson's image in the industry—but not for the better. This chart-topper's tantalizingly lustful view of sex is bound to undermine teens' moral purity and leave an unhealthy impression. And it's distributed by a label that calls itself Virgin? Don't dance with *janet*.

Jagger, Mick

◆ ◆ ◆ ◆ ◆ ◆ ◆ ◆ ◆ ◆ ◆ ◆ ◆ ◆ ◆ ◆ ◆ ◆ ◆

Born in Dartford, England, Jagger has performed as lead singer with The Rolling Stones since 1963. He has also recorded three solo projects. Jagger married model Bianca Peres Norena de Macias in 1971 and, after divorcing her in 1980, went on to marry model and actress Jerry Hall *(Batman)*. His brief film career includes a role in the 1992 sci-fi actioner *Freejack*.

Title: *Wandering Spirit* (1993)
Label: Atlantic
Genre: Rock
Pro-Social Content: None
Objectionable Content: Lyrics on "Use Me," "Sweet Thing," and "Wired All Night" embrace sexual obsession ("We were at each other night and day . . . you were so sensual and so inventive" and "I'm as hard as a brick, hope I never go limp"). The title cut's anti-religious sentiment leaves Jagger seeking direction while whining about being a lost and lonely soul. "Mother of a Man" talks of packing an Uzi and refers to a woman as "little b—ch." He also invites his ex to "stick a knife right in [his] chest." "Evening Gown" and "Wired All Night" glorify drunkenness.

Summary/Advisory: This Rolling Stone still hasn't grown up, shouting and growling his way through songs of debauchery, pessimism, and despair. And after all these years he still gets no satisfaction. Avoid this downer from an artist who should know better. (SEE ALSO: Rolling Stones, The)

Jars of Clay

◆ ◆ ◆ ◆ ◆ ◆ ◆ ◆ ◆ ◆ ◆ ◆ ◆ ◆ ◆ ◆ ◆ ◆ ◆ ◆

The Grammy-winning band Jars of Clay consists of Dan Haseltine, Stephen Mason, Matt
Odmark, and Charlie Lowell. They have
received numerous awards, including Dove's
1996 Group of the Year.

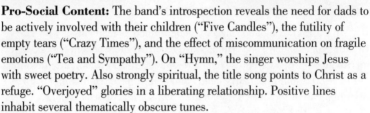

Title: *Much Afraid* (1997)
Label: Essential
Genre: Alternative/Rock
Pro-Social Content: The band's introspection reveals the need for dads to
be actively involved with their children ("Five Candles"), the futility of
empty tears ("Crazy Times"), and the effect of miscommunication on fragile
emotions ("Tea and Sympathy"). On "Hymn," the singer worships Jesus
with sweet poetry. Also strongly spiritual, the title song points to Christ as a
refuge. "Overjoyed" glories in a liberating relationship. Positive lines
inhabit several thematically obscure tunes.
Objectionable Content: None
Summary/Advisory: This sophomore disc from CCM's Jars of Clay (which
sold more than 500,000 copies and hit the pop Top 10) seems incomplete.
The weary traveller is well represented, but the abundant joy of John 10:10
is not; abundant soul-searching predominates. That's fine if the band wants
secular listeners to know that it empathizes with their daily struggles. And
as a pop album, *Much Afraid* is a winner. But Christian teens expecting
edifying answers to these same deep questions will need to look elsewhere.

Jewel

◆ ◆ ◆ ◆ ◆ ◆ ◆ ◆ ◆ ◆ ◆ ◆ ◆ ◆ ◆ ◆ ◆ ◆ ◆ ◆

Jewel Kilcher is a native of Homer, Alaska. At age six, she began joining
her singing parents onstage and on the road. Jewel attended Michigan's
Interlochen Fine Arts Academy on a vocal scholarship. *Pieces of You* (1996)
has sold more than 8 million copies. Viewers of Superbowl XXXII saw the
Denver Broncos beat the Green Bay Packers, but not before they heard
Jewel perform the national anthem for a worldwide audience.

Title: *Pieces of You* (1996)

Label: Atlantic
Genre: Rock/Folk
Pro-Social Content: With sweetly heartfelt
vocals, the artist elevates ideals such as honesty, clean living, relational sensitivity, and
an appreciation for the arts ("Foolish
Games"). "Painters" relates a widowed
woman's affectionate reflections on her marriage. The refusal to give up on a semi-comatose
young man's life is the subject of "Adrian." "Angel Standing
By" further illustrates unconditional love and devotion. Jewel
prefers handshakes and hugs to pain and drugs on her optimistic call to
arms, "Little Sister."
Objectionable Content: She talks of saving our own souls and having a
paranoid fear of God on the huge hit single "Who Will Save Your Soul."
The title cut calls for tolerance, falsely equating a disgust for homosexuality
with discrimination based on race or gender. Jewel imagines ripping out her
father's throat and bashing in his teeth ("Daddy").
Summary/Advisory: Despite some sparkling sentiments, this Jewel suffers from a few glaring flaws. Appraisal: Not worth the investment.

Jodeci

◆ ◆ ◆ ◆ ◆ ◆ ◆ ◆ ◆ ◆ ◆ ◆ ◆ ◆ ◆ ◆ ◆ ◆ ◆

Jodeci is two sets of brothers: Devante and Dalvin Degrate; K-Ci and JoJo
Hailey. *The Show, The After Party, The Hotel* was a number-1 R&B album,
peaking at number 2 on the pop chart.

Title: *The Show, The After Party, The Hotel* (1995)
Label: MCA
Genre: Hip-hop
Pro-Social Content: "Love U 4 Life" desires
a marriage that lasts "for eternity."
Objectionable Content: The rest of this project focuses more on lust than on commitment.
Sexually suggestive slang (such as "pumping,"
"getting freaky," and "feeling so horny") is the
rule, not the exception. These obscenity-strewn lyrics give an approving nod
to pornography ("Room 577"), multiple sex partners ("Fun 2 Nite"), and

other lascivious activity. Hormones rage on the half-million-selling radio single, "Freak'n You" ("I don't give a d—- about nothing else/Freak'n you is all I need/Tonight I need your body").

Summary/Advisory: This follow-up to Jodeci's appropriately titled *Diary of a Mad Band* will send young fans hazardous messages about sex. One member of the group, K-Ci, told the media, "My parents still don't listen to our albums." Smart folks. Avoid *The Show*.

Title: *Diary of a Mad Band* (1994)
Label: MCA
Genre: Pop/Hip-hop
Pro-Social Content: None
Objectionable Content: Lack of sexual self-control dominates this disc. One after another, testosterone-induced tunes talk about "gettin' sweaty" and "sticky," "lickin' thighs," "humping," getting naked and doin' some "freaky s—." Expletives abound. Also, the opening of "Feenin" promotes marijuana use with the line, "Hit me. [Sound of someone inhaling deeply.] All the chronic in the world couldn't even mess with you; you're the ultimate high."
Summary/Advisory: Worthless trash from start to finish. What's more, one member of Jodeci thanks "everybody at Christ Gospel Church 4 their constant prayers," though it's doubtful their intercession had anything to do with this smut reaching store shelves. The disc's title says it all. This group needs therapy. (SEE ALSO: K-Ci & JoJo)

Joel, Billy

◆ ◆ ◆ ◆ ◆ ◆ ◆ ◆ ◆ ◆ ◆ ◆ ◆ ◆ ◆ ◆ ◆ ◆ ◆

This Rock 'n' Roll Hall of Famer from Hicksville, Long Island, formed several bands and played with others before signing with Columbia Records as a solo artist in 1973. Since then, the native New Yorker has sold nearly 60 million albums. Joel has been honored with Grammy's Living Legends Award and *Billboard*'s Century Award. Married for nearly 10 years to supermodel Christie Brinkley, he is the proud father of their daughter, Alexa Ray. The couple has since divorced. With the release of his *Greatest Hits Volume III* project in late 1997, Joel announced he would be leaving pop music and returning to his classical roots. "I started out learning classical music from the age of four," Joel told *Rolling Stone* [10/2/97]. "Then, when I got to be 13, this hot seductress in shredded fishnet stockings swept me away: I had a passionate affair with rock 'n' roll. But I'm 48 now and it's getting old."

Title: *River of Dreams* (1993)
Label: Columbia
Genre: Pop/Rock
Pro-Social Content: Joel skewers superficial materialism on "No Man's Land," which also questions the media's love affair with bizarre lusts. "All About Soul" honors his wife's strength (model Christie Brinkley, though they have since divorced). His daughter's curiosity about death inspired the sweet but hollow "Lullabye."
Objectionable Content: Joel's soul-searching on "Blonde Over Blue" takes a dim view of spirituality and people of faith ("These days not a d— soul prays and there is no faith 'cause there's nothing to believe in"). He drowns the pain with wine on "A Minor Variation." "Shades of Grey" reflects a sense of futility, giving in to relativism over his youthful belief in right and wrong.
Summary/Advisory: Despite some thoughtful, positive sentiments, the album portrays both faith and truth as philosophical red herring. The good news is that, for all of his searching, Joel seems to have set aside the partying and casual sex glorified on earlier albums for a deeper look at life and human relationships. Unfortunately, *River of Dreams* is a mire of questions that will remain unanswered apart from God.

John, Elton

◆ ◆

Elton John was born Reginald Kenneth Dwight in Pinner, Middlesex, England. He won a scholarship to the Royal Academy of Music when he was 11. John was inducted into the Rock 'n' Roll Hall of Fame in 1994 and knighted by Queen Elizabeth II in 1998. He won a Grammy for "Candle in the Wind 1997," his tribute to Princess Diana.

Title: *Made in England* (1995)
Label: Rocket
Genre: Rock/Pop
Pro-Social Content: "Please" models romantic commitment as it asks a love, "Let me grow old with you." On "Blessed," the artist sensitively promises his love to a child not yet

conceived. "Belfast" denounces Ireland's civil unrest while honoring the city itself for its bravery and strength.

Objectionable Content: "Believe" suggests that the church is just another decaying institution. Elton identifies religion, love, purity, and peace as "Pain." "Lies" posits that dishonesty is a regrettable yet normal part of daily existence, admitting in the process, "I've lied for a drug or two." Upset with an unnamed individual, he sings, "Well, here's my middle finger" ("Made in England"). The tune also refers to his homeland as a place where "you can still say homo and everybody laughs . . . but the joke's on you."

Summary/Advisory: A mixed bag. Even the positive love songs are hard to enjoy knowing Elton John's own sexual preference.

Jordan, Montell

◆ ◆ ◆ ◆ ◆ ◆ ◆ ◆ ◆ ◆ ◆ ◆ ◆ ◆ ◆ ◆ ◆ ◆

Montell Jordan, a 6'8" native of Compton, California, made his musical debut with the platinum effort *This Is How We Do It*.

Title: *This Is How We Do It* (1995)
Label: PMP/RAL
Genre: R&B/Hip-hop
Pro-Social Content: Jordan rejects gun use on "Introducing Shaunta."
Objectionable Content: Lots of talk about casual, lewd, and explicit sex. On "I Wanna," he tells his libidinous prey, "I don't even have to know your name . . . I wanna get laid; it ain't about love tonight." More of the same on "I'll Do Anything," "Payback," "Comin' Home," and "Somethin' 4 Da Honeyz," which adds alcohol to the mix. "Down on My Knees" lecherously propositions a woman whose man often leaves her alone. Jordan brags of wealth on the half-million-selling "This Is How We Do It," and uses profanity throughout the disc's 15 tracks.

Summary/Advisory: Montell is a raging libido in search of an outlet. As for sex, the Bible clearly states that this is how we *don't* do it. Smooth sounds, but lyrically crude to the core. Avoid this dreck at all costs.

Journey

◆ ◆ ◆ ◆ ◆ ◆ ◆ ◆ ◆ ◆ ◆ ◆ ◆ ◆ ◆ ◆ ◆ ◆ ◆

Journey united in 1973 with George Tickner, Aynsley Dunbar, Ross Valory, and Gregg Rolie. By 1986, the group also consisted of lead vocalist Steve Perry (added in 1978), Neal Schon, and Jonathan Cain (added in 1981). From 1978's *Infinity* to the band's *Greatest Hits* collection a decade later, Journey watched all eight of its albums go platinum or better.

Title: *Trial by Fire* (1996)
Label: Columbia
Genre: Rock
Pro-Social Content: "Message of Love" cries out for relational reconciliation. Lead singer Steve Perry pledges to help a woman pick up the pieces of a failed romance ("If He Should Break Your Heart"). Elsewhere, he uses biblical metaphors in a musical prayer for help during a "Trial by Fire" and condemns shallow faith in God ("Easy to Fall"). While "Don't Be Down on Me Baby" warns partners not to be critical of one another, "Castles Burning" reminds listeners that the glamor of beauty, fame, and passion can be empty. Falling in love is described as "a joy that lasts forever" on the band's AC radio staple, "When You Love a Woman."
Objectionable Content: None
Summary/Advisory: Adults familiar with Journey's '80s résumé (which includes the hits "Open Arms" and "Who's Crying Now") will be impressed with this modern resurrection—one likely to bridge a musical chasm in some homes. A driving presentation that's also lyrically sound. (SEE ALSO: Perry, Steve)

Judd, Wynonna

◆ ◆ ◆ ◆ ◆ ◆ ◆ ◆ ◆ ◆ ◆ ◆ ◆ ◆ ◆ ◆ ◆ ◆

Originally half of the Grammy-winning mother-daughter country duo The Judds, Wynonna launched her solo career in 1992.

Title: *Revelations* (1996)
Label: Curb
Genre: Country
Pro-Social Content: Numerous tracks exalt love and devotion as a basic

human need worth fighting for ("To Be Loved by You"), sacrificing and praying for ("Heaven Help My Heart"), and making oneself vulnerable for ("Somebody to Love You"). "Love by Grace" celebrates commitment as one-half of a quarrelling couple returns home to mend the relationship. "Dance! Shout!" points to Jesus as a faithful friend worthy of praise.

Objectionable Content: "Old Enough to Know Better," about a woman's inability to resist a man, could be based on the country diva's own poor decisions which led to an out-of-wedlock pregnancy.

Summary/Advisory: While lyrically sound, much of Wynonna's comeback album rings hollow in light of the moral compromises she made public at the time of its release. Otherwise, *Revelations* is a solid pick.

Title: *Tell Me Why* (1993)
Label: MCA
Genre: Country/Pop
Pro-Social Content: "Let's Make a Baby King" reverently refers to Jesus as the answer to the world's problems ("We need a Lord to guide us, to teach us wrong and right/And we need a lamb to lead us into the land of light"). "Rock Bottom" makes the hope-filled observation that "a dead-end street is just a place to turn around." With sweet reflection reminiscent of her Judds hit "Grandpa," Wynonna revisits the home of her youth where "Cokes were just a nickel" ("I Just Drove By"). "Father Sun" decries empty, iconic religiosity and pleads for forgiveness and salvation from the One who "will be coming back."

Objectionable Content: None
Summary/Advisory: Whether singing about spiritual truth, girls and guitars, and Elvis's Cadillac or lamenting over love lost, Wynonna injects plenty of energy into her second solo effort. A lyrically solid collection.

K-Ci & JoJo

◆ ◆ ◆ ◆ ◆ ◆ ◆ ◆ ◆ ◆ ◆ ◆ ◆ ◆ ◆ ◆ ◆ ◆ ◆ ◆

Brothers K-Ci (Cedric Hailey) and JoJo (Joel Hailey) first achieved celebrity as two members of the raunchy R&B group Jodeci. The pair hail from Tiny Grove, North Carolina.

Title: *Love Always* (1997)
Label: MCA
Genre: R&B
Pro-Social Content: The Haileys sing about
deep, committed romantic love on the hit single
"All My Life," the retro "Love Ballad," and
"Now and Forever," which states, "I'm a firm
believer in trusting, caring and loving." A man
expresses his love for a lady on "Last Night's Letter." In the midst of
emotional pain, he cries out to God for relief ("How Could You"), and says
he will do anything to make up for wronging a romantic partner ("Just for
Your Love").
Objectionable Content: Sexual references taint "Still Waiting" ("Can't
that be I kissin' your lips and rubbin' your thighs . . . Let me knock it with
ease") and "Don't Rush (Take Love Slowly)" ("You got buck wild . . .
started rubbing my legs").
Summary/Advisory: Compared to the duo's explicit, sexually charged
work with Jodeci, K-Ci & JoJo have toned things down considerably here.
With the noted exceptions, a focus on wholesome romance weaves its way
through *Love Always*. (SEE ALSO: Jodeci)

Kelly, R.

◆ ◆ ◆ ◆ ◆ ◆ ◆ ◆ ◆ ◆ ◆ ◆ ◆ ◆ ◆ ◆ ◆ ◆ ◆

R. (Robert) Kelly made music history when "You Are Not Alone," a song
he wrote and produced for Michael Jackson's *HIStory* CD, *debuted* at number 1 on *Billboard*'s Hot 100 singles chart—the first song ever to accomplish that. Kelly's *12 Play* held onto the number-1 R&B album position for
more than 10 weeks. His self-titled album debuted at number 1.

Title: *R. Kelly* (1995)
Label: Jive
Genre: R&B
Pro-Social Content: Kelly urges his urban brothers to respect women in
the prayerful "As I Look Into My Life." He asks forgiveness and wants to
restore relationships on "Heaven If You Hear Me" and "I Can't Sleep
Baby." "Trade in My Life" points listeners to God for guidance and comfort
("The Bible says He'll watch and prepare the way . . . Thank you Jesus for
being the head of my life").

Objectionable Content: With a smattering of profanity, this disc confuses love and sex, often using Christianity to justify hormonally charged behavior. "Intro—The Sermon" claims, "Even the Statue of Liberty wants to bump and grind. Can I get a witness?" Euphemisms fly everywhere. The hit single "You Remind Me of Something" likens a woman to a car, a jeep, and a stereo system. "Hump Bounce" expresses a desire for cheap sex, as do a number of smooth tunes designed to lure young women into bed ("Step in My Room," "Tempo Slow"). "Down Low" speaks of smoking marijuana and portrays the Koran as a book of truth.

Summary/Advisory: Believe it or not, this disc isn't as offensive as Kelly's 4 million-selling *12 Play*—but it's still way out of bounds with its disturbing blend of sexuality and spirituality.

Title: *12 Play* (1993)
Label: Jive
Genre: Pop/Hip-hop/Rap
Pro-Social Content: "Sadie" pays tribute to the artist's departed mother. "For You" pledges romantic commitment. One line in "Summer Bunnies" states, "I won't call 'em hos, 'cause in the '90s, you gotta respect the ladies."
Objectionable Content: Kelly's *dis*respect for women speaks much louder. Crude sexual references dominate this disc, including talk of "freakin' that body," sex "from behind," and so on. "Homie Lover Friend" alludes to using pornography. "Summer Bunnies" approves of group sex and getting an alcohol buzz. Gangsta violence takes center stage on "Back to the Hood A' Things."
Summary/Advisory: It's understandable that young R&B fans would find R. (Robert) Kelly's smooth vocal style and catchy melodies attractive. Too bad he's prostituting himself by producing audio porno. Don't let teens be seduced.

Kenny G

◆ ◆ ◆ ◆ ◆ ◆ ◆ ◆ ◆ ◆ ◆ ◆ ◆ ◆ ◆ ◆ ◆ ◆ ◆ ◆

This Seattle-born fusion saxophonist (born Kenny Gorelick) has sold more than 30 million albums in his 14-year career—one-third of them coming from his popular disc, *Breathless*. He also holds an accounting degree and various academic honors from the University of Washington.

Title: *Breathless* (1992)
Label: Arista
Genre: Jazz/Adult contemporary
Pro-Social Content: Only two songs on this mostly instrumental album contain lyrics. Both are romantic ballads, sung by soul artists Peabo Bryson ("By the Time This Night Is Over") and Aaron Neville ("Even If My Heart Would Break").
Neville's tune pledges a deep and everlasting love despite circumstances.
Objectionable Content: Bryson, on the other hand, hopes that "two lovers . . . will be together in the morning" without explaining whether or not they're married.
Summary/Advisory: Virtuoso saxophonist Kenny G's first album in four years features ultramellow instrumental sounds. A light collection of romantic mood music that is sure to be enjoyed by a wide audience—including some teens.

King Missile

◆ ◆ ◆ ◆ ◆ ◆ ◆ ◆ ◆ ◆ ◆ ◆ ◆ ◆ ◆ ◆ ◆ ◆ ◆ ◆

King Missile is a band comprised of John S. Hall, Dave Rick, Chris Xefos, and Roger Murdock. The CD cover for *Happy Hour* has been purposely omitted due to extremely graphic imagery.

Title: *Happy Hour* (1993)
Label: Atlantic
Genre: Alternative
Pro-Social Content: None
Objectionable Content: "Take Me Home" glorifies sadomasochism ("throw me down, tie me up, spit in my face, kick me hard"). "Martin Scorsese" details acts of violence the singer fantasizes about inflicting upon

the famous film director, including ripping off an ear, chewing off lips, sucking out an eye, and kicking in his teeth. "It's Saturday Night" inspires revolt and encourages people to "f— sh— up." One of the most ridiculous cuts is titled "Detachable Penis" and relates the story of a man whose genitalia are often removed and misplaced (or rented out). Unbelievably, it received radio airplay as well as exposure on MTV. The band's dark side comes through on "Ed," "Heaven" (which is anything *but)*, "Happy Hour," and "The Evil Children." The warning label is well-deserved for obscenity. **Summary/Advisory:** Very nihilistic, this record also includes vile and antireligious imagery. What isn't downright nonsensical is patently offensive. Don't take in *Happy Hour*.

Kirk Franklin and the Family

◆ ◆ ◆ ◆ ◆ ◆ ◆ ◆ ◆ ◆ ◆ ◆ ◆ ◆ ◆ ◆ ◆ ◆ ◆

Kirk Franklin was appointed minister of music at Mt. Rose Baptist Church at the age of 11. It was at this time he began to write, arrange, and rearrange Christian music. His debut album was certified platinum.

Title: *Whatcha Lookin' 4* (1996)
Label: GospoCentric
Genre: R&B/Gospel
Pro-Social Content: Every joy-filled track boldly gives praise, glory, and honor to Jesus Christ. Themes range from simple praise and worship choruses to up-tempo tunes celebrating God's faithfulness, mercy, and saving grace. "Melodies  from Heaven" invites the warm embrace of the Holy Spirit. On "Mama's Song," Franklin pays tribute to the aunt who raised him (the artist's teenage parents abandoned him at age three). When God seems distant, the singer reaches for the hem of His garment ("Let Me Touch You"). Outstanding messages!
Objectionable Content: None
Summary/Advisory: Another fine Top-40 project from Kirk and the clan. Best of all, this music is both unapologetically Christian and accepted by mainstream R&B radio! One syndicated radio host told *USA Today* [3/8/95], "We've played so-called gospel music before—BeBe and CeCe Winans, Sounds of Blackness—but this is truly gospel. [Kirk] says 'Jesus' a lot, which inspirational songs don't dare do." And they love it! A soulful addition to any family's music collection.

Title: *Kirk Franklin and the Family* (1995)
Label: GospoCentric
Genre: Gospel/R&B
Pro-Social Content: From simple praise and worship choruses to electrifying urban "salvation celebrations," this disc seeks to glorify God and introduce people to the Savior. "Why We Sing" testifies that Christ is the reason for the group's rejoicing. Other songs point to Him as a help in times of trouble ("Call on the Lord," "He Can Handle It," "He's Able") and cherish His worth ("Silver and Gold," "Speak to Me," "Real Love," and others).
Objectionable Content: None
Summary/Advisory: This project was released in 1993 but didn't hit the mainstream until more than a year later when one secular radio station played "Why We Sing." Others followed. The self-titled effort penetrated pop's Top 100 and was the first traditional gospel album to hit R&B's Top 10 since Aretha Franklin's *Amazing Grace* in 1972. It may have taken a year and a half, but Kirk Franklin and his 17 backup singers have become an overnight sensation with uncompromising messages that exalt Jesus—not a watered-down attempt to attain pop success.

Korn

◆ ◆ ◆ ◆ ◆ ◆ ◆ ◆ ◆ ◆ ◆ ◆ ◆ ◆ ◆ ◆ ◆ ◆ ◆ ◆

Korn consists of Jonathan Davis, Brian Welch, James Shaffer, Reginald Arvizu, and David Silvera. The band's self-titled debut album has sold nearly 1 million copies.

Title: *Life Is Peachy* (1996)
Label: Immortal/Epic
Genre: Metal/Industrial
Pro-Social Content: Not a single kernel
Objectionable Content: Explicit lyrics abound. "K@#0%!" rattles off a dozen obscenities in succession for pure shock value (Davis told *Interview* [6/97], "I was p——ed off at radio stations censoring my s—— because I have a bad mouth, so we were going to send 'K@#0%!' out as the first single and say, 'Censor this.' I just wanted something that was violent and full of cusswords"). The f-word appears throughout this sick disc. On "Kill

You," lead growler Jonathan Davis uses grisly detail to express hatred for his stepmother, whom he wants to see dead. He's also bitter toward beloved children's-TV host "Mr. Rogers" ("What a f—ing neighbor/I hate you!"). Spewing blasphemous obscenities from start to finish, "Good God" appears to blame the Lord for an empty existence. Masturbation and sex with strangers are advocated on "A.D.I.D.A.S.," which stands for "All Day I Dream About Sex." The rap cut "Wicked" blends sex and violence. **Summary/Advisory:** Deserving of two explicit lyric stickers, *Life Is Peachy* is pure trash. Davis, a horror film buff, enrolled in mortuary college and was recently quoted as saying, "I just got off on cutting people open. I could do things that serial killers did and get paid for it." His statement reflects this album's nasty disposition. Don't let teens feed on Korn.

Kris Kross

◆ ◆ ◆ ◆ ◆ ◆ ◆ ◆ ◆ ◆ ◆ ◆ ◆ ◆ ◆ ◆ ◆ ◆ ◆ ◆

Kris Kross teamed up teenagers Chris Kelly and Chris Smith. Their first album sold more than 4 million copies, while their first single went double platinum. The duo has been nominated for an MTV award and two Grammy awards and won two American Music Awards. The duo's debut album, *Totally Krossed Out*, sold in excess of 4 million units, followed up by *Da Bomb*, selling 1 million. *Young, Rich & Dangerous* went gold.

Title: *Young, Rich & Dangerous* (1996)
Label: Ruffhouse/Columbia
Genre: Rap
Pro-Social Content: None
Objectionable Content: Casual sex with multiple partners is a recurring theme ("Tonite's the Night," "Some Cut Up," "It's a Group Thang," "Mackin' Ain't Easy"). "Tonite's the Night," which spent over a month as rap's hottest single, recommends getting drunk, as does the title track. There's nothing subtle about the come-on: "My whole thing is to get inside your body" ("Live and Die for Hip Hop"). On "Da Streets Ain't Right," the duo raps about toting a gun for defense. Frequent use of the n-word is inappropriate.

Summary/Advisory: Remember when Kris Kross made it hip for kids to wear their pants backwards? But as they grew up, the boys' rebellion escalated to truly dangerous levels. Like rutting animals in a zoo, they proudly parade beastly hormonal urges before an adoring public. Kris Kross—and their handlers—should be ashamed.

Title: *Da Bomb* (1993)
Label: Ruffhouse/Columbia
Genre: Rap/Hip-hop
Pro-Social Content: Not much this time. "A Lot 2 Live 4" acknowledges the challenges of inner-city life while it encourages daily prayer and perseverence.
Objectionable Content: The boys brag about everything from their income ("It Don't Stop"), talent ("Take Em Out," "Freak Da Funk"), and how tough they are ("Da Bomb") to ways they've impacted youth fads, including braided hair for guys and wearing their pants backward. The title track sanctions weapons use ("give me a 30-30 half caliber half gauge"). Haughty rebellion throughout.
Summary/Advisory: Although Chrises Smith and Kelly haven't crossed the line into explicit gangsta rap, Kris Kross has sold out to a more aggressive street sound that *Entertainment Weekly* called "harder, less mall-friendly." *Da Bomb* lacks the positive pop elements of the duo's first record, and publicists say the change resulted from the boys growing up. At this rate, future releases will require a parental advisory sticker.

Lawrence, Tracy

◆ ◆ ◆ ◆ ◆ ◆ ◆ ◆ ◆ ◆ ◆ ◆ ◆ ◆ ◆ ◆ ◆ ◆ ◆

Since bursting onto the country music scene in 1991 with the hit "Sticks and Stones," Lawrence has sold more than 5 million albums, produced 11 chart-topping hits, and won several national awards, including the 1993 Academy of Country Music's Top New Male Vocalist crown. *Time Marches On* achieved gold status.

Title: *Time Marches On* (1996)
Label: Atlantic
Genre: Country
Pro-Social Content: A lonely Lawrence
regrets pursuing worldly success at the expense
of loving relationships on "Somewhere Between

the Moon and You." With similar disdain for material wealth, "From What We Give" values giving more highly than receiving. Tender love songs ("Stars Over Texas," "Different Man," "If You Loved Me") repent of past mistakes and vow eternal devotion.

Objectionable Content: "Excitable Boy" boasts of womanizing and a rebellious streak ("skip a little school . . . bend another rule") and suggests that date rape is acceptable if the boy is "raring to go." A rebel spirit also fuels "Speed of a Fool." On the title song, the singer shares some family history, accepting that his brother's days of smoking marijuana—and dad's committing adultery—were normal and bound to happen over time. A mild profanity mars "Is That a Tear." "Different Man" finds the artist drowning his sorrows at a bar.

Summary/Advisory: At barely 33 minutes in length, this brief project has a lot to say. Too bad its positive messages are overshadowed by unruliness. For more edifying country music, young fans of Tracy Lawrence should sample CCM soundalikes Ken Holloway and Jeff Silvey.

Lennox, Annie

◆ ◆

Born in Aberdeen, Scotland, on Christmas Day, 1954, Lennox was trained as a classical flutist at the Royal Academy of Music in London. She broke into the music biz in the late 1970s with a band called the Tourists. But it wasn't until she signed on as the lead singer with the '80s pop band Eurythmics that her career really took off. As a solo artist, the double-platinum *Diva* (1992) spawned two Top-10 hits and received three Grammy nominations. *Medusa* (1995) proceeded to sell a million copies.

Title: *Medusa* (1995)
Label: Arista
Genre: Adult contemporary
Pro-Social Content: "Something So Right" explains how a partner's love can dissolve emotional barriers. Other cuts also explore the ups and downs of romantic relationships ("Take Me to the River," "Train in Vain," "Downtown Lights," "No More 'I Love You's").
Objectionable Content: Youngsters could interpret casual references to

smoking and drinking as endorsements. "I Can't Get Next to You" boasts the ability to control nature and one's own immortality in godlike fashion. On "Thin Line Between Love and Hate," a victim of infidelity accuses her partner of indifference ("You don't give a d— about me") and uses violence to even the score.

Summary/Advisory: *Medusa* consists of 10 tunes previously released by other artists. Lennox breathes new life and passion into many of them. While two songs are problematic, much of the disc is innocuous fun.

Lewis, Donna

◆ ◆ ◆ ◆ ◆ ◆ ◆ ◆ ◆ ◆ ◆ ◆ ◆ ◆ ◆ ◆ ◆ ◆ ◆

Born in Cardiff, Wales, Lewis started playing the piano when she was six years old and was writing music at age 14. Her 1996 release *Now in a Minute* sold more than 500,000 copies. "I Love You Always Forever" reached number 2 on the pop singles chart.

Title: *Now in a Minute* (1996)
Label: Atlantic
Genre: Pop
Pro-Social Content: The pop smash "I Love You Always Forever" pledges lifelong commitment. A lovely tribute, "Mother" honors the faithfulness of Lewis's mom and her ability to provide strength and shelter. Amid mourning, the artist longs to be reunited with a loved one in heaven on "Silent World." She advises a friend haunted by childhood trauma to let go of the hurt and never look back ("Simone") and examines relational ups and downs on "Love and Affection," "Without Love," "Fool's Paradise," and "Nothing Ever Changes."

Objectionable Content: Minor. Overcome by romantic emotion, Lewis asks, "How can I retain my self-control?" ("Love and Affection").

Summary/Advisory: Families can feel good about the sweetly serene, celestial strains of Donna Lewis. The Welsh-born singer and songwriter avoids off-color themes and has said, "If I can move people with my songs, that's great." It sure is. With one small exception, Lewis moves listeners in the right direction on *Now in a Minute*.

Lil' Kim

◆ ◆ ◆ ◆ ◆ ◆ ◆ ◆ ◆ ◆ ◆ ◆ ◆ ◆ ◆ ◆ ◆ ◆ ◆ ◆

Lil' Kim grew up in The Bronx, New York, and witnessed the divorce of her parents when she was nine years old. Rapper Biggie Smalls (a.k.a. Notorious B.I.G.), a friend of Kim's brother, helped launch her music career—eventually hooking her up with the rapping team Junior M.A.F.I.A. *Hardcore* sold more than a half-million copies.

Title: *Hardcore* (1997)
Label: Atlantic
Genre: Gangsta rap
Pro-Social Content: None
Objectionable Content: Unflinchingly pornographic, the disc's many explicit references to sex include the artist recalling anal sex with a promiscuous man ("Crush on You") and oral sex ("Not Tonight," "We Don't Need It," "Schemin'"). "Take It!" incorporates spoken obscenities as men brag about their libidinous conquests. Most tracks rely on the f-word and lewd anatomical slang. On "We Don't Need It," Kim resents her "date" for falling asleep before bringing her to climax, whereupon she is "forced" to masturbate. Three cuts deal with either drugs or alcohol. "M.A.F.I.A. Land," one of several attempts by Kim to prove she can be as violent as male rappers, features murderous threats and gunshots.
Summary/Advisory: Appropriately titled, *Hardcore* takes listeners on a seedy trek through rap's red-light district—especially disturbing since the tour guide objectifies herself in graphic fashion. Sick and sad.

Live

◆ ◆ ◆ ◆ ◆ ◆ ◆ ◆ ◆ ◆ ◆ ◆ ◆ ◆ ◆ ◆ ◆ ◆ ◆ ◆

Live (pronounced using a long "i") consists of Edward Kowalcyzk, Chad Taylor, Patrick Dahlheimer, and Chad Gracey, who began playing together as teenagers. The band is lead by Kowalcyzk, who is known for a non-deist spirituality which serves as the basis for his lyrics.

Title: *Secret Samadhi* (1997)
Label: Radioactive

Genre: Alternative
Pro-Social Content: A few isolated lines that don't add up to much.
Objectionable Content: The Samadhi of the title is
Sanskrit for a divine state achieved through meditation. Eastern mysticism continues to be a
preoccupation of this band, which gives a
nod to pantheism ("Gas Hed Goes West")
and the worship of a Hindu goddess
("Lakini's Juice"). On "Ghost," a boy "can't
help eyein' up the whores." The artist dreams of
killing people who wronged him ("Heropsycho-
dreamer") and tells the listener, "Forget your
mother and your father; they aren't important, son" ("Graze"). The f-word
appears on "Freaks," a disturbing song about incest. Several cuts mention
drugs or alcohol.
Summary/Advisory: The band's last album, *Throwing Copper*, sold more
than 6 million copies. This one's equally irksome. Grinding guitars and
angry vocals inject these tunes with added bitterness. If per chance your
teen already owns this disc, it's one *Secret* they should *not* keep.

Title: *Throwing Copper* (1994)
Label: Radioactive
Genre: Alternative
Pro-Social Content: Some isolated lines, but they're all shrouded in
lyrical obscurity.
Objectionable Content: No warning sticker, but several f-words and
assorted profanities appear. A vague reference to Christ's death seems to
miss its true significance on "Setting the Drama." Other songs conjure
mental pictures that, taken at face value, result in pessimistic images of
family (an untitled track), waitresses ("Waitress"), and small towns ("Sh—
Towne"). Relational angst and a general sense of hopelessness are woven
throughout.
Summary/Advisory: Live's press bio reads, "Taylor's guitar and
Kowalczyk's [vocals] can subtly guide you into dark, thoughtful places."
Dark is the operative word. Ambiguous, brooding poetry? Profane, miserable nonsense is more like it. Either way, *Throwing Copper* is an oppressive
disc with nothing of value to communicate to teens.

L.L. Cool J

◆ ◆ ◆ ◆ ◆ ◆ ◆ ◆ ◆ ◆ ◆ ◆ ◆ ◆ ◆ ◆ ◆ ◆ ◆

This two-time Grammy award-winning rapper also won 15 New York Music Awards, 10 Soul Train Awards, a *Billboard* Music Award, and was nominated for Favorite Album at the 1992 American Music Awards. He has also appeared on the UPN-TV show *In the House.*

Title: *14 Shots to the Dome* (1993)
Label: Columbia
Genre: Rap
Pro-Social Content: Very little. "Diggy Down" bemoans a troubled society where kids carry guns.
Objectionable Content: That message is effectively squelched by "Funkadelic Relic," "Ain't No Stoppin' This" ("I carry a 9mm and a stiletto"), and other references to weapon use. "Soul Survivor" threatens censors with grisly violence ("I'll wake you up with an axe . . . I'll leave your bullet-riddled body on the curb"), while "How I'm Comin'" advocates further brutality. Graphic sexual references dominate "Back Seat." Meanwhile, "All We Got Left Is the Beat" is a pessimistic rap diatribe about the current plight of blacks in a world where even God can't offer hope.
Summary/Advisory: Lewd and violent themes, numerous expletives, and a generally rotten attitude make L.L. Cool J an artist to avoid. Columbia Records' decision not to include a warning label is downright irresponsible.

Loeb, Lisa

◆ ◆ ◆ ◆ ◆ ◆ ◆ ◆ ◆ ◆ ◆ ◆ ◆ ◆ ◆ ◆ ◆ ◆ ◆

With the single "Stay (I Missed You)," Loeb became the first (and, to date, only) artist to have a song hit number 1 before signing a record deal. This song from the soundtrack of the film *Reality Bites* stayed three weeks in that position during August 1994. This song resulted in Loeb being nominated for a Grammy for Best Pop Performance by Duo or Group.

Title: *Tails*
Label: Geffen
Genre: Folk/Rock/Pop

Pro-Social Content: "Snow Day" suggests that everyday setbacks can be overcome. On "Hurricane," a man warns the artist not to turn her heart over to a dangerous, witchy woman. Though not clearly in the context of marriage, "Sandalwood" conveys a romantic hunger in poetic terms akin to the Bible's Song of Solomon. Several of Loeb's tunes deal with being separated from the man she loves.

Objectionable Content: A muddled "Garden of Delights" expresses hatred for a lover described as Jesus ("You are my Jesus boy; you're laying on a bedly cross").

Summary/Advisory: Mostly neutral material. Lots of lyrical obscurity. Fortunately, Loeb's soul-searching avoids the dark, brooding nihilism embraced by many of her cryptic peers (Live, The Smashing Pumpkins, Veruca Salt). Teens could do much worse than this Grammy nominee's *Tails*, but an even better option is something by CCM duo Out of the Grey.

Lost Boyz

◆ ◆ ◆ ◆ ◆ ◆ ◆ ◆ ◆ ◆ ◆ ◆ ◆ ◆ ◆ ◆ ◆ ◆ ◆ ◆

This foursome includes Mr. Cheeks, DJ Spigg Nice, Freaky Tah, and Pretty Lou. Their popularity is based, in part, on their claim to be "real" gangstas raised in the ghetto.

Title: *Legal Drug Money* (1996)
Label: Universal
Genre: Gangsta rap
Pro-Social Content: None
Objectionable Content: "The Yearn" brags about a drug- and alcohol-enhanced sexual conquest with a new acquaintance. So does the popular radio single "Renee," which includes the line, "I started feelin' on her breasts." Amid frequent use of the racially charged n-word, "Straight from da Ghetto" justifies cold-blooded murder. Other cuts also glorify gangsta violence ("All Right," "Keep It Real," "Jeeps, Lex Coups, Bimaz & Benz," "1 2 3," "Legal Drug Money"). "Da Game" boasts of killing police ("We're blasting coppers in the face"). Marijuana is the group's drug of choice on at least eight tracks. They blame

government and the white man for their homicidal depravity ("Straight from da Ghetto," "Channel Zero"). Obscenities fly like unwanted Tater Tots in a grade school cafeteria.

Summary/Advisory: Crude, lewd, and rude. These libidinous, hateful, substance-abusing Boyz are Lost in more ways than one. Even laundering can't clean up *Legal Drug Money*.

LSG

◆ ◆ ◆ ◆ ◆ ◆ ◆ ◆ ◆ ◆ ◆ ◆ ◆ ◆ ◆ ◆ ◆ ◆ ◆ ◆

LSG is Gerald Levert, Keith Sweat, and Johnny Gill. Levert has performed as a solo artist and with the group that bears his name. Sweat established himself as both a performer and producer. His platinum, self-titled solo effort reached number 5 on the pop chart. Gill entered the R&B scene 10 years ago at age 16 as a member of New Edition (the sextet reunited in 1996 to record *Home Again*).

Title: *Levert.Sweat.Gill* (1997)
Label: EastWest
Genre: R&B/Rap

Pro-Social Content: The artists want to fix rocky romances on "Where Did I Go Wrong?" "Drove Me to Tears," and "My Side of the Bed" (though the latter lacks marital context). "Love Hurts" pledges devotion to a woman stung by the unfaithfulness of another man.

Objectionable Content: Steamy sexuality motivates most of the songs on this salacious collaboration ("Door #1," "Round & Round," "Curious"). Two tracks get pretty explicit. "Let a Playa Get His Freak On" croons, "I'll make you hot like a wet dream . . . I'll lick you from head to toe . . . make you scream." On the million-selling number-1 R&B hit "My Body," the singer asks a girl, "Would you like it if I was to sex you down? . . . Wanna fill you up till your river flows all over me." Sex, sex, and more sex.

Summary/Advisory: Individually, Gerald Levert, Keith Sweat, and Johnny Gill have carved out successful R&B careers. With the creation of *Levert.Sweat.Gill,* they've teamed up for a sensual, velvet-tongued project that deserves its own 900 number. Clearly, three sets of hormones are *not* better than one. Teens should avoid this libidinous trio. (SEE ALSO: New Edition)

Madonna

◆ ◆ ◆ ◆ ◆ ◆ ◆ ◆ ◆ ◆ ◆ ◆ ◆ ◆ ◆ ◆ ◆ ◆ ◆

Madonna Louise Ciccone performed in various venues before releasing her self-titled LP in 1983. Over the course of her career, she has sold approximately 40 million records, the most popular being 1984's *Like a Virgin*. Madonna has appeared in numerous films, including *Dick Tracy, Evita, A League of Their Own*, and the documentary *Truth or Dare*. She was married to actor Sean Penn from 1985–89, and generated headlines in 1992 with her pornographic picture book, *Sex*. Also the entertainer's shameless conduct on CBS's *The Late Show* in 1997 inspired host David Letterman to ban her from future appearances.

Title: *Ray of Light* (1998)
Label: Maverick/Warner Bros.
Genre: Pop/Electronica
Pro-Social Content: This new mom appears to address her baby on "Swim" as she enumerates societal ills and longs to escape them. "Sky Fits Heaven" exalts giving, love, and caring for children, and credits "the Gospel" with speaking to her. Madonna encourages a man to let go of hate, regret, and pain ("Frozen"). She treasures her daughter as a "present from God" ("Little Star") and admits that misplaced priorities nearly caused her to miss out on love ("Drowned World/Substitute for Love" and "Nothing Really Matters").
Objectionable Content: "Candy Perfume Girl"'s vague lines yearn for "moist warm desire" and instruct a man, "devour me when you're with me." Liner photos show the artist clothed (sort of) in a see-through top revealing her breasts.
Summary/Advisory: This disc marks a musical makeover for The Material Girl. She has converted to a techno beat and embarked on a pseudospiritual quest (reportedly, yoga and Eastern mysticism). Regarding her new attitude, she told *Spin* [4/98], "Now I feel like everything we do—the movies we make, the music, the stuff that's on television—affects society in a potent way. I feel a sense of responsibility because my consciousness has been raised and I would like to impart the wisdom I have to others without being corny or preachy." It's a step in the right direction. And Madonna's lyrical reformation really is a *Ray of Light*, though there's no excuse for the soft porn CD booklet.

Title: *Bedtime Stories* (1994)
Label: Maverick/Sire
Genre: R&B-flavored pop/Dance
Pro-Social Content: "Inside of Me" thanks a love for his support and reliability, but . . .
Objectionable Content: . . . it is underscored by heavy breathing, reinforcing a sexual double entendre. Shallow eroticism with virtual strangers is a recurring theme ("I'd Rather Be Your Lover," "Forbidden Love," "Human Nature"). The title track dwells on the fact that the artist is "leaving logic and reason, traveling in the arms of unconsciousness." The hedonistic anthem "Human Nature" repeatedly tells the listener, "Express yourself; don't repress yourself . . . I'm not your b—ch, don't lay your s— on me."
Summary/Advisory: In the January 1994 issue of *Spin*, the artist stated, "I somehow equate God and religion and sacrifice with taboo and sexuality. All of those things are sort of mixed up in a stew for me. . . . I'm a role model for those who dare to be different. . . . I definitely think I inspire people." Ignore anything you've heard about an "image change" on this particular project. Madonna's *Bedtime Stories* are still a far cry from Mother Goose and Aesop's Fables.

Makaveli

◆ ◆ ◆ ◆ ◆ ◆ ◆ ◆ ◆ ◆ ◆ ◆ ◆ ◆ ◆ ◆ ◆

(SEE: Shakur, Tupac)

Manson, Marilyn

◆ ◆ ◆ ◆ ◆ ◆ ◆ ◆ ◆ ◆ ◆ ◆ ◆ ◆ ◆ ◆ ◆

Marilyn Manson is both the name of the band and the name of its frontman. The quintet (all of whom have adopted stage names by blending the names of movie starlets and serial killers) also features Twiggy Ramirez, Madonna Wayne Gacy, Daisy Berkowitz, and Ginger Fish. Throughout 1997, communities across America were embroiled in grass-roots battles to keep the band's concerts *out* of their towns. In 1998, Manson (born Brian Warner) published his twisted, explicit biography, *The Long Hard Road Out of Hell*.

Title: *Antichrist Superstar* (1996)
Label: Interscope

Genre: Rock/Metal
Pro-Social Content: None
Objectionable Content: Angry lyrics promote murder, suicide, perverse eroticism, and a
satanic distaste for Christianity. Lines include,
"You can kill yourself now because you're dead
in my mind" ("Man That You Fear"), "I am the
faggot anti-pope" ("1996"), "Saw heaven and
hell were lies/When I'm God everyone dies"

("The Reflecting God"), "I've got abortions in my eyes . . . I wasn't born
with enough middle fingers" ("Irresponsible Hate Anthem"), "I am the
dinner whore. . . . The world spreads its legs for another star" ("Little
Horn"), "I will bury your God in my warm spit" ("Deformography")—a
small sampling of nearly 80 obscenity-strewn minutes of nihilistic trash.
Summary/Advisory: This band is spiritually oppressive, socially irresponsible, and downright hateful. One line from their song "The Minute of
Decay" betrays Manson's destructive course and dangerous agenda for
teens: "I'm on my way down now/I'd like to take you with me." Bad news!

Title: *Smells Like Children* (1995)
Label: Interscope
Genre: Rock
Pro-Social Content: An isolated line on "I Put a Spell on You" expresses
love. That's it.
Objectionable Content: Manson refers to himself as "the god of f——"
("Everlasting C——sucker") and "the face of p——, and s—— and sugar"
("Kiddie Grinder"). Beyond the profanity and its talk of sodomy, the former
could also be interpreted as applauding date rape. "White Trash" enumer-
ates a teen girl's sexual proclivities. A racial slur is central to "Rock & Roll
N-gger," on which the artist lays claim to the title "all-American
Antichrist" before concluding the track with screams of "f—— you!" "F——
Frankie" repeats the song's title ad nauseam. On the mocking "Sympathy
for the Parents," a female voice conveys concerns about satanic music in a
religiously self-righteous tone.
Summary/Advisory: Outrageous, androgynous makeup. Inflammatory
stage antics. Anti-Christian rhetoric and a satanic pose. Toss in lyrics such
as the ones on *Children* and there's ample reason to keep kids away from
this band. The artist issued this devilish warning to parents in *Rip* magazine
[2/95]: "Raise your kids better or I'll be raising them for you." *Heed it.*

Marcy Playground

◆ ◆ ◆ ◆ ◆ ◆ ◆ ◆ ◆ ◆ ◆ ◆ ◆ ◆ ◆ ◆ ◆ ◆ ◆ ◆

Minneapolis, Minnesota, native John Wozniak had to travel all the way to New York City to meet Dylan Keefe and Dan Reiser, the musicians who would eventually partner with him in the band known as Marcy Playground. Wozniak is the group's principal songwriter and lead vocalist.

Title: *Marcy Playground* (1997)
Label: Capitol
Genre: Acoustic rock/Alternative
Pro-Social Content: "Saint Joe on the School Bus" grieves over the cruelty inflicted upon a young boy. A line on "Dog and His Master" asserts that people can choose their own futures.
Objectionable Content: Though obscure, "Sex and Candy" (the video for which was a big hit on MTV) involves the singer eyeing a curvaceous lady. A despondent boy and his distraught mother both drown themselves while clutching their Bibles ("One More Suicide")—a bad model that romanticizes death for despairing teens and portrays Christianity as ineffectual. Two tracks boldly applaud recreational drug use ("Opium," "Poppies"), while the more subtle "Ancient Walls of Flowers" may carry a similar message. A dabbler in black magic talks of dressing in occultic garb and owning "sixteen books on magic spells" ("A Cloak of Elvenkind"). Listeners are told to visit the Big Apple to see prostitutes and maybe take in a murder ("The Vampires of New York").
Summary/Advisory: Wozniak named his band after the schoolyard where he was picked on as a child—an experience he claims inspired these songs. But his bizarre ideological swings (from the joys of opium, to suicide, to casting spells) may push young fans down a slippery slide, making this *Playground* a dangerous hangout.

Mase

◆ ◆ ◆ ◆ ◆ ◆ ◆ ◆ ◆ ◆ ◆ ◆ ◆ ◆ ◆ ◆ ◆ ◆

Throughout his young life, Mase (Mason Betha) moved back and forth between Florida and New York. After high school, he attended State University of New York on a basketball scholarship and eventually recorded a rap demo that was heard by Sean "Puffy" Combs (a.k.a. Puff Daddy). *Harlem World* has sold more than 2 million copies.

Title: *Harlem World* (1997)
Label: Bad Boy Entertainment
Genre: Gangsta rap
Pro-Social Content: One line on the hit single "Feel So Good" asks feuding rappers to "bury the hate."
Objectionable Content: Other tracks continue to glamorize gangstas burying *each other* ("Will They Die 4 You," "The Player Way," and "Take What's Yours," which says, "A lot of blood gonna be spilled/We ain't discriminatin'/ Even thugs gonna be killed"). This disc is also extremely misogynistic. On "Lookin' at Me," a married man secretly solicits group sex in a hotel room, requesting, "Please no hickies 'cause my wifey's with me." Corrupt slang with explicit descriptions of sexual acts scar at least seven cuts. Other problems include obscenities, references to smoking marijuana, and a fantasy about killing city officials in a suicide bombing.
Summary/Advisory: There's nothing artistic about obnoxious bragging, anonymous sex, murderous gunplay, or being able to rhyme things with the f-word. Keep teens out of Mase's *World!*

Master P

◆ ◆ ◆ ◆ ◆ ◆ ◆ ◆ ◆ ◆ ◆ ◆ ◆ ◆ ◆ ◆ ◆ ◆

Billboard magazine has never seen a higher debut from street-date violations than the one Master P made September 13, 1997, when the advance sale of 8,000 units placed him at number 137. No surprise that after a full week of "legal" retailing, *Ghetto D* debuted at number 1 with sales exceeding 256,000 units.

Title: *Ghetto D* (1997)
Label: Priority
Genre: Gangsta rap
Pro-Social Content: "Stop Hatin'" calls for
an end to bitterness and hostility.

Objectionable Content: The artist admits he's
"full of hatred" on the violent "Only Time Will
Tell" ("grab my [gun] and kill off my enemies").
In addition, the lyrics find him committed to
drinking Hennessey and smoking marijuana. Nearly a dozen of the album's
19 tracks glorify drugs and alcohol in the form of blunts, weed, crack, dope,
or cocaine. Coarse language—f-word included—is heard throughout. On
"Going Through Some Thangs," a street thug shoots a woman (yes, there are
gunshots) after robbing a safe ("I never trust a b—ch 'cause nowadays these
b—ches carry an extra clip"). On "Let's Get 'Em," the rapper threatens to
urinate on an enemy's porch and defecate in his house. Truly awful stuff.
Summary/Advisory: From his vicious disrespect for human life to his
boneheaded blueprint for getting out of the ghetto (selling drugs), Master P's
Ghetto D is worse than empty: It's dangerous. Keep teens out of this *Ghetto*.

Matchbox 20

◆ ◆ ◆ ◆ ◆ ◆ ◆ ◆ ◆ ◆ ◆ ◆ ◆ ◆ ◆ ◆ ◆ ◆ ◆ ◆

Matchbox 20 consists of Rob Thomas, Kyle Cook, Adam Gaynor, Paul
Doucette, and Brian Yale. The band's debut disc has gone multiplatinum.

Title: *Yourself or Someone Like You* (1997)
Label: Lava
Genre: Rock/Alternative
Pro-Social Content: Isolated lines make an
appeal for relational harmony ("Argue"), recog-
nize the need for "amazing grace" ("Busted"),
and acknowledge God as the source of hope
("Long Day"). But they don't add up to much.

Objectionable Content: Profanities, including blasphemous uses of God's name, fly through these songs like bottles in a barroom brawl. Speaking of which, alcohol use appears on "Kody" and "Girl
Like That." The latter also considers a bad romance better than none at
all—a dangerous message for insecure teens desperate for acceptance.

Despite a desire for close relationships, the singer broods over failures and frustrations that have gotten in his way ("Kody," "Back 2 Good," "Shame," "Long Day," "Girl Like That," "D—n"). The group claims its MTV hit "Push" condemns lovers manipulating each other, but lines such as, "I wanna push you around . . . I wanna take you for granted" could easily send the opposite message.

Summary/Advisory: Emptiness. Misery. Fans of this musical style would do better to sample the Christ-centered tunes of CCM artists Big Tent Revival or Third Day.

McBride, Martina

◆ ◆ ◆ ◆ ◆ ◆ ◆ ◆ ◆ ◆ ◆ ◆ ◆ ◆ ◆ ◆ ◆ ◆ ◆

Born Martina Schifft in Medicine Lodge, Kansas, McBride has captured several country music awards. Her previous CDs, *The Way That I Am* and *Wild Angels*, went platinum and gold, respectively.

Title: *Evolution* (1997)
Label: RCA
Genre: Country
Pro-Social Content: "Whatever You Say" reminds listeners that ladies need to hear "I love you." With "Happy Girl," the artist casts off a pessimistic past and decides to see the glass as half-full ("The world won't change just 'cause I complain"). A woman finds courage to leave an abusive relationship on the chart-topping ballad, "A Broken Wing." The desire to move past romantic conflicts is central to "Some Say I'm Running" and "Be That Way." Fans could interpret "One Day You Will" from the perspective of God waiting for someone to accept His love ("I am timeless, I am patient/I'm beside you and above"). The sweet "Valentine" celebrates enduring romance. Neutral tracks share the pain of lost love.

Objectionable Content: None

Summary/Advisory: Sincere and generally upbeat, the million-selling *Evolution* resists honky-tonk turn-offs (such as drinking or carousing) in favor of home-cooked matters of the heart. A solid option for young country music lovers.

McCartney, Paul

◆ ◆ ◆ ◆ ◆ ◆ ◆ ◆ ◆ ◆ ◆ ◆ ◆ ◆ ◆ ◆ ◆

This founding member of The Beatles (together from 1964–70) was born in Liverpool, England. McCartney later formed the band Wings (1971–81) and, over the course of his 34 years in the business to date, has written more than 50 Top-10 singles and won Grammy's Lifetime Achievement Award.

Title: *Flaming Pie* (1997)
Label: Capitol
Genre: Rock
Pro-Social Content: "Somedays" ponders the meaning of life, concerned for "those who live in fear." The artist relates his reformation from an unprincipled past, advocates maintaining a positive attitude, and credits God with the masterpiece of creation on "Used to Be Bad." "Souvenir" pledges to "ease the pain" of another and love that person "like a friend." McCartney wrote the comforting lullaby "Little Willow" for the grieving children of a friend who passed on. Other tracks convey confidence and optimism about life ("Great Day") and express deep affection ("Really Love You").
Objectionable Content: Minor. Stray lines allude to "praying to the voice inside," "making love underneath the bed," and "smok[ing] a pipe."
Summary/Advisory: Every so often, a disc comes along destined to bond teens and their boomer parents. Enter the former Beatle and his Grammy-nominated, predominantly acoustic effort, *Flaming Pie*. Positive messages far outweigh its few negative hiccups. Listen for artistic contributions from Steve Miller, Ringo Starr, and ELO's Jeff Lynne.

Title: *Off the Ground* (1993)
Label: Capitol
Genre: Pop/Rock
Pro-Social Content: "Looking for Changes" promotes the ethical treatment of animals. Society is rallied to "make the best of all we have and more" and love one another in "C'mon People." "Peace in the Neighborhood" imagines a world where the "best thing I ever saw was a

man who loved his wife" and people were "helping each other out."
Objectionable Content: Depending on how the song is received, "Biker
Like an Icon" could serve to justify rebellious behavior.
Summary/Advisory: Mostly upbeat and optimistic in lyrical tone,
McCartney celebrates the beauty and tranquility of nature, the need for
peace on earth, and other sentiments reminiscent of the Beatles's "peace
and love" era. With only minor flaws, a good overall pick. (SEE ALSO:
Beatles, The)

McCready, Mindy

◆ ◆ ◆ ◆ ◆ ◆ ◆ ◆ ◆ ◆ ◆ ◆ ◆ ◆ ◆ ◆ ◆ ◆ ◆

Mindy McCready moved to Nashville when she was 18. She gave herself a
year, promising her mother that if her music career didn't take off, she
would attend college. One week before her self-imposed deadline,
McCready signed a record contract. Her debut album, *Ten Thousand
Angels,* sold more than 500,000 units. "Guys Do It All the Time" was a
number-1 country single.

Title: *Ten Thousand Angels* (1996)
Label: BNA
Genre: Country
Pro-Social Content: Mature listeners will appreciate McCready's prayerful
struggle to resist sexual temptation on "Ten
Thousand Angels." "All That I Am" appreciates
and pledges devotion to a caring man ("You
bring out what's inside of me . . . I love the way
you understand all that I am"). Temporary separation of the "tough love" ilk motivates "Maybe
He'll Notice Her Now" and "Without Love."
Objectionable Content: With tit-for-tat
irresponsibility, "Guys Do It All the Time"
finds the artist imitating her man's carousing. "It Ain't a
Party" celebrates social drinking at the local honky-tonk.
Summary/Advisory: With a sweetly pleasing voice akin to Music Row
predecessors Faith Hill, Sylvia, and Marie Osmond, 20-year-old McCready
confidently belts out some tunes with positive themes, such as self-control
and self-respect. If only she (and her many peers in the business) could
resist defaulting to watering-hole anthems that promote alcohol use.

McEntire, Reba

◆ ◆ ◆ ◆ ◆ ◆ ◆ ◆ ◆ ◆ ◆ ◆ ◆ ◆ ◆ ◆ ◆ ◆

Reba McEntire is one of country's best-known and most-beloved female performers. Her list of successes includes more than 30 million records sold, best-selling female country act of all time, highest grossing country tour of 1994, and at least 54 major awards. Reba has appeared in several made-for-TV movies since making her big-screen acting debut in the sci-fi/horror/comedy hit *Tremors*. Reba's sister is Christian recording artist Susie Luchsinger.

Title: *Read My Mind* (1994)
Label: MCA
Genre: Country
Pro-Social Content: On the bittersweet "She Thinks His Name Was John," a woman contracts AIDS from a one-night stand. This moving slice-of-life clearly illustrates that sin ("In her heart she knew it was wrong . . . too much wine") has consequences. "Why Haven't I Heard from You" playfully reminds the man in her life about the importance of communication. On "I Won't Stand in Line," Reba demands loyalty from a beau prone to wander. Elsewhere, she quells the desire to rekindle an old flame when she finds the man is married ("And Still").
Objectionable Content: "The Heart Is a Lonely Hunter" implies that adultery is wrong, but casual sex between single adults who meet in a bar is okay—dangerously hypocritical advice in light of her life-and-death AIDS ballad, "She Thinks His Name Was John."
Summary/Advisory: With this one glaring exception, Reba delivers a decent disc laced with the vocal calisthenics her fans love.

Title: *It's Your Call* (1993)
Label: MCA
Genre: Country
Pro-Social Content: The title track and others ("For Herself," "Will He Ever Go Away") call unfaithful partners to account. "Straight from You" finds Reba demanding of her man, "Now I've been told you've gone and let me down/I need to hear it straight from you." "He Wants to Get Married" communicates a standard of commitment and "teaching values."

Objectionable Content: The hit "Take It Back" appears to condone unmarried cohabitation ("You talked me into movin' in and giving you my key").

Summary/Advisory: In this follow-up to her 2-million-selling album, *For My Broken Heart*, Reba empathizes with those stinging from broken relationships. Still, she doesn't hold out a lot of hope, except in "One Last Good Hand" and "For Herself." With only minor exceptions, a good overall selection.

McGraw, Tim

◆ ◆

The son of former National League pitcher Tug McGraw, Tim has won Academy of Country Music awards for Album of the Year and Top New Male Vocalist. Only one other artist, Clint Black, has achieved this feat. Collectively, his discs have sold more than 9 million copies. McGraw recently married fellow country crooner Faith Hill.

Title: *Everywhere* (1997)
Label: Curb
Genre: Country
Pro-Social Content: Joined by his new bride, singer Faith Hill, McGraw credits her love with making him "happier than ever" ("It's Your Love," which spent a month as country's top single). The sweet "You Just Get Better All the Time" sends a similar message. Amicable partings and sacrificial love dominate "Just to See You Smile" and "For a Little While." "Where the Green Grass Grows" longs for the simple pleasures of rural life, including knowing one's neighbors and raising children "where the good Lord's blessed." The artist struggles to forgive himself and find peace, plagued by memories of the emotional pain he caused others ("One of These Days").

Objectionable Content: A philanderer is condemned less for his behavior than for his carelessness ("Ain't That the Way It Always Ends").

Summary/Advisory: An extremely positive effort by McGraw. With the one subtle exception noted above, *Everywhere*'s down-on-the-farm charm makes it a worthwhile option for fans of this genre.

Title: *All I Want* (1995)
Label: Curb
Genre: Country
Pro-Social Content: A man in love discovers manners and sacrifices bachelor pleasures for his girl ("I Like It, I Love It"). McGraw takes pride in his homespun values ("That's Just Me"). When tempted to be jealous, he trusts his attractive partner to resist the flirtatious advances of others ("She Never Lets It Go to Her Heart"). "The Great Divide" is a hopeful reminder that it takes two to restore a marriage ("They could still get back all the love they lost, but only if they both will reach across"), but . . .
Objectionable Content: . . . it rings hollow when McGraw himself abandons a relationship on "When She Wakes Up (And Finds Me Gone)."
Summary/Advisory: Overall, this disc applauds sound marriages, a solid work ethic, respect for parents, open communication and not-so-common courtesy. Concerns are minor. A bold, fun-loving follow-up to *Not a Moment Too Soon.*

Title: *Not a Moment Too Soon* (1994)
Label: Curb
Genre: Country
Pro-Social Content: McGraw affirms his woman's value on "Wouldn't Want It Any Other Way." The country chart-topper "Don't Take the Girl" speaks of a man's self-sacrifice when faced with losing his love to outside forces. The title track alludes to the saving power of love.
Objectionable Content: On "Refried Dreams," the artist admits to being "sick as a dog" and "shootin' tequila, wantin' to kill" the woman who left him. "Ain't That Just Like a Dream" recalls a wild young romance. Although not explicit, "Down on the Farm" alludes to drinking and sexual situations in the context of a rowdy tailgate party. A clever tribute to the blues tunes of George Strait is spoiled by dependence on a bottle in a bar ("Give It to Me Strait"). "It Doesn't Get Any Countrier Than This" winks approvingly at immodesty and premarital sex.
Summary/Advisory: This disc spent its first *three months* as a number-1 country album and several weeks atop the pop chart. Musically sound, but lyrically McGraw lives on the wild side, retreating into alcohol when times get hard.

McKennitt, Loreena

◆ ◆ ◆ ◆ ◆ ◆ ◆ ◆ ◆ ◆ ◆ ◆ ◆ ◆ ◆ ◆ ◆ ◆ ◆

This internationally respected artist was born and raised in Morden, Manitoba, a town of Irish, Scottish, German, and Icelandic peoples located in the Canadian prairies. McKennitt's rural upbringing gave way to significant travel and research into ancient tribes and Celtic traditions. She briefly studied veterinary sciences before dedicating herself to folk music. The self-managed singer and record company head (she is her label's only property) resides in Stratford, Ontario.

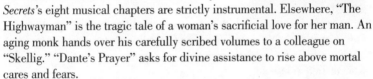

Title: *The Book of Secrets* (1997)
Label: Quinlan Road
Genre: New Age/Celtic/Adult contemporary
Pro-Social Content: Three of *The Book of Secrets*'s eight musical chapters are strictly instrumental. Elsewhere, "The Highwayman" is the tragic tale of a woman's sacrificial love for her man. An aging monk hands over his carefully scribed volumes to a colleague on "Skellig." "Dante's Prayer" asks for divine assistance to rise above mortal cares and fears.
Objectionable Content: Nothing in the lyrics. Unfortunately, McKennitt explains her music—and the theological hodgepodge that inspired it—in the liner notes. Her spiritualism ranges from Celtic origins and Sufiism (a blend of Islam and Eastern mysticism) to Christian gnosticism.
Summary/Advisory: A cross between Enya and Celine Dion, this gifted artist leans on classical literature and her own nomadic ponderings to capture a bygone era. Very pleasant listening. However, McKennitt's written allusions to ancient texts and spurious spiritualism will, for many families, taint the beauty of the music itself.

McKnight, Brian

◆ ◆ ◆ ◆ ◆ ◆ ◆ ◆ ◆ ◆ ◆ ◆ ◆ ◆ ◆ ◆ ◆ ◆ ◆

The youngest of five brothers, McKnight grew up singing gospel in his hometown of Buffalo, New York. He formed a jazz-fusion group at age 17 and signed a solo deal with Mercury Records at age 19. The artist may be best known for his chart-topping duet with Vanessa Williams, "Love Is."

Title: *Anytime* (1997)
Label: Mercury
Genre: R&B/Rap
Pro-Social Content: McKnight wishes to
reinvest in strained romantic relationships
("Show Me the Way Back to Your Heart," the
number-one hit "Anytime") and lobbies a
woman to give him a chance to treat her better

than her current boyfriend ("You Should Be Mine"). The artist
seems to value marriage as he considers a potential mate ("Could"). "When
the Chariot Comes Home" examines the brevity of life for the purpose of
turning listeners to the Lord ("Satan's a cheater, Christ is the teacher/And
life's the test . . . I gotta be ready when Jesus comes"). A great final cut!
Objectionable Content: McKnight is willing to pursue "lust or love"
("Hold Me") and repeats the expression "I'll be d—ned" ("Til I Get Over
You"). An ambiguous sexual proposition mars "Everytime We Say
Goodbye."
Summary/Advisory: While not nearly as explicit or troublesome as most
of his peers, McKnight's million-selling CD still has a few rough edges.
Families reluctant to work through them may want to introduce teens to the
music of Take 6 instead.

McLachlan, Sarah

◆ ◆

McLachlan launched the summer music festival known as Lilith Fair—the
two-stage, multi-artist bill featuring a host of female-fronted acts. Her 1997
disc, *Surfacing*, debuted at number 2 on the pop chart and led to two
Grammy awards.

Title: *Surfacing* (1997)
Label: Arista
Genre: Rock/Folk/Alternative
Pro-Social Content: "I Love You"
empathizes with a woman desperate to find the
words to tell her man how much she cares.
Pondering the nature of heaven, the singer longs
to be lifted "out of the darkness of doubt"
("Witness"). On "Angel," McLachlan seeks

sanctuary from the world's "vultures and thieves" in her man's embrace. Battling depression, she desperately pursues virtues that will elevate her to a better place ("Full of Grace").

Objectionable Content: McLachlan's use of the f-word is inexcusable as she speaks of a theologically confused lover (a man decked out in rasta clothing who sleeps with voodoo dolls) on the song "Building a Mystery." In addition, several lines weakened by vague contexts could be interpreted as anti-Christian.

Summary/Advisory: Known for giving fans a window into her occasionally tortured soul, McLachlan says of her early work, "It was almost as if I needed to be depressed to be creative." Not so here. The Canadian-born artist is generally upbeat. Even though most of these songs deal with unstable relationships, she manages to project a glass-is-half-full attitude. Unfortunately, a few caveats hold *Surfacing* under the threshold of acceptability.

Meat Loaf

◆ ◆

Born Marvin Lee Aday, Meat Loaf made his chart debut in 1971 and has sold more than 45 million albums. *Bat Out of Hell*, one of the most profitable albums ever recorded, is certified by the *Guinness Book of World Records* as the longest charting album in British pop music history. *Bat Out of Hell II: Back Into Hell* soared to number 1 on the pop chart within four weeks of its release. The album sold 12 million copies worldwide and earned Meat Loaf a Grammy.

Title: *Welcome to the Neighborhood* (1995)
Label: MCA
Genre: Rock
Pro-Social Content: The artist offers a romantic partner forgiveness on "Amnesty Is Granted." The obscure "Where Angels Sing" dreams of a virtuous place devoid of hate, pain, pity, spite, materialism, and hunger.
Objectionable Content: If Loaf-man really desires heaven, you'd never know it from songs like "Original Sin" which, bored with all the old vices, searches for new ones. His utopia consists of casual sex without precautions or consequences ("Where the Rubber Meets the Road"), specifically with an intoxicated Mexican prostitute ("Runnin' for the Red Light"). On "Left in the Dark," he

accuses his lover of being unfaithful and then demands sexual intimacy from her. The hit single "I'd Lie for You (And That's the Truth)" sends mixed messages about honesty. "45 Seconds of Ecstasy" is an ode to an orgasm.

Summary/Advisory: This Meat Loaf consists of half-baked sexual rock 'n' roll leftovers sure to give discerning teens spiritual indigestion. His *Neighborhood* is on the seedy side of town.

Title: *Bat Out of Hell II: Back Into Hell* (1993)
Label: MCA
Genre: Rock
Pro-Social Content: None
Objectionable Content: The number-1 radio single "I'll Do Anything for Love" promotes casual sex ("I'll never forgive myself if we don't go all the way tonight") and Mr. Loaf "pray[s] to the god of sex and drums and rock 'n' roll." Elsewhere, sex is a synonym for salvation and the "answer to every prayer" is a one-night stand. On "Wasted Youth," the singer screams about smashing his guitar "against the body of a varsity cheerleader" and refuses to ponder the meaning of life ("Forget the questions! Someone gimme another beer!"). This rebellious, self-destructive imagery not only flies in the face of biblical principles but also thumbs its nose at common sense.

Summary/Advisory: In 1978, *Bat Out of Hell* raced up the charts. With *Back Into Hell*, it's the same old rancid Meat Loaf heated up and dished out 15 years later. Leftovers like this we can do without.

Megadeth

◆◆◆◆◆◆◆◆◆◆◆◆◆◆◆◆◆◆◆◆◆

This California-based heavy-metal group was conceived in 1985 by one-time Metallica guitarist Dave Mustaine, Marty Friedman, Dave Ellefson, and Nick Menza. To date, the band has watched four of its albums sell more than 1 million copies each.

Title: *Youthanasia* (1994)
Label: Capitol
Genre: Heavy metal
Pro-Social Content: "Family Tree" explores the "living hell" endured by sexually abused children. "Addicted to Chaos" urges perseverance during difficult times.
Objectionable Content: The album cover

alone speaks volumes. Inside, another offensive photo depicts Jesus wearing what looks like a crown of worms and the band's T-shirt. "Reckoning Day" mocks those who would "beg salvation from the empty skies." This cut and "Train of Consequences" take pride in causing others pain. The muddled "Elysian Fields" blends biblical allusions with references to ancient mythology. The band expresses comfort in having "the devil by our side" on "Blood of Heroes." Two profanities further darken this project.

Summary/Advisory: One of the genre's most popular acts, Megadeth assaults decency and good taste once again on *Youthanasia*. Fans of this musical style should give CCM acts Michael Sweet, Bride, or Tamplin a listen.

Mellencamp, John

◆ ◆ ◆ ◆ ◆ ◆ ◆ ◆ ◆ ◆ ◆ ◆ ◆ ◆ ◆ ◆ ◆ ◆ ◆

John Mellencamp began recording for MCA in 1975. His biggest hit was "Jack & Diane," a teen-sex-in-the-heartland anthem that spent four weeks at number 1 in the summer of '82. This Indiana native has now sold more than 20 million records. Mellencamp also directed and starred in the 1992 movie *Falling from Grace.*

Title: *Human Wheels* (1993)
Label: Mercury
Genre: Rock
Pro-Social Content: "Case 795 (The Family)" uses a tragic Texas murder as evidence that our culture is suffering from deteriorating relationships in the home ("It's easy . . . to pretend that everything's all right with the family . . . the ruin of a nation lies at our feet"). Other songs explore the fleeting nature of possessions and the fallacy of valuing a man based on his clothing, appearance, or acquaintances.

Objectionable Content: John mocks salvation, self-control, and pure living, choosing debauchery on "When Jesus Left Birmingham." Other songs ("To the River" and "Junior") shed additional light on his misguided theology. Also, his MTV video for the title track combines deviant sexuality with an all-American picnic scene.

Summary/Advisory: With the release of *Human Wheels*, the cat's out of the bag—and the name. Formerly John "Cougar" Mellencamp, this artist continues to speak to the blue-collar crowd. Unfortunately, some positive themes are clouded by an anti-Christian worldview.

Merchant, Natalie

◆ ◆ ◆ ◆ ◆ ◆ ◆ ◆ ◆ ◆ ◆ ◆ ◆ ◆ ◆ ◆ ◆ ◆ ◆ ◆

Before going solo, Merchant recorded six albums with the New York-based band 10,000 Maniacs (1981–83). *Tigerlily* sold more than 2 million copies.

Title: *Tigerlily* (1995)
Label: Elektra
Genre: Mellow Alternative
Pro-Social Content: Merchant warns an aspiring actress of Hollywood's fickle nature on "San Andreas Fault" ("O promised land, O wicked ground, build a dream and tear it down"). On the touching "Beloved Wife," a man mourns the death of his partner of 50 years. "Cowboy Romance" uses a slice-of-life tale to denounce one-night stands. A miracle child is gifted with love, patience, and faith—all presented as virtues ("Wonder"). Listeners will also find several references to prayer.
Objectionable Content: "Seven Years" curses a betrayer, refusing to forgive. A glowing, grieving tribute to River Phoenix ("River") glosses over the drug abuse that killed him.
Summary/Advisory: This is Merchant's first solo project. With very minor exceptions, it's a good one. While she sings about sleepless nights, unrequited love, and the pain of losing a spouse, she doesn't wallow in despair. (SEE ALSO: 10,000 Maniacs)

Metallica

◆ ◆ ◆ ◆ ◆ ◆ ◆ ◆ ◆ ◆ ◆ ◆ ◆ ◆ ◆ ◆ ◆ ◆ ◆ ◆

Metallica was formed in 1982 by James Hetfield, Lars Ulrich, Kirk Hammett, and Jason Newsted. The band won three consecutive Grammys between 1989 and 1991. A favorite act of MTV's animated slackers Beavis and Butt-head, Metallica has sold more than 30 million albums over the past 16 years, including the number-1 debuts *Load* and *Reload*.

Title: *Reload* (1997)
Label: Elektra
Genre: Metal

Pro-Social Content: The band testifies to the vanity and emptiness of fame ("The Memory Remains") and urges an innocent individual to impact this troubled world ("Where the Wild Things Are").

Objectionable Content: "Better Than You" is wholly consumed by covetous pride and one-upmanship. On "Fixxxer," the vocalist ponders the power of voodoo and reaches hopelessly for inner healing. Though he appears to be speaking figuratively, his desire to "kill" someone on "Attitude" lingers like a bad aftertaste. On a song sung from Satan's perspective, the band invites young fans to join in the "Devil's Dance" ("Let me make your mind, leave yourself behind/Be not afraid/I've got what you need, hunger I will feed"). An embittered "Fuel" includes the line, "F—- 'em, man." Amidst growling and yelling, the central figure on "Prince Charming" claims to be the source of pain, suffering, isolation, addiction, murder, and suicide. Several tracks allude to drug use.

Summary/Advisory: This angry, edgy band still has enough fan support to debut at number 1. Unfortunately, *Reload* once again fills the chamber with musical shells of dark, despairing torment.

Title: *Load* (1996)
Label: Elektra
Genre: Heavy metal
Pro-Social Content: Who is being addressed is unclear, but "The Thorn Within" seeks forgiveness for sins from someone called "Father." "King Nothing" alludes to the emptiness of fame.

Objectionable Content: A tormented mixture of depression and demons haunts this band ("The House That Jack Built," "Until It Sleeps," "Bleeding Me"). Elsewhere, lyrics promote emotional isolation ("Hero of the Day"), self-pity and agony ("Poor Twisted Me"), and bitter self-loathing ("Wasting My Hate"). After nearly 79 minutes of such obsessive moaning, some listeners might volunteer to put the band out of its misery.

Summary/Advisory: Metallica's last studio album, a self-titled disc, sold more than 9 million copies. More of the same this time. Grinding guitars and growled vocals give oppressive personality to dark, hopeless lyrics that molest the psyche. With minor exceptions, this *Load* should have been left at the curb on trash day.

Michael, George

◆ ◆ ◆ ◆ ◆ ◆ ◆ ◆ ◆ ◆ ◆ ◆ ◆ ◆ ◆ ◆ ◆ ◆ ◆

George Michael was originally one-half of the '80s pop duo Wham! He has sold 60 million records worldwide, notched six U.S. number-1 singles, nine British number-1 singles, and five number-1 albums. In 1998, Michael was "arrested after performing a 'lewd act' in front of an undercover cop in a well-known gay hang-out" [*Newsweek*, 4/20/98], an event that led him to publicly declare his homosexuality.

Title: *Older* (1996)
Label: DreamWorks
Genre: Pop
Pro-Social Content: Michael demonstrates "tough love" on "Spinning the Wheel" as he walks out on an adulterous partner. Later, he lays aside painful relational failures and confidently presses forward ("Move On"). "To Be Forgiven" sounds like a prayer for purpose, direction, and self-control. Celebrity is portrayed as a shallow addiction on "Star Power."
Objectionable Content: While acknowledging that Christ's sweet love for children is praiseworthy, it seems shadowy here as it is equated with a lover's physical passion ("Jesus to a Child"). Michael beckons a lover to have sex ("The Strangest Thing") and uses strong profanity on two songs. The most sexually irresponsible tune is the hit single "Fastlove," which follows the exploits of a man who prefers casual sex to commitment ("My friends got their ladies/They're all havin' babies/But I just want to have some fun").
Summary/Advisory: George Michael is the guy who sang the crude come-on "I Want Your Sex" in 1987. This effort is *Older*, but there's no indication its creator is any wiser.

Mighty Mighty Bosstones, The

◆ ◆ ◆ ◆ ◆ ◆ ◆ ◆ ◆ ◆ ◆ ◆ ◆ ◆ ◆ ◆ ◆ ◆ ◆

Eight individuals make up this ska band: Dicky Barrett, Joe Sirois, Dennis Brochenborough, Nate Albert, Tim Burton, Ben Carr, Kevin Lenear, and Joe Gittleman. Their fifth album, *Let's Face It*, sold more than a million copies.

Title: *Let's Face It* (1997)
Label: Big Rig/Mercury
Genre: Punk rock/Ska
Pro-Social Content: Strong anti-drug lyrics
are central to "Royal Oil" ("When you smoke
or poke the poison, you lose the chance to be
tomorrow"). "Nevermind Me" finds the victim
of a holdup mourning for the drug addict who
robbed him. Gang violence leads to murder, which leads to
prison on the cautionary tale "Numbered Days." Fed up with society's
scandals and lies, "Desensitized" longs for truth. "Noise Brigade" values
higher education and learning a trade. The title song condemns racial
hatred, sexism, and bigotry . . .
Objectionable Content: . . . but it also seems to sanction homosexuality
by urging listeners to tolerate others' "preferences." "That Bug Bit Me"
includes one use of the word *sh—*. "Another Drinkin' Song" condemns
drunkenness, but only after a first-person diatribe that seems to revere it.
Summary/Advisory: This band has a good heart. Sadly, its lyrical execution leaves something to be desired. Not a terrible disc, but The Insyderz or
Supertones are better ska options.

Montgomery, John Michael

◆ ◆

John Michael Montgomery's *Life's a Dance*
(1992) sold more than 2 million copies, while
Kickin' It Up (1994) went triple platinum.
Among his many hit singles, "I Swear" (an
R&B success for All-4-One) picked up a
Grammy in 1994.

Title: *John Michael Montgomery* (1995)
Label: Atlantic
Genre: Country
Pro-Social Content: The smash single "I Can Love You Like That" as
well as "Long As I Live" pledge undying romantic love. The latter also
recognizes that every day is a gift from God ("Til the Lord says it's time to
go with him, I'm yours as long as I live"). On "No Man's Land," a once-
married working mother of three courageously handles the pressures of

single parenthood. A high school sweetheart's ongoing commitment earns praise on "High School Heart." Though it fails to mention God by name, "Heaven Sent Me You" credits "someone up there" with sending a loving partner. "It's What I Am" recalls a father's advice ("He said work hard and let the good Lord do the rest").

Objectionable Content: "Cowboy Love" invites a stranger to share "some southern homemade wine" and "lovemakin'."

Summary/Advisory: This self-titled project features a nice blend of bouncy backroad melodies and tender ballads. With the one noted exception, a good effort.

Title: *Kickin' It Up* (1994)
Label: Atlantic
Genre: Country
Pro-Social Content: Several of JMM's songs pay tribute to marriage ("She Don't Need a Band to Dance," "Oh, How She Shines," the hit single "I Swear"). Refreshing lyrics focus on the character of the woman in his life rather than on her physical attributes. A recurring theme finds him grateful for her encouragement and faith in his abilities despite his own doubts. "If You've Got Love" claims that anything is possible with love, even standing "your ground when the devil's at your door." On "Oh, How She Shines," he honors his mate, positively comparing her to an old flame.

Objectionable Content: "Friday at Five" talks of partying away a week that's "been hell" with a "girl on my arm and a beer in my hand." The lust of the eyes and romantic urges take control on "Be My Baby Tonight."

Summary/Advisory: Montgomery's take on marriage and devotion are terrific. But the weekend recreation he advocates keeps *Kickin' It Up* from getting a thumbs-up.

Morissette, Alanis

◆ ◆ ◆ ◆ ◆ ◆ ◆ ◆ ◆ ◆ ◆ ◆ ◆ ◆ ◆ ◆ ◆ ◆ ◆

Morissette, a native of Canada, began writing songs and made her recording debut at the age of nine. Her debut album, *Jagged Little Pill*, earned four Grammys and five Canadian Juno awards. The album sold more than 15 million copies.

Title: *Jagged Little Pill* (1995)
Label: Maverick/Reprise
Genre: Alternative

Pro-Social Content: On "All I Really Want," Morissette longs for peace, patience, and calm. The love song "Head Over Feet" thanks a friend for his manners, love, and devotion.
Objectionable Content: On "You Oughta Know," the artist uses the f-word while cursing a lover who left her for another. Other profanities appear on "Right Through You" (a tune in which Alanis mention's her date's desire for alcohol and oral sex) and "Hand in My Pocket," which claims no one knows the meaning of life. Catholic-bashing takes center stage throughout "Forgiven."
Summary/Advisory: *Rolling Stone* [11/2/95] described this album as "uncensored documentation of her psychosexual former-Catholic-girl torments." A musical hybrid of The Cranberries and Sinead O'Connor, Alanis Morissette trades mostly on cynicism and angst, making this bitter *Pill* hard to swallow. Prescription: Skip it.

Morrison, Van

◆ ◆ ◆ ◆ ◆ ◆ ◆ ◆ ◆ ◆ ◆ ◆ ◆ ◆ ◆ ◆ ◆ ◆ ◆

This Irish folk/rock artist was born George Ivan in 1945. He began his solo career in the late '60s. Known for hit singles such as "Brown-Eyed Girl" and "Gloria," Morrison was inducted into the Rock 'n' Roll Hall of Fame in 1993. He was also the leader of the rock band Them.

Title: *Too Long in Exile* (1993)
Label: Polydor
Genre: Rock/Blues
Pro-Social Content: "Till We Get the Healing Done" acknowledges that life is guided by divine purpose. It speaks of sowing, reaping, giving thanks, and spending eternity with God. The artist repents of past mistakes and rejects foolish living on "Wasted Years." Elsewhere, he says to "look up and see your maker before Gabriel blows his horn." "Ball and Chain" expresses romantic love and commitment.
Objectionable Content: On one cut, self-control is deemed impossible due to the sway of a female. Van joins John Lee Hooker to reprise the

'60s hit about an insatiable woman named "Gloria." Also, although it attempts to convey spiritual truth, the album's theology is questionable at times.

Summary/Advisory: Soulful, energetic tunes mix godly themes with raging hormones, resulting in tainted truth. *Exile* this disc; teens can do better.

Nas

◆ ◆

The first release by native New Yorker Nasir Jones (known to his friends and fans as Nas or Nasty Nas) was 1994's *Illmatic*.

Title: *It Was Written* (1996)
Label: Columbia
Genre: Gangsta rap
Pro-Social Content: None
Objectionable Content: Variations on the f-word get quite a workout, making the warning sticker more than justified. The hit "If I Ruled the World" envisions a planet under Nas's control—no rules, plenty of drugs and condomless sex, and all prisoners set free. Lewd references to oral sex ("Shootouts," "Street Dreams") and other casual encounters appear throughout, peppered with salacious slang. Numerous cuts glorify getting drunk and high. Drugs of choice include cocaine, marijuana, heroin, PCP, and hashish. Tracks place faith in Islamic doctrines and leaders ("Album Intro," "Nas Is Coming"). On "Shootouts," the gang kills a policeman and a woman who betrayed them. The artist's conclusion is that "every day crime pays" ("Live N-gga Rap").

Summary/Advisory: This number-1 debut disc spent its first month atop the pop and R&B charts. Amid a flurry of expletives, Nasir Jones promotes drug use, gang violence, misogynistic sex, cop-killing, and related vices. Nas-ty stuff. *It Was Written* that teens should avoid this sleaze (Psalm 101:3, Philippians 4:8).

Naughty By Nature

◆ ◆ ◆ ◆ ◆ ◆ ◆ ◆ ◆ ◆ ◆ ◆ ◆ ◆ ◆ ◆ ◆ ◆ ◆

Naughty By Nature is Vinnie, Treach, and Kay Gee. The group picked up a Grammy in 1992. NBN's first two albums sold more than a million copies each.

Title: *Poverty's Paradise* (1995)
Label: Tommy Boy
Genre: Rap
Pro-Social Content: "Shout Out" thanks the band's friends and supporters in the media.
Objectionable Content: Violence, drugs, sexual perversion, misogyny, lewd urban slang, and graphic scatological references abound. Gun-

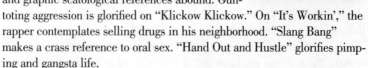

toting aggression is glorified on "Klickow Klickow." On "It's Workin'," the rapper contemplates selling drugs in his neighborhood. "Slang Bang" makes a crass reference to oral sex. "Hand Out and Hustle" glorifies pimping and gangsta life.
Summary/Advisory: These guys have sold millions of albums (this one went to number 1 on the R&B chart) and won several awards, including a Grammy. Stickered for explicit content, this sleazy project is a fool's *Paradise*.

Title: *19 Naughty III* (1993)
Label: Tommy Boy
Genre: Gangsta Rap
Pro-Social Content: None
Objectionable Content: Multiple partners and oral sex are encouraged on "Cruddy Clique" ("f— any b—ch who can hang out with a cruddy clique"). "Knock Em Out Da Box" conveys disrespect for the home ("f— your family!") and rallies new recruits for gang violence ("follow in my footsteps . . . my goal is disaster"). "The Hood Comes First" and "Sleepin' on Jersey" inspire loyalty to friends, but at the expense of others, including police and politicians.
Summary/Advisory: Profanity pervades this tribute to rebellion, gangsta violence, and sexual misconduct. This number-1 R&B disc differs very little from the group's self-titled debut, which sold more than a million copies. Awful stuff that can only benefit society as *landfill*.

Neil, Vince

◆ ◆ ◆ ◆ ◆ ◆ ◆ ◆ ◆ ◆ ◆ ◆ ◆ ◆ ◆ ◆ ◆ ◆ ◆ ◆

Lead singer of the pop metal act Mötley Crüe, Neil went solo in 1993, only to return to his old band several years later.

Title: *Exposed* (1993)
Label: Warner Bros.
Genre: Hard rock
Pro-Social Content: Not much. "Can't Have Your Cake" recalls Mom's advice to "stand tall" and "live your life by the golden rule." "Forever" is a love song written to Neil's wife (before she filed for divorce).
Objectionable Content: "Sister of Pain" features a woman squealing in ecstasy as Neil talks of sadomasochistic sex with a minister's daughter. Hormones rage on with "Fine, Fine Wine." Murder is glorified on "The Edge" and "Look in Her Eyes" ("You can feel excitement in your veins . . . the thrill, the kill, and you know that it is over"). Other themes include prostitution, marijuana use, and sentiments about being "better off dead."
Summary/Advisory: Neil's screaming vocals and wailing guitars underscore equally grating messages. Don't be *Exposed*.

Neville, Aaron

◆ ◆ ◆ ◆ ◆ ◆ ◆ ◆ ◆ ◆ ◆ ◆ ◆ ◆ ◆ ◆ ◆ ◆ ◆ ◆

Aaron Neville is the youngest of three siblings who comprised the classic New Orleans, Louisiana, family group, The Neville Brothers.

Title: *The Grand Tour* (1993)
Label: A&M
Genre: Adult contemporary
Pro-Social Content: Neville clearly conveys a concern for others, devotion to God, and commitment to family. He expresses appreciation to his stagehands on "The Roadie Song," honors the woman in his life with "I Owe You One," and expresses love to his brother on "My Brother, My Brother." A remake of The

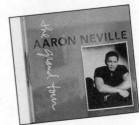

Stylistics's 1972 hit "Betcha by Golly, Wow" focuses on enduring love. The disc concludes with a beautiful rendition of "The Lord's Prayer."
Objectionable Content: None
Summary/Advisory: A winning combination of musical genres, including Motown, country, and '50s rock 'n' roll, make *The Grand Tour* worth taking. But it's Neville's honest, soulful lyrics that really set this album apart.

New Edition

◆ ◆ ◆ ◆ ◆ ◆ ◆ ◆ ◆ ◆ ◆ ◆ ◆ ◆ ◆ ◆ ◆ ◆ ◆ ◆

New Edition began in 1983 with Ronnie DeVoe, Bobby Brown, Ricky Bell, Mike Bevins, and Ralph Tresvant. Johnny Gill joined the group in 1986 at the age of 16.

Title: *Home Again* (1996)
Label: MCA
Genre: R&B/Hip-hop
Pro-Social Content: "Try Again," "I'm Still in Love with You," and "One More Day" all desire relational reconciliation. "Thank You (The J.G. Interlude)" is a gospel tune thanking God for His protection, blessing, and peace.
Objectionable Content: These jet-setters brag about a high-rollin' night on the town filled with gambling and drinking ("Oh Yeah, It Feels So Good"). The popular single "Hit Me Off" is one long sexual proposition. On "How Do You Like Your Love Served," the singers use innuendo to ask a woman her preferred sexual positions and activities. "Shop Around" promotes sex with multiple partners ("A man's got to do every woman he can 'cause it's in our nature") while reducing courtship to hormonally charged browsing.
Summary/Advisory: The disc's velvety vocals and urban grooves sound great. Too bad New Edition's few positive themes get lost amid silver-tongued advances and lewd prowling. Wise families will run away from *Home*. (SEE ALSO: LSG)

Next

◆ ◆ ◆ ◆ ◆ ◆ ◆ ◆ ◆ ◆ ◆ ◆ ◆ ◆ ◆ ◆ ◆ ◆ ◆

Hailing from Minnesota's Twin Cities, Next is a male R&B trio whose members go by the nicknames R.L., T-Low, and Tweety (the latter two are brothers). This group began rehearsing in the home of T-Low's godmother, Sounds of Blackness lead singer Ann Nesby, who trained and managed the group for a while. The act eventually signed with Arista Records' Divine Mill label, owned by Kay Gee of the rap group Naughty By Nature.

Title: *Rated Next* (1998)
Label: Arista
Genre: R&B/Rap
Pro-Social Content: "You Are My High" honors a partner for strength and inspiration, and "I Still Love You" pledges lasting devotion.
Objectionable Content: These guys are *obsessed* with sex. They croon obscene propositions and offer play-by-play analysis of intercourse and oral sex in terms much too explicit to repeat here.
"Penetration," a song performed with the group Naughty By Nature, uses the f-word to describe a sexual escapade featuring a ménage à trois and bondage. Some titles, such as "Phone Sex," pretty much say it all: "Just imagine that it's me inside . . . Scream as loud as you want." "Stop, Drop & Roll" asks a woman for "some in and out" and "freakin'." On "Taste So Good," the singer describes oral sex. Verbal foreplay on "Next Experience," a duet with Adina Howard, also alludes to phone sex and oral sex. "Cozy" adds alcohol to the mix. Sexual infidelity is central to "Problems" and "Sexitude," while the platinum single "Butta Love" talks of "enticing thighs" and erections.
Summary/Advisory: *Rated Next is* nothing short of audio pornography. A couple love songs can't redeem more than 70 minutes of wanton ruttishness. Believe it or not, in the CD's liner notes these guys have the unmitigated temerity to credit "God" and "Jesus Christ" with inspiring this dreck. Families should pass on Next.

Nine Inch Nails

◆ ◆ ◆ ◆ ◆ ◆ ◆ ◆ ◆ ◆ ◆ ◆ ◆ ◆ ◆ ◆ ◆ ◆

NIN is a one-man industrial rock act created by Trent Reznor. Known for his depressingly nihilistic image and music, Reznor was quoted in *Rolling Stone* [3/6/97] as saying, "I think my music's more disturbing than Tupac's—or at least I thought some of the themes of *The Downward Spiral* were more disturbing on a deeper level—you know, issues about suicide and hating yourself and God and people and everything else." Reznor has sold more than 5 million records and contributed dreary music to a number of gothic film soundtracks.

Title: *The Downward Spiral* (1994)
Label: Interscope/Atlantic
Genre: Industrial
Pro-Social Content: None
Objectionable Content: This disc is obscenely mean-spirited. A man holds a gun to a woman's head and demands oral sex ("Big Man with a Gun"), saying he may kill her anyway, just for kicks. On "Closer," lead singer Trent Reznor rants, "I want to f— you like an animal/I want to feel you from the inside . . . My whole existence is flawed/You get me closer to God." He refers to a female as his "precious whore" ("Reptile") and viciously attacks Christianity ("Heresy," "Mr. Self Destruct"). Sentiments such as "Find you, taste you, f— you, use you, scar you, break you" pass for sweet nothings on "Eraser." This disc is strewn with obscenities. The title cut promotes suicide as a means of solving one's woes ("He put the gun into his face/Bang!/So much blood for such a tiny little hole/Problems have solutions/A lifetime of f—ing things up fixed in one determined flash"). Truly awful stuff.

Summary/Advisory: In *Spin* magazine [2/96], Trent Reznor admitted, "I think *The Downward Spiral* actually could be harmful, through implying and subliminally suggesting things." He's right. Anyone connected with this hateful sewage should be ashamed. So should the millions of young fans who bought copies. Pray that your teen isn't one of them.

Title: *Broken* (1992)
Label: Interscope/Atlantic
Genre: Industrial/Alternative metal
Pro-Social Content: "Slave Screams" accurately comprehends the phoniness of conformity for conformity's sake.
Objectionable Content: Trent Reznor's despair is not merely an unimpassioned commentary on the state of youth. It's real, personal hopelessness that says there's "nothing more f—-ed up" than "putting faith in god [*sic*]." Ultimately, he concludes that momentary hedonistic escape ("let me inside of you . . . this is for right now") on "Last" or self-hatred ("gonna smash myself") on "Gave Up" are preferable to unbearable angst.
Summary/Advisory: Nine Inch Nails is part of the "industrial" movement, which typically relies on the metal-tinged, sample-laden dance music often associated with underground clubs. This expletive-filled, angry music could lead some young fans to self-destructive ends. A very poor choice.

Nirvana

◆ ◆ ◆ ◆ ◆ ◆ ◆ ◆ ◆ ◆ ◆ ◆ ◆ ◆ ◆ ◆ ◆ ◆ ◆ ◆

This grunge act, fronted by lead singer and cultural icon Kurt Cobain, sold more than 22 million albums. Cobain (who wed Courtney Love, leader of the band Hole) committed suicide in April 1994. The surviving members of the trio, Chris Novoselic and Dave Grohl (who went on to form Foo Fighters), elected to dissolve Nirvana. *Kurt and Courtney*, a 1998 documentary by Nick Broomfield, chronicles Cobain's tragic life and death.

Title: *In Utero* (1993)
Label: Geffen
Genre: Grunge rock
Pro-Social Content: None
Objectionable Content: The boys from Seattle recommend getting high and ending up with a hangover on the appropriately titled "Dumb." Worse yet, "Rape Me" is destined to be an accessory in violent crimes against women by suggesting that they enjoy being sexually assaulted—repeatedly ("Rape me my friend . . . hate me, do it and do it again"). Tongue in cheek? Hard to tell. Other dangerous messages involve hating enemies, committing suicide ("Milk It"), and the normalcy of homosexuality ("All Apologies").

Obscene and grotesque references appear throughout.
Summary/Advisory: *In Utero* is noxious noise with no redeeming value.
Kmart and Wal-Mart even refused to stock it. The band's bassist was
quoted as saying, "I'm just waiting for some right-wing Christian group to
deem the record satanic. That would really move some units." (SEE ALSO:
Foo Fighters)

No Doubt

◆ ◆ ◆ ◆ ◆ ◆ ◆ ◆ ◆ ◆ ◆ ◆ ◆ ◆ ◆ ◆ ◆ ◆ ◆ ◆

Originally formed in 1987 as a punk/ska band in
Anaheim, California, No Doubt is comprised of Tom Dumont, Gwen Stefani,
Adrian Young, and Tony Kanal. Lead singer
Stefani has been known to shock audiences
by shouting obscenities from stage. For example, when performing "I'm Just a Girl," she
frequently leads female concert-goers in the
singing of the chorus as "F—- you. I'm just a
girl."

Title: *Tragic Kingdom* (1996)
Label: Trauma
Genre: Pop/Rock
Pro-Social Content: Perseverance in the quest to achieve lofty goals
("The Climb") and maintaining a healthy self-image through uncomfortable
adolescent years ("Sixteen") are among the project's more optimistic cuts.
The ability of common folks to do uncommon things and leave a mark on
their world is the focus of "Different People" ("You don't have to be a
famous person . . . A mother can be an inspiration to her little son").
Objectionable Content: The singer takes a cynical view of marriage,
throwing a wet blanket on a bride's hopes for happiness ("Hey You"). She
lets loneliness and a lack of self-respect lead her to grovel for a man's affection on the contextually vague "Excuse Me Mr."
Summary/Advisory: An interesting blend of musical influences escorts
lead singer Gwen Stefani—passion oozing from the confident cry in her
voice—through *Tragic Kingdom*'s 14 tracks. Noted exceptions aside, No
Doubt delivers a generally upbeat and worthwhile release.

Notorious B.I.G.

◆ ◆ ◆ ◆ ◆ ◆ ◆ ◆ ◆ ◆ ◆ ◆ ◆ ◆ ◆ ◆ ◆ ◆ ◆ ◆

Brooklyn-born Christopher Wallace, better known to music fans as gangsta rapper Notorious B.I.G. (a.k.a. Biggie Smalls), released his first album in 1994 *(Ready to Die)*. His messages proved to be prophetic. Wallace, a one-time crack dealer, was gunned down on March 9, 1997 in a gang-related drive-by shooting.

Title: *Life After Death* (1997)
Label: Jive
Genre: Gangsta rap
Pro-Social Content: None
Objectionable Content: Smalls sentimentalizes his crack-dealing youth on "Miss U," while "Ten Crack Commandments" provides a how-to guide for peddling cocaine. He promotes drug use (mainly marijuana and cocaine) throughout. Perverse sexuality is a recurring theme as well. Amid a strafing of obscenities, the artist talks of oral sex ("Another," "Goin' Back to Cali"), vicious group sex ("Kick in the Door," "The World Is Filled"), and boasts of abusiveness ("F—— You Tonight"). Bloody gangsta violence flows from nearly a dozen cuts. "N-ggas Bleed" says, "I saw her brains hit the floor . . . shot the chick in the breast/She cryin', head shots put her to rest." The line "baptize rap guys with the Holy Ghost" means blowing away rival musicians on "Long Kiss Goodnight." Vile from beginning to end.

Summary/Advisory: Debuting at number 1, this posthumous double disc by B.I.G. sold nearly 700,000 copies its first week and more than 6 million overall. *Life After Death* provides a shameful epitaph to a sad, squandered existence. Furthermore, following his murder, an unnamed music industry source told *USA Today* [3/10/97], "People might think this is one more nail in [rap's] coffin, but what it does for the kids involved in gangsta rap is it makes it even more attractive." May it not be so in your home.

Oasis

◆ ◆ ◆ ◆ ◆ ◆ ◆ ◆ ◆ ◆ ◆ ◆ ◆ ◆ ◆ ◆ ◆ ◆ ◆ ◆

Oasis, from Manchester, England, is brothers Liam and Noel Gallagher, along with Paul Arthur, Paul McGuigan, and Tony McCarroll. The band enjoys an enormous following, having sold more than 20 million albums.

Title: *Be Here Now* (1997)
Label: Epic
Genre: Rock

Pro-Social Content: The singer encourages listeners to "believe in life" ("D'You Know What I Mean"), look toward a brighter future ("It's Gettin' Better Man"), and share their optimism with others ("All Around the World"). Though the band is unsure how to address the God of creation, they acknowledge His existence ("D'You Know What I Mean," "My Big Mouth"). Frontman Noel Gallagher wants to "make things right" in the wake of relational discord ("Don't Go Away") and admits he has "a lot of things to learn" about life ("Stand By Me"). Generally, uplifting messages.

Objectionable Content: Profanity mars "Be Here Now," "The Girl in the Dirty Shirt," and "Don't Go Away." The otherwise upbeat "All Around the World" tells someone, "If you're lost at sea, I hope that you've drowned."

Summary/Advisory: This amazingly popular band has shown steady improvement over its last few projects. *Be Here Now* is an optimistic step up. However, Gallagher and the boys still have room for growth, both in their lyrics and in their vain, boldly rebellious lifestyle, which has been well documented in the mainstream press.

Title: *(What's the Story) Morning Glory?* (1995)
Label: Epic
Genre: Rock

Pro-Social Content: "Don't Look Back in Anger" points out the destructiveness of bottled-up anger, and that material things will fade away. Other tracks ("Some Might Say," "Cast No Shadow," "Hey Now!") are thought-provokingly philosophical, but fail to offer real answers to life's questions.

Objectionable Content: The singer looks forward to getting drunk and high on "Champagne Supernova" (not surprising considering the songwriter's creative formula of "me and a guitar and a bottle of Jack Daniels" [*USA Today*, 2/24/95]). A profanity mars "Hello." "Roll with It" advises against self-sacrifice ("don't ever be denied . . . don't let anybody get in your way . . . don't ever stand aside").

Summary/Advisory: It's an improvement over the band's last album, *Definitely Maybe*, but these British rockers still need to make changes, lyrically. In addition, their concerts and private lives have been characterized by much-publicized arrogance and excursions into vice. What's the story? Oasis needs to clean up its act.

Title: *Definitely Maybe* (1994)
Label: Epic
Genre: Rock
Pro-Social Content: A few isolated lines could be interpreted positively, but that's about it.
Objectionable Content: The sarcastic "Up in the Sky" shows no sympathy for someone who's hurting ("I heard the shine's gone out of your life/Well that's just too bad/Welcome to my world"). But apathy may be better than the solutions they offer. "Cigarettes and Alcohol" devalues gainful employment while suggesting that the substances mentioned in the title are all one needs in life. The tune also alludes to drug use. There's more drinking on "Supersonic," which drones "give me gin and tonic." A spirit of spitefulness and one thinly disguised profanity mar "Married with Children."
Summary/Advisory: Hyped as the hottest British rock band since The Beatles, Oasis is proud of its irreverent debauchery. There's no doubt teens should skip *Definitely Maybe*.

Offspring, The
◆ ◆ ◆ ◆ ◆ ◆ ◆ ◆ ◆ ◆ ◆ ◆ ◆ ◆ ◆ ◆ ◆ ◆ ◆ ◆

The Offspring is Bryan "Dexter" Holland, Ron Welty, Kevin Wasserman, and Greg Kriesel. In 1994, their breakthrough single "Come Out and Play" and pop hit "Self-Esteem" helped make their third album, *Smash*, the best selling independent record of all time (9 million plus).

Title: *Ixnay on the Hombre* (1997)
Label: Columbia
Genre: Punk rock
Pro-Social Content: "Gone Away" mourns the death of a loved one.
Objectionable Content: From its sarcastic opening "Disclaimer" (which

mocks the notion of parental discretion), this obscenity-strewn album plummets toward punk-rock bottom. The artist spends all day in bed bingeing on wine and oral sex on "Me & My Old Lady." "Mota" promotes marijuana use and driving under the influence. Anti-authority anthems ("I Choose," "All I Want") encourage teens to rebel. Before claiming "I'm only happy when I'm in my misery," "Cool to Hate" lashes out against teachers, jocks, cheerleaders, and school in general (a hypocritical and insincere disrespect for education, considering the lead singer is working on a Ph.D. in microbiology). "Amazed" and "Way Down the Line" convey hopelessness, the latter assuring young listeners, "You'll f—- up just like your parents did."

Summary/Advisory: This follow-up to the record-breaking *Smash* is one bad *Hombre*. Take the facetious warning of "Disclaimer" seriously and "just don't listen to it."

Title: *Smash* (1994)
Label: Epitaph
Genre: Alternative/New wave
Pro-Social Content: "What Happened to You?" condemns a drug user for self-destructive insensitivity. "Come Out and Play" seems to condemn gangs and guns; however . . .
Objectionable Content: . . . the singer awaits a chance to gun down rude drivers on "Bad Habit" ("I open the glove box, reach inside; I'm gonna wreck this f—-er's ride"). Other cuts wallow in despair and dis-illusionment ("Self Esteem," "Something to Believe In," "Nitro," "Not the One"). "Self Esteem" alludes to a girlfriend's alcohol abuse and sexual appetite ("Late at night she knocks on my door, drunk again and she's lookin' to score"). Shouting the sentiments "Kill! Rape! Die!" at the end of "So Alone" ruins an otherwise neutral song. Hateful obscenities make regular appearances.
Summary/Advisory: Inconsistent at best, this disc deserves to be *Smash*ed (in the interest of family harmony, it may be wise to *discuss* the album's problems with your teen before taking a sledgehammer to it). If it hasn't already invaded your home, skip it.

O'Neal, Shaquille

◆ ◆

Shaquille O'Neal was chosen as the first pick in the 1992 NBA draft by the Orlando Magic. After four seasons with Orlando, he signed a seven-year, $150 million contract with the Los Angeles Lakers. Music is strictly a "moonlighting" gig for this sports superstar, who also dabbles in roles for the big screen. His films include *Blue Chips*, *Kazaam*, and *Steel*.

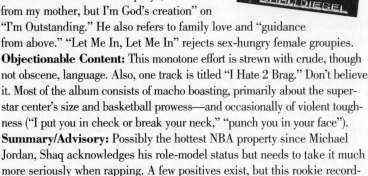

Title: *Shaq Diesel* (1993)
Label: Jive
Genre: Rap
Pro-Social Content: Shaq says, "I'm born from my mother, but I'm God's creation" on "I'm Outstanding." He also refers to family love and "guidance from above." "Let Me In, Let Me In" rejects sex-hungry female groupies.
Objectionable Content: This monotone effort is strewn with crude, though not obscene, language. Also, one track is titled "I Hate 2 Brag." Don't believe it. Most of the album consists of macho boasting, primarily about the superstar center's size and basketball prowess—and occasionally of violent toughness ("I put you in check or break your neck," "punch you in your face").
Summary/Advisory: Possibly the hottest NBA property since Michael Jordan, Shaq acknowledges his role-model status but needs to take it much more seriously when rapping. A few positives exist, but this rookie recording effort travels out of bounds.

Osborne, Joan

◆ ◆

A native of Anchorage, Kentucky, Osborne began her singing career at a neighborhood bar. She released her first album, *Soul Show*, in 1992. Whan asked by *Details* magazine [May, 1996] what drugs have taught her, Osborne replied, "Definitely a good thing. Certainly the hallucinogens I've taken have helped me get over the idea of being Miss Perfect."

Title: *Relish* (1995)

Label: Mercury
Genre: Folk/Alternative
Pro-Social Content: "Crazy Baby" shows compassion for a close friend struggling with unnamed emotional problems. "One of Us" croons "God is great/God is good."
Objectionable Content: That same contagious hit song also perceives coming "face-to-face" with God as a negative if it means "having to believe in heaven, Jesus, the saints and all the prophets." Spiritually confused at best, *Relish* also contains grim, moping tunes like "Dracula Moon," "Let's Just Get Naked," and others that endorse escaping into sex and drugs. Mild profanity punctuates these dreary themes.
Summary/Advisory: Osborne's vocal interpretation of her often obscure poetry drips with attitude and angst. In her press bio she says, "Sexuality and spirituality are so closely related that to me, it's not a contradiction . . . to put the two right next to each other in the same song." What god is *she* worshipping? Teens tempted to spice up their music collections should save their money and hold the *Relish*.

Overstreet, Paul

◆ ◆ ◆ ◆ ◆ ◆ ◆ ◆ ◆ ◆ ◆ ◆ ◆ ◆ ◆ ◆ ◆ ◆ ◆

Since 1986, Paul Overstreet has racked up 10 Top-10 hits as a recording artist. He has also written hits for musicians such as Randy Travis, The Judds, and Kathy Mattea. Overstreet has grabbed many of music's top accolades, including CMA "Song of the Year," CCMA "Country Songwriter of the Year," and several Grammy and Dove awards.

Title: *Time* (1996)
Label: Integrity Music
Genre: Country
Pro-Social Content: Overstreet celebrates lifelong marital commitment, referring to his wife as his best friend ("We've Got to Keep on Meeting Like This"), keeping conjugal conflicts in perspective ("Even When It Don't Feel Like It"), and alluding to the pleasure of lovemaking in the proper context ("Let's Go to Bed Early"). Worldly romance loses its luster compared to one woman's willingness to wait for her "One in a Million" man. An aspiring groom explains his plans to propose to his girlfriend on "I'm Gonna Ring Her." "Mr. Miller" is

Overstreet's posthumous tribute to the father of his bride. A dad's time is prized above riches on "You Gave Me Time." "My Rock" enthusiastically calls listeners to find salvation in the Lord.

Objectionable Content: None

Summary/Advisory: Fun, wholesome, and substantive. The wisdom contained in *Time* is as relevant, eternal, and warmly communicated as life lessons passed down from generation to generation on a country porch (lemonade not included). An outstanding release.

Pantera

◆ ◆ ◆ ◆ ◆ ◆ ◆ ◆ ◆ ◆ ◆ ◆ ◆ ◆ ◆ ◆ ◆ ◆ ◆ ◆

Pantera is comprised of Philip Anselmo, Dimebag Darrell, Vinnie Paul, and Rex. Their album *Far Beyond Driven* debuted at number 1 and sold more than 2 million copies worldwide. *The Great Southern Trendkill* (1996) peaked at number 4, selling more than 500,000 copies. Anselmo was clinically dead for five minutes in 1996 as the result of a heroin overdose. According to *Kerrang!* magazine, he admitted to having done the drug for approximately six months prior to the incident.

Title: *The Great Southern Trendkill* (1996)
Label: EastWest/Atlantic
Genre: Thrash/Metal
Pro-Social Content: Though plagued with problems of their own, cuts do denounce hateful violence by skinheads ("13 Steps to Nowhere") and undue leniency toward criminals ("Drag the Waters").

Objectionable Content: Growling and screaming, this obnoxious band spews all sorts of vile sludge. Listeners are urged to solve problems with "pills that kill" and a "gun up to the mouth" on "Suicide Note (Parts 1 & 2)." A vicious verbal attack is launched against the media and the world in general on "War Nerve," just one of many tracks punctuated with the f-word. The title assault (to call it a "song" would be much too kind) uses obscenities to condemn the alternative/punk-rock movement. Elsewhere, the lead vocalist vomits forth a string of dark pleasures including oral lust, angel dust, anal whore, VD ecstasy, and lesbian love.

Summary/Advisory: On this maddening disc, Pantera claims to be "in position to wage teenage mayhem." It's true. Keep this venomous snake in the grass far away from your home.

Title: *Far Beyond Driven* (1994)
Label: EastWest
Genre: Death metal
Pro-Social Content: None
Objectionable Content: Philip Anselmo's mangled, throaty vocals are powered by an ungodly vengeance, promoting all sorts of deviancy. He proudly admits to profiting from drugs on "Strength Beyond Strength" ("I'm helping to legalize dope on your pristine streets and I'm making a fortune"). Several tracks consider the merits of suicide ("Becoming," "Shedding Skin," "Good Friends and a Bottle of Pills," "Slaughtered"). On "25 Years," he hatefully threatens his father with violence ("we're f—ing you back"). The f-word peppers this entire album and is used in shocking descriptions of sexual perversion. Other lyrics promoting dangerous behavior include, "I drink all day, I smoke all day . . . a hangover is inspiration" ("Hard Lines, Sunken Cheeks").
Summary/Advisory: Dark, obscene, occultic. *Far Beyond Driven* should be driven far beyond civilization as we know it—and *trashed.*

Pearl Jam

◆ ◆ ◆ ◆ ◆ ◆ ◆ ◆ ◆ ◆ ◆ ◆ ◆ ◆ ◆ ◆ ◆ ◆ ◆ ◆

Eddie Vedder, Stone Gossard, Jeff Ament, Jack Irons, and Mike McCready currently make up the group Pearl Jam. Former members have included Dave Krusen and Dave Abbruzzese. Prior to the release of their 1998 CD, *Yield*, this alternative act had sold nearly 22 million albums since 1992.

Title: *Yield* (1998)
Label: Sony
Genre: Alternative
Pro-Social Content: Lead singer/guitarist Eddie Vedder's predominantly neutral stream of consciousness gives way to positive sentiments about the world's ability to change ("Brain of J."), self-improvement ("Wishlist"), and the liberation found in loving others unconditionally ("Given to Fly"). God hears men's prayers on "Faithful." Vedder condemns "taking pills to get along" ("All Those Yesterdays"). In contrast to his former angst, the artist surveys life and claims to be "fine" on "Push Me, Pull Me"—an improvement.

Objectionable Content: Obscenities. The f-word appears on "MFC" and "Given to Fly." "Do the Evolution" is unsettling due to the unclear context of lines such as "I'm at peace with my lust/I can kill 'cause I trust in God" and "I'll do what I want, but irresponsibly."

Summary/Advisory: With the release of *No Code,* Vedder and the boys finally began to appreciate the daily gift of taking in oxygen, expressing less angst and despair. This disc reflects that introspective progress as well. In fact, *Entertainment Weekly* [2/6/98] described Pearl Jam's latest as "less pretentious than in the past, reflecting a looser, even marginally whimsical, worldview." Sadly, *Yield's* obscenities and ambiguity signal "do not enter."

Title: *No Code* (1996)
Label: Sony
Genre: Alternative
Pro-Social Content: This band has evolved, shifting from unmitigated misery to burgeoning optimism. Lead singer Eddie Vedder talks about how great life is ("In My Tree") even "when the sun don't shine" ("Smile"). "Hail Hail" acknowledges the value of close relationships. On "Sometimes," Vedder ponders his place in the world, reverently pointing to God as the omnipotent guide ("You're God and you got big hands/The challenges you give me/Seek my part, devote myself/My small self—like a book amongst the many on a shelf"). He also urges fans to forget about past mistakes and move on ("Present Tense") while cautioning them to consider the consequences of dangerous behavior ("Habit"). Some really good themes here.

Objectionable Content: Harsh language (including an occasional f-word) mars "Off He Goes," "Who You Are," and "Lukin." Though vague, lines on "I'm Open" and "Present Tense" convey dubious philosophies reminiscent of New Age.

Summary/Advisory: Since storming onto the pop scene in 1992, this band has elevated angst, despair, and bellyaching to an artform (*Ten, Vs.,* and *Vitalogy*). But not here. *No Code* is surprisingly upbeat. Sadly, the noted caveats prohibit an enthusiastic thumbs-up, but this is a step in the right direction for Vedder and Co.

Title: *Vitalogy* (1994)
Label: Epic
Genre: Alternative
Pro-Social Content: "Nothingman" reminds the listener that actions have

consequences and that "some words, when spoken, can't be taken back." That's about it.

Objectionable Content: Despair. Misery. Isolation. On one track ("Bugs"), Eddie Vedder contemplates eating insects "raw or well done." He welcomes visits from the devil on "Satan's Bed," which relies on profanity and a reference to oral sex for added shock value. Vedder also shouts "f—- you" to fans unwilling to grant him privacy ("Not For You") and, on at least two tracks, speaks of suicide as a viable solution to life's problems.

Summary/Advisory: Why would anyone dream of being a rock star if it all adds up to this? Glum and self-destructive, the chart-topping *Vitalogy* is anything *but* vital listening.

Title: *Vs.* (1993)
Label: Epic
Genre: Alternative
Pro-Social Content: None
Objectionable Content: Amid expletives and references to rebellious, crude sex without standards ("Leash," "Rearviewmirror"), Pearl Jam slams both decency and authority. "W.M.A." comes off as anti-police. Rodents are esteemed higher than mankind on "Rats." And, while several songs attempt to shed light on social problems such as child abuse, drug use, and gun-toting mobsters, listeners could just as easily interpret them as promoting those same antisocial elements.

Summary/Advisory: This number-1 disc set a first-week sales record of 950,000 copies. Pearl Jam speaks fluently to angry youths from dysfunctional homes. But rather than offer them hope, this confused band chooses to wallow in the same despair. According to *Time* magazine, *Vs.* "combines politically correct views with punk-inspired belligerence." Clearly, one to avoid.

Perry, Steve

◆ ◆ ◆ ◆ ◆ ◆ ◆ ◆ ◆ ◆ ◆ ◆ ◆ ◆ ◆ ◆ ◆ ◆ ◆

A native of Hanford, California, Perry joined the band Journey in 1978. He released his first solo project (the 2 million-selling *Street Talk*) in 1984 and scored his biggest single with a cut from that record, "Oh Sherrie."

Title: *For the Love of Strange Medicine* (1994)
Label: Columbia
Genre: Rock

Pro-Social Content: With faith and hope, Perry sings of commitment and truthfulness, clinging to love in an age of disposable relationships. On "I Am" and "Anyway," he repents of selfishness and dishonesty, seeking restoration with a lover and a "brother," respectively. "Stand Up (Before It's Too Late)" rises to defend a romance and make it succeed. "Somewhere There's Hope" may not point to God, but it assures angst-ridden teens that trials are only temporary—a refreshing message considering the number of pro-suicide bands charting today.

Objectionable Content: None

Summary/Advisory: Perry has taken a distinctly positive path in his journey as a solo artist. This lyrically sound effort—which sold more than 500,000 copies—is welcome *Medicine.* (SEE ALSO: Journey)

Petty, Tom

◆ ◆

The artist formed the successful rock band Tom Petty and The Heartbreakers in 1975. He was also a member of The Traveling Wilburys, along with Roy Orbison, Bob Dylan, George Harrison, and ELO's Jeff Lynne. Career album sales have topped 17 million.

Title: *Wildflowers* (1994)
Label: Warner Bros.
Genre: Rock
Pro-Social Content: Several songs value lifelong love ("House in the Woods") and show a willingness to work through relational trials ("A Higher Place," "Only a Broken Heart"). Adultery is called "bad" and "sad" on "To Find a Friend," which describes the aftermath of a failed marriage. "Wake Up Time" discourages dreaming that ignores life's realities.

Objectionable Content: The Top-40 hit "You Don't Know How It Feels" irresponsibly promotes using marijuana and driving under the influence ("Let's roll another joint/Let's head on down the road"). Petty also endorses getting stoned on "It's Good to Be King." His moral stand on adultery doesn't carry over to premarital sex, which gets an approving nod on "Honey Bee."

Summary/Advisory: In addition to confusing sexual standards, problems stem from pro-drug lyrics, making *Wildflowers* a mixed bouquet. Better *leaf* this one *bee*.

Phair, Liz

◆ ◆ ◆ ◆ ◆ ◆ ◆ ◆ ◆ ◆ ◆ ◆ ◆ ◆ ◆ ◆ ◆ ◆ ◆

Born and raised in Chicago, Illinois, both Liz and her brother were adopted. While attending Oberlin College, she released a series of homemade audio-cassettes that found their way into the hands of Matador Records, which signed her in 1993.

Title: *Whip-smart* (1994)
Label: Matador
Genre: Rock/Folk
Pro-Social Content: On the title cut, the artist pledges motherly protection for her son.
Objectionable Content: Raunchy and profane, Phair endorses irresponsible, casual sex ("Chopsticks," "Supernova") in terms that would make Hugh Hefner blush. On "May Queen," a potential lover asks, "Got any warts?" "X-ray Man" describes a lustful male who undresses women with his eyes. The f-word appears frequently. The album also condones drug and alcohol use ("Crater Lake," "Supernova," "May Queen"), which is consistent with reports of Phair's own recreational lifestyle.
Summary/Advisory: In a *Rolling Stone* [10/6/94] interview, Phair professed a fascination with the occult. And Lisa Palac, editor of the porn magazine *Future Sex*, has stated that Phair will help reshape the next generation's sexual values. Let's hope not.

Phish

◆ ◆ ◆ ◆ ◆ ◆ ◆ ◆ ◆ ◆ ◆ ◆ ◆ ◆ ◆ ◆ ◆ ◆

Members of Phish include Page McConnell, Trey Anastasio, Jon Fishman, and Mike Gordon. For a band that enjoys phenomenal concert attendance—including sold-out shows at Madison Square Garden and Boston Garden and a cult following akin to that of the Grateful Dead—Phish's album sales have been lackluster. This act also has the distinction of having a flavor of Ben & Jerry's ice cream named after it—Phish Food.

Title: *Billy Breathes* (1996)
Label: Elektra
Genre: Rock
Pro-Social Content: The acoustic "Bliss" and jazzy "Cars Trucks Buses" are instrumental. A true friend's companionship is esteemed more highly than other activities ("Waste") and valued above possessions ("Theme from the Bottom"). "Swept Away" and "Steep" express frustration with the pressures of celebrity. The artist bemoans his inability to communicate on "Talk" ("I can't talk my talk with you/Nothing's ever soaking through/. . . I can't sing my song with you"). Other songs are lyrically obscure.
Objectionable Content: Lacking relational context, an invitation to cohabitate on "Taste" appears to be sexually motivated.
Summary/Advisory: Described by *Entertainment Weekly* as "rock's largest-living cult band." Could this group be the next Grateful Dead? That's what industry analysts are predicting. Such popularity is unfortunate considering the act's decadent résumé and reports of mass drug use at live shows. On the plus side, *Billy Breathes* all but avoids disturbing content.

Pink Floyd

◆ ◆ ◆ ◆ ◆ ◆ ◆ ◆ ◆ ◆ ◆ ◆ ◆ ◆ ◆ ◆ ◆ ◆

In 1965, this English rock band was made up of Roger Waters, Nick Mason, Rick Wright, and Syd Barrett. Before the band hit stride in the early '70s, Barrett was replaced by David Gilmour. Waters embarked on a solo career in 1984. In its more than 25-year career, Pink Floyd has charted a dozen platinum albums and sold nearly 50 million records. *The Dark Side of the Moon* (1973) sold 13 million. *The Wall* (1979) sold 10 million. The band was inducted into the Rock and Roll Hall of Fame in 1996.

Title: *The Division Bell* (1994)
Label: Columbia
Genre: Synthesized rock
Pro-Social Content: With a sense of hope, "A Great Day for Freedom" condemns pride, bitterness, and bloodshed. On "Wearing the Inside Out" and "Coming Back to Life," the artist reflects on life struggles from which he has learned lessons and successfully emerged on the other side. "Keep Talking" points out that healthy relationships require solid communication.

Objectionable Content: A potentially positive message on "Lost for Words" is sunk by one expletive ("they tell me to please go f—— myself"). "Take It Back" is selfish and suspicious about love—perhaps even abusive ("I spy on her, I lie to her . . . I take all that I can take, and I push her to the limit to see if she will break"). In stark contrast to several other cuts, "High Hopes" describes the human experience as emptiness without answers.

Summary/Advisory: This disc spent its first month as the nation's top album. Pink Floyd is musically sharp, but the aged band fluctuates between lyrical optimism and poetic pessimism.

P.M. Dawn

◆ ◆ ◆ ◆ ◆ ◆ ◆ ◆ ◆ ◆ ◆ ◆ ◆ ◆ ◆ ◆ ◆ ◆ ◆ ◆

P.M. Dawn is two brothers from Jersey City, New Jersey: Attrel and Jarrett Cordes (better known as Prince Be and DJ Minutemix).

Title: *Jesus Wept* (1995)
Label: Gee Street/Island
Genre: Hip-hop/Pop
Pro-Social Content: If there's a strength here, it's emotional commitment ("Miles from Anything," "Apathy . . . Superstar"), even to the point of loving someone who shows only hatred in return ("Forever Damaged").

Objectionable Content: Talk of God becomes a liability when it strays from biblical truth—which is often. Numerous lines promote polytheism and the belief that each of us has a Christ within ("I'll Be Waiting for You," "Why God Loves You," "Sometimes I Miss You So Much"). The artists also suggest that they've experienced multiple lives and/or personalities ("Why God Loves You," "Downtown Venus," "A Lifetime," "Sonchyenne").
Summary/Advisory: *Jesus Wept* will lead teens into spiritual error. This creative, musically pleasant project is mired in theological confusion: Mysticism. Reincarnation. Self-deification. New Age "Christ consciousness." The one thing missing from this smorgasbord is the historical Jesus of John 11:35. Skip it.

Title: *The Bliss Album . . . ?* (1993)
Label: Island
Genre: Hip-hop/Pop/Rap
Pro-Social Content: None
Objectionable Content: This album strongly promotes Eastern mysticism and occultic themes. From the introduction (an astrological reading) to the final cut, P.M. Dawn weaves New Age thought, enlightenment philosophy, reincarnation, and self-deification through rap and catchy love ballads. One of the rap cuts ("The Nocturnal Is in the House") describes the rapper's evangelistic purpose: "I'm spreading that Nocturnal [new age] juice." "Beyond Infinite Affections" paints an unbiblical picture of eternity and human destiny.
Summary/Advisory: Spiritual themes in secular music can be refreshing. Unfortunately, this project peddles cosmic consciousness and other unhealthy New Age propaganda. Stick with Christian artists committed to communicating truth.

Poison

◆ ◆

Bret Michaels, Bobby Dall, Rikki Rockett, and C.C. DeVille formed this explosive rock band in Harrisburg, Pennsylvania. Poison's first three discs each sold at least 3 million copies. Prior to the release of *Native Tongue*, Richie Kotzen replaced C.C. DeVille at guitar.

Title: *Native Tongue* (1993)
Label: Capitol
Genre: Hard rock

Pro-Social Content: "The Scream" cries of a world in pain ("Lord praise the soul who can hear the scream") and asks forgiveness for sins. "Stay Alive" opposes hate and cocaine use. The album's first single, "Stand," urges people to keep from making gods out of lies and money and to stand up for what they believe. **Objectionable Content:** "Body Talk" is one long proposition from a sex-starved male. Obscenities pepper an angry response to thoughtless politicians on "Bring It Home." They are also prominent on "Strike Up the Band," a tribute to masochistic machismo. "Ride Child Ride" fondly recalls drinking Jack Daniels and smoking weed as youngsters. Preachers are deemed useless on "Ain't That the Truth."

Summary/Advisory: This long-awaited project from the multimillion-selling party band glorifies wild times, hard living, and alcohol and marijuana use and employs enough obscenities to effectively squelch any spirituality it attempts to convey on its first two cuts. Offensive material far outweighs any positive elements.

Porno for Pyros

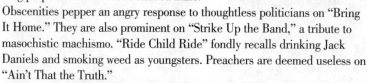

Porno for Pyros, a band that rose from the ashes of the defunct group Jane's Addiction, has played numerous major music events, including Lollapalooza and Woodstock II.

Title: *Good God's Urge* (1996)
Label: Warner Bros.
Genre: Alternative
Pro-Social Content: Despite its faulty theology, the title cut relates a son's earnest prayer for his ailing father. The singer associates times when he's not "thinking of god" with the sensation of being "dead inside" ("Wishing Well").

Objectionable Content: A casual attitude toward sex creeps into several tunes. During a tribute to man's best friend, the guys admire canines because "when it's time to mate, they're not too particular" ("Dogs Rule the Night"). The dreary "Porpoise Head" desires a submissive lover. "Bali

Eyes" relates a drug-induced spiritual journey. A jealous man threatens his girlfriend ("Say you love me or I'll kill us!") on the dark, empty "Freeway." Even more bleak, "Thick of It All" ponders life with the hopeless conclusion that a person might do well just "to die and to get off this planet."

Summary/Advisory: The disc's few positive sentiments get lost amid sexual musings, polytheism, bitter attitudes, and hallucinogenic mushroom use. Teens tempted to sample Porno for Pyros should resist the *Urge*—as well as this warped band's other neurotic efforts.

Title: *Porno for Pyros* (1993)
Label: Warner Bros.
Genre: Alternative
Pro-Social Content: None
Objectionable Content: "Orgasm" relates the band's squalid sexual fantasies while "Bad Sh—" glorifies drug use and the resulting "trip." Murderous revenge dominates "Packin' .25" ("dreamt all yesterday how I might make a man feel with a gun up to his face"). The album's title cut describes masturbation during the L.A. riots ("I took off my clothes and came four times—could not leave myself alone") and advocates the violence that devastated that community.

Summary/Advisory: From its first words ("I got the devil in me") to its last, *Porno for Pyros* delivers nothing but offensive content—and hit number 3 on the pop chart its first week! *Rolling Stone* asked band leader Perry Farrell for the key to personal happiness. He said, "Besides 'Do drugs' or anything obvious like that, I'd say, 'Move as far away from your parents as you could.'" Farrell is also the man behind the popular multiact summer music festival, Lollapalooza. Avoid both.

Presidents of the U.S.A.

◆ ◆ ◆ ◆ ◆ ◆ ◆ ◆ ◆ ◆ ◆ ◆ ◆ ◆ ◆ ◆ ◆ ◆ ◆ ◆

This Seattle-based group includes Chris Ballew, Dave Dederer, and Jason Finn. As part of the band's rapid rise to fame, the trio played a Democratic rally in downtown Seattle for the real president of the U.S.A. in November 1994.

Title: *II* (1996)
Label: Columbia
Genre: Rock
Pro-Social Content: Inoffensive cuts string together musings about

Matchbox cars ("Mach 5"), insects ("Bug City"), and skinny chickens ("Puffy Little Shoes"). Innocuous nonsense.

Objectionable Content: Unfortunately, the group's weird, detached stream of consciousness flows into forbidden territory. Several tunes include profanity ("Tiki God," "Twig," "Bath of Fire"). The singer longs to get a lover "home in my room between my sheets" on "Lunatic to Love" and boasts of ridding himself of an unfaithful girl-friend through a "Tiki God" ("My tiki god made sure I'd live in peace/One day I read they found her body in the river"). "Bath of Fire" portrays hell as a place of cleansing—one where band members reunite for jam sessions. "Twig" speaks of being "drunk in a bar," though the context is hard to make out. A girl is said to be the "love child of Genghis Khan and a beauti-ful busty Amazon" on "Supermodel."

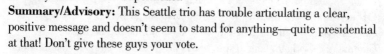

Summary/Advisory: This Seattle trio has trouble articulating a clear, positive message and doesn't seem to stand for anything—quite presidential at that! Don't give these guys your vote.

Title: *The Presidents of the U.S.A.* (1995)
Label: Columbia
Genre: Alternative/Punk rock
Pro-Social Content: Several upbeat, nonsensical tunes (about everything from "froggies and fishies" to old men rocking on a back porch) avoid offen-sive elements but provide little more than ear candy.

Objectionable Content: Crude sexual innuendo characterizes both "Kitty" and "Peaches." The former repeats the line "F— you, kitty." Profanities also appear on "Dune Buggy," "Boll Weevil," and "Kick Out the Jams." On "Stranger," a man propositions a stripper working in a porno house ("You seem cool for a naked chick in a booth/Let's be pals some-day"). The boys voice excitement about being "naked and famous" on the song of the same name.

Summary/Advisory: Musically, The Presidents of the United States of America. lighten up the alternative scene, resisting the temptation to mope. These guys are out to enjoy life. The problem is *how* they get their kicks. Silly songs aside, the band's preoccupation with sex sends a dangerous message to teens.

Prince

◆ ◆

Prince Roger Nelson was born in 1958. In addition to a host of platinum-plus albums, the artist has starred in a number of films (most notably, *Purple Rain*). For a time, he jettisoned his royal moniker in favor of an androgynous symbol, but recently returned to calling himself Prince. The Artist-Once-Again-Known-As-Prince has sold a combined 32 million albums during his career.

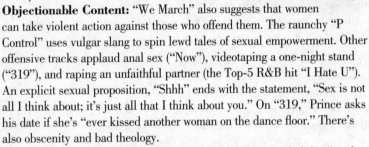

Title: *The Gold Experience* (1995)
Label: Warner Bros.
Genre: R&B
Pro-Social Content: "The Most Beautiful Girl in the World" admires a woman's inner beauty. "We March" calls for racial harmony.
Objectionable Content: "We March" also suggests that women can take violent action against those who offend them. The raunchy "P Control" uses vulgar slang to spin lewd tales of sexual empowerment. Other offensive tracks applaud anal sex ("Now"), videotaping a one-night stand ("319"), and raping an unfaithful partner (the Top-5 R&B hit "I Hate U"). An explicit sexual proposition, "Shhh" ends with the statement, "Sex is not all I think about; it's just all that I think about you." On "319," Prince asks his date if she's "ever kissed another woman on the dance floor." There's also obscenity and bad theology.
Summary/Advisory: Prince (also referred to as "The Symbol Guy" and "The Artist Formerly Known As Prince") has a long history of lyrical perversity. In fact, his *Dirty Mind* album even included a song celebrating incest. This latest effort is musical fool's *Gold*—and the few positive nuggets aren't worth panning for.

Prodigy

◆ ◆

Prodigy, originally from Essex, England, consists of Liam Howlett, Keeti Palmer, Leeroy Thornhill, and Keith Flint. Their *The Fat of the Land* disc debuted at number 1, and its smash single, "Breathe," has sold nearly 2 million copies worldwide.

Title: *The Fat of the Land* (1997)
Label: Maverick
Genre: Techno/Electronica
Pro-Social Content: None
Objectionable Content: The artist repeatedly shouts, "Smack my b——ch up!" on the disturbing groove of the same title. A trip-hop rap cut puts faith in astrology and human intellect ("Diesel Power"), while the Eastern chants on "Narayan" give a nod to transcendental meditation. Another track ("Funky S——") repeats the profane phrase, "Oh my god, that's the funky s——!" "Breathe" finds a vindictive man eager to victimize a mentally unstable other. "Fuel My Fire" expresses rage and unforgiveness ("I got a bad attitude . . . got a grudge that I'm holding for as long as I live"). With "Serial Thrilla," the artist boasts of being a "serious killa."
Summary/Advisory: Lyrics take a backseat to dark, pulsating, computer-generated beats. What lyrics do appear on *The Fat of the Land* radiate hostility and pessimism. A big hit within the rave subculture, this British band has nothing of value to export.

Puff Daddy & The Family

◆ ◆ ◆ ◆ ◆ ◆ ◆ ◆ ◆ ◆ ◆ ◆ ◆ ◆ ◆ ◆ ◆ ◆ ◆ ◆

Puffy Combs (a.k.a. Puff Daddy), the CEO and founder of Bad Boy Entertainment, has produced a handful of number-1 rap singles. Combs was named Songwriter of the Year at ASCAP's Rhythm & Soul Awards in 1996.

Title: *No Way Out* (1997)
Label: Bad Boy
Genre: Gangsta rap
Pro-Social Content: Asking forgiveness for himself and for his enemies, a deceased gangsta reverently prays to God, requesting divine protection for his family ("Intro").
Objectionable Content: However, this disc also suggests that Christian faith is compatible with the gangsta lifestyle ("I'll Be Missing You," "Pain"). Frequent glorifications of violence—including the line "stripped his a—naked, then I put a slug in him" ("I Got the Power")—are aggravated by obscenities, suicidal thoughts, and explicit, perverse sexuality. Tracks promote

drugs and alcohol in the form of weed, acid, coke, crack, meth, and malt liquor.

Summary/Advisory: This rookie debut hit number 1 and sold 561,000 copies its first week. *No Way Out* busts its lewd rhymes over familiar background tracks ranging from David Bowie's "Let's Dance" to the theme from *Rocky II*. While musically engaging at times, it's ultimately 78 minutes of the same tired lyrical trash this genre has become infamous for. Don't let teens drop in on Puff Daddy and his dysfunctional Family. The Christian band E.T.W. is a good alternative for young rap fans.

Queensrÿche

◆ ◆ ◆ ◆ ◆ ◆ ◆ ◆ ◆ ◆ ◆ ◆ ◆ ◆ ◆ ◆ ◆ ◆ ◆ ◆

Queensrÿche is a five-man metal band from Washington state. Prone to explore political issues in their music, Geoff Tate, Chris DeGarmo, Michael Wilton, Eddie Jackson, and Scott Fockenfield have collectively sold more than 6 million records.

Title: *Promised Land* (1994)
Label: EMI
Genre: Rock/Heavy metal
Pro-Social Content: "Out of Mind" condemns a society eager to forget its mentally ill. An absentee father tries in vain to re-enter his adult son's life on "Bridge." "My Global Mind" reflects the frustration of hearing about worldwide injustices in this information age, yet feeling helpless to effect change.

Objectionable Content: "Lady Jane" could, metaphorically, be promoting marijuana use. "Disconnected" refers to taking pills to overcome a "loathsome state." The title track, "One More Time," and "I Am I" seek fresh guidance after being disappointed by the promises of family and organized religion. A fall from grace gives the singer a sense of purpose on "Someone Else."

Summary/Advisory: Despite some thought-provoking themes, pessimism, alienation, and spiritual disillusionment inhabit *Promised Land*. One band member told *Kerrang!* [10/15/94] "I don't remember drinking as much as we did when making this album." It shows.

Radiohead

◆ ◆ ◆ ◆ ◆ ◆ ◆ ◆ ◆ ◆ ◆ ◆ ◆ ◆ ◆ ◆ ◆ ◆ ◆ ◆

This unique alternative band is made up of Thom Yorke, Jonny and Colin Greenwood, Ed O'Brien, and Phil Selway. Radiohead's *OK Computer* earned the act a Grammy in 1998 for Best Alternative Music Performance.

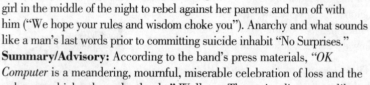

Title: *OK Computer* (1997)
Label: Capitol
Genre: Alternative/Industrial
Pro-Social Content: An isolated line on "Paranoid Android" states, "God loves his children."
Objectionable Content: "Exit Music (For a Film)" finds lead singer Thom Yorke waking a girl in the middle of the night to rebel against her parents and run off with him ("We hope your rules and wisdom choke you"). Anarchy and what sounds like a man's last words prior to committing suicide inhabit "No Surprises."
Summary/Advisory: According to the band's press materials, *"OK Computer* is a meandering, mournful, miserable celebration of loss and the unknown which aches relentlessly." Well put. The entire disc seems like the soundtrack for a despairing hallucination—dark and bleak. Even positive thoughts on "Lucky" and "Filter Happier" seem sarcastic the way they're moaned. Don't let youngsters log onto *OK Computer*.

Rage Against the Machine

◆ ◆ ◆ ◆ ◆ ◆ ◆ ◆ ◆ ◆ ◆ ◆ ◆ ◆ ◆ ◆ ◆ ◆ ◆ ◆

Rage Against the Machine is Zack de la Rocha, Tom Morello, Timmy C., and Brad Wilk. Their mix of metal and rap provides an armor-plated vehicle for communicating political angst and a call to anarchy.

Title: *Evil Empire* (1996)
Label: Epic
Genre: Metal/Rap
Pro-Social Content: "Wind Below" accuses members of the media of perpetuating lies. Other tracks empathize with exploited farmers, questioning the practices that oppress them.

Objectionable Content: Numerous uses of the f-word punctuate angry lyrics. "Year of the Boomerang" claims the "doctrines of the right" enslave people with dogma. The same is true of "Vietnow" and "Roll Right," which include the church among the band's targets. That bitterness turns ugly on "Down Rodeo" as society's "have nots" are encouraged to lash out violently against the "haves."

Summary/Advisory: Radical left-wing political rhetoric galore. True to the band's moniker, its members angrily rail against the establishment, recommending hatred toward the wealthy and violent conflict as a means of "improving" society. Don't let 'em blow off steam in your home.

Raitt, Bonnie

◆ ◆ ◆ ◆ ◆ ◆ ◆ ◆ ◆ ◆ ◆ ◆ ◆ ◆ ◆ ◆ ◆ ◆ ◆ ◆

Raitt is a veteran blues-rock singer, guitarist, and daughter of Broadway actor/singer John Raitt. Her 1989 project, *Nick of Time,* won four Grammys. Career album sales now exceed 12 million units.

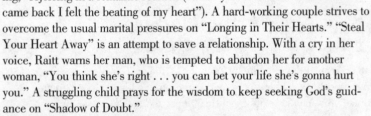

Title: *Longing in Their Hearts* (1994)
Label: Capitol
Genre: Rock/Pop
Pro-Social Content: The tender ballad "You" refers to love as what "keeps us breathing," rejoicing in a romantic reunion ("when you came back I felt the beating of my heart"). A hard-working couple strives to overcome the usual marital pressures on "Longing in Their Hearts." "Steal Your Heart Away" is an attempt to save a relationship. With a cry in her voice, Raitt warns her man, who is tempted to abandon her for another woman, "You think she's right . . . you can bet your life she's gonna hurt you." A struggling child prays for the wisdom to keep seeking God's guidance on "Shadow of Doubt."

Objectionable Content: "Hell to Pay" refers to karma and employs the phrase "ain't it a b—ch." Ambiguous lyrics on several tracks indicate a possible lack of self-control as Raitt gives herself over to feelings of romantic love and/or passion (not explicit).

Summary/Advisory: Laid-back blues rock. Pleading ballads. With only the noted exceptions, this 12-track collection (featuring the hit single "Love Sneakin' Up on You") is as solid lyrically as it is musically.

Rancid

◆ ◆ ◆ ◆ ◆ ◆ ◆ ◆ ◆ ◆ ◆ ◆ ◆ ◆ ◆ ◆ ◆ ◆ ◆ ◆

The punk band Rancid is made up of Tim Armstrong, Matt Freeman, Brett
Reed, and Lars Frederiksen. Their *And Out Come the Wolves* CD went gold.

Title: *And Out Come the Wolves* (1995)
Label: Epitaph
Genre: Punk rock
Pro-Social Content: "11th House" reminds
"little sister" that it's up to her to take the first
step off a destructive path. "As Wicked" shows
concern for the homeless and abandoned, while
"Avenues and Alleyways" condemns racial
hatred.

Objectionable Content: This disc contains several uses of the f-word.
The song "Listed M.I.A." repeatedly takes the Lord's name in vain.
Amid a guitar-driven whirlwind of hopelessness, the band promotes
getting high ("Maxwell Murder"), public drunkenness ("Roots Radicals")
and unmarried sex ("Ruby Soho"). A teen contemplating suicide could
get a push in that direction from a line on "Time Bomb" ("The secret to a
good life is knowing when you're through"). "Daly City Train" pays tribute to a dead drug addict whose lifestyle is never truly condemned.
Similarly, the title character on "Junkyman" is lauded for rebellion,
"shootin' up," and arson.
Summary/Advisory: According to the band, this project includes "personal tales of drugs, vagrancy and lonely East Bay and South Bay street
life." A few positive sentiments, but they can't compensate for deafening
tracks filled with profanity, drugs, and despair.

Raye, Collin

◆ ◆ ◆ ◆ ◆ ◆ ◆ ◆ ◆ ◆ ◆ ◆ ◆ ◆ ◆ ◆ ◆ ◆ ◆ ◆

Native Arkansan Collin Raye has three platinum albums to his credit—*All
I Can Be, In This Life,* and *Extremes.* His press bio explains that his music
is purposeful, embodying a "commitment to songs that touch and heal."

Title: *I Think About You* (1995)
Label: Epic

Genre: Country

Pro-Social Content: The hit "One Boy, One Girl" is a warm retelling of a young couple's meeting, marrying, and having twins together. On the title track, the father of an eight-year-old daughter values every woman he sees as the little girl she used to be. Raye also pledges eternal devotion to a woman ("I Volunteer") and describes a man's loving attempts to melt icy emotional walls ("Heart Full of Rain"). A struggling couple learns to appreciate one another's uniqueness on "Not That Different." "What If Jesus Came Back Like That" considers Christ's humble birth and crucifixion as it urges listeners to care for their fellow man.

Objectionable Content: Drinking is a means of escape on "The Time Machine." "Sweet Miss Behavin'" exalts a carousing woman.

Summary/Advisory: Raye has a way with songs about warm, loving relationships. More of the same here. Two unfortunate tunes mar an otherwise excellent project.

Title: *Extremes* (1994)

Label: Epic

Genre: Country

Pro-Social Content: Raye recalls the loving advice his mother offered when he left to follow his dreams on "A Bible and a Bus Ticket Home" ("One will get you where you're going . . . and one will bring you back, son, if your dreams ain't waiting there"). On "Little Rock," he tells his woman how much he regrets having left her, and, describing how he has cleaned up his act, pleads for reconciliation. "That's My Story" uses humor to preach the need for honesty in marriage. Several other songs convey a deep commitment to romantic love—and to personal integrity ("Man of My Word").

Objectionable Content: Just one minor blemish. "To the Border and Beyond" brags of wild living with a character who's a "push-it-to-the-limit kind of guy."

Summary/Advisory: In addition to being an enjoyable listen, Collin Raye's *Extremes* gives two-stepping teens and their parents plenty of positive themes to discuss together. Overall, a solid option.

Real McCoy

◆ ◆ ◆ ◆ ◆ ◆ ◆ ◆ ◆ ◆ ◆ ◆ ◆ ◆ ◆ ◆ ◆ ◆ ◆ ◆

This Berlin-based group consists of Olaf Jeflitza (O-Jay), Patricia (Patsy) Peterson, and Vanessa Mason. Infectious bass grooves makes this dance-club music especially popular in Europe.

Title: *Another Night* (1995)
Label: Arista
Genre: Dance/Techno-pop
Pro-Social Content: Several tunes describe a deep and lasting love ("Love and Devotion," "Sleeping with an Angel," "I Want You"). A female forgives her partner for wrongs committed on "If You Should Ever Be Lonely." "Run Away" says to "keep the faith" and flee controlling influences such as materialism and sex.
Objectionable Content: Space aliens intent on "saving" the human race monitor earthly activity on "Operator." Reincarnation and a lack of sexual self-control appear on "Automatic Lover," in which a woman invites a man to feel her "super-magic, space-erotic x-tasy."
Summary/Advisory: This Berlin-based band boasts universal appeal. Too bad lyrical shortcomings mar a musically upbeat effort. Fans of the genre should try early Eric Champion or Code of Ethics instead.

Red Hot Chili Peppers

◆ ◆ ◆ ◆ ◆ ◆ ◆ ◆ ◆ ◆ ◆ ◆ ◆ ◆ ◆ ◆ ◆ ◆ ◆ ◆

This band, which has made animated cameo appearances on *The Simpsons*, includes Anthony Kiedis, Flea, Chad Smith, and Dave Navarro (formerly the guitarist for Jane's Addiction and Porno for Pyros). Navarro left the band in 1998 and was replaced by John Frusciante. In regard to *One Hot Minute*, Kiedis told *Rolling Stone* [6/1/95], "I've been on a blistering roller-coaster of mental health ups and downs . . . This is the darkest Chili Peppers record."

Title: *One Hot Minute* (1995)
Label: Warner Bros.
Genre: Alternative
Pro-Social Content: "My Friends" pledges support to discouraged and lonely companions.

Objectionable Content: Though not stickered for explicit content, this disc employs highly offensive language throughout, including hateful epithets on "Pea." The singer invites a woman to "illuminate my lust" with a steamy sex romp ("Coffee Shop"). An angry diatribe, "Shallow Be Thy Game" seeks to trash God and the church at every turn ("I was not created in the likeness of a fraud . . . I prefer a loving god" and "You're not born into sin/The guilt they try to give you/Puke it in the nearest bin"). "Aeroplane" approves of "pleasure spiked with pain," while other tunes seem to be basking in New Age euphoria. "Deep Kick" glorifies the antics of two thieves who get "drugged up" and hitch a ride with a transvestite.

Summary/Advisory: Hedonistic sludge. At one point, the band tells fans, "It's better to regret something you did than something you didn't do." A shaky philosophy. Don't allow this warped group into your home . . . you *won't* regret it.

R.E.M.

◆ ◆ ◆ ◆ ◆ ◆ ◆ ◆ ◆ ◆ ◆ ◆ ◆ ◆ ◆ ◆ ◆ ◆ ◆

R.E.M. is a four-piece band that formed in 1980 in Athens, Georgia, consisting of Michael Stipe, Mike Mills, Bill Berry, and Peter Buck. On August 24, 1996, it was announced at an annual meeting of Warner Bros. Music executives that the label had re-signed R.E.M. to a five-record deal worth $80 million, making history as the largest recording contract signed to date. Berry left the band in October 1997, claiming that a brain aneurysm led him to reevaluate his priorities. He was replaced by drummer Barrett Martin of the Screaming Trees.

Title: *New Adventures in Hi-Fi* (1996)
Label: Warner Bros.
Genre: Alternative
Pro-Social Content: "Be Mine" pledges to meet the needs of another and desires to end worldly greed. Other lyrics are poetically vague.
Objectionable Content: Anti-Christian sentiment runs like a polluted tributary through this disappointing disc. The singer views himself as "godless" ("How the West Was Won and Where It Got Us"), dismisses salvation,

heaven, and religion ("Undertow"), and claims
no love for Christ except for His command not
to judge others ("New Test Leper"). When interviewed about his sexuality, frontman Michael
Stipe has left the door open to all sorts of possi-
bilities, as one might gather from "So Fast, So
Numb," on which Stipe calls himself the "lover"
of someone called "motel boy." Obscenities

appear on "Departure" and the enigmatically sexual "Binky the Doormat."
Lines such as "I lost myself in sorrow/I lost myself in pain . . . That's what
keeps me down" underscore the disc's sense of emptiness.

Summary/Advisory: This melancholy effort was released on the heels of
R.E.M. inking the largest contract in music history. Will that cheer them
up? Don't count on it. Young fans of this musical style should try CCM's
The Waiting instead.

Title: *Monster* (1994)
Label: Warner Bros.
Genre: Alternative
Pro-Social Content: "Strange Currencies" and "Crush with Eyeliner"
ponder the complexities of human relationships. Other songs denounce
greed ("King of Comedy") and jealousy ("Circus Envy").
Objectionable Content: Crude sexual slang shows up on "Bang and Blame,"
"Tongue," and "I Don't Sleep, I Dream." Amid "Tongue"'s obscure lyrical
stream of consciousness is the line, "Ugly girls know their fate/Anybody can
get laid." Clergy get no respect on "King of Comedy," which portrays religious
leaders as money-hungry hypocrites. Profanity appears in liner notes.
Summary/Advisory: Don't let the teddy-bear cover fool you. Despite a few
positive cuts, R.E.M. has created a *Monster* that feeds on sexual preoccupation and anti-Christian sentiment. Fans of this musical style should instead
check out CCM's Newsboys or The Waiting.

Rimes, LeAnn

◆ ◆ ◆ ◆ ◆ ◆ ◆ ◆ ◆ ◆ ◆ ◆ ◆ ◆ ◆ ◆ ◆ ◆ ◆ ◆

Rimes began her singing career performing in a Mississippi talent contest
at age five. She cut her first independent album at 11. Already, Rimes has
captured numerous music industry statuettes and generated a following
among both young and old country music fans.

Title: *Sittin' on Top of the World* (1998)
Label: Curb
Genre: Country
Pro-Social Content: This starry-eyed teenager
uses five songs to tell the object of her affection
just how irreplacable he really is ("Undeniable,"
"Feels Like Home," "Nothin' New Under the
Moon," "Sittin' on Top of the World," and her

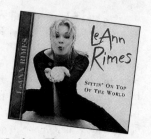

contribution to the *Quest for Camelot* soundtrack, "Looking Through
Your Eyes"). On the Top-20 country hit "Commitment," she holds out for a
long-term love. Other love songs express a broad range of emotions: uncertainty,
gratitude, melancholy, and hope. Amid pain, the singer anticipates a heavenly
reunion with a departed loved one ("When Am I Gonna Get Over You").
Objectionable Content: Allusions to physical intimacy spoil
"Insensitive" and "Rock Me" ("All night long we lay where heaven lies/He
takes me all the way to paradise when he rocks me in the cradle of love").
Summary/Advisory: "I don't think I have to live anything to sing it," the
teen told *Entertainment Weekly* [5/8/98]. Perhaps not, but parents may
bristle at the thought of their daughters taking some of LeAnn's subtle cues
about romance. Apart from those caveats, her disc is a winner.

Title: *You Light Up My Life: Inspirational Songs* (1997)
Label: Curb
Genre: Country/Gospel
Pro-Social Content: Inspirational melodies range from the patriotic
("National Anthem," "God Bless America") to the profoundly spiritual.
Rimes imagines that it must have looked like rain when "Ten Thousand
Angels Cried" at Jesus' crucifixion. She also ponders the depth of God's
love ("Amazing Grace," "On the Side of Angels") and longs to walk with
the Savior ("I Know Who Holds Tomorrow," "Clinging to a Saving Hand").
"Bridge Over Troubled Water" pledges faithful friendship during hard
times. "I Believe" testifies that trials can yield triumphs, prayers are heard,
and prodigals get second chances. "How Do I Live" is a beautiful love song
that quickly scaled the pop singles chart. Great stuff!
Objectionable Content: One line on "You Light Up My Life" states, "It
can't be wrong if it feels so right."
Summary/Advisory: This number-1 album went multiplatinum in just
over a month. Warmth, optimism, and a predominantly Christian worldview
characterize this extremely worthwhile effort.

Title: *Blue* (1996)
Label: Curb
Genre: Country
Pro-Social Content: LeAnn encourages listeners to remain optimistic during trials on "The Light in Your Eyes" ("Keep on shining, keep on smiling/Don't lose faith and don't lose heart"). A drifting partner is urged to trust and communicate as a step toward restoration ("Talk to Me"). "I'll Get Even with You" promises to repay affection with lifelong love.
Objectionable Content: The artist looks forward to drinking champagne on "One-Way Ticket." She confuses love and lust on "Good Lookin' Man." "My Baby" praises a "full-grown lover" who gives her "satisfaction"—a particularly awkward theme in light of the fact that the singer was only *13 years old* when she recorded this multiplatinum disc.
Summary/Advisory: Some of this disc's friskier tunes seem inappropriate when sung by a girl who, by many parents' standards, isn't even old enough to date. While generally positive, this disc could send mixed messages to LeAnn's peers about mature matters of the heart.

Robyn

◆ ◆

A native of Stockholm, Sweden, Robyn Carlsson was motivated to write her first song at age 11 out of the sadness of her parents' divorce. This street-smart artist was 19 when she recorded her million-selling album *Robyn Is Here*.

Title: *Robyn Is Here* (1997)
Label: RCA
Genre: R&B
Pro-Social Content: Expressions of romantic love dominate "Show Me Love" and "You've Got That Somethin'." Robyn demands commitment from her man on "The Last Time," "Just Another Girlfriend," and "Do You Know (What It Takes)?" She also refuses to put up with dishonesty from a boyfriend ("Don't Want You Back"). "Do You Really Want Me?" suggests specific ways men and women can improve their relationships. "Bumpy Ride" encourages listeners to persevere through difficult circumstances . . .
Objectionable Content: However, profanities *ruin* this song. Also, a lack of sexual self-control characterizes "Here We Go" ("Here we go makin' love

again . . . though we both know this is not right . . . It feels so right, it can't be wrong"). Similar lapses in judgment hurt "How" and "Robyn Is Here" (which talks of being "horny" and in a "freaky mood").

Summary/Advisory: Robyn has some worthwhile things to say. Too bad her smooth, sweet vocals and bouncy melodies occasionally succumb to overheating hormones.

Rolling Stones, The

◆ ◆

This band formed in 1963 in London, England. The original members included Mick Jagger, Keith Richards, Brian Jones, Bill Wyman, and Charlie Watts. Various members have come and gone through the years, but Jagger and Richards remain the crux of the band. They were inducted into the Rock and Roll Hall of Fame in 1989 and received Grammy's Lifetime Achievement Award in 1986.

Title: *Bridges to Babylon* (1997)
Label: Virgin
Genre: Rock
Pro-Social Content: A man longs to revive a failed relationship ("Always Suffering"). One line on the otherwise troubling "Saint of Me" says, "St. Paul the persecutor was a cruel and sinful man/Jesus hit him with a blinding light and then his life began."
Objectionable Content: Lead singer Mick Jagger maliciously threatens to maim and kill an unfaithful lover before leaving town "in a state of grace" ("Gunface"). "Out of Control" relates a life of poor choices, including drunkenness. Alcohol washes away pain on "Might As Well Get Juiced" and "Too Tight" (which also promotes marijuana). Jagger prays to the shrine of a sex partner ("Are You Already Over Me") and refuses to place faith in Christ ("Saint of Me"). Deluded into thinking he's ready to face eternity, he taunts death and hell on "Flip the Switch." Occasional profanities. The f-word is used.
Summary/Advisory: The founding members of The Rolling Stones have been on a 34-year musical journey leading to *Babylon*—and to the insolent assertion that inner peace lies in sex, drinking, hatred, violence, and a general hostility toward God. *That's* the key to happiness and satisfaction? Despite a positive sentiment or two, parents will be tempted to burn *Bridges*.

Title: *Voodoo Lounge* (1994)
Label: Virgin
Genre: Rock
Pro-Social Content: Tearing down relational walls and denouncing foolish pride are advised on "Baby Break It Down." In a reasonably neutral context, "Blinded by Rainbows" reminds listeners about "the pain He felt upon the cross" and asks, "Do you fear the final hour, do you kneel before the cross?" "Sweethearts Together" rejoices in a committed relationship, pledging, "I will stay right by your side."
Objectionable Content: "Sparks Will Fly" crudely prepares a woman for a wild sexual encounter. Equally offensive, "Suck on the Jugular" encourages orgies and alludes to homosexual dabblings. Sexual double entendres abound on "Brand New Car." Even thematically positive songs are spoiled by explicit and unnecessary lines like "'cause now I get those f——ing blues."
Summary/Advisory: Although slightly more pro-social than past Stones efforts, this disc carries on the band's tradition of glorifying sex in lewd terms. You won't "get no satisfaction" from a visit to the *Voodoo Lounge.* (SEE ALSO: Jagger, Mick)

Run-D.M.C.

◆ ◆ ◆ ◆ ◆ ◆ ◆ ◆ ◆ ◆ ◆ ◆ ◆ ◆ ◆ ◆

Joseph Simmons (Run), Darryl McDaniels (D.M.C.), and DJ Jason Mizell (Jam Master J) comprise this rap trio that released its first disc in 1984. Six more followed. Five of them went either gold or platinum, including the 3-million-selling 1986 release, *Raising Hell. Down with the King* debuted at number 1 on *Billboard*'s R&B chart.

Title: *Down with the King* (1993)
Label: Profile
Genre: Rap
Pro-Social Content: "Three Little Indians" claims "wisdom is more precious than gold." A valid, biblically based statement, but one the rest of the album fails to support.
Objectionable Content: This album should carry a warning label since many tracks are peppered with expletives, obnoxious street slang, and references to women as whores. "What's Next"

uses a hip-hop/reggae beat to request sex from a woman after an initial meeting ("I'm rubbin' her down till she started to frown . . . baby, where do I go now?").

Summary/Advisory: Even more disturbing than the album itself is the claim by band members of being new Christians. Their lyrics certainly don't bear that out. Perhaps a line from their song "Big Willie" epitomizes their conversion experience: "I'm born again, I got a Friend, but other than that. . . there ain't nothin' changed." Avoid this one.

Sade

◆ ◆ ◆ ◆ ◆ ◆ ◆ ◆ ◆ ◆ ◆ ◆ ◆ ◆ ◆ ◆ ◆ ◆ ◆ ◆

This Nigerian-born artist changed her name from Helen Folasade Adu to Sade (pronounced "shaw-day"). She moved to England at a young age and designed menswear before winning a Grammy in 1985 for Best New Artist. Her first three albums sold at least 1 million copies each.

Title: *Love Deluxe* (1992)
Label: Epic
Genre: Pop
Pro-Social Content: "No Ordinary Love" seeks to preserve a relationship. Likewise, "I Couldn't Love You More" vows not to "lay with or love another." Toward that end, "Cherish the Day" promises not to "go astray." "Feel No Pain" pleads the case of the unemployed, urging the listener to help them strive, move on, live long, have some future, smile, and live life. "Pearls" relates the sad scene of a Somalian mother gathering grains of rice for her starving children.

Objectionable Content: None

Summary/Advisory: This Anglo-African songstress sings mostly of committed love. Despite a fairly racy cover photo of a nude woman with arms folded across her breasts, this smooth collection is socially responsible and thought-provoking. There's a lot to *Love*.

Salt-N-Pepa

◆ ◆ ◆ ◆ ◆ ◆ ◆ ◆ ◆ ◆ ◆ ◆ ◆ ◆ ◆ ◆ ◆

This Queens, New York-based female rap trio is comprised of single moms Cheryl "Salt" James, Sandy "Pepa" Denton, and Dee Dee "DJ Spinderella LaToya" Roper. The group has produced several albums (four going platinum and *Brand New* going gold) and racked up numerous awards.

Title: *Brand New* (1997)
Label: PolyGram
Genre: R&B/Hip-hop
Pro-Social Content: "Imagine" condemns violence, racial prejudice, and selling drugs. The girls promote self-respect and tough love in the midst of an abusive situation ("The Clock Is Tickin'") and preach about putting God first and honoring our mothers ("Hold On").

Objectionable Content: Unfortunately, any spirituality is squelched by crude sexual slang and profanity ("R U Ready," "Knock Knock"). "Gitty Up" invites sodomy. On "Boy Toy," the singer eagerly awaits a tryst with a married man. "Do Me Right" finds a woman willing to give sex to anyone "attracted to the God" in her. The girls boast incessantly of their wealth, and three tracks glorify alcohol use (twice connected to driving).

Summary/Advisory: This follow-up to 1994's *Very Necessary* shows some improvement, but the girls have a long way to go. Especially disturbing is how they confuse spirituality and sexuality. Sample CCM's Out of Eden instead.

Title: *Very Necessary* (1993)
Label: London
Genre: Rap/Reggae
Pro-Social Content: None
Objectionable Content: The opening song from this popular female rap trio prepares the listener for a "rumpshaker flavor with the nasty rhymes." On that sorry promise, it delivers. Like the male artists who dominate the genre, these bad girls seek, perform, and boast about sex in a variety of immoral contexts. They refer to prostitution ("If she wants to be a freakin'

and sell it on the weekend, it's none of your business"), acts of violence ("Ask me any questions and my Smith & Wesson will answer"), and masturbation. The album ends with several minutes of pro-condom propaganda under the guise of an AIDS message.

Summary/Advisory: The girls attempt to get spiritual in the liner notes, giving thanks to Jesus for "guidance." But it's safe to say He had absolutely nothing to do with this hedonistic smut. Pass on the Salt-N-Pepa.

Sandler, Adam

◆ ◆ ◆ ◆ ◆ ◆ ◆ ◆ ◆ ◆ ◆ ◆ ◆ ◆ ◆ ◆ ◆ ◆ ◆ ◆

After getting his start cohosting an MTV quiz show, this *Saturday Night Live* alum sold 500,000 copies of his first music/comedy CD, *They're All Gonna Laugh at You.* He has also starred in motion pictures such as *Billy Madison, Happy Gilmore,* and *The Wedding Singer.*

Title: *They're All Gonna Laugh at You* (1993)
Label: Warner Bros.
Genre: Comedy
Pro-Social Content: None
Objectionable Content: Sophomoric humor and scatological references abound. Crude, unfunny jokes involve bestiality, oral sex, masturbation, urination, murder, drug use, and voyeurism. Four "The Beating of . . ." 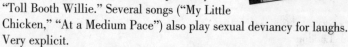 tracks use screams and sound effects to simulate violence against various high school staffers. A "priest" uses abusive profanity on "Toll Booth Willie." Several songs ("My Little Chicken," "At a Medium Pace") also play sexual deviancy for laughs. Very explicit.

Summary/Advisory: Twisted, raunchy stuff. As puerile as *Beavis and Butt-head,* Sandler doesn't even have the sense to hide behind animation. No shame and desperate for attention—a truly pitiful combination. Skip it.

Savage Garden

◆ ◆ ◆ ◆ ◆ ◆ ◆ ◆ ◆ ◆ ◆ ◆ ◆ ◆ ◆ ◆ ◆ ◆ ◆ ◆

This group from Down Under consists of Daniel Jones and Darren Hayes. In addition to the pair's success in the States, "I Want You" became the biggest-selling Australian single of 1996.

Title: *Savage Garden* (1997)
Label: Columbia
Genre: Pop
Pro-Social Content: "To the Moon & Back" correctly implies that parental rejection can make a girl lonely, bitter, withdrawn, and eager for a romantic surrogate. On "Santa Monica," the singer ponders the value society places on outward appearances ("On the telephone line, I am anyone . . . any height, any age"). Several neutral tunes examine dynamic relationships ("I Want You," "Carry on Dancing") and the emotional upheaval that occurs when they end ("Tears of Pearls," "A Thousand Words").
Objectionable Content: Mild profanity taints "Promises" and "Violet." A sexual encounter is the center of "Universe" ("Our clothes are on the floor . . . entwined to perfection . . . when you wake up, I won't be found"). Similarly, "Truly Madly Deeply" speaks of bathing and lying together.
Summary/Advisory: Sweet and bitter fruit from the same *Garden*. Musically, this Australian duo is terrific, but fans of their energized beats and smooth vocals will reap a better lyrical harvest with CCM's East to West or Tony Vincent.

Scarface

◆ ◆ ◆ ◆ ◆ ◆ ◆ ◆ ◆ ◆ ◆ ◆ ◆ ◆ ◆ ◆ ◆ ◆ ◆ ◆

Born Brad Johnson, this rapper was one of the original members of the Geto Boys.

Title: *The World Is Yours* (1993)
Label: Priority
Genre: Gangsta rap
Pro-Social Content: None
Objectionable Content: The first song alone

includes 46 uses of the f-word. It is indicative of things to come on this totally depraved record. Nearly every track describes murder or promotes violence—often directed at police. Lyrics include "I'm a born killer" ("Comin' AGG"), "I used to pack a pistol, but Uzis do it better . . . AK-47 to your face" ("Still That Aggin #"), and "Always look a man in the eye before you kill him" ("He's Dead"). Scarface also relates—in explicit and sadistic detail—deviant and violent sexual acts, often abusive to women. On "I Need a Favor," he asks his girl to "do" [have sex with] a friend. She consents after he claims it will make him respect her more. Also, numerous songs point to alcohol and marijuana as problem-solvers.

Summary/Advisory: Priority Records continues to specialize in antisocial material. Keep young rap fans out of Scarface's *World*.

Seal

◆ ◆ ◆ ◆ ◆ ◆ ◆ ◆ ◆ ◆ ◆ ◆ ◆ ◆ ◆ ◆ ◆ ◆ ◆ ◆

Seal was born Sealhenry Samuel in Paddington, England, and is of Nigerian/Brazilian descent. He picked up a Grammy in 1996 for both song and record of the year ("Kiss from a Rose").

Title: *Seal* (1994)
Label: Warner Bros.
Genre: Pop/Adult contemporary
Pro-Social Content: On the Grammy-winning hit single, "Kiss from a Rose," the artist refers to a woman as a positive influence in his life ("the light on the dark side of me"). Seal also credits someone's unconditional love with giving him a sense of purpose and peace ("Bring It On"). He points to Christ's death as personally relevant on "I'm Alive" ("Blood on the cross . . . it changed my life") and seeks relational peace and reconciliation on "Dreaming in Metaphors."

Objectionable Content: In the liner notes, Seal mentions how he sought advice from a palm reader. Though unclear, "Newborn Friend" includes the line, "I would dance with a total stranger and hold *him* in my arms" [emphasis added].

Summary/Advisory: Most of *Seal*'s lyrics are obscure thoughts bridged by a melody—a disjointed stream of consciousness that results in generally pleasant, inoffensive listening. This gifted artist has described his music as "very idealistic." Cryptic maybe, but it is optimistic.

Selena

◆ ◆ ◆ ◆ ◆ ◆ ◆ ◆ ◆ ◆ ◆ ◆ ◆ ◆ ◆ ◆ ◆ ◆ ◆

A native of Lake Jackson, Texas, Selena Quintanilla began her singing career as the 10-year-old lead singer of Selena y Los Dinos. Her Grammy-nominated 1994 release *Amor Prohibido* went platinum, and two other albums went gold. Selena was shot and killed by a disgruntled former employee on March 31, 1995.

Title: *Selena* (1997)
Label: EMI Latin
Genre: Latin pop/Adult contemporary
Pro-Social Content: As part of a disco medley, Selena covers Gloria Gaynor's 1979 hit about a jilted woman determined to persevere ("I Will Survive"). A woman tempted to flee a troubled

relationship (presumably a marriage) returns home on "Only Love." An inno-cent young lady guards her heart and successfully resists the lure of a pas-sionate fling, stating, "I know it's not right" ("I Could Fall in Love"). Singing the urgent, cautionary words of Anita from *West Side Story*, Selena describes a man guilty of murder who cannot love and warns a friend to avoid "A Boy Like That." Guitar licks punctuate Lil' Ray's upbeat reminiscence of Selena on "One More Time" ("So many miles, so many places . . . leavin' smiles on their faces/What I wouldn't give to hear her sing one more time").
Objectionable Content: None
Summary/Advisory: This collection, recorded by the late Tejana singer and revived for the 1997 film about her life, peaked at number 7. Tender, roman-tic ballads. Energetic live performances. The result is a fitting tribute to this wholesome Latina songstress for whom the curtain fell much too soon. [This album review also appears in the "Soundtrack" section.]

Title: *Dreaming of You* (1995)
Label: EMI
Genre: Latin/Adult contemporary
Pro-Social Content: Selena resists giving in to the temptation of physical intimacy on "I Could Fall in Love," stating, "I know it's not right." Songs express love over emotional ("Dreaming of You") and geographical ("Missing My Baby," "Wherever You Are") distance. Other cuts explore the ups and downs of romance ("Como La Flor," "I'm Getting Used to You," "Bidi Bidi Bom Bom").

Objectionable Content: The artist tries to drown her sorrows in alcohol ("You, Only You") and knowingly pursues a perilous infatuation ("Captive Heart").

Summary/Advisory: Selena's predominantly positive path to stardom came to a sudden halt when the artist was tragically murdered. Her final, chart-topping effort includes five songs performed in English, two bilingual duets, and the balance in Spanish (liner notes include translations). With the noted exceptions, *Dreaming of You* is a solid pick. *Nuestra última despedida, Selena.*

Seven Mary Three

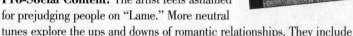

Seven Mary Three is Jason Ross, Jason Pollock, Casey Daniel, and Giti Khalsa. In 1992, the two Jasons met while attending the same college. The remaining band members were added later. Seven Mary Three first skyrocketed into public awareness when Orlando radio station WJRR added the song "Cumbersome" to its playlist.

Title: *American Standard* (1995)
Label: Atlantic
Genre: Alternative
Pro-Social Content: The artist feels ashamed for prejudging people on "Lame." More neutral tunes explore the ups and downs of romantic relationships. They include the hit "Cumbersome," which wants to put an end to "stone throwing."

Objectionable Content: "Water's Edge" contains the album's lone use of the f-word. On "Margaret," a 70-year-old man tells the singer how he was recently seduced by a 16-year-old girl who wants to marry him and have 15 children ("Before she knew my name, she was in my bed"). "Roderigo" could inspire teen rebellion against parental authority. "I'm only one ciga-rette away from mobility," croons the waking artist on "Punch in Punch Out." On "Devil Boy," he jabs at the Catholic church for harrassing him about missing holiday masses.

Summary/Advisory: Try to imagine John Mellencamp with an alternative growl. That's the sound of Seven Mary Three, a band whose *American Standard* won't meet discerning parents' *family* standards. A lyrically dis-appointing effort.

Shai

◆ ◆ ◆ ◆ ◆ ◆ ◆ ◆ ◆ ◆ ◆ ◆ ◆ ◆ ◆ ◆ ◆ ◆ ◆ ◆

Shai (pronounced "shy") is a vocal quartet consisting of Garfield Bright, Marc Gay, Carl Martin, and Darnell Rensalier. The members met at Howard University in Washington, D.C.

Title: *If I Ever Fall in Love* (1993)
Label: Gasoline Alley/MCA
Genre: R&B
Pro-Social Content: Shai attempts to be sensitive in the heavily sentimental "If I Ever Fall in Love," "Comforter," "Together Forever," and "Baby I'm Yours."
Objectionable Content: The group turns from sensitivity to sensuality on "Sexual Interlude" and "Sexual" ("I perspire with desire when I see your naked skin"). "Waiting for the Day" increases the sexual pressure ("I want . . . to feel your body close to mine . . . stay all night") as it ascribes meaning to saying "I do" that has *no* connection to marriage.
Summary/Advisory: Sweet-sounding quartet Shai sends mixed signals by salting its album of mostly harmless romantic ballads with sexual pandering. One wonders how the group reconciles its profuse liner-note thanks to God—and its claim to have been "shown the way" on "Lord I've Come"—with this kind of attitude.

Shakur, Tupac

◆ ◆ ◆ ◆ ◆ ◆ ◆ ◆ ◆ ◆ ◆ ◆ ◆ ◆ ◆ ◆ ◆ ◆ ◆ ◆

Rapper/actor Tupac Shakur's gangsta rap albums have gone gold, platinum, or multiplatinum. He also recorded under the names 2Pac and Makaveli, but it's all of the same ilk. The deaths of at least two police officers have been blamed on Shakur's lyrics glamorizing cop-killing. The hostile rapper was himself murdered in a drive-by shooting on September 13, 1996, as he and his manager were motoring down a busy Las Vegas street. It fulfilled a prediction Shakur made in *Details* [4/96]: "I know I'm going to die in violence. . . . All the good n——ers who change the world die in violence." Shakur costarred in films including *Poetic Justice* and *Gang Related*.

Title: *R U Still Down? (Remember Me)* (1997)
Label: Interscope
Genre: Gangsta rap
Pro-Social Content: None
Objectionable Content: Near-constant use of the f-word on this double disc is just the beginning. Twelve of the project's 26 tracks glamorize either drugs or alcohol, occasionally in conjunction with driving a car ("Definition of a Thug N-gga," "F—- All Y'all"). The former also alludes to gang members having tag-team sex with the same girl. Tupac treats women like cigarettes—an impersonal source of momentary pleasure to be discarded on the street ("I'm lookin' for a b—ch to f—-," "Got the d—- and now you get the pistol, honey"). Hair-trigger black-on-black brutality and cop-killing rears its ugly head on at least 11 cuts ("Should I shoot his b—ch," "Every n-gger on my block dropped two cops," "I put the n-gger in his casket"). The rapper places faith in suicide and reincarnation on "Only Fear of Death."
Summary/Advisory: From the grave, Tupac terrorizes families with this, his second posthumous release (which sold more than 4 million copies). It's nearly two hours of drugs, misogyny, alcohol, gang violence, anarchy, and rutting sexuality. Until Shakur's record label runs out of squirreled-away recordings, parents won't be able to rest in peace.

Title: *The Don Killuminati: The 7 Day Theory* (1996)
(Released under the alias "Makaveli")
Label: Death Row
Genre: Gangsta rap
Pro-Social Content: "Blasphemy" finds a preacher accurately describing salvation and Christ's return and a woman reciting the Lord's Prayer.
Objectionable Content: The song's lyrics also include a man asking, "Is God just another cop waitin' to beat my a—?" On "Bomb First," the rapper wants to kill people and send them to hell and refers to the "holy Koran." Other tracks showcase explicit sexual references ("Me and My Girlfriend," "Toss It Up") and glorify drugs and alcohol ("To Live & Die in L.A.," "Hail Mary," "Krazy"). Tupac, who died by the gun, lives by the gun throughout. For example, the late rapper boasts, "Enemies bleed when I hold my

chrome" ("Hold Ya Head"). A constant flow of obscenities makes his back-
alley saber rattling even more hateful.
Summary/Advisory: This posthumous Tupac Shakur disc hit number 1
with first-week sales of 646,000 copies. During his life, Shakur made a
fortune exploiting drugs, violence, and sexual perversion. *Theory* delivers
more of the same from this bitter, misogynistic hoodlum.

Title: *All Eyez on Me* (1996)
Label: Death Row/Interscope
Genre: Gangsta rap
Pro-Social Content: None
Objectionable Content: As offensive as 2Pac's work has been in the past,
All Eyez on Me steps up the sexual braggadocio and perversity. Raunchy
themes range from oral and anal sex ("Whatz Ya Phone #," "Check Out
Time") to multiple partners ("Run Tha Streetz," "Can't C Me") and sex with
minors. Several cuts refer to suicide. One states, "Play your game of
Russian roulette and have a blast" ("Got My Mind Made Up"). The f-word
is used literally hundreds of times throughout. Murder is a way to resolve
conflict on "Ain't Hard 2 Find," "2 of Amerikaz Most Wanted," "No More
Pain," "Ambitionz Az a Ridah," "When We Ride," "Tradin' War Stories,"
and others. 2Pac raps about "smoking weed," "getting drunk," and "sellin'
narcotics." His warped theology includes a belief in reincarnation ("No
More Pain," "Only God Can Judge Me").
Summary/Advisory: This 132-minute double-disc—which has sold
more than 7 million copies—spent its first two weeks at number 1. On
"Got My Mind Made Up" the artist boasts, "My lyrics motivate the
planet." Let's hope not. A reviewer for *USA Today* actually praised *All
Eyez on Me* as "a thug-a-thon of . . . tough raps about mean streets, guns,
drugs and 'b—ches.'" But blindness is better than having all eyes on
2Pac.

Title: *Me Against the World* (1995)
Label: Interscope
Genre: Gangsta rap
Pro-Social Content: On "Dear Mama," 2Pac thanks his mother (a mem-
ber of the Black Panther Party) for doing her best to raise him.
Objectionable Content: Seven cuts glorify smoking marijuana or
"blunts" (hollowed out cigars stuffed with pot). On "Death Around the
Corner," Shakur proudly recalls drinking liquor from a very young age. "It
Ain't Easy" and "Temptations" make crude sexual references. Obscenities

appear throughout. Numerous tracks venerate the violent, including "So Many Tears" ("You wanna last? Be the first to blast!"). "Outlaw" talks of shooting a district attorney and tells gangsta wannabes, "Keep it real—pack that steel." Hatred oozes from this disc, which one might surmise from the song title "F——- the World."

Summary/Advisory: When this album debuted, 2Pac (known by the penal system as Tupac Shakur) was serving a prison term for sexually assaulting a fan. He preached what he practiced, making the popularity of *World* especially disturbing. Avoid this trash at all costs.

Silk

◆ ◆

The Atlanta, Georgia, R&B quintet is Timothy Cameron, Jimmy Gates, Jonathan Rasboro, Gary Jenkins, and Gary Glenn.

Title: *Lose Control* (1993)
Label: Keia/Elektra
Genre: R&B
Pro-Social Content: Only the album's final cut, "I Gave to You," could be interpreted as platonic, innocent romance.
Objectionable Content: Otherwise, hormones rage throughout. The group's hit "Happy Days" begs, wheedles, and cajoles "dope honeys" whose "sex has got it goin' on" to "gimme what I want," which is to "lick you up and down." The follow-up single, "Freak Me," offers more of the same, panting "let me make you real hot" by using whipped cream. In the aptly-titled "Don't Keep Me Waiting," the boys insist on making it "hurt so good" while the girl wants them to "slow down" and "talk." Even the innocent-sounding "Girl U 4 Me" feels the need to add "freak ya" and "make love."
Summary/Advisory: Smooth-talking Silk (much like Boyz II Men) has chiseled out its niche with a set of syrupy love ballads and hip-hop tunes tainted by an abundance of sexual come-ons.

Silkk the Shocker

◆ ◆ ◆ ◆ ◆ ◆ ◆ ◆ ◆ ◆ ◆ ◆ ◆ ◆ ◆ ◆ ◆ ◆ ◆

New Orleans native Silkk the Shocker and his two brothers (Master P and C-Murder) recorded together as TRU before all three embarked on solo careers. Silkk's sophomore disc, *Charge It 2 Da Game*, went platinum in less than a month. The rapper also appeared in the 1998 film *I Got the Hook Up*.

Title: *Charge It 2 Da Game* (1998)
Label: Priority
Genre: Gangsta rap
Pro-Social Content: None
Objectionable Content: Three of this chart-topping R&B disc's 20 tracks boast of dealing drugs ("Give Me the World," "What Gangstas Do," "Mama Always Told Me"). Many others celebrate using them with lines such as, "I go smoke some bud," "sit back and maintain the coke," and "keep the weed lighted." Explicit references to sexual intercourse appear on the ill-spirited "Thug 'N' Me," "Ummm," and "Tell Me," a cut about violent, anonymous sex that degrades women ("Some b—ches let you f— 'em till they bleed"). Snoop Doggy Dogg appears on "Give Me the World" to promote slapping women as a sign of manliness. Violent threats include "Cut off one of your fingers, send it in the mail," "Slammin' jive b—ches like you dead in the pavement," and "My pops say look 'em in the eye before I kill 'em."
Summary/Advisory: Obscenity-strewn trash from start to finish. Drugs. Misogyny. Murder. Sexual perversion. Teens could pay a very high price if they let this gangsta *Charge It* at their expense. Keep youngsters away from Silkk the Shocker.

Silverchair

◆ ◆ ◆ ◆ ◆ ◆ ◆ ◆ ◆ ◆ ◆ ◆ ◆ ◆ ◆ ◆ ◆ ◆ ◆

The Australian teenage trio Silverchair made waves in the music industry when its debut album, *Frogstomp*, sold more than two million copies in the U.S. alone. The band consists of Daniel Johns, Chris Joannou, and Ben Gillies.

Title: *Freak Show* (1997)
Label: Epic

Genre: Alternative
Pro-Social Content: A friend's self-destructive
addiction to drugs and alcohol is clearly condemned on "Pop Song for Us Rejects." In the
same vein, one line on "Learn to Hate" says,
"As you pump drugs into your bloodstream, I
sit observing in disgust."
Objectionable Content: This song also
relates and encourages deep animosity toward others ("Hating you
should be introduced as a new law/Take the time to learn to hate")—an irrec-
oncilable attitude in light of 1 John 3:15. While outwardly hostile, "Abuse
Me" also solicits cruelty. In fact, self-loathing is a recurring theme. The 17-
year-old lead singer admits to "contemplating suicide" ("No Association")
and, believing he has "lived too long," insists of someone, "Take me to a
place where I can die" ("Slave"). Life is compared to living in a "Cemetery,"
a hopelessness echoed on "Roses," "The Closing," and "Petrol & Chlorine."
Summary/Advisory: Malicious anger. Self-pity. Nihilism. Despair.
"We've always liked dark, aggressive music," Silverchair's Daniel Johns
told *Entertainment Weekly* [2/7/97]. "When I write lyrics, I just like to focus
on the negative side of what's happened to us. We're not interested in
happy pop music." It shows. Avoid this aberration.

Title: *Frogstomp* (1995)
Label: Epic
Genre: Alternative
Pro-Social Content: "Faultline" is a tribute to victims of natural disas-
ters. "Pure Massacre" mourns families needlessly torn apart. Perseverance
is urged on "Findaway" ("Don't give in, don't give in . . . thinking negative
. . . is eating you down to the bone"). Those in emotional pain are encouraged to seek help ("Shade").
Objectionable Content: "Cicado" describes growing up as a downhill
journey filled with boredom. "Suicidal Dream" seems to advocate suicide as
the singer fantasizes about hanging himself. Hatred for others takes the fore
on "Israel's Son."
Summary/Advisory: This paradoxical teen trio (the oldest member was 16
when the disc was released) has some worthwhile things to say. Too bad
those upbeat messages are packaged alongside dark, disturbing tracks.
Johns told *Rip* [12/95], "Every time I come up with a good idea for a song,
it's about death." An inconsistent effort.

Sister Hazel

◆ ◆ ◆ ◆ ◆ ◆ ◆ ◆ ◆ ◆ ◆ ◆ ◆ ◆ ◆ ◆ ◆ ◆ ◆

This five-man band consists of Andrew Copeland, Ken Block, Jeff Beres, Ryan Newell, and Mark Trojanowski. Their disc *Somewhere More Familiar* went gold and spent nearly a year on *Billboard*'s pop album chart.

Title: *Somewhere More Familiar* (1997)
Label: Universal
Genre: Acoustic rock
Pro-Social Content: A man expresses love and gratitude to the woman who believed in him enough to marry him ("Cerilene"). "Look to the Children" believes we can recapture the innocence of youth after "hav[ing] seen a storm or two" in life. A contented, cheerful person claims to be

"Happy." The singer recalls a sweet haunt where children laughed and romance bloomed before the site was covered by an office building ("Just Remember"). According to "Concede," loving behavior includes faithfulness, flexibility, comforting, and listening. When interpersonal trials ensue, the artist examines his own heart ("So Long"), tries to improve ("All for You"), and isn't bitter toward a partner who calls it quits ("Wanted It to Be").
Objectionable Content: None
Summary/Advisory: This act maintains a positive outlook on life. Lyrically solid. Several cuts succumb to poetic silliness, but the disc never veers out of bounds. For teens partial to acoustic rock, parents can safely encourage them to explore *Somewhere More Familiar*.

Slayer

◆ ◆ ◆ ◆ ◆ ◆ ◆ ◆ ◆ ◆ ◆ ◆ ◆ ◆ ◆ ◆ ◆ ◆ ◆

Slayer is a California-based death metal band (Tom Araya, Jeff Hanneman, Kerry King, Paul Bostaph) whose lyrics glamorize mass murderers and exalt the devil. The fans of Slayer have been known to carve the act's name into their forearms.

Title: *Divine Intervention* (1994)
Label: American
Genre: Death metal

Pro-Social Content: None

Objectionable Content: Plenty. "Serenity in Murder" refers to killing as "spiritual ecstasy"—a sick lust for violence that is also prominent on "Killing Fields," "Dittohead," and "213" (a title inspired by Jeffrey Dahmer's apartment number). The latter attempts to titillate listeners with morbid descriptions of sexualized homicide. On "Sex. Murder. Art," the singer taunts a woman, screaming threats at her in graphic detail regarding the sadistic rape he's about to commit ("Can't rid the sexual fascination . . . You're nothing, an object of animation . . . beaten into submission, raping again and again"). Anti-Christian hatred is the sole focus of "Circle of Beliefs."

Summary/Advisory: Wallowing in violent, occultic, and sexual themes is common to this exploitive genre. What's even scarier is that this was a Top-10 disc by a band whose lyrics have been connected with violent real-life crimes. Slay teens' requests for this reprehensible trash.

Smash Mouth

◆ ◆ ◆ ◆ ◆ ◆ ◆ ◆ ◆ ◆ ◆ ◆ ◆ ◆ ◆ ◆ ◆ ◆ ◆ ◆

Based in San Jose, California, Smash Mouth is Steve Harwell, Gregory Camp, Paul DeLisle, and Devin Coleman. The band's big break came in 1996 when a local modern rock radio station played a track from the then-unsigned foursome's demo. It was well received and led to a record contract with a major label.

Title: *Fush Yu Mang* (1997)
Label: Interscope
Genre: Punk/Retro rock
Pro-Social Content: A young girl selling sex for drugs is said to be living a "sad" existence ("Nervous in the Alley"). One line on the band's remake of the 1975 War hit "Why Can't We Be Friends" promotes racial harmony.
Objectionable Content: The chart-topping modern rock single "Walkin' in the Sun" denounces crack cocaine but advocates marijuana use. Similarly, "Heave-Ho" glamorizes pot-smoking and alcohol. Lead vocalist Steve Harwell spews the f-word on "Let's Rock," a celebration of vice that

disregards "the prices that I'll later have to pay." At a bar, he indiscriminately tries to pick up a woman—*any woman*—for cheap sex ("Beer Goggles"). On "The Fonz," a man contemplates suicide and the reaction it might get ("When you pulled your own trigger/They all gathered around to watch"). The explicit advisory sticker is much deserved. Also, the singer's bisexual girlfriend upsets him by continually calling out the name of her lesbian lover while they're having sex ("Flo"). **Summary/Advisory:** Drugs. Alcohol. Suicide. Sex with anything that moves. Smash Mouth's grinding, over-amplified rhythms are drowned out only by the band's sick, selfish hedonism.

Smashing Pumpkins, The

The original Smashing Pumpkins consisted of Billy Corgan, James Iha, D'Arcy Wretzky, and Jimmy Chamberlain (replaced because of his chronic heroin use). The double disc *Mellon Collie and the Infinite Sadness* sold more than 8 million units.

Title: *Mellon Collie and the Infinite Sadness* (1995)
Label: Virgin
Genre: Alternative
Pro-Social Content: Sincerity and reconciliation get positive nods on "Tonight Tonight," while romantic fidelity is valued on "Beautiful" and "Galapogos." The optimistic "Thirty-three" testifies to the permanence of love, and "Take Me Down" attributes love to God.
Objectionable Content: However, those upbeat songs must compete with "Bodies" ("Love is suicide"), "Jellybelly" ("Living makes me sick, so sick I wish I'd die"), and other nihilistic tunes. On "F— You (An Ode to No One)," the singer brags about losing his virginity "to a no good girl." This cut also uses the name of the Virgin Mary in an unflattering context. "Zero" characterizes God as empty and powerless. Though not stickered for obscenities, harsh language crops up throughout.

Summary/Advisory: This two-disc set is only the third double-length project in history to debut as *Billboard's* top pop album. Two hours of music. Twenty-eight songs. Very little worth a listen. From the screaming guitars of James Iha to the whining screams of lead singer Billy Corgan, the dark side dominates this disc's split personality. In the end, there's entirely too much melancholy on *Mellon Collie.*

Title: *Pisces Iscariot* (1994)
Label: Virgin
Genre: Alternative
Pro-Social Content: "Whir" laments "wasted years" and considers a love's desire to settle down ("She says she wants to marry me/She says she wants a family").
Objectionable Content: Angst-ridden lines about a life devoid of purpose are strewn throughout. "Pissant" combines anger and apathy. On "Plume," lead singer Billy Corgan moans, "My boredom has outshined the sun." "La Dolly Vita" is a being who grants wisdom and visions (probably either a mystic or a metaphor for drugs). The f-word appears in several places.
Summary/Advisory: *Pisces* embodies the obscure poetry of Generation X to the tune of grinding guitars and acoustic ballads. By mumbling cryptic lyrics, the band veils many of its messages. And most of what *is* discernable isn't worth listening to.

Title: *Siamese Dream* (1993)
Label: Virgin
Genre: Alternative
Pro-Social Content: A few positive lines scattered throughout the project are ultimately squelched by overriding themes of negativity and despair. For example, "your life is a prize, renew and revive" is soon followed by the line "life's a bummer when you're a hummer, yeah, life's a drag."
Objectionable Content: Dark themes dominate this disc. "Quiet" portrays life as a mess, humans as fossils and relics, and God as an uncaring being who has turned a deaf ear to His creation. The offensively titled "Silverf——" disturbingly describes the violence resulting from dysfunctional living. Escape from misery is the focus of "Rocket," though the song's journey through space could easily be interpreted by troubled teens as a metaphor suggesting suicide.
Summary/Advisory: The words are often hard to make out, but parents can contact Virgin for a lyric sheet. Ultimately, despair and self-loathing (lines such as "I never liked me anyway") will perpetuate the hopelessness felt by disillusioned adolescents.

Smith, Will

◆ ◆ ◆ ◆ ◆ ◆ ◆ ◆ ◆ ◆ ◆ ◆ ◆ ◆ ◆ ◆ ◆ ◆ ◆ ◆

The rapper/actor grew up in middle-class Philadelphia, Pennsylvania, and was nicknamed Prince by his teachers because he was always charming his way out of trouble. Later, he added "Fresh" to it and, at age 12, started rapping as part of the duo DJ Jazzy Jeff and the Fresh Prince. He has since won several Grammys. In 1989, NBC cast him in the role he was born to play—a street-smart kid from West Philly transplanted in Beverly Hills—in the television sitcom *The Fresh Prince of Bel-Air*. After small parts in several films, Will Smith hit the jackpot with roles in the sci-fi adventure movies *Independence Day* and *Men in Black*. On December 31, 1997, he married actress Jada Pinkett.

Title: *Big Willie Style* (1997)
Label: Columbia
Genre: Rap
Pro-Social Content: On "It's All Good," Smith anticipates arriving home to his boy's hugs. He prays to be a good dad and advises his son to turn vengeful anger over to God "'cause hate in your heart will consume you, too" ("Just the Two of Us"). Romantically, he's hesitant to pursue a woman until he knows for sure he's not "home-wreckin'" ("Candy"). . . .

Objectionable Content: However, the same song makes sexual advances by erotically sampling the names of favorite sweets ("He tryin' to get a Reese's piece of the Kit-Kat . . . we could Snicker all night at my Jolly Ranch"). Dancing and sex are one and the same on "Y'all Know." Five tracks find Smith boasting of his fortune and fame, while "Gettin' Jiggy Wit It" and "Miami" revel in the casual sex available to stars. The couple on "Chasing Forever" has cohabited for several years.

Summary/Advisory: This likable actor/musician isn't as raunchy as most of his rapping peers. Still, he's far from wholesome. A few pro-social ideals can't rescue multiplatinum *Big Willie*.

Snoop Doggy Dogg

◆ ◆ ◆ ◆ ◆ ◆ ◆ ◆ ◆ ◆ ◆ ◆ ◆ ◆ ◆ ◆ ◆ ◆ ◆

Born Calvin Broadus, he spent several years in and out of prison after graduating from high school. His first solo record, *Doggystyle,* has sold more than 4 million copies. Its violent, misogynistic lyrics provided the primary evidence for pro-family activist Dr. C. Delores Tucker, who aggressively approached Interscope's then-parent company Time-Warner with a call for social responsibility. Time-Warner

later dropped Interscope, a troublesome label that has changed hands several times since. Snoop appeared in the 1998 film *Half Baked,* a feature-length tribute to its main character—marijuana.

Title: *Tha Doggfather* (1996)
Label: Death Row/Interscope
Genre: Gangsta rap
Pro-Social Content: Although Snoop maligns women on numerous tracks, "Doggyland" calls mothers "righteous" and "queens."
Objectionable Content: This lost Dogg is as rabid as ever. A woman is deemed worthless except for her ability to perform oral sex ("You Thought"). "Blueberry," "Gold Rush," "Groupie," and "Freestyle Conversation" glamorize marijuana smoking. Several cuts convey extreme disrespect for women, calling them "b—ches" and "whores." The artist boasts of engaging in perverted sex with a fan ("Groupie"). Violence—including a drive-by shooting—is required to protect a cocaine business on "Downtown Assassins" ("Murder's an everyday thing in the city . . . Circle 'round the block, let 'em have it"). The need to carry a gun is also mentioned on "Snoop's Upside Ya Head," "2001," "Gold Rush," "Snoop Bounce," and "(Tear 'Em Off) Me & My Doggz." Obscenities abound, most notably the f-word and crude anatomical slang.
Summary/Advisory: Once clothed exclusively in baggy jeans and baseball caps, this artist donned Italian suits for *Tha Doggfather.* But a well-dressed thug is still a thug. Despite attempts by record execs to position this project as the urban ruminations of a more positive, socially conscientious Snoop, it's still immoral propaganda.

Title: *Doggystyle* (1993)
Label: Death Row/Interscope
Genre: Gangsta rap
Pro-Social Content: None
Objectionable Content: Misogynistic, violent, sexually explicit lyrics take center stage on this offensive collection. "Ain't No Fun" brags about oral and group sex, valuing women no further than the act itself ("The b—ch ain't s— to me . . . give me ten b—chs, then I'll f— all ten"). As the record's thinly veiled title suggests, Snoop also hounds after anal intercourse. Marijuana use (often referred to by the street term *chronic*) is glorified on at least five tracks. "The Shiznit" and "Who Am I" advocate murdering police officers.
Summary/Advisory: This Dogg has fleas, but no one seems to care. The media has praised the album as urban art, and more than a million copies followed listeners home in record time (802,000 in *one week*). Avoid this trash at all costs.

Snow

◆ ◆ ◆ ◆ ◆ ◆ ◆ ◆ ◆ ◆ ◆ ◆ ◆ ◆ ◆ ◆ ◆ ◆ ◆ ◆

This white male reggae singer was born Darren O'Brien in 1969. His one album went platinum.

Title: *12 Inches of Snow* (1993)
Label: EastWest
Genre: Reggae/Rap
Pro-Social Content: "Ease Up" advises a drug addict to give up a lifestyle of prostitution and robbery for the sake of her young son.
Objectionable Content: The value of women is cheapened throughout this disc. "Uhh in You" is a crudely brazen sexual proposition. Love is frequently confused with sex or mere infatuation. On "Runaway," Snow makes a vulgar reference to oral sex to demean a girl he claims is "nothin' but a fat fool."
Summary/Advisory: Catchy melodies and stylish production help explain the singer's appeal. But the content misses the mark. Snow describes himself on "Creative Child" as "wicked as a tyrant." He's not kidding, having once been on probation for attempted murder. That attitude shows on this album—one that deserves to be buried in a 10-foot drift.

Soul Asylum

◆ ◆ ◆ ◆ ◆ ◆ ◆ ◆ ◆ ◆ ◆ ◆ ◆ ◆ ◆ ◆ ◆ ◆

This band consists of David Pirner, Sterling Campbell, Karl Mueller, and Dan Murphy. Soul Asylum signed with Columbia Records in 1991 and soon after released the platinum *Grave Dancer's Union*.

Title: *Let Your Dim Light Shine* (1995)
Label: Columbia
Genre: Rock
Pro-Social Content: A mother values each of her 13 children on "Eyes of a Child."
Objectionable Content: Instead of counting life's blessings, the hit single "Misery" dreams of creating a company that manufactures despair. A prostitute figures prominently in the bizarre chain of events on "String of Pearls." When a despondent girl has second thoughts about suicide, the band suggests that she "chickened out" ("Just Like Anyone"). "Crawl" glorifies getting too drunk to walk. Taking drugs to deal with life is portrayed as normal rather than self-destructive ("Eyes of a Child"). Nihilism leads to hedonism on "Hopes Up," which claims, "There's just no substitute for fun." Lying and stealing are justified by employing situational ethics and blaming the past ("I Did My Best").
Summary/Advisory: Misery, disappointment, and insecure disillusionment have become lyrical staples for this moody bunch. A light *this* dim serves no purpose. Just turn it off.

Title: *Grave Dancers Union* (1992)
Label: Columbia
Genre: Rock
Pro-Social Content: Not much. "Get on Out" considers worrying worthless ("Cast all your frustrations to the bottomless sea").
Objectionable Content: The fatalistic "New World" claims, "You can't believe in yourself, you can't believe in anyone else." Although the video for "Runaway Train" has been credited with restoring families, the lyrics tell kids that running away is "easier than dealing with the pain" and suggest there can be no return home ("No one can help me now; I'm in too

deep . . . never going back"). The singer "falls in love with a hooker" on "Without a Trace," and "99%" recommends cohabitation.

Summary/Advisory: Like so many modern bands, Soul Asylum carves its niche by singing about disenchantment and alienation. And while the lyrics themselves don't promote drug use, *Rolling Stone* referred to the band as "a half-step away from a number of 12-step programs." A vacuous effort.

Soundgarden

◆ ◆ ◆ ◆ ◆ ◆ ◆ ◆ ◆ ◆ ◆ ◆ ◆ ◆ ◆ ◆ ◆ ◆ ◆ ◆

Soundgarden consists of band members Chris Cornell, Kim Thayil, Ben Shepherd, and Matt Cameron. They have won an MTV video music award ("Black Hole Sun") and a Grammy for the album *Superunknown*. The band called it quits in April 1997.

Title: *Down on the Upside* (1996)
Label: A&M
Genre: Alternative
Pro-Social Content: None
Objectionable Content: "Ty Cobb" spews obscenities as it promotes revenge and hatred. "Switch Opens" advises slaves to hang their owners (a far cry from Ephesians 6:5). On "Burden in My Hand," the singer tells listeners to "drown in alcohol" and commit suicide ("kill your health and kill yourself and kill everything you love"). He admits to having a death wish ("Blow Up the Whole World"), denounces authority and conformity ("Boot Camp," "No Attention"), and claims he only finds pleasure in the pain of others ("Rhinosaur"). On "Tighter & Tighter," he hopes for "one last sin" before he dies, presumably a night of hedonistic sex. The f-word punctuates lines filled with hopelessness, bitterness, and musings about suicide.

Summary/Advisory: Named after a Seattle pipe sculpture that makes unearthly howling noises in the wind, the band Soundgarden produces a similar but less edifying racket with *Down on the Upside*. Even its few innocuous tracks get lost in a pessimistic flurry of darkness, depression, anger, and hateful obscenities. There is no upside to this disc—except possibly that, after 66 minutes, it's over.

Title: *Superunknown* (1994)
Label: A&M

Genre: Hard rock
Pro-Social Content: Two songs on this number-1 pop debut incorporate elements of hope. "Head Down" encourages listeners to keep their chins up and smile in the face of adversity. "Half" reminds them that, despite the odds, "we still have a chance."
Objectionable Content: "Like Suicide" blends the concepts of love, murder, and suicide so it's hard to tell where one ends and another begins. "Fell on Black Days," "The Day I Tried to Live," "Superunknown," and other cuts portray life as hopelessly devoid of meaning. "Let Me Drown" squeals, "Give up to greed . . . give up to fate." With a similarly defeatist attitude, "My Wave" tells people, "hate if you want to hate." By not identifying such attitudes as harmful, the band could fuel antisocial behavior.
Summary/Advisory: This bleak, empty effort from Soundgarden is full of weeds. Don't let teens venture into the *Superunknown*. CCM bands such as Liaison and Whitecross are better options for fans of this musical style.

Soundtracks

◆ ◆

Title: *Anastasia* (1997)
Label: Atlantic
Genre: Adult contemporary/Pop/Instrumental
Pro-Social Content: On "Journey to the Past," the character Anastasia sings, "Home, love, family/I will never be complete until I find you." Her memory is stirred by images from her childhood, leading her to recall the reassuring embrace of kin ("Once Upon a December"). The disc also includes pop radio versions of these two melodies—by Aaliyah and Deana Carter respec-  tively. Richard Marx and Donna Lewis team up for "At the Beginning," a sweet love song about companionship and renewed hope. A half-dozen tunes are strictly instrumental.
Objectionable Content: Men dream of pulling off "the biggest con in history" as townsfolk long for gossip ("A Rumor in St. Petersburg").
Summary/Advisory: In an attempt to out-Disney Disney, Fox has created a stylish soundtrack for its animated film about the orphaned Romanov princess. With only minor caveats, a positive pick with pop panache!

Title: *The Apostle* (1998)
Label: October/Sparrow
Genre: Country/Gospel
Pro-Social Content: Steven Curtis
Chapman's CCM hit "I Will Not Go Quietly"
finds a man eager to preach the things of God
until his dying day. With similar evangelical
zeal, Emmylou Harris and Robert Duvall (the
film's producer/director/star) team up for the gospel classic "I
Love to Tell the Story." Other time-honored spiritual songs include "In the
Garden" (Johnny Cash), "There Is Power in the Blood" (Lari White), "Softly
& Tenderly" (Rebecca Lynn Howard), "There Is a River" (Gaither Vocal
Band), "I'll Fly Away" (Gary Chapman & Wynonna), and "There Ain't No
Grave" (Russ Taff). On "Two Coats," Patty Loveless gladly casts off the old
nature and adorns herself with the Savior. Lyle Lovett leads a foot-stompin'
celebration of life in Christ's service ("I'm a Soldier in the Army of the
Lord"). Similarly, Sounds of Blackness uses hand-claps and tambourines to
praise God, declaring, "Victory Is Mine."
Objectionable Content: None
Summary/Advisory: It's rare that a mainstream motion picture would rely
so heavily on music celebrating Christian faith. But this one does. Every
edifying cut overflows with enthusiasm, optimism, and Southern-fried conviction. As soundtracks go, *The Apostle* is cause for great rejoicing.

Title: *Batman & Robin* (1997)
Label: Warner Bros.
Genre: Rock/Rap/Alternative
Pro-Social Content: Jewel praises a man's depth of character on "Foolish
Games." Eric Benet's "True to Myself" exalts God, family and personal
integrity. "Gotham City," by R. Kelly, longs for a city of justice, love, and
peace.
Objectionable Content: A woman blasphemously
complains about her monthly menstrual
cycle (Lauren Christy on "Breed"). Bone
Thugs N Harmony promotes gangsta violence
and marijuana use on the theologically confused "Look Into My Eyes." Several tracks
enlist lyrical pessimism and a bleak worldview.
Moloko shares her own devilish nightmares

("Fun for Me"). Goo Goo Dolls's "Lazy Eye" moans about lies and emptiness. The Grammy-winning song "The End Is the Beginning Is the End" (by The Smashing Pumpkins) relates a "disastrous" relationship amid despondent, apocalyptic ramblings.

Summary/Advisory: Often as dark and eerie as Gotham City itself. Inky. Brooding. There are a few bright spots, but they get lost in murky melancholy. Furthermore, this soundtrack will undoubtedly inspire young *Batman & Robin* fans to sample other music by these 14 popular artists—some of which is extremely objectionable.

Title: *Batman Forever* (1995)
Label: Atlantic
Genre: Rock/Rap/R&B
Pro-Social Content: The human longing for meaningful relationships is central to Eddie Reader's "Nobody Lives Without Love." "Crossing the River" speaks of faith and trust between two people taking a chance on romance.
Objectionable Content: Any song that invites a lover to commit murder in a fit of passion (U2's "Hold Me, Thrill Me, Kiss Me, Kill Me") is trouble, especially when it derides Christian faith in the process. Destructive anger fuels The Offspring's "Smash It Up," while "Bad Days" (by The Flaming Lips) tells listeners to perform hateful, violent acts in their dreams as a form of catharsis. Death, murder, hopelessness, and evil provide the focus for "The Riddler" (Method Man) and "There Is a Light" (Nick Cave). The latter portrays God and preachers as apathetic or impotent when it comes to solving the world's problems. Meanwhile, 16-year-old Brandy fondly recalls weeks of making love "so sweet and pure" ("Where Are You Now?").
Summary/Advisory: A couple of clean cuts can't compensate for considerable crudities on this caped crusader collection (holy alliteration!). Assorted artists. A sordid disc.

Title: *Blues Brothers 2000* (1997)
Label: Universal
Genre: Blues/Soul
Pro-Social Content: By definition, the blues are inherently melancholy. Still, Matt Murphy reflects on how blues music bonded him to his father

("The Blues Don't Bother Me"). And The Paul Butterfield Blues Band's "Born in Chicago" uses the genre to mourn victims of street violence. "Cheaper to Keep Her" (by The Blues Brothers Band) counts the financial cost of marital infidelity and decides it's not worth it. Addressing her man, Aretha Franklin demands love and "R-E-S-P-E-C-T." The gospel number "John the Revelator" speaks of Adam and the Garden of Eden and refers to Christ as God risen from the dead. Several artists team up for "634-5789," a song on which a man tells a woman to call if she needs affection.

Objectionable Content: A mild profanity mars "Cheaper to Keep Her." While not explicit, "Looking for a Fox" finds John Goodman and Dan Aykroyd on the prowl for female companionship.

Summary/Advisory: The film that inspired it has endured a critical thrashing, but there's very little not to like about the soundtrack to *Blues Brothers 2000*. Of the 18 featured tracks, three are jazzy instrumentals. Others seek refuge in relationships or acknowledge the lordship of Christ— the *only* sure cure for the blues!

Title: *The Bodyguard* (1992)
Label: Arista
Genre: R&B/Pop
Pro-Social Content: Houston's multimillion-selling remake of Dolly Parton's "I Will Always Love You" pledges lasting devotion. Her single "Run to You" is also a positive tune about support-ive romance, as are Joe Cocker's "Trust in Me"

and Lisa Stansfield's "Someday (I'm Coming Back)." S.O.U.L. System's breezy rap, "It's Gonna Be a Lovely Day" and Curtis Stiger's rendition of "(What's So Funny 'Bout) Peace, Love and Understanding" are similarly upbeat. Houston delivers a lovely, biblically faithful version of "Jesus Loves Me."

Objectionable Content: "Queen of the Night" takes an aggressive sexual posture, as does Whitney's hit "I'm Every Woman," though to a lesser degree.

Summary/Advisory: Whitney Houston's multiplatinum single "I Will Always Love You" spent 10 weeks atop *Billboard*'s "Hot 100." A couple of minor flaws, but otherwise there's lots to like about this synergistic collec-tion anchored by Houston, who also starred in the film.

Title: *The Crow: City of Angels* (1996)
Label: Miramax/Hollywood
Genre: Metal/Rock/Rap
Pro-Social Content: Seven Mary Three's
"Shelf Life" recognizes how anger can destroy
a relationship. On "Knock Me Out," Linda
Perry thanks someone for keeping her sober.
Objectionable Content: Iggy Pop, Deftones,

and PJ Harvey all shout obscenities on their tracks (s——,
f——, ——damn). Above the Law raps, "As I reload, I'm all alone, set to
explode like an illogical murderer" ("City of Angels"). Ghostly images invade
Toadies's "Paper Dress." Even the cuts that avoid offensive lyrics rock with
swarthy anger and a nihilistic pose.
Summary/Advisory: *The Crow: City of Angels* is the film sequel to *The
Crow,* a 1994 tale of black-mass vengeance in which a dead man returns to
exact justice on his killers. This soundtrack reflects the eerie, macabre
mood of both movies. But even more disturbing than its aura of death-metal
masochism is the possibility that teens will pursue albums by the out-of-
bounds bands appearing on it. White Zombie. Hole. Above the Law. Bush.
In short, *Angels* can't possibly bless Christian families.

Title: *Dangerous Minds* (1995)
Label: MCA
Genre: Gangsta rap/R&B
Pro-Social Content: Two contributions by
Rappin' 4-Tay ("A Message for Your Mind,"
"Problems") contain lines that applaud self-
reliance and motherhood while condemning
violence and illiteracy.
Objectionable Content: "Gin and Juice" (by
DeVante) celebrates partying with marijuana and alcohol at an orgy-like
"freak fest." A cut by Mr. Dalvin & Static ("True O.G.") also models drug
use, but more in the context of black-on-black street violence. Sista uses
disgusting slang and profanity on "It's Alright." The Coolio hit "Gangsta
Paradise" makes violent threats ("Your homies might be lined in chalk").
The materialistic "Havin' Thangs" rails against school, police, and prisons.
Summary/Advisory: Except for a few isolated lines, this collection of
bitter urban anthems is morally bankrupt. Exposing young minds really is
dangerous. By the way, the R-rated hit movie that spawned this disc was
released by a Walt Disney subsidiary.

Title: *Evita* (1996)
Label: Warner Bros.
Genre: Rock opera/Latin/Adult contemporary
Pro-Social Content: Themes woven
through this narrative project include rising
above one's circumstances, the emptiness of
fame and fortune without love, the need to
respect others regardless of social standing and
the dangers of selfish ambition.
Objectionable Content: Teens taking cues from
Eva Perón (given voice by pop star Madonna) will be led to believe that, in
areas of morality, the end justifies the means. The disc's heroine—labeled
promiscuous on several cuts—uses sex for career advancement. "Goodnight
and Thank You" cynically insists that all lovers are looking for opportunities
to manipulate each other. Dishonest financial dealings are excused for the
"good" they accomplished. Several of the 31 tracks make crude references.
Summary/Advisory: Overall, this modern opera paints a much too flatter-
ing picture of Argentina's infamous political despots, Eva and Juan Perón.
Revisionism aside, *Evita*'s positive messages are overshadowed by its
attempt to defend indefensible behavior.

Title: *Friday* (1995)
Label: Priority
Genre: Rap
Pro-Social Content: The 1977 Rose Royce
hit "I Wanna Get Next to You" tenderly
expresses romantic affection.
Objectionable Content: No fewer than six
cuts toss in obscenities and other explicit language (with frequent use of the f-word). Tunes glorify
gangsta violence (Ice Cube's "Friday," E-A-Ski's "Blast If I Have To"), illicit
sex ("Friday," Bootsy Collins and Bernie Worrell's "You Got Me Wide Open,"
2 Live Crew's "Hoochie Mama," and "Friday Night" by Scarface), consumption of marijuana and/or alcohol ("Friday Night," Cypress Hill's "Roll It Up,
Light It Up, Smoke It Up," Mack 10's "Take a Hit," The Alkaholiks's "Coast
II Coast," Dr. Dre's "Keep Their Heads Ringin'"). 2 Live Crew also speaks of
whoring, ejaculation, and lesbian encounters, all in lewd terms.
Summary/Advisory: TGIF—There's Garbage in *Friday*. Namely, sex,
drugs, and violence.

Title: *Gridlock'd* (1997)
Label: Death Row/MCA
Genre: Gangsta rap/R&B
Pro-Social Content: "It's Over Now," one of the two tracks by Danny
Boy, promises to safeguard a woman from a hurtful man.
Objectionable Content: Violence. Drug use. Sexual perversity.
Hundreds of uses of the f-word. This stickered
disc features notorious gangsta rappers Snoop
Doggy Dogg, Dat Nigga Daz, the late Tupac
Shakur, and other musical menaces to society.
"Don't Try to Play Me Homey" celebrates
marijuana, cocaine, and oral sex. Four cuts
focus on gunplay and murder, including "Out
the Moon," which talks of cop-killing. "Lady
Heroin" and "Body and Soul" worship the
rush delivered by heroin, the latter stating, "The ultimate high is when you die." Women are referred to as "b—ches"
and "hos" (whores).
Summary/Advisory: At the 1997 Grammy Awards, National Academy of
Recording Arts and Sciences president Michael Green made a politically
correct appeal for artists to "carefully consider their position on art that
promotes violence, degrades women or glorifies the use of drugs." He could
have been speaking directly to the producers of this sleazy, irresponsible
disc—though it's doubtful their "position" would change.

Title: *The Hunchback of Notre Dame* (1996)
Label: Walt Disney
Genre: Pop/Liturgical/Choral
Pro-Social Content: Several tunes further the film's premise that beauty
is found within. "Out There" finds Quasimodo eager to sample the "normal"
existence we can easily take for granted. On "God Help the
Outcasts," a Gypsy's humble prayer puts the needs of
others at the fore ("I ask for nothing; I can
get by/But I know so many less lucky than
I"). "A Guy Like You" offers friendly
encouragement.
Objectionable Content: A pious villain
struggles with lust on "Hellfire," abdicating
responsibility for his sin ("It's not my fault if in

God's plan He made the devil so much stronger than a man"). Elsewhere in the song, he threatens to either possess or destroy a Gypsy girl. "Topsy Turvy" celebrates rebellion and "breaking rules" on the day "the devil in us gets released" and "the beer is never stoppin'."

Summary/Advisory: Composer Alan Menken and lyricist Stephen Schwartz have created a stylish musical backdrop for what is, at times, a rather tenebrous tale. Some cuts are warm and uplifting. Still, young children may have trouble applying context to the ones that aren't. Use discretion.

Title: *The Jerky Boys* (1995)
Label: Atlantic/Select
Genre: Rock/Rap/Punk rock/Comedy
Pro-Social Content: Tom Jones's (yes, *that* Tom Jones) contribution, "Are You Gonna Go My Way," decries violence, urging mankind to rediscover peace and brotherly love.
Objectionable Content: Several crank phone calls by The Jerky Boys—and sound bites from the movie—employ abusive language, crude humor, and talk of violence. The disc's lyrical vocabulary is equally offensive. Amid profanity, "Dirty Dancing" (by The Wu-Tang Clan) applauds smoking marijuana. "Hurricane" (Four Fly Guys) also spews blasphemy and raw slang. House of Pain's "Beef Jerky" yells "F— life!" while it boasts sexual dash ("I can keep it on and on") and murderous skill ("I'll smoke you like a pig's head").
Summary/Advisory: High-energy tunes, yes, but most are lyrically bankrupt. Also, it was rather disappointing to see Collective Soul's name among the various artists listed in the credits. The band's connection to this slime is troublesome in light of its own positive first and third projects. As a whole, like the film that inspired it, this *Jerky* compilation is a major wrong number. Don't pick it up.

Title: *The Lion King* (1994)
Label: Walt Disney
Genre: Pop/Instrumental
Pro-Social Content: Both the film and radio versions of "Can You Feel the Love Tonight" speak tenderly of romance. "Circle of Life" ponders finding our place in this majestic world we call home.

Objectionable Content: "Hakuna Matata" makes light of the warthog's compulsive gassiness. "I Just Can't Wait to Be King" sounds haughty out of its positive cinematic context.

Summary/Advisory: This is the first time since *Mary Poppins* (1964) that a Disney soundtrack has topped the pop music chart. An upbeat, fun collection. Mostly neutral, these messages gain meaning in their film habitat. Four of the 12 tracks are instrumental. Three pop melodies appear twice; once as they do in the film, and once as performed by Elton John.

Title: *Lost Highway* (1997)
Label: Nothing/Interscope
Genre: Metal/Industrial/Rock

Pro-Social Content: Despite its dismal sound, Lou Reed's remake of "This Magic Moment" retains the romantic lyrics of the 1960 original.

Objectionable Content: Relational angst and personal emptiness lead Trent Reznor to compare a lover to "The Perfect Drug." "Heirate Mich," by the German band Rammstein, translates into the story of a man who digs up a woman's corpse, which falls apart as he tries to kiss it. Amid obscure ramblings, gothic rocker Marilyn Manson longs for someone to die with him ("Apple of Sodom") and threatens an unfaithful woman by stating, "If I can't have you, no one will" ("I Put a Spell on You"). Insomnia-riddled Smashing Pumpkins frontman Billy Corgan utters, "To the gates of hell-dom/To myself be d—-ned" on "Eye." David Bowie builds a song around the proud admission, "I'm Deranged." Dark, angry tracks reinforced by 14 bizarre instrumentals.

Summary/Advisory: This compilation, showcasing various artists, spent nearly two months in the pop Top 40. Cult film director David Lynch (*Twin Peaks, Blue Velvet*) has created an eerie score for his warped tale. Even more unsettling is the thought that teens might sample other musical expressions by these morose whiners. Definitely pass on this *Highway*.

Title: *Men in Black* (1997)
Label: Columbia
Genre: R&B/Hip-hop/Rap

Pro-Social Content: On "Just Cruisin'," Will Smith asks, "Am I bein' the best daddy I can?"

Objectionable Content: That line rings hollow as Smith shamelessly

ogles a woman in short shorts and applauds the
hateful music of Tupac Shakur and Biggie
Smalls. De La Soul spews profanity and vulgar
slang for male genitalia on "Chanel No. Fever."
In addition to glamorizing drugs and alcohol,
"We Just Wanna Party with You" (by Snoop
Doggy Dogg) boasts of casual sexual conquests in explicit detail ("After we push, I
leave her 'cause I don't love her"). Other cuts allude to
group sex (Emoja's "Erotik City") and encourage infidelity (Trey Lorenz's
"Make You Happy"). Nasty stuff.

Summary/Advisory: Apart from this number-1 pop disc's three innocuous
instrumental tracks, this collection deserves to be launched into deep
space. Fans of the hit sci-fi movie who buy the disc for Danny Elfman's
theme music or Will Smith's neutral "Men in Black" rap will be blasted by
songs with a serious hormonal imbalance.

Title: *Mighty Morphin Power Rangers: The Movie* (1995)
Label: Fox/Atlantic
Genre: Rock/Pop
Pro-Social Content: "Go Go Power Rangers" reminds kids that their
colorful heroes only use their weapons in self-defense. Devo's "Are You
Ready" and Van Halen's "Dreams" both encourage youngsters to work hard
and hang tough in pursuit of life's goals.

Objectionable Content: Minor. A boastful rapper
states, "Stay off my back or I will attack"
("The Power"). Though *renamed* "Kung Fu
Dancing," a techno-pop version of Carl
Douglas's 1974 hit still refers to kung fu
fighting in the song itself.

Summary/Advisory: Lyrically, the disc
keeps in mind the age of its audience, though
some of the artists *on it* have developed a fol-
lowing based on raunchy material. Fans of the soundtrack may also wish to
see the *film*, which features a barely-dressed woman imparting New Age
animal spirits to the Rangers for guidance and empowerment. Ample reason
to be wary of where this disc could lead children, assuming parents haven't
already made their homes a Morphin-free zone.

Title: *Mortal Kombat* (1995)
Label: TVT Records
Genre: Techno/Industrial/Heavy metal
Pro-Social Content: Though short on solutions, Geezer's "Invisible" speaks up for social
outcasts. Several cuts are strictly instrumental.
Objectionable Content: Despite the variety of
artists (mostly unknowns), darkness and aggression are consistent themes. Obscenities, including

the f-word, appear on "What You See" (by Mutha's Day Out) and "Goodbye"
(Gravity Kills). The latter also rejects the need for forgiveness and boasts the
skill of mind control. Type O Negative's contribution, "Blood and Fire,"
alludes to a lesbian relationship. "I Reject" finds the singer for Bile claiming
to be the living dead, and stating, "I crush, you bleed . . . I kill."
Summary/Advisory: This dark, sinister disc provides a platform for bands
who make a living peddling disturbing muck. Meanwhile, the hit film that
inspired it trades heavily in violent hand-to-hand combat. Avoid both.

Title: *Philadelphia* (1994)
Label: Epic
Genre: Various artists and styles
Pro-Social Content: On "It's in Your Eyes,"
Pauletta Washington sings of everlasting love
and devotion. A number of songs also
chronicle the ups and downs of life and
relationships ("Have You Ever Seen the
Rain" by Spin Doctors, and Indigo Girls's
"I Don't Wanna Talk About It").
Objectionable Content: Nothing explicit, but since the
movie focuses on homosexual relationships, some of the disc's love songs
could easily be interpreted in that context. Thinly veiled references on
Sade's "Please Send Me Someone to Love" ("show the world how to get
along, peace will enter when hate is gone") and Bruce Springsteen's Oscar-
winning single "Streets of Philadelphia" ("so receive me brother with your
faithless kiss") are vague but questionable.
Summary/Advisory: The term "city of brotherly love" takes on new
meaning in this film about a sympathetic gay character battling AIDS.
Fortunately, the *Philadelphia* soundtrack itself avoids blatant pro-
homosexual sermonizing.

Title: *Pocahontas* (1995)
Label: Walt Disney
Genre: Pop/Instrumental
Pro-Social Content: Pocahontas counts the
cost of bold dreaming on "Just Around the
Riverbend," realizing that truly living requires
calculated risks. "Colors of the Wind" teaches
respect for others and the environment. The

pop duet "If I Never Knew You" applauds the power of love. Mutual
hatred between settlers and native Americans is portrayed as socially unde-
sirable on "Savages."
Objectionable Content: "Mine, Mine, Mine" and "The Virginia Company"
revel in gold-induced greed. The latter also says, "We'll kill ourselves an
Injun, or maybe two or three," combining such lusts with service to God.
Indian/New Age theology (praying to a mountain, spirits in rocks, trees, earth,
sky) infects several tracks, including the Oscar-winning "Colors of the Wind."
Summary/Advisory: This disc earned much wampum as Disney's follow-up
to the million-selling *Lion King* soundtrack. But *Pocahontas*'s spiritual confusion should send smoke signals to discerning parents. A disappointment.

Title: *The Preacher's Wife* (1996)
Label: Arista
Genre: Gospel/Adult contemporary
Pro-Social Content: The hit single "I Believe
in You and Me" is a tender melody that pledges
lifelong love to a romantic partner. Aerobically
upbeat, "Step by Step" embraces the challenges
of living day by day. Whitney Houston exuberantly captures the joy of meeting a special some-
one on "My Heart Is Calling." "You Were Loved" reminds listeners to share
their feelings with loved ones. The rest of this project is charged with a
dynamic spiritual energy. Heartfelt gospel tunes extol God's faithfulness
("Hold on, Help Is on the Way," "The Lord Is My Shepherd," "I Go to the
Rock," "Somebody Bigger Than You and I"). They also acknowledge Christ
as King ("Who Would Imagine a King," "Joy to the World," "Joy").
Objectionable Content: None
Summary/Advisory: Perfect. This Top-3 pop disc showcases the talents of
Whitney Houston on all but one song. Her brilliant vocals, backed by a
soulful gospel choir, drive home edifying lyrics. *The Preacher's Wife* is a
heaven-sent winner from start to finish!

Title: *Pure Country* (1992)
Label: MCA
Genre: Country
Pro-Social Content: "Heartland" promotes a solid work ethic and traditional values in a place where folks "still know wrong from right" and
"simple people livin' side by side still wave to their neighbor as they're
driving by." Men are encouraged to show their love in a tender, tangible
way on "Baby Your Baby." "I Cross My Heart" is a commitment to unconditional love.
Objectionable Content: The sexually suggestive (though not explicit) "Overnight Male" and
"She Lays It All on the Line" aren't clearly
sung in the context of marriage.
Summary/Advisory: This soundtrack album
is all George Strait—from a generally family-
friendly movie that starred the singer in his
first dramatic role. Fans will enjoy these
songs of devotion as well as the painfully crooned blues
that have become Strait's trademark. There's plenty of pedal steel
guitar, but no glorification of alcohol or blatant sexual carousing. A positive pick that has sold more than 5 million copies.

Title: *Romeo + Juliet* (1996)
Label: Capitol
Genre: Rock/Alternative/Metal
Pro-Social Content: Quindon Tarver's quasi-choral "Everybody's Free
(To Feel Good)" offers to help a friend ease inner pain.
Objectionable Content: There's nothing Garbage won't do for a lover on
the band's song "#1 Crush"—including steal, lie, kill, and die (which is
especially disturbing in the context of a film that romanticizes suicide). The
f-word punctuates Everclear's rebellious anthem "Local God." That obscenity also appears on "You and Me Song" (The Wannadies) and
"Talk Show Host" (Radiohead). Jesus travels
down to Mexico as a drug courier for the
deceased Juliet on the Butthole Surfers's cut
"Whatever." Kim Mazelle fatalistically urges
women to view marriage as an institution of
pain and oppression on "Young Hearts Run
Free" ("Just another lost and lonely wife/You

count up the years, they will be filled with tears"). She also suggests that men are all chronic adulterers.

Summary/Advisory: Dysfunction weaves its way through this compilation like the nihilistic rhymes of a tragic sonnet. Instead of love songs, the tunes gathered for this downer of a soundtrack focus on the tortured, ultimately doomed relationship of Shakespeare's star-crossed lovers.

Title: *Selena* (1997)
Label: EMI Latin
Genre: Latin pop/Adult contemporary
Pro-Social Content: As part of a disco medley, Selena covers Gloria Gaynor's 1979 hit about a jilted woman determined to persevere ("I Will Survive"). A woman tempted to flee a troubled relationship (presumably a marriage) returns home on "Only Love." An innocent young lady guards her heart and

successfully resists the lure of a passionate fling, stating, "I know it's not right" ("I Could Fall in Love"). Singing the urgent, cautionary words of Anita from *West Side Story*, Selena describes a man guilty of murder who cannot love and warns a friend to avoid "A Boy Like That." Guitar licks punctuate Lil' Ray's upbeat reminiscence of Selena on "One More Time" ("So many miles, so many places . . . leavin' smiles on their faces/What I wouldn't give to hear her sing one more time").
Objectionable Content: None
Summary/Advisory: This collection, recorded by the late Tejana singer and revived for the recent film about her life, peaked at number seven. Tender, romantic ballads. Energetic live performances. The result is a fitting tribute to this wholesome Latina songstress for whom the curtain fell much too soon.

Title: *Sleepless in Seattle* (1993)
Label: Epic
Genre: Adult contemporary/Jazz/
Big band/Country
Pro-Social Content: A bevy of ballads for the truly romantic. Nat King Cole's inspirational "Stardust." Louis Armstrong's hopeful "A Kiss to Build a Dream On." "A Wink and a Smile," Harry Connick Jr.'s tribute to the "perfect match." Nearly every song is a classic

recalling a bygone era that celebrated romance over one-night stands. Several cuts pledge everlasting love and devotion ("Stand By Your Man," "Make Someone Happy," "When I Fall in Love").

Objectionable Content: "Makin' Whoopee" repeats the title as a euphemism for sex, and adultery is implied.

Summary/Advisory: Although the film itself isn't entirely family-friendly, the soundtrack for *Sleepless in Seattle* delivers a refreshing sound that, with just one exception, is warm and welcome. Some teens may not find this mellow collection to their liking, but in other homes, it will bond generations. Overall, a positive pick.

Title: *Soul Food* (1997)
Label: LaFace
Genre: R&B/Rap
Pro-Social Content: The members of Boyz II Men honor their mothers on "A Song for Mama." Earth Wind & Fire's "September" and Milestone's "Care 'Bout You" are wholesome songs about romantic relationships.

Objectionable Content: A sexually neglected man tells his woman, "I dream of lovers past" (Dru Hill's "We're Not Making Love No More"). Both male and female groups either recall or fantasize about sexual escapades (Blackstreet's "Call Me," Xscape's "Let's Do It Again," and En Vogue's "You Are the Man"). A new mother uses crude language to describe the "shady" father of her child who chases other girls (Total's "What About Us?"). On Outkast's "In Due Time," the guys glamorize peddling marijuana. Though numerous obscenities are technically "bleeped," even listeners whose minds aren't in the gutter will have no trouble filling in the blanks. Crude stuff.

Summary/Advisory: Sex, sex, *more* sex . . . and drugs. That kind of soul food can only lead to spiritual heartburn. Avoid this double-platinum soundtrack *and* the R-rated movie that inspired it.

Title: *Space Jam* (1996)
Label: Atlantic
Genre: R&B/Rap
Pro-Social Content: A remake of the 1977 Steve Miller Band hit "Fly Like an Eagle" finds Seal longing to provide food, shoes, and shelter to those less fortunate. Several tracks encourage young listeners to work hard,

dream, overcome obstacles, and impact their world (R. Kelly's Grammy-winning "I Believe I Can Fly," Coolio's "The Winner"). Monica's sweet ballad, "For You I Will," scores a slam-dunk by expressing a willingness to meet another's needs at any cost.

Objectionable Content: Alien hoopsters brag of aggressive on-court dominance ("My tactic's unsportsmanlike conduct") on "Hit 'Em High," a rap that uses what sounds like the s-word. A string of street slang on Salt-N-Pepa's "Upside Down" relates a hormonal infatuation. Chris

Rock double dribbles when he uses mild profanity twice on his duet with Barry White, "Basketball Jones." R. Kelly mentions cruising clubs for women, and a female singer offers her man "anything to turn [him] on" ("All of My Days"). A bitter Bugs Bunny raps on the attitude-laden "Buggin'."

Summary/Advisory: Only a few cuts are inherently problematic, but this Top-5 disc is destined to introduce young fans to hip-hop artists famous for recording explicit material (R. Kelly, Coolio, L.L. Cool J, Salt-N-Pepa, and Spin Doctors). A flagrant foul in light of *Space Jam*'s pre-adolescent target audience.

Title: *That Thing You Do* (1996)
Label: Epic
Genre: Sixties rock/Pop
Pro-Social Content: With refreshing innocence, this soundtrack captures various stages of love and romance in 1960s fashion: Starry-eyed infatuation ("All My Only Dreams"). Taking a bold risk on a new love ("She Knows It"). Tender courtship ("Lovin' You Lots and Lots," "Hold My Hand, Hold My Heart"). The pain of a broken heart ("That Thing You Do," "My World Is Over"). No weighty social issues or psychological probing. Just good, clean fun. Instrumental tracks lend additional retro flavor.
Objectionable Content: "Drive Faster" could inspire recklessness ("I wanna have some fun/Run every red light"). The singer two-times his girl with a "Little Wild One."

Summary/Advisory: Instead of recycling hits from 1964, the filmmakers commissioned all-new '60s soundalikes. Styles range from The Beatles and Beach Boys to Bobby Darin and the Shangri-Las. Five of these tunes were penned by Scott Rogness and CCM artist Rick Elias. With minor exceptions, this journey back in time is well worth the trip.

Title: *Titanic* (1998)
Label: Sony
Genre: Instrumental/Celtic/Adult contemporary
Pro-Social Content: Celine Dion's chart-topping single, "My Heart Will Go On," celebrates true love and the enduring nature of romantic devotion ("Love can touch us one time and last for a lifetime/And never let go till we're gone . . . Near, far, wherever you are/I believe that the heart does go on"). The rest of this disc (more than an hour of music) is strictly instrumental. Styles range from relaxed Celtic strings to sweeping orchestral overtures to pulse-pounding tracks designed to energize onscreen action.
Objectionable Content: None
Summary/Advisory: This predominantly lyricless album sold more than 7 million copies in its *first eight weeks* of release. Amazing. Since 1980, James Horner has written the scores to more than 70 motion pictures and won Grammys, Oscars, and Golden Globes for his work. Though parents may take issue with some elements of the highest-grossing film of all time, *Titanic*'s soundtrack won't be one of them. An outstanding effort.

Title: *Waiting to Exhale* (1995)
Label: Arista
Genre: R&B/Pop
Pro-Social Content: Describing the man in her life, Chaka Khan keeps his physical attractiveness in perspective on a jazzed-up remake of "My Funny Valentine" ("your looks are laughable, unphotograph-able"). Songs such as For Real's "Love Will Be Waiting at Home" and Patti LaBelle's "My Love, Sweet Love" express undying trust and devotion. The duet "Count on Me" (Whitney Houston and CeCe Winans) is a celebration of

friendship reminiscent of "Bridge Over Troubled Water."

Objectionable Content: TLC's lewd "This Is How It Works" refers to oral sex and uses the f-word numerous times. "All Night Long" (by SWV) is one long sexual proposition.

Summary/Advisory: Mostly smooth and enjoyable—quite a collection of female talent. But what knothead invited TLC and SWV to the party? Those two cuts ruin an otherwise praiseworthy disc.

Spice Girls

◆ ◆ ◆ ◆ ◆ ◆ ◆ ◆ ◆ ◆ ◆ ◆ ◆ ◆ ◆ ◆ ◆ ◆ ◆

This British all-girl act includes members Emma Bunton, Geri Halliwell (who left the group in mid-1998), Melanie Chisholm, Melanie Brown, and Victoria Adams. Not only has the quintet sold more than 14 million records worldwide, but Spicemania has led to the spin-off of a number of other U.K. projects as well: a Spice Girls magazine, Spice Girls action figures, a Pepsi endorsement deal, two TV shows, the feature film *Spice World,* and more. Regrettably, Halliwell has released *Spice Exposed,* a video featuring the singer in more than 200 pornographic poses. At the same time, Ray Cooper of Virgin Records proudly told *Forbes* [9/22/97], "The Spice Girls seem to be the first group ever that have got 4-, 5- and 6-year-old girls and boys to own music."

Title: *Spice World* (1997)
Label: Virgin
Genre: Pop
Pro-Social Content: An antidote to the angst of alternative rock, these blithe, buoyant tunes advocate glass-is-half-full positivity. The hit single "Spice Up Your Life" recommends smiling and dancing to chase away the blues. The girls advise young fans to pick themselves up, hold onto good times, and trust in love ("Never Give Up"). "Move Over"—adopted by Pepsi as a jingle in its "Generation Next" ad campaign—tries to rally baby-busters to universal togetherness. The singers want romantic partners who are true friends on "Too Much."

Objectionable Content: Beyond the group's sex-kitten stage presence, a handful of songs use mild profanity ("h—," "a—") and what could be interpreted as hip euphemisms for sex. "Do It" tells young girls, "make your own rules to live by," which includes defying parents and having sex. **Summary/Advisory:** Since their rookie release, *Spice*, the Girls have throttled back on inappropriate content. But what little *does* show up is inexcusable. If preteens ask you to give them this album, remember "Do It" . . . then *don't.*

Title: *Spice (1997)*
Label: Virgin
Genre: Pop/Hip-hop/R&B
Pro-Social Content: "Mama" expresses love for a caring mother whose wisdom was once met with rebellion. The singer asks a man for a promise of devotion on "Say You'll Be There."
Objectionable Content: Sexual propositions and innuendo drive the vast majority of these tracks: "Wanna make love to ya, baby . . . Get it on, get it on" ("2 Become 1"); "If you wanna be my lover . . . slam your body down and wind it all around" ("Wannabe," which spent over a month as the nation's top single); "Undress you with her eyes . . . She wants to get naked" ("Naked"). The Girls long for lovers with "gentle hands" and "dirty minds" on the double-entendre-laden "Last Time Lover." They also issue a vague threat to any guy who comes between them ("Love Thing"). While not as explicit as some acts in this genre, the Spice "ladies" aren't any more acceptable.
Summary/Advisory: These five Brits take pride in their rowdy, raunchy image as "unrepentant swearers, drinkers and smokers; broads who speak frankly about sex and are not averse to the occasional frontal flash at a male passerby" [*Entertainment Weekly*, 2/21-28/97]. It shows on *Spice*. Fans should try CCM trio Out of Eden's equally spicy sound—with much sweeter lyrics.

Spin Doctors
◆ ◆ ◆ ◆ ◆ ◆ ◆ ◆ ◆ ◆ ◆ ◆ ◆ ◆ ◆ ◆ ◆ ◆ ◆ ◆

This rock quartet was formed at New York's New School of Jazz. The group was originally comprised of Christopher Barron, Eric Schenkman, Mark White, and Aaron Comess. By 1994, Anthony Krizan replaced Schenkman.

Title: *Turn It Upside Down* (1994)
Label: Epic

Genre: Rock/Funk
Pro-Social Content: "At This Hour" condemns greed and shows compassion for the homeless. Patience in romance is the theme of "You Let Your Heart Go Too Fast," while "Indifference" denounces relational apathy.
Objectionable Content: Sexual entendres and activity outside marriage dominate "Big Fat Funky Booty." On "Laraby's Gang," the singer urges, "Buy a beer . . . smoke a couple of your favorite brand." Earth-mother theology appears on "More Than Meets the Ear" and "Beasts in the Woods." Disguised as a love song, "Mary Jane" promotes marijuana as an escape from emotional pressures.
Summary/Advisory: If these guys fancy themselves "doctors," it's time for a second opinion. Despite finding more positive elements here than on *Pocket Full of Kryptonite*, the band's drug- and sex-charged ballads are reason enough to avoid it.

Title: *Pocket Full of Kryptonite* (1992)
Label: Epic
Genre: High-energy funk
Pro-Social Content: None
Objectionable Content: "Little Miss Can't Be Wrong" bids good riddance to a "b—ch" who totes a shotgun ("I hope you hear this song and it p—ed you off"). Superman's sidekick propositions Lois Lane to dump the Man of Steel on "Jimmy Olson's Blues" ("Come on downtown and make love to me . . . I got a pocket full of kryptonite"). "Refrigerator Car" refers to a woman blowing her brains out. "Hard to Exist" pessimistically suggests alcohol as a means of escape.
Summary/Advisory: Weird, bizarre stuff. This 5-million-selling album's dismal tone is accompanied by lyrics that devalue meaningful relationships and the establishment in general. In addition, Spin Doctorism has become a psychedelic cultural phenomenon with fans traveling across the country to take in concerts, an appeal due mostly to the group's high-energy, R&B-infected funk. Spin past this downer of a disc.

Squirrel Nut Zippers

Seven diverse talents make up Squirrel Nut Zippers, a band "confection-ately" named after an old-fashioned chewy, peanut-flavored candy. The North Carolina-based group is Jim Mathus, Katharine Whalen, Ken Mosher, Chris Phillips, Tom Maxwell, Steward Cole, and Je WindenHouse.

Title: *Hot* (1997)
Label: Mammoth
Genre: Ska/Jazz/Big band
Pro-Social Content: "The Bad Businessman"
warns of a dangerous solicitor peddling lies
("Beware of what he sells . . . ain't no bottom in
that wishing well"). "It Ain't You, Baby"
implies that healthy marriages require long-

term commitment. Taking a cue from Matthew 5:9, a man steps in to defuse a potential brawl ("Put a Lid on It"). Unlike pop songs that portray hell as a place to party, SNZ offers a sobering glimpse at an afterlife sepa-rated from God on "Hell" ("People listen attentively/I mean about future calamity/I used to think the idea was obsolete/. . . Eternally fire is applied to the body/In the afterlife, you could be headed for some serious strife"). "Twilight" and "Meant to Be" paint romantic pictures of true love. Three tracks are entirely instrumental.
Objectionable Content: None
Summary/Advisory: Experimenting with a unique, high-energy musical hybrid has earned this band a loyal teen following. In other words, *Hot* is cool. So are its lyrics. Let's hope the members of Squirrel Nut Zippers have stored away *more* upbeat acorns for future albums.

Stewart, Rod

Rod Stewart has spent three decades as one of rock music's leading hit-makers. He won Grammy's Living Legends Award in 1989 and was inducted into the Rock and Roll Hall of Fame in 1994. He spent time in the Jeff Beck group as well as with the band Faces. Career album sales as a solo artist exceed 28 million.

Title: *Unplugged . . . and Seated* (1993)
Label: Warner Bros.
Genre: Pop/Rock/Blues
Pro-Social Content: Stewart dedicates his
romantic hit single "Have I Told You Lately
(That I Love You)" to his wife. The chorus
repeats the line, "At the end of the day, we
should give thanks and pray to the One, to
the One." "People Get Ready" is a time-honored spiritual
that calls people to faith because "Jesus is coming."
Objectionable Content: Several of his "greatest hits" dredge up offensive
themes, including one-night stands ("Stay With Me," "Hot Legs") and
casual, self-indulgent sex with a young girl on "Tonight's the Night" ("Don't
say a word my virgin child, just let your inhibitions run wild").
Summary/Advisory: This 15-track collection is an installment in MTV's
acoustic *Unplugged* series. In spite of references to spiritual things, there's
little evidence Rod takes them to heart. Several ballads and sound instrumental work are praiseworthy, but any redeeming elements are squelched
by this veteran rocker's warped view of sex.

Sting

◆ ◆ ◆ ◆ ◆ ◆ ◆ ◆ ◆ ◆ ◆ ◆ ◆ ◆ ◆ ◆ ◆ ◆ ◆

Sting was born Gordon Sumner in Wallsend,
England. He was a member of rock's The
Police (which formed in 1977 and sold more
than 13 million records). Sting's first solo
album, *The Dream of the Blue Turtles*, went
platinum. He has also played roles in the films
Quadrophenia, Dune, The Bride, Plenty, and
others. He was nicknamed "Sting" because the
yellow-and-black jersey he liked to wear resem-
bled a bumble bee.

Title: *Mercury Falling* (1996)
Label: A&M
Genre: Rock/Pop
Pro-Social Content: Sting wishes to share another's hurt and model his
courage on "Let Your Soul Be Your Pilot." "I Was Brought to My Senses"

credits heaven with the beauty of creation and affirms a lasting love. A sobering scene from the Old West finds the artist deeply sorry for accidentally shooting a man, retelling his story as he faces the gallows ("I Hung My Head"). "I'm So Happy I Can't Stop Crying" uses first-person testimony to express the painful consequences of divorce—from custody battles and loneliness to thinking of his bride with other men and being a long-distance dad ("She says the kids are fine and that they miss me/Maybe I could come and babysit sometime"). Despite losing a love, Sting focuses on the good times they shared ("The Hounds of Winter").

Objectionable Content: None

Summary/Advisory: No need for parents to police this upbeat Top-10 disc endowed with cautionary tales. Smartly written and produced, *Mercury* rises to artistic and lyrical heights.

Title: *Ten Summoners' Tales* (1993)
Label: A&M
Genre: Pop/Rock
Pro-Social Content: "Heavy Cloud No Rain" conveys the genuine despair of being so close, yet so far. Loyalty and devotion are the focus of "It's Probably Me," which assures a friend of faithfulness in times of need. On the playful "Seven Days," Sting contemplates competing with a "six-foot-ten Neanderthal" for the woman he loves.

Objectionable Content: "Love Is Stronger Than Justice" tells of a cowboy who murders his six brothers because the town they ride into has only one woman ("ethical stuff never got in my way"). Elsewhere, alcohol is recommended as a stress-management tool. Sting also expresses a lack of faith in the Church.

Summary/Advisory: This disc landed at number 2 on the pop chart. Unfortunately, dreary imagery and cryptic lyrics abound.

Stone Temple Pilots

◆ ◆ ◆ ◆ ◆ ◆ ◆ ◆ ◆ ◆ ◆ ◆ ◆ ◆ ◆ ◆ ◆ ◆ ◆

The band features Scott Weiland, Dean DeLeo, Robert DeLeo, and Eric Kretz. According to Weiland, the band was conceived "as a way of making a living, and to tour with our music. That was our goal: to have enough money so we could eat, buy a few beers, and get some good grass" [*Kerrang!*, 11/26/94]. STP's second album, *Purple*, entered the charts at number 1 and stayed there three consecutive weeks. The band has won a

Grammy, two American Music Awards, one *Billboard* Music Award, two *Billboard* Video Awards, and an MTV Music Video Award.

Title: *Tiny Music . . . Songs from the Vatican Gift Shop* (1996)
Label: Atlantic
Genre: Alternative
Pro-Social Content: In addition to two instrumental cuts, "Adhesive" encourages listeners to "grab the hate and throw it down." The need to love one's wife and children is mentioned on "Pop's Love Suicide."
Objectionable Content: Restlessness on "Tumble in the Rough" is expressed as a quest for artificial highs ("I can booze, steal your shoes . . . I'm looking for a new stimulation"). Alcohol also flows on "Trippin' on a Hole in a Paper Heart," which paints a fairly bleak picture of life, as does "Big Bang Baby." "Art School Girl" refers to the partying exploits of a makeup-wearing man and his leather-clad girlfriend. The band's history of drug use suggests that "Adhesive" may be referring to opium when it states, "Flyin' high across the plain/Purple flowers ease the pain."
Summary/Advisory: Not the absolute worst of the genre, but *Tiny Music* is big on negativity. Its few expressions of hope seem to seek salvation in drugs and alcohol, making it one teens could do without.

Title: *Purple* (1994)
Label: Atlantic
Genre: Rock
Pro-Social Content: Isolated lines condemn envy, search for meaning in life, value personal relationships, and reject conformity.
Objectionable Content: A sense of hopelessness pervades "Lounge Fly," which refers to alcohol use and repeatedly rages, "I wanna f——!" The bleak "Unglued" searches for meaning amid confusion, which could lead to reckless self-indulgence. People are compared to flies stuck in "Vasoline," trapped and incapable of improving their fate. "Army Ants" involves violence ("You kick me . . . you hit me"). "Still Remains" alludes to sex with no marital context ("making love . . . I become you, flesh is warm with naked feet").
Summary/Advisory: Despite a few commendable ideas, STP's offbeat, garbled lyrics are still predominantly pessimistic, though not as blatantly offensive as the band's last disc, *Core*.

Title: *Core* (1993)
Label: Atlantic
Genre: Rock
Pro-Social Content: None
Objectionable Content: This album has an unhealthy preoccupation with death and life's dark side as it wallows in pain and suffering ("Sin," "Dead and Bloated," "Naked Suffering"). "Sex Type Thing," which suggests a date rape is about to occur, received heavy play on MTV. "Creep" and "Crackerman" both romanticize carrying—and using—a gun.
Summary/Advisory: A real downer. This band celebrates pain and misery as a sign of artistic status. The dark side of existence is their promised land. Rotten to the *Core*.

Strait, George

◆ ◆ ◆ ◆ ◆ ◆ ◆ ◆ ◆ ◆ ◆ ◆ ◆ ◆ ◆ ◆ ◆ ◆ ◆

Since 1981, George Strait has consistently been on top of the country music charts. He has accumulated more than two dozen number-1 singles, 10 gold albums and 4 platinum discs. Credited with bringing the "hat fad" back into country music and reviving western swing, Strait tried his hand at film acting in 1993 with *Pure Country*, a movie about a troubled western singing star.

Title: *Carrying Your Love with Me* (1997)
Label: MCA
Genre: Country
Pro-Social Content: Movin' with "the good Lord's speed," Strait reflects on his woman's love for him as he travels ("Carrying Your Love with Me"). On "The Nerve," he considers how his family tree grew as the result of men from generation to generation courageously courting women. Suffering the pain of divorce, a man goes directly to a church to pray for God's help on a remake of Vern Gosdin's 1983 hit, "Today My World Slipped Away."
Objectionable Content: An uncommitted couple shares "love all night" in a series of rendezvous (the chart-topping "One Night at a Time"). On "Won't You Come Home (And Talk to a Stranger)," Strait plays the role of a married man prone to drinking with the boys and flirting with "every woman in town."

Summary/Advisory: Musically, this award-winning crooner hasn't changed much since breaking into the biz in '81. Same Texas twang. Same fiddles and pedal steel guitar. And lyrically, he still has some good things to say but proceeds to taint those sentiments with a few songs steeped in a fast-lovin', honky-tonk livin' mentality. So much for the Strait and narrow.

Title: *Lead On* (1994)
Label: MCA
Genre: Country
Pro-Social Content: "The Big One" is an upbeat look at falling in love ("On the Richter Scale of romance, you hit a twelve"). Two songs, "Lead On" and "Nobody Has to Get Hurt," seek to restore broken relationships. The latter song finds Strait accepting the blame and asking for forgiveness. A man recalls a vow of faithfulness on "I'll Always Be Loving You" ("I made a promise long ago and it still stands").
Objectionable Content: Alcohol pours freely on "I Met a Friend of Yours Today."
Summary/Advisory: Strait delivers what fans have come to expect—a blend of romance, pedal steel country blues, and the standard bouncy tune with a hummable hook. With the one noted exception, a positive pick.

Title: *Easy Come, Easy Go* (1993)
Label: MCA
Genre: Country
Pro-Social Content: "We Must Be Loving Right" and "The Man in Love with You" celebrate long-term commitment. A married man rejects the advances of another woman on "Stay Out of My Arms" ("Stop now while there's still strength to see . . . turn your eyes and run away from me").
Objectionable Content: A love returns to the honky-tonk atmosphere she had left behind where "the wine flows free" ("That's Where My Baby Feels at Home").
Summary/Advisory: Several tunes mourn lost love in the country tradition, but the album is nicely balanced by songs that offer a sense of hope for enduring love against all odds. Overall, a solid pick.

Title: *Pure Country* (1992)
Label: MCA
Genre: Country
Pro-Social Content: "Heartland" promotes a solid work ethic and traditional values in a place where folks "still know wrong from right" and

"simple people livin' side by side still wave to their neighbor as they're driving by." Men are encouraged to show their love in a tender, tangible way on "Baby Your Baby." "I Cross My Heart" is a commitment to unconditional love.

Objectionable Content: The sexually suggestive (though not explicit) "Overnight Male" and "She Lays It All on the Line" aren't clearly sung in the context of marriage.

Summary/Advisory: This soundtrack album is all George Strait—from a generally family-friendly movie that starred the singer in his first dramatic role. Fans will enjoy these songs of devotion, as well as the painfully crooned blues that have become Strait's trademark. There's plenty of pedal steel guitar, but no glorification of alcohol or blatant sexual carousing. A positive pick that has sold more than 5 million copies. [This album review also appears in the "Soundtrack" section.]

Sublime

◆ ◆

Sublime consists of Brad Nowell (now deceased), Bud Gaugh, Eric Wilson, Mike "Miguel" Happoldt and Marshall Goodman. Nowell died of a heroin overdose on May 26, 1996. Originally recorded for under $1,000, the band's independent debut album, *40 oz. to Freedom,* charted for more than 50 weeks.

Title: *Sublime* (1996)
Label: MCA
Genre: Punk/Reggae
Pro-Social Content: A line on "What I Got" supports giving charitable donations.
Objectionable Content: That same song also mentions "smok[ing] pot" and "hit[ting] the bottle" while the singer spouts the f-word. It's typical of this stickered album. The artist tells of his corrupt relationship with a 12-year-old prostitute who is being sexually exploited by her family ("Wrong Way"). Perverse allusions to sodomy are further aggravated by the comparison of a tavern to a church ("Same in the End"). Other sexually explicit tracks describe outercourse ("Caress Me

Down") and a routine of getting high and masturbating with pornography ("Burritos"). Sick stuff. Elsewhere, life is depressing and meaningless ("Garden Grove") unless the chance arises to pull out a .9mm handgun and shoot a few narcotics officers ("Get Ready"). The violence continues on "Santeria," and the artist boasts of looting conquests during the L.A. riots on "April 29, 1992 (Miami)."

Summary/Advisory: After completing this disc, lead singer Brad Nowell died of a heroin overdose. But that hasn't stopped MTV from making Sublime a huge success with young fans. Don't let teens drink from this stagnant pool.

Sugar Ray

◆ ◆ ◆ ◆ ◆ ◆ ◆ ◆ ◆ ◆ ◆ ◆ ◆ ◆ ◆ ◆ ◆ ◆ ◆ ◆

Mark McGrath, Murphy Karges, Rodney Sheppard, Stan Frazier, and DJ Homicide make up Sugar Ray. Their 1995 Lava/Atlantic debut, *Lemonade and Brownies,* stirred up a hornet's nest of debate about its cover art featuring an unclothed woman in a risqué pose.

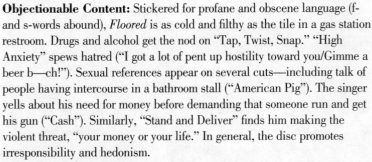

Title: *Floored* (1997)
Label: Lava/Atlantic
Genre: Metal/Punk rock/Rock/Reggae
Pro-Social Content: Individual lyrics value perseverance ("Anyone"), honesty, and motherly advice ("Fly").

Objectionable Content: Stickered for profane and obscene language (f- and s-words abound), *Floored* is as cold and filthy as the tile in a gas station restroom. Drugs and alcohol get the nod on "Tap, Twist, Snap." "High Anxiety" spews hatred ("I got a lot of pent up hostility toward you/Gimme a beer b—ch!"). Sexual references appear on several cuts—including talk of people having intercourse in a bathroom stall ("American Pig"). The singer yells about his need for money before demanding that someone run and get his gun ("Cash"). Similarly, "Stand and Deliver" finds him making the violent threat, "your money or your life." In general, the disc promotes irresponsibility and hedonism.

Summary/Advisory: In the band's press bio, Sugar Ray's Mark McGrath states that his goals in life are to "drink, scream and f—." It shows on this pointless tribute to trashy self-indulgence. Despite incorporating various musical styles, the band keeps singing the same sour note.

Suicidal Tendencies

◆ ◆ ◆ ◆ ◆ ◆ ◆ ◆ ◆ ◆ ◆ ◆ ◆ ◆ ◆ ◆ ◆ ◆ ◆ ◆

This Venice, California, metal band was formed in 1982 by Mike Muir, Rocky George, Mike Clark, and Robert Trujillo. Muir and Trujillo went on to create another group, Infectious Grooves.

Title: *Suicidal for Life* (1994)
Label: Epic
Genre: Punk rock
Pro-Social Content: "Love vs. Loneliness" examines adolescent angst and self-hatred, encouraging self-respect.
Objectionable Content: "Love vs. Loneliness" goes on to exclude God from the healing process, leaving confused teens to find the answers within themselves ("only you can cure the loneliness"). Worse yet, 94 uses of the f-word pepper this stickered disc, with variations appearing in four song *titles.* "Suicyco Muthaf——a" promotes self-destructiveness, stating "If you ain't suicidal, you ain't s——!" On "I Wouldn't Mind," the artist's favorite things include "hearing you scream in pain" and "seeing blood squirting from your veins." Taking unfair advantage of people is the focus of "What You Need's a Friend." "Evil" revels in the twisted inner workings of a reprobate soul.
Summary/Advisory: The closing lyric, "We ain't trying to tell you how to think; we're just trying to get you to think," rings hollow after 49 minutes of perverted preachiness. Muir told *Rip* [6/96], "Hate can be a good thing if you let it . . . and I let it. Hate is to motivation what gasoline is to the engine." Drain the tank.

Sweat, Keith

◆ ◆ ◆ ◆ ◆ ◆ ◆ ◆ ◆ ◆ ◆ ◆ ◆ ◆ ◆ ◆ ◆ ◆ ◆ ◆

Keith Sweat was born in Harlem, New York. He graduated from New York's City College and worked as a brokerage assistant at the New York Stock Exchange before the song "I Want Her" launched his music career in 1987. Sweat's five albums have collectively sold more than 8 million copies.

Title: *Keith Sweat* (1996)
Label: Elektra

Genre: R&B/Rap

Pro-Social Content: On the R&B chart-topper "Twisted," Sweat admits to his lady, "I was downright foolish and stupid." He later vows, "I'll treat you right your whole life long" ("Show Me the Way").

Objectionable Content: Crass sexual proposals abound. Among the less explicit are "I've been wondering, can you satisfy me?/Here we go, bring it on/Let it flow" ("Nature's Rising") and "Drop them clothes so we can clown/Girl your body's mine for the sticking/Let's do it now" ("Funky Dope Lovin'"). Smooth vocals seductively attempt to convince women that they are more than just the spoils in a macho quest for flesh. "Freak With Me" alludes to anal intercourse. "In the Mood" practically diagrams a sexual encounter ("Back and forth, forth and back").

Summary/Advisory: Raunchy sexual braggadocio seems to be Keith's trademark—enough reason for parents to cry "No *Sweat!*" Teens partial to this musical style (which also includes mainstream's New Edition, Jodeci, R. Kelly, and Montell Jordan) should check out the Christ-centered rhythms of LaMore or Take 6. (SEE ALSO: LSG)

SWV

◆ ◆ ◆ ◆ ◆ ◆ ◆ ◆ ◆ ◆ ◆ ◆ ◆ ◆ ◆ ◆ ◆ ◆

SWV is a multiplatinum vocal trio comprised of Cheryl "Codo" Gamble, Tamara "Taj" Johnson, and Leanne "Lelee" Lyons. Their three albums have sold more than 4 million copies. SWV stands for "Sisters With Voices."

Title: *It's About Time* (1993)
Label: RCA
Genre: Pop/Hip-hop
Pro-Social Content: "You're Always on My Mind" and "Weak" are hopeful, dreamy ballads of romantic love.

Objectionable Content: Half of this album dwells on sexual themes, getting explicit at times. On "Downtown," the girls coach a lover to

"put your mouth on me . . . baby move on down." Men are encouraged to be hormonally aggressive on "Give It to Me" and "Anything." Meanwhile, "Blak Pudd'n" is a highly offensive rap duet performed by two sex-starved partners that alludes to oral sex by using various crude metaphors.

Summary/Advisory: SWV's generally pleasing vocal work is spoiled by a foul lyrical aftertaste. Their unhealthy preoccupation with lewd sex wastes considerable talent. Not recommended listening.

Take 6

◆ ◆ ◆ ◆ ◆ ◆ ◆ ◆ ◆ ◆ ◆ ◆ ◆ ◆ ◆ ◆ ◆ ◆ ◆ ◆

This group, signed by Warner Bros. in 1987, has included members Claude McNight, Mark Kibble, Mervyn Warren (later replaced by Joey Kibble), Alvin Chea, Cedric Dent, and David Thomas. Several of their albums have gone either platinum or gold. The group has won eight Grammys and a host of other honors.

Title: *Brothers* (1996)
Label: Warner Bros.
Genre: R&B/Gospel
Pro-Social Content: "Chance of a Lifetime" embraces life as a wellspring of purpose and possibility. The singer vows to care for a dear friend sacrificially on "Don't Let Go," "You Don't Have to Be Afraid," "I'll Be There," and "Can't Stop Thinking 'Bout You" (all could be interpreted from a spiritual perspective, though God is never mentioned). "Delilah" uses the image of a temptress to urge listeners who are "playin' with fire" to cast off habits that will ensnare them. The inspirational "Jesus Makes Me Happy" is a straightforward expression of the joy that comes from knowing Christ.

Objectionable Content: None

Summary/Advisory: This winner of 1998's Grammy for Best Contemporary Soul Gospel Album kicks off with a remake of Earth, Wind & Fire's jubilant 1976 hit "Sing a Song." That track prescribes music as a cure for the blues. It *is* if teens turn to the tunes of Take 6. This sextet is a fun, soulful alternative for fans of Montell Jordan, R. Kelly, Usher, and Jodeci—secular R&B artists whose lyrics are usually far less edifying. *Brothers* is a keeper!

Title: *Join the Band* (1994)
Label: Warner Bros.
Genre: Gospel/Jazz
Pro-Social Content: With strong vocal harmonies, Take 6 builds upbeat rhythms around bold, positive, and often Christ-centered messages. Ray Charles guests on "My Friend," a tribute to brotherly love. "It's Gonna Rain" expresses the need for repentance, while "I've Got Life" reflects the abundant life promised in John 10:10. "Harmony" is a call to racial unity ("Black and white together, we can face all kinds of weather, no storm can sever when we're one family"). This uplifting effort concludes with the prayerful "Lullaby."
Objectionable Content: None
Summary/Advisory: *Join the Band* has sold more than a million copies to date. With this effort, the five-time Grammy winners depart from a cappella exclusivity but remain true to their gospel roots. A wholesome alternative for fans of All-4-One.

Tears for Fears

◆ ◆ ◆ ◆ ◆ ◆ ◆ ◆ ◆ ◆ ◆ ◆ ◆ ◆ ◆ ◆ ◆

The first hit album by Tears for Fears (the British duo of Roland Orzabal and Curt Smith) was *Songs from the Big Chair*. It debuted in 1985 and remained at number 1 for five weeks. By 1992, Smith had left the band.

Title: *Elemental* (1993)
Label: Mercury
Genre: Alternative
Pro-Social Content: Not much. "Cold" acknowledges that love requires work (although the singer is unwilling to put forth the effort).
Objectionable Content: "Power" speaks of "sacrific[ing] the Virgin white/Her death will be the life of me." Antireligious sentiment appears

throughout. The title cut asks (apparently in the context of seduction) if the girl has lost her faith in God and if her conscience gets her down, claiming "it's all in the mind." Another song promotes New Age theology with references to a "force" and praying to a "power," though clearly not God. "Brian Wilson Said" devalues women ("girls are ten a penny"), while "Cold" wallows in loneliness and self-pity ("I don't long to belong").

Summary/Advisory: More nihilistic noise with virtually no redeeming value. Lots of dark questions, but no answers. Direct young fans to a solid alternative from the Christian band The Choir.

10,000 Maniacs

◆ ◆ ◆ ◆ ◆ ◆ ◆ ◆ ◆ ◆ ◆ ◆ ◆ ◆ ◆ ◆ ◆ ◆ ◆

This quintet from Jamestown, New York, includes Natalie Merchant, Dennis Drew, Robert Buck, Steven Gustafson, and Jerome Augustyniak. In 1993, Merchant left the group to embark on a solo career.

Title: *Our Time in Eden* (1992)
Label: Elektra
Genre: Alternative folk
Pro-Social Content: "These Are the Days" is an inspirational tune that speaks of being "blessed" with life and all the potential it holds. Making peace with yesterday and "building a future" are themes on "Few and Far Between." Wrought with symbolism, "Eden" encourages us to love one another and see the good in people.
Objectionable Content: "Candy Everybody Wants" tolerates worldliness ("If lust and hate is the candy . . . give 'em what they want"). On "Jezebel," parents who regret ever marrying talk to their child about an impending divorce.
Summary/Advisory: The group's mellow rock sound and poetic lyrics leave a generally positive, if somewhat ambiguous, impression. (SEE ALSO: Merchant, Natalie)

Third Eye Blind

◆ ◆ ◆ ◆ ◆ ◆ ◆ ◆ ◆ ◆ ◆ ◆ ◆ ◆ ◆ ◆ ◆ ◆ ◆

This band, formed in 1994, consists of Stephan Jenkins, Kevin Cadogan, Arion Salazar, and Brad Hargreaves.

Title: *Third Eye Blind* (1997)
Label: Elektra
Genre: Rock/Alternative
Pro-Social Content: Positive themes include overcoming past pain ("Jumper") and supporting others as they endure hard times ("Good for You").

Objectionable Content: A partially veiled celebration of oral sex and amphetamine use is central to the Top-10 single "Semi-Charmed Life." "Thanks a Lot" shows disrespect for the parents of a girl the singer likes for "all the dirty things" she likes to do. Alcohol numbs angst on "Narcolepsy" and "God of Wine." "Losing a Whole Year" finds the artist spending "the whole d—ned day in bed" with his girlfriend, who takes Prozac and wants "to try a life of sin" with "pierced queer teens in Cyberspace." Sex and the suggestion that there are "people Jesus couldn't save" mar "I Want You."

Summary/Advisory: This Frisco-based band falls prey to self-destructive hedonism and grim fascinations. Stephan Jenkins told *Entertainment Weekly* [9/19/97] that he considers it funny that people have embraced "Semi-Charmed Life," a song "about snorting speed and [oral sex]." A few bright spots, but most of the project's 14 tracks are trouble. Don't let teens be led by the *Blind*.

311

◆ ◆ ◆ ◆ ◆ ◆ ◆ ◆ ◆ ◆ ◆ ◆ ◆ ◆ ◆ ◆ ◆ ◆ ◆ ◆

Members of this quintet include Nicholas Hexum, Timothy Mahoney, Aaron Charles Wills, Douglas Vincent Martinez, and Chad Sexton. The group has headlined for both the Warped and H.O.R.D.E. tours and performed on *Late Night with Conan O'Brien*. The band's self-titled album has sold more than 2 million copies.

Title: *Transistor* (1997)
Label: Capricorn
Genre: Rock/Rap/Reggae
Pro-Social Content: The singer asks a friend to stick close through hard times ("Jupiter"). Isolated lines on otherwise disturbing tunes call for love and unity.

Objectionable Content: Listeners will find themselves machine-gunned by obscenities, including the f-word. "Beautiful Disaster" states that "people really suck," and that many of them deserve "the axing." The theory of evolution is presented as fact ("Electricity"). Consistent with the

band's campaign to legalize marijuana, "Starshines," "Stealing Happy
Hours," and "Tune In" glorify pot-smoking. At least seven tracks promote a
warped, pantheistic worldview couched in cosmic consciousness.
Summary/Advisory: 311 lead vocalist Nicholas Hexum asserts, "We try
to talk about positive things." Don't buy it. Though these guys may see
themselves as anti-angst crusaders, abusive language, drug use, and sus-
pect theology overshadow any pro-social messages. Teens should tune out
Transistor's offensive static.

Title: *311* (1995)
Label: Capricorn
Genre: Rap/Metal/Hip-hop
Pro-Social Content: Isolated lines denounce consuming heroin, cocaine,
and Jim Beam.
Objectionable Content: These vocal supporters of NORML (the
National Organization for the Reform of Marijuana Laws) glorify pot-
smoking and hallucinogenic mushroom trips on "Brodels" and "Loco,"
respectively. The singer shouts the f-word and presents reincarnation as
fact on "Random," while describing himself as a "rude boy . . . sick as a
porno flick." His ability to "wiggle jiggle" is likened to "a huge sperm" on
the crude "Hive." The boys justify violence in cases where a person is
pushed too far ("DLMD," "T&P Combo"). Obscenities and vulgarities
abound.
Summary/Advisory: *311* blends elements of rap and metal for a sound
and attitude similar to The Beastie Boys, Rage Against the Machine, and
Red Hot Chili Peppers. The band's name comes from a police code for
indecent exposure, appropriate since young fans of this profane nonsense
will be exposed to various forms of indecency. It's a musical frat party—
pointless and puerile.

TLC

◆ ◆ ◆ ◆ ◆ ◆ ◆ ◆ ◆ ◆ ◆ ◆ ◆ ◆ ◆ ◆ ◆ ◆ ◆ ◆

TLC is a female rap group from Atlanta, Georgia (Tionne "T-Boz" Watkins,
Lisa "Left Eye" Lopes, Rozonda "Chilli" Thomas). Even though the trio's
two albums have sold in excess of 14 million copies, the group filed for
bankruptcy in 1995.

Title: *CrazySexyCool* (1994)

Label: LaFace/Arista
Genre: Rap/Hip-hop
Pro-Social Content: "Case of the Fake People" bids farewell to "back-stabbers." The tragic consequences of AIDS, cocaine use, and urban violence are described on "Waterfalls."
Objectionable Content: Sex, sex, and more sex. The number-one R&B smash "Creep" excuses promiscuity as a way of meeting the needs of "affection" and "attention." "Switch" advises, "If your man starts actin' up, switch and take his friend." Other tracks are of the basic "urge to merge" variety ("Kick Your Game," "Red Light Special," "Let's Do It Again," "Take Our Time"). A prank phone call combines phone sex  with bathroom humor on "Sexy." Profanity appears on "Sumthin' Wicked This Way Comes," which despairingly admits, "Sometimes I feel like there's nothing to live for."
Summary/Advisory: In 1992, TLC turned condoms into a fashion statement. On *CrazySexyCool*, the trio proves only that female rappers can succumb to the same erotic filth as their rutting male peers.

Tonic

◆ ◆

Los Angeles-based Tonic is comprised of Emerson Hart, Jeff Russo, Dan Lavery, and Kevin Shepard. The group has performed on NBC's *Late Night with Conan O'Brien* and toured with The Verve Pipe.

Title: *Lemon Parade* (1997)
Label: Polydor
Genre: Rock
Pro-Social Content: The singer differentiates between one woman's true love for him and another's lies and manipulations ("If You Could Only See"). People are encouraged to wait out life's trials ("Open Up Your Eyes") or to forget them and press on ("Soldier's Daughter"). On "Thick," the artist offers his love to a girl stinging from the

hurts of the world. Similarly, the title track finds him empathizing with a woman who, as a child, was forced to endure the scorn and ridicule of her peers ("I would have kept you underneath my wing/I would protect you from everything"). An Irish immigrant, lead vocalist Emerson Hart ponders the merging of his two cultures ("Celtic Aggression").

Objectionable Content: Though it is implied that he ultimately resists temptation, a man battles lust on "Mountain."

Summary/Advisory: Some lyrics are a bit obscure, but there's a lot to like about *Lemon Parade:* Selflessness. Commitment. Keeping things in perspective. For fans of Counting Crows and other acoustic guitar-driven rock/pop, Tonic may be the perfect musical elixir.

Tony! Toni! Toné!

◆ ◆ ◆ ◆ ◆ ◆ ◆ ◆ ◆ ◆ ◆ ◆ ◆ ◆ ◆ ◆ ◆ ◆ ◆ ◆

Comprised of brothers Dwayne and Raphael Wiggins, with cousin Timothy Christian, this R&B/funk trio's first Top-40 album, *The Revival,* was released in 1990.

Title: *Sons of Soul* (1993)
Label: Wing/Mercury
Genre: Hip-hop/Soul
Pro-Social Content: Very little. "Anniversary" recognizes the special days a couple shares as part of their life together.

Objectionable Content: On "I Couldn't Keep It to Myself," the singer not only recounts his sexual experience but also the compulsion to tell his friends about it. Another song ("Lay Your Head on My Pillow") likens sex to treasure and genitalia to pearls. A hormonally controlled boy tries to convince his girlfriend to defy her parents and live with him on "Leavin'" ("You know how it feels when we're alone; you blow me like a saxophone"). Women are referred to as whores and treated as sexual playthings.

Summary/Advisory: Yet another attempt by a pack of lustful urbanites to convince teens that sex is a commodity to be worshiped. Deceptively smooth vocals sugarcoat lyrics that can only lead to a distorted view of sex.

Too Short

◆ ◆ ◆ ◆ ◆ ◆ ◆ ◆ ◆ ◆ ◆ ◆ ◆ ◆ ◆ ◆ ◆ ◆ ◆ ◆

Rapper Todd Shaw was born in Los Angeles, California, in 1966. His stage name refers to his modest height of 5'7". Too Short has scored five platinum records since making the R&B scene in 1989.

Title: *Cocktails* (1995)
Label: Jive
Genre: Rap
Pro-Social Content: "Thangs Change" decries society's slide into the sewer since the 1950s.
Objectionable Content: Meanwhile, the rest of this disc *dwell*s in the sewer. Amid enough hateful profanity to earn it a warning label, *Cocktails* is mysogynistic from cover to core. Numerous tracks boast about the sexual domination of "b—ches" and "hos" ("Don't F— for Free," "Paystyle," "We Do This," "Coming Up $hort," "Giving Up the Funk"). Forced oral sex appears on the title cut, among others. Alcohol and drug use—from pot to angel dust—is glorified on "Top Down," "We Do This," and "Ain't Nothing Like Pimpin'." It also advocates gangsta violence and murderous threats against police.
Summary/Advisory: Obscene, insulting sleaze that arrogantly degrades women (including the CD cover). On "Thangs Change," Too Short admits, "If this was 1950, do you think I'd sell?/No, they'd probably throw me straight in jail." Hmmmm.

Title: *Get In Where You Fit In* (1993)
Label: Jive
Genre: Rap
Pro-Social Content: None
Objectionable Content: This thoroughly corrupt record promotes the use of marijuana, cocaine, alcohol, and various forms of pornography. It also advocates violent behavior and abortion. Women exist strictly as perverse playthings for men to abuse emotionally and physically ("b—ch tried to front me for f—in' her cousin, I took one step back and went straight to her jaw"). "Money in the Ghetto" recommends getting ahead by selling drugs rather than by earning a degree. Explicit lyrics abound.
Summary/Advisory: That someone would produce such irresponsible, offensive trash is amazing. That this record achieved best-selling status (it hit number 1) is a sad commentary on our culture's demand for it.

Tool

◆ ◆ ◆ ◆ ◆ ◆ ◆ ◆ ◆ ◆ ◆ ◆ ◆ ◆ ◆ ◆ ◆ ◆ ◆

Formed in 1990, Tool consists of Danny Carey,
Maynard James Keenan, Adam Jones, and Justin
Chancellor. The band, which owes much of its
commercial success to the Lollapalooza music
festival, picked up a Grammy for Best Metal
Performance for work on *Ænima*.

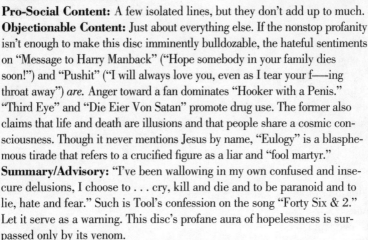

Title: *Ænima* (1996)
Label: Zoo/Volcano Entertainment
Genre: Alternative metal
Pro-Social Content: A few isolated lines, but they don't add up to much.
Objectionable Content: Just about everything else. If the nonstop profanity
isn't enough to make this disc imminently bulldozable, the hateful sentiments
on "Message to Harry Manback" ("Hope somebody in your family dies
soon!") and "Pushit" ("I will always love you, even as I tear your f——ing
throat away") *are.* Anger toward a fan dominates "Hooker with a Penis."
"Third Eye" and "Die Eier Von Satan" promote drug use. The former also
claims that life and death are illusions and that people share a cosmic consciousness. Though it never mentions Jesus by name, "Eulogy" is a blasphemous tirade that refers to a crucified figure as a liar and "fool martyr."
Summary/Advisory: "I've been wallowing in my own confused and insecure delusions, I choose to . . . cry, kill and die and to be paranoid and to
lie, hate and fear." Such is Tool's confession on the song "Forty Six & 2."
Let it serve as a warning. This disc's profane aura of hopelessness is surpassed only by its venom.

Tractors, The

◆ ◆ ◆ ◆ ◆ ◆ ◆ ◆ ◆ ◆ ◆ ◆ ◆ ◆ ◆ ◆ ◆ ◆ ◆

A country/rock band from Tulsa, Oklahoma, The Tractors are driven by
Steve Ripley, Walt Richmond, Ron Getman, Casey Van Beek, and Jamie
Oldaker. Their two albums have sold more than 2 million copies.

Title: *The Tractors* (1994)
Label: Arista
Genre: Country blues

Pro-Social Content: The working class gets its due on "The Little Man."
A number of fun, neutral tunes ("Badly Bent," "Tryin' to Get to New
Orleans," "The Blue Collar Rock") celebrate
rural life with a refreshingly unique cajun/blues
musical style.

Objectionable Content: Innuendo suggesting a sexual proposition appears on "Baby
Likes to Rock It," which showcases a "go-go
dancer busy showin' off her chest." A man
longs for sex on "Fallin' Apart." "Doreen"
is a tribute to a teasing 17-year-old who wears tight
jeans and sweaters. The artist enlists a Gypsy woman to cast a
voodoo spell ("Thirty Days").

Summary/Advisory: A high-energy collection that's musically enjoyable.
It's too bad The Tractors's talent gets plowed under by a handful of sexually
charged themes.

Travis, Randy

◆ ◆ ◆ ◆ ◆ ◆ ◆ ◆ ◆ ◆ ◆ ◆ ◆ ◆ ◆ ◆ ◆ ◆ ◆ ◆

Travis (born Randy Bruce Traywick) hails from North Carolina. He started
singing at age 10 and moved to Nashville in 1981, but it wasn't until 1985
that his career really took off. Travis was embraced by the Grand Ole Opry
in 1986, the year he won the Country Music Association's Horizon Award.
In '87 and '88, he was voted Male Vocalist of the Year. In the mid-'90s he
caught the acting bug, with appearances on television's
Evening Shade and *Touched by an Angel*.

Title: *This Is Me* (1994)
Label: Warner Bros.
Genre: Country
Pro-Social Content: "Before You Kill Us
All" humorously conveys relational repentance
as everything in the house is dying without the
woman he loves ("I know I had it comin' and it's
all my fault . . . baby, come back before you kill
us all"). On a remake of the O'Kanes's "Gonna Walk That Line," a man
expresses his romantic commitment and a desire to settle down. The bouncy
"Small Y'all" warns couples to control their tempers and tongues when

resolving conflict ("The neighbors all know that you're at it again, and two little kids just a few feet away hear every word that you say"). Rummaging through his dead father's mementos, a son sees the softer side of a man who was never able to express his love ("The Box"). The title cut pledges unconditional support to a romantic partner.

Objectionable Content: Minor. Although there's not a single mention of alcohol, "Honky Tonk Side of Town" prescribes a barroom jukebox as the cure for the blues.

Summary/Advisory: Travis's rich, earnest baritone is in top form here and is perfectly matched to these wholesome, traditional themes. Overall, a positive choice for young fans.

Tribe Called Quest, A

◆ ◆

The Queens, New York-based A Tribe Called Quest consists of rappers Q-Tip, Ali Shaheed Muhammad, and Phife. Their first album was released in 1990 and sold more than 500,000 units. Their next two CDs both went platinum.

Title: *Beats, Rhymes and Life* (1996)
Label: Jive
Genre: Rap
Pro-Social Content: "Keeping It Moving" admits that R&B music "doesn't tell you how to raise a child or treat a wife."
Objectionable Content: Morally bankrupt, "The Hop" raps about getting high, beating a man and leaving him for dead, committing arson, and making lewd sexual advances to women. Tracks give an approving nod to alcohol and marijuana use ("Jam," "Motivators") while promoting casual sex ("Jam"). Violent threats spew forth with no regard to consequences on "1nce Again" ("Tonight we gettin' off like O.J. [Simpson]"). Gun shots ring out after the rapper catches his wife having sex with another man ("Crew"). Despite the absence of a warning sticker, the f-word and other obscenities punctuate numerous songs.

Summary/Advisory: The Tribe promotes itself as a "positive" alternative to raunchy gangsta rappers such as Nas, Snoop, and 2Pac. Don't believe it. Foul language, sex, drugs, and braggadocio put this trio in the same miserable class.

Twain, Shania

◆ ◆ ◆ ◆ ◆ ◆ ◆ ◆ ◆ ◆ ◆ ◆ ◆ ◆ ◆ ◆ ◆ ◆ ◆ ◆

The second oldest of five children, this Timmins, Ontario, native was drawn to music at a very early age. After Twain's parents were tragically killed in an automobile crash when she was 21, she found herself singing at a resort to support her teenage siblings. She eventually landed a recording contract and married music producer Jeff "Mutt" Lange (Def Leppard, The Cars, Foreigner). Twain's last two albums have combined for sales exceeding 15 million copies.

Title: *Come on Over* (1997)
Label: Mercury
Genre: Country
Pro-Social Content: Through thick and thin, Twain swears devotion to her man on "From This Moment On," a duet with Bryan White. "Black Eyes, Blue Tears" decries domestic violence, promising better days for women who refuse to remain victims. A guide to winning a woman's heart includes listening, friendship, giving, and tenderness ("If You Wanna Touch Her, Ask"). The title track tells listeners, "Be happy to be who you are." Other love songs are just giddy fun.
Objectionable Content: A profanity punctuates the sarcastically bossy role-reversal "Honey I'm Home." Twain longs to "go totally crazy" and "forget I'm a lady" during a night on the town ("Man! I Feel Like a Woman"). The "lovemaking" on "You've Got a Way" lacks marital context. An isolated line equates a good time with an alcohol buzz.
Summary/Advisory: Catchy country hooks make this ample disc (16 songs) an upbeat follow-up to Twain's 10-million-selling *The Woman in Me*. Lyrically, she's moving in the right direction but still has a few rough edges.

Title: *The Woman in Me* (1995)
Label: Mercury
Genre: Country
Pro-Social Content: "Is There Life After Love?" expresses a belief in "angels in heaven and God up above" as Twain repents for doing her man wrong. She asks the Lord to help suffering humanity on "God Bless the

Child." "(If You're Not in It for Love) I'm Outta Here" finds a woman rejecting offers for a one-night stand.

Objectionable Content: The song also implies that hanging out in bars— and giving in sexually to a *sincere* man—are okay. "Whose Bed Have Your Boots Been Under?" casually requests information about one affair while it reels off a list of past offenses. The best-selling country single "Any Man of Mine" presents a relational double standard.

Summary/Advisory: More than *10 million* sold—a very warm reception for this artist, who seemed to come out of nowhere with *The Woman in Me*. Musically, her foot-stompin' honky-tonk style and pedal steel blues have appeal, but Twain dwells on tales of unfaithfulness and heartache without much to counter the downer. Also, sexual ethics lack clarity.

2Pac

◆━◆━◆━◆━◆━◆━◆━◆━◆━◆━◆━◆━◆

(SEE: Shakur, Tupac)

UB40

◆━◆━◆━◆━◆━◆━◆━◆━◆━◆━◆━◆━◆

UB40 stands for Unemployment Benefits, form 40. This interracial reggae octet from Britain was formed in 1978.

Title: *Promises and Lies* (1993)
Label: Virgin
Genre: Reggae
Pro-Social Content: There's an emphasis on serving, blessing, and relieving the suffering of others on "C'est La Vie," "It's a Long, Long Way" and "Desert Sand." The band expresses its love and devotion to one another on "Reggae Music." "Bring Me Your Cup" is a song of romantic love.

Objectionable Content: Several tunes take a pessimistic view of life ("Promises and Lies," "Now and Then," and "Things Ain't Like They Used to Be"), treating the world's problems as insurmountable obstacles.

"Sorry" coldly refuses to accept a mere apology from non-blacks for slavery in England, demanding retribution and "400 years back pay" ("No value in your talking; money speaks and bulls——'s walking").

Summary/Advisory: The synthetic reggae sound of UB40 contains some positive messages. Unfortunately, they are tainted by a handful of less desirable tracks.

Usher

◆ ◆ ◆ ◆ ◆ ◆ ◆ ◆ ◆ ◆ ◆ ◆ ◆ ◆ ◆ ◆ ◆ ◆ ◆

This teenage artist first surfaced in 1994. Managed by his mother, Jonetta Patton (who was also his childhood choir director), Usher went on to record a national Christmas jingle for Coca-Cola in 1995. He has performed during the American Music Awards, presented at the Grammys, and appeared on *Oprah*.

Title: *My Way* (1997)
Label: LaFace
Genre: Hip-hop/R&B
Pro-Social Content: "You Make Me Wanna" suggests that the finest romance occurs between "best friends."
Objectionable Content: A duet with raunchy female rapper Lil' Kim ("Just Like Me") speaks of oral sex, masturbation, gunplay, and cocaine. Usher boasts to another man that he's having sex with his woman ("[I] make your girl say ooh-ooh/. . . She beeps me whenever she wanna get freaky"). Similar encroachment characterizes "One Day You'll Be Mine," a track that also reinforces the rape myth ("You say you 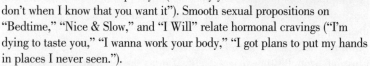 don't when I know that you want it"). Smooth sexual propositions on "Bedtime," "Nice & Slow," and "I Will" relate hormonal cravings ("I'm dying to taste you," "I wanna work your body," "I got plans to put my hands in places I never seen.").

Summary/Advisory: Seductively sleek vocals and pleasant melodies make these libidinous come-ons particularly troublesome. *My Way* went multiplatinum and peaked at number 4, yielding *simultaneous* Top-10 pop hits with "Nice & Slow" and "You Make Me Wanna." But successful or not, families should show Usher the door.

U2

◆ ◆

This group employs Bono (real name Paul Hewson), The Edge (real name Dave Evans), Larry Mullen, and Adam Clayton. The band formed in 1978 when all four Irishmen were still students at Dublin's Mount Temple School. Worldwide, the band has sold more than 69 million copies of its various albums. *Joshua Tree* (1987) sold more than 15 million copies. *Achtung Baby* (1991) sold more than 10 million. U2's 1997 Pop Mart tour ranked as one of the most expensive productions of its kind in concert history.

Title: *Pop* (1997)
Label: Island/Polygram
Genre: Rock/Pop
Pro-Social Content: The band denounces materialism and greed ("Gone," "Last Night on Earth"). Asking his woman "Do You Feel Loved?" a man longs to apply the relational adhesives of love and support. "Discotheque" and "Please" grapple with the concept of love.
Objectionable Content: U2 dreams of visiting Hugh Hefner's hedonistic haven on "Playboy Mansion." Casual acquaintances "get hot in a photo booth" ("Miami"). Spiritual confusion about the character of the Creator undermines "Staring at the Sun" ("God is good, but will He listen?"), "If God Will Send His Angels" ("God has got His phone off the hook, babe/Would He even pick it up if He could?"), and "Wake Up Dead Man," which seems to be a blasphemous address to an impotent Christ ("Jesus . . . I know you're looking out for us, but maybe your hands aren't free"). The latter includes the f-word.
Summary/Advisory: Some fans vehemently defend the notion that U2 is a Christian band. It's time to face reality. During the 1994 Grammy Awards, lead singer Bono announced, "I'd like to give a message to the young people of America. That is, we shall continue to abuse our position and f——up the mainstream." Whose gospel did *that* come from? Don't drink U2's flat *Pop*.

Title: *Zooropa* (1993)
Label: Island
Genre: Rock
Pro-Social Content: The incessant assault on our sensibilities by empty media messages motivates "Numb." Likewise, "Zooropa" refers to those "ridiculous voices" that beckon us to follow status symbols and adopt the values of popular advertising.
Objectionable Content: U2 weaves dark, enigmatic themes throughout. "The First Time" talks of a father (God) who gives the singer keys to a coming kingdom, which he apparently rejects ("But I left by the back door and I threw away the key"). Also, the insert photos contain female nudity.
Summary/Advisory: This confused album is characterized by cryptic soul-searching in the image of the band's last effort, *Achtung Baby*. But instead of offering answers, it merely rehashes the same questions with less sincerity. Just when it appears that U2 is conveying a positive principle (as in "The Wanderer"), the lyrics get lost in a poetic fog that negates or neutralizes the message. Evidently, this hot group *still* hasn't found what it's looking for.

Vandross, Luther

◆ ◆ ◆ ◆ ◆ ◆ ◆ ◆ ◆ ◆ ◆ ◆ ◆ ◆ ◆ ◆ ◆ ◆

Luther Vandross has 12 platinum or double-platinum albums to his credit, as well as a series of awards, including Best R&B Vocal Performance of 1990, 1991, and 1997. Total career album sales exceed 15 million.

Title: *Songs* (1994)
Label: Epic
Genre: Adult contemporary/1970s R&B
Pro-Social Content: A number of these oldie hits by musical predecessors celebrate romantic commitment that lasts a lifetime ("Endless Love," "Always and Forever," "Evergreen"). "Ain't No Stoppin' Us Now" relishes the idea of leaving the past behind and moving forward. In the same vein, "The Impossible Dream" expresses a willingness to fight to make the world a better place.
Objectionable Content: "Love the One You're With" argues for one-night stands. Luther remakes Roberta Flack's "Killing Me Softly" without

changing the gender pronouns, leaving the impression he is "flush with fever" over another man.

Summary/Advisory: Except for these two sour notes, *Songs* is right on key—an enjoyably mellow and predominantly positive disc.

Van Halen

◆ ◆

Named after two of the members, brothers Eddie and Alex, this hard rock band formed in 1974. David Lee Roth was the lead singer until 1985, when he was replaced by Sammy Hagar, who has in turn been replaced by Gary Cherone of Extreme. The first 11 albums by Van Halen have gone at *least* double-platinum. The popularity of *III* should push total career album sales for the band past 50 million copies.

Title: *III* (1998)
Label: Warner Bros.
Genre: Rock
Pro-Social Content: Tracks examine the power of true love ("Once"), satisfaction in a relation-ship ("One I Want"), and the emotional strain of a committed long-distance romance ("From Afar"). "Fire in the Hole" borrows from James 3 as it describes the tongue's ability to cause tremendous damage ("Rudder of a ship which sets the course/Does not the bit bridle the horse?/Great is the forest set by a small flame/Like a tongue on fire, no one can tame"). New lead singer Gary Cherone asserts, "You got to give more than you take" ("Without You"). On "Josephina," a young woman is urged to put the past behind her and move on. "How Many Say I" chides men who fail to meet the needs of their spouses, the homeless, and the hungry.

Objectionable Content: Two stray lines on "Dirty Water Dog" could be interpreted as rejections of Christianity ("I don't wanna find religion" and the astrological inquiry, "What's your sign?").

Summary/Advisory: This Top-5 disc sounds a lot like Van Halen's early arena-rock projects fronted by former lead singer David Lee Roth—but *without* their rebellion and sexuality. A welcome shift. Pained vocals aside, the band's latest guitar-heavy release is lyrically solid.

Title: *Balance* (1995)
Label: Warner Bros.
Genre: Rock
Pro-Social Content: "Can't Stop Lovin' You" and "Not Enough" commit to faithfully loving a romantic partner over time. On "Feelin'," the band urges listeners to "pay attention, watch your back/pay your dues, stay on track" in a fallen culture. . . .
Objectionable Content: This same pessimistic cut offers no hope—especially when weighed against the album's anti-Christian and pro-drug messages. With chanting supplied by Buddhist monks, "The Seventh Seal" misuses religious terminology as sexual double entendre. Prayer and salvation are equated with weakness on the MTV favorite "Don't Tell Me," which implies that "bear[ing] the cross just like Jesus Christ" can include violence and heroin use. "Amsterdam" glorifies getting high on marijuana ("Score me some Panama Red . . . stone you like nothin' else can"). "Big Fat Money" screeches about premature ejaculation.
Summary/Advisory: There's nothing balanced about *Balance*, an unstable project toppled by offensive, irresponsible content. Skip it.

Veruca Salt

◆ ◆ ◆ ◆ ◆ ◆ ◆ ◆ ◆ ◆ ◆ ◆ ◆ ◆ ◆ ◆ ◆ ◆ ◆ ◆

The band Veruca Salt started when Louise Post and Nina Garden met in 1992 and decided to get serious about their music. They added Steve Lack and Stacey Jones several months later.

Title: *American Thighs* (1994)
Label: Minty Fresh/Geffen
Genre: Rock
Pro-Social Content: From a unique vantage point, "All Hail Me" denounces crimes that too often earn the criminals celebrity status. A spirit of forgiveness pervades "Celebrate You." Other tracks ("Wolf," "Fly") share the honest pain of relationships, inviting the listener to identify with—or learn from—those mistakes and the resulting heartache.
Objectionable Content: The battle to control anger would seem unwinnable according to

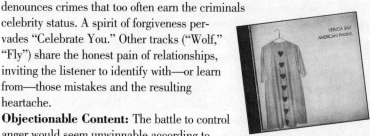

"Seether." A snapshot of childhood abuse appears on "25," with the artist resigning herself to live in its shadow indefinitely ("I'm afraid I will never change").

Summary/Advisory: Melancholy strains. Obscure lyrics. While not explicit or offensive, there's not much optimism here, either. Every member of this act is a product of divorce, possibly explaining why they see the hole instead of the doughnut. But it's doubtful teens will be any better off after tasting Salt's pain-filled worldview.

Verve, The

◆ ◆ ◆ ◆ ◆ ◆ ◆ ◆ ◆ ◆ ◆ ◆ ◆ ◆ ◆ ◆ ◆ ◆ ◆

Hugely popular in Great Britain, this band from Lancashire, England, started out as Verve in 1990 with Richard Ashcroft, Nick McCabe, Simon Jones, and Peter Salisbury. They later added Simon Tong to their ranks and a "The" to their name. The Verve performed as part of the touring Lollapalooza festival in the summer of '94.

Title: *Urban Hymns* (1997)
Label: Virgin
Genre: Rock
Pro-Social Content: Recognizing a lifetime of mistakes, the singer resolves to put the past behind him and "rise into the light" on "This Time." "Catching the Butterfly," "Lucky Man," and "One Day" (which puts an arm around a friend suffering romantic disappointment) are equally optimistic. "Sonnet" prayerfully longs for the day when a special young lady becomes more than just a friend. A distraught woman seeking refuge in medication is told by her boyfriend that "The Drugs Don't Work," and will actually make things worse.

Objectionable Content: However, the boyfriend seems to be contemplating suicide should he lose her ("If heaven calls, I'm coming, too . . . You leave my life, I'm better off dead"). Similarly, "Weeping Willow" alludes to people keeping pills and a gun beneath their pillows—tools to liberate them from their agony. The apparent anti-drug message on "The Drugs Don't Work" falls flat alongside "Come On" and "Velvet Morning," which both talk of taking pills. Also, the vocalist concludes "Come On" by repeating, "This is a big f—— you!" Disappointing.

Summary/Advisory: *Urban Hymns* features some truly inspirational themes. But The Verve swerves. A disturbing detour into obscenities, drugs, and suicide makes this disc inappropriate listening.

Verve Pipe, The

◆ ◆ ◆ ◆ ◆ ◆ ◆ ◆ ◆ ◆ ◆ ◆ ◆ ◆ ◆ ◆ ◆ ◆ ◆ ◆

The Verve Pipe from East Lansing, Michigan, consists of Brad and Brian Vander Ark, Donny Brown, A.J. Dunning, and Doug Corella. *Villains* marks the band's first release on a major label.

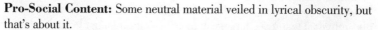

Title: *Villains* (1996)
Label: RCA
Genre: Alternative
Pro-Social Content: Some neutral material veiled in lyrical obscurity, but that's about it.
Objectionable Content: "Cup of Tea" implies that life is dull and hopeless. "Villains" finds the artist lusting over "a pair of blazing thighs" before giving the female in question a thorough ogling. On "Barely (If At All)," the singer announces that he "bought a lover." Casual sex is also suggested on "Ominous Man" ("sleep on the pillow that reeks of another") and "Reverend Girl" ("another lover wakes me up"). Other isolated lines range from the bleak to the bizarre.
Summary/Advisory: *Villains* reflects elements of Live, Bush, and other alternative acts built around muddled musings and musical moping. Obscurity is the rule. While not patently offensive, this disc includes precious little worth piping into teens' systems.

Walker, Clay

◆ ◆ ◆ ◆ ◆ ◆ ◆ ◆ ◆ ◆ ◆ ◆ ◆ ◆ ◆ ◆ ◆ ◆ ◆ ◆

Clay Walker's musical career was launched in 1993. He has sold more than 4 million albums, with platinum certifications for each of his first three Giant discs. He has charted no fewer than seven number-1 singles.

Title: *Rumor Has It* (1997)
Label: Giant

Genre: Country
Pro-Social Content: The title cut basks in the
transparent exuberance of a man in love—and
his knowledge that his affection is returned.
On "I'd Say That's Right," Walker respectfully assures a girl's father of his commitment
to her. "One, Two, I Love You" chronicles a
life of devotion to one lady that began in
preschool. God gets the credit for uniting two very different people ("That's Us"), though the artist realizes his own ability to
"love" and "give" is vital to keeping romance alive ("Watch This"). A
calypso beat undergirds "Then What," a warning to avoid infidelity. Other
songs ("You'll Never Hear the End of It," "Heart Over Head Over Heels")
merrily remind listeners what it feels like to be hopelessly in love.
Objectionable Content: To summon memories of better days, Walker
turns to alcohol ("I Need a Margarita").
Summary/Advisory: With Joe Diffie-style vocals, this brief disc (31-
plus minutes) features simple, catchy tunes with hummable hooks. And
with the one noted exception, there's a lot of truth to this *Rumor*. Good
stuff.

Wallflowers, The

◆ ◆ ◆ ◆ ◆ ◆ ◆ ◆ ◆ ◆ ◆ ◆ ◆ ◆ ◆ ◆ ◆ ◆ ◆

Jakob Dylan (son of Bob Dylan) formed The Wallflowers in 1990. The
band's other four members include Michael Ward, Mario Calire, Greg
Richling, and Rami Jaffee. The Wallflowers were nominated for two
Grammys in 1996 and *won* a pair in 1998 for the hit single "One
Headlight."

Title: *Bringing Down the Horse* (1997)
Label: Interscope
Genre: Rock/Folk

Pro-Social Content: Obscurity is the rule.
Isolated lines speak of faith, honesty, and
other virtues. Despite references to death,
loneliness, and heartache, the band keeps its
chin up with pearls of optimism such as "When
all this night time vision fails, I'll lose all these

chains and slip out of this jail" ("Laughing Out Loud"). The singer extends a hand of friendship for the purpose of mutual healing on "Josephine." He expresses concern for a homeless musician who disappears ("6th Avenue Heartache") and mourns the loss of a friend to cancer ("I Wish I Felt Nothing").

Objectionable Content: The artist becomes infatuated with a girl he first saw "behind the glass at a peep show" ("God Don't Make Lonely Girls").

Summary/Advisory: This band brings to mind the folk rock sounds of Eric Clapton, Bruce Springsteen, and Bruce Hornsby. Not bad lyrically, but in the end, *Horse* is more neutral than positive.

Warren G

◆ ◆ ◆ ◆ ◆ ◆ ◆ ◆ ◆ ◆ ◆ ◆ ◆ ◆ ◆ ◆ ◆ ◆ ◆ ◆

Warren Griffin III was born in Long Beach, Calif., and is the half-brother of rapper Dr. Dre. He has also written, performed and produced for Mista Grimm and Slick Rick. His *Regulate . . . G Funk Era* disc has sold more than 3 million copies.

Title: *Regulate . . . G Funk Era* (1994)
Label: Violator/Ral
Genre: Rap
Pro-Social Content: None
Objectionable Content: Two versions of this disc are littering the streets. On one, portions of offensive words are "dropped out" (though it takes no imagination to fill in the blanks), while the other is disgustingly explicit. Numerous tracks promote indo (marijuana) and alcohol use ("Runnin' wit No Breaks," "So Many Ways," "Gangsta Sermon"). Gangsta-style brutal-ity shows up on "This Is the Shack," "And Ya Don't Stop," "Do You See," and "What's Next." Degrading sexual references are also par for this coarse course.

Summary/Advisory: Run-of-the-mill gangsta garbage. A close friend of Snoop Doggy Dogg, Warren G wallows in the same lyrical swill. Avoid both versions of *Regulate*.

Weezer

◆　◆　◆　◆　◆　◆　◆　◆　◆　◆　◆　◆　◆　◆　◆　◆　◆　◆

Weezer consists of Patrick Wilson, Matt Sharp, Brian Bell, and Rivers
Cuomo. The West Coast band signed with Geffen Records in 1993 and
released their 2 million-selling, self-titled debut one year later.

Title: *Weezer* (1994)
Label: Geffen
Genre: Rock/Alternative
Pro-Social Content: The artist credits "finding
Jesus" as the solution to his dad's alcoholism on
"Say It Ain't So." Despite unattractive physical
attributes that cause friends to poke fun at the
singer's girlfriend, he pledges devotion to her
("I don't care what they say . . . I'm always near"). On "No One Else,"
the artist desires a woman who will remain faithful.
Objectionable Content: "In the Garage" refers approvingly to *Dungeons
& Dragons* and the rock band KISS. A sexual fantasy is replayed in the
artist's mind on "The World Has Turned and Left Me Here." On "Holiday,"
he wants to go "where they speak no word of truth." Beer and blasphemy
open "Undone—The Sweater Song."
Summary/Advisory: A handful of positive themes and neutral tunes can't
revive this disappointing, inconsistent disc. Within two tracks, the band
alludes to Jesus' healing power *and* spews the profanity "g—d—n." *Weezer*
belongs on a respirator, not in teens' music libraries.

White, Bryan

◆　◆　◆　◆　◆　◆　◆　◆　◆　◆　◆　◆　◆　◆　◆　◆　◆　◆

A native of Lawton, Oklahoma, Bryan White was lauded with numerous
awards in 1996 as a promising newcomer to country music. The
singer/songwriter wants "to show people who don't dig country that it's not
all songs about drinking and cheating on your wife" [*TV Guide*, 4/18/98].
White also encourages young fans to persevere academically as part of his
Stay in School campaign.

Title: *The Right Place* (1997)
Label: Asylum

Genre: Country
Pro-Social Content: Several tunes mourn a
loss of female companionship, ranging in
tone from playful procrastination ("Never
Get Around to It") to regretful reflections
("We Could Have Been," "Bad Day to Let
You Go," "Call Me Crazy"). Afraid of losing a
love, a man asks God to follow up His miracles
of giving sight to a blind man and changing
water into wine by healing the romance ("One
More Miracle"). A couple's lifelong love—from childhood to old age—is
chronicled on White's "Tree of Hearts." He credits God with the creation
of a phenomenal female on "What Did I Do (To Deserve You)?" and
celebrates the joy of being in love ("Love Is the Right Place"). Co-written
with Skip Ewing, "Leave My Heart Out of This" shows wisdom as the
singer cautiously waits for a girl to get over a heartache before getting
involved with her.
Objectionable Content: None
Summary/Advisory: On this Top-10 country disc, Bryan White shifts
effortlessly between AC/pop stylings and songs sure to satisfy pedal-steel
purists. Families looking for country music with good-hearted lyrics will
find it in *The Right Place*.

White Zombie

◆ ◆ ◆ ◆ ◆ ◆ ◆ ◆ ◆ ◆ ◆ ◆ ◆ ◆ ◆ ◆ ◆ ◆ ◆

White Zombie came together in 1985 and consists of Rob Zombie, Sean
Yseult, John Tempesta, and Jay Yuenger. In support of their major label
debut, *La Sexorcisto: Devil Music Vol. One*, released in March 1992, the
band toured two and a half years *nonstop*—helping to
push record sales past the million mark. They
have also received a Grammy nomination.

Title: *Astro-Creep: 2000* (1995)
Label: Geffen
Genre: Heavy metal
Pro-Social Content: None
Objectionable Content: Just in case its
numerous uses of the f-word and truly sick lines

illustrations weren't enough to earn it a warning label, this sewage takes every opportunity to slam Christianity and further a satanic agenda. Infuriating. On "I Zombie," the artist calls himself a "kill machine." "Super-Charger Heaven" portrays Jesus as evil and shouts, "inbreed the witches and worship the dogs." Other tracks spew forth more explicitly twisted content—including sex with demons.

Summary/Advisory: The band's press bio says it all: "An album seething with uninhibited imagery of dark obsessions with sex, death and other bizarre, barren landscapes of the human condition. As always, these night-marish visions drip with black humor that sucks listeners deep into the belly of The Beast." Any questions?

Williams, Vanessa

◆ ◆ ◆ ◆ ◆ ◆ ◆ ◆ ◆ ◆ ◆ ◆ ◆ ◆ ◆ ◆ ◆ ◆ ◆

Born in New York to a pair of music teachers, Williams was the first African American to win the Miss America title (in 1983). She was later stripped of her crown when it was dis-covered that she had posed nude in *Penthouse* magazine. The scandal didn't seem to affect her budding career. In addition to hit albums of her own, Williams sang "Colors of the Wind" for Walt Disney's *Pocahontas* soundtrack, earning an Oscar and a Golden Globe in the process. She also costarred with Arnold Schwarzeneggar in the movie *Eraser*.

Title: *The Sweetest Days* (1994)
Label: Mercury
Genre: R&B/Adult contemporary
Pro-Social Content: On "Higher Ground," Williams regrets a period of greed, seeking restoration in the arms of God. The need for relational com-mitment and the strength that results are themes of "You Can't Run" and the title song, respectively. A few tunes are simply light, romantic fare without any offensive elements. "Long Way Home" tells of a bold dreamer who must return to her previous way of life in the wake of failure. Williams encourages her by saying, "It happens to the best of us." "Ellamental" honors jazz legends.
Objectionable Content: "The Way That You Love" is a steamy come-on,

inviting "unspoken pleasure." On "Betcha Never," a jealous woman quickly finds a new lover in an attempt to get even with her man.

Summary/Advisory: The former Miss America has softened her image a bit on this album (her third), which emphasizes smooth, Natalie Cole-style vocals. Still, two disappointing tracks sour *The Sweetest Days.*

Willie D

◆ ◆

Formerly a member of Geto Boys, William James Dennis (Willie D) released his lone solo project, *I'm Goin' Out Like a Soldier,* in 1992.

Title: *I'm Goin' Out Like a Soldier* (1992)
Label: Rap-a-Lot
Genre: Rap
Pro-Social Content: Willie urges youngsters off the streets in "Go Back 2 School." "U Still a N-gga" notes that racial prejudice doesn't end when blacks gain education or status in a community.
Objectionable Content: Plenty. D's message on "School" is thoroughly muddled by a constant flow of vulgarity and by advocating violent crime, as in "Trenchcoats N' Ganksta Hats"— where women and even babies are fair game. On "F— Rodney King," D sides with Los Angeles rioters and calls for Rodney King to be murdered. He also threatens to slap and rape gold-digging "b—ches" and "hoes" ("Little Hooker" and "Yo P—— My D—") and condones smoking marijuana on "Pass Da Piote."
Summary/Advisory: "I'd love to stick the tape in and say, 'Listen to what Daddy did.' But then Hugh Hefner can't show off his magazines to kids, either," Willie D told *USA Today* [6/8/95]. "My fans expect me to be a certain way, and that's what I give them. I have to put food on the table." This former Geto Boy once rapped about having sex with a woman after slitting her throat. Here, ceaseless, explicit references to oral sex, forcible sodomy, and graphic violence make this one entirely out of bounds. Any A+ record library is minus D. (SEE ALSO: Geto Boys)

Wonder, Stevie

◆ ◆

Stevie Wonder, once dubbed the 12-year-old genius because of his musical talent, had his first hit with "Fingertips (Pt. II)" on the Motown label before his teen years. He was born Steveland Morris on May 13, 1950, and was renamed Little Stevie Wonder in 1962. Stevie has won 17 Grammy awards and was inducted into the Rock 'n' Roll Hall of Fame in 1989. In 1998, he recorded "True to Your Heart" for the soundtrack to Disney's *Mulan.*

Title: *Conversation Peace* (1995)
Label: Motown
Genre: Pop/R&B
Pro-Social Content: "Rain Your Love Down" prays for God to cleanse the world of drugs, disease, crime, and pain. The feeling of salvation birthed from true love is compared to "a Christian who's been born again" on "I'm New." "Take Time Out" urges listeners to love and assist the less fortunate. Background vocals on "Treat Myself" borrow from Philippians 4:8. The title cut promotes world-wide unity and love, trusting the one "who gave the ultimate sacrifice."
Objectionable Content: "Cold Chill" describes a woman as "someone to get into" by boys "hot to trot and about to pop." Using crude slang for inter-course, "Edge of Eternity" boasts of sexual prowess. On "Sensuous Whisper," Stevie glories in a woman's ability to "get him hot."
Summary/Advisory: Some solid messages and characteristically smooth vocals, but a few sexually charged hip-hop tracks spoil what could have been a "Wonder"ful return to the charts.

Wreckx-n-Effect

◆ ◆

The rap group was originally composed of Aqil Davidson, Markell Riley, and Brandon Mitchell. Mitchell died in 1990, a victim of gunfire. Riley is the brother of producer Teddy Riley. The group's million-selling *Hard or Smooth* penetrated the pop Top 10.

Title: *Hard or Smooth* (1992)
Label: MCA
Genre: Rap
Pro-Social Content: "New Jack Swing II" objects to "other rappers get[tin'] high to survive." "Tell Me How You Feel" is a clean, respectful love ballad.
Objectionable Content: The million-selling single "Rump Shaker" (which made going "zooma-zoom in the boom boom" famous) rewards posterior motion with something "like a long, sharp sword . . . a surprise that's a back-breaker." Even more potently offensive is "Knock-n-Boots," which makes an explicit, vulgar reference to male body fluids and promotes sex with multiple partners. Several other tracks use profanity, and a few ("New Jack," "Wreckx-n-Effect," "Hard") contain metaphorical threats of violence.
Summary/Advisory: Although produced by the talented Teddy Riley, the material contained in this disc does little to reform rap's less-than-puritanical image. Detour *around* Wreckx.

Wu-Tang Clan

◆ ◆ ◆ ◆ ◆ ◆ ◆ ◆ ◆ ◆ ◆ ◆ ◆ ◆ ◆ ◆ ◆ ◆ ◆ ◆

Wu-Tang Clan was formed in 1992 and consists of nine members: RZA, The Genius (a.k.a. GZA), Ol' Dirty Bastard, Inspector Deck, Chef Raekwon, U-God, Ghost Face Killer, Method Man, and Master Killer. At the 1998 Grammys, Ol' Dirty Bastard (upset that his group wasn't awarded a statuette) jumped on stage, grabbed the microphone, and proceeded to brag about Wu-Tang before security personnel escorted him from the building.

Title: *Wu-Tang Forever* (1997)
Label: Loud/RCA
Genre: Gangsta rap
Pro-Social Content: "A Better Tomorrow" mourns the state of urban life, warning that kids imitate their parents' vices.
Objectionable Content: This song also includes lewd slang with nods to pot-smoking and oral sex.

"Reunited" speaks of drinking vodka, beer, and moonshine while making scores of sexual conquests. "The Projects" glorifies sodomy in graphic fashion. On "Older Gods," the artist boasts of sex with "thousand-dollar lesbians." Violent threats ("I'm going to chop off your arm") and faulty theology ("There's no heaven above . . . no hell below") characterize the raps "Severe Punishment" and "Wu-Revolution," respectively. Numerous cuts promote drug use, and the f-word appears throughout these 27 tracks.

Summary/Advisory: Obscenities, arrogance, materialism, drugs, misogyny, and sexual perversion overwhelm this double disc's few instances of social conscience. It hit number 1 on the pop and R&B charts and sold a whopping 612,000 copies its first week alone. It's a shame, but trash sometimes floats to the top.

Wynonna

◆ ◆

(SEE: Judd, Wynonna)

Yankovic, Weird Al

◆ ◆

"Weird Al" Yankovic's professional stint as a comic began in 1979. He has been nominated for eight Grammys and awarded two. He's also had 14 gold and platinum records in the U.S. and Canada, his own feature film (*UHF*), three best-selling videos, and his own specials on Showtime and MTV.

Title: *Bad Hair Day* (1996)
Label: Rock-n-Roll/Scotti Bros.
Genre: Rock satire
Pro-Social Content: Mild crudities aside, funny parodies include a tribute to Forrest Gump ("Gump"), a caution about making prank telephone calls ("Phony Calls"), an ode to television addiction ("Syndicated Inc."), and a white-knuckle visit to the dentist ("Cavity Search").

Objectionable Content: On "I Remember Larry," the singer reminisces about a friend he killed in retaliation for mean practical jokes. "Amish Paradise" belittles the Amish as prideful, "technologically impaired" hypocrites who live joyless existences, deriving their greatest pleasure from their piety ("I'll be laughing my head off when he's burning in hell"). Kris Kringle is a liquored-up psycho who butchers his reindeer in graphic fashion on "The Night Santa Went Crazy."

Summary/Advisory: What could have been a short-lived, nasal-toned novelty has grown into a multi-album career for Yankovic, an extremely talented pop-culture satirist. But too often this gifted manic strays into areas of questionable taste, as he does on *Bad Hair Day*. Teens should instead comb the CD bins for *Mouth in Motion*, a fun alternative by Christian comedian Mark Lowry.

Yearwood, Trisha

◆ ◆ ◆ ◆ ◆ ◆ ◆ ◆ ◆ ◆ ◆ ◆ ◆ ◆ ◆ ◆ ◆ ◆ ◆ ◆

Country singer Trisha Yearwood was born in Monticello, Georgia, and lent background vocals to Garth Brooks's first album. She appeared on Brooks's 1997 release, *Sevens*, where she performed the Grammy-winning duet "In Another's Eyes." Her own album sales exceed 5 million copies.

Title: *Thinkin' About You* (1995)
Label: MCA
Genre: Country
Pro-Social Content: As an expression of grief, a woman prays in church and weeps "in the arms of Jesus" ("On a Bus to St. Cloud"). "Those Words We Said" points out that a sharp tongue can inflict deep relational wounds. On the title cut, Yearwood makes a romantic late-night phone call to express her affection. Optimism in spite of past disappointments is also a recurring theme ("Fairytale," "Till I Get It Right").

Objectionable Content: "I Wanna Go Too Far" longs to irresponsibly throw caution to the wind. On "The Restless Kind," Yearwood boasts, "I can hold my wine."

Summary/Advisory: Generally positive, but the noted exceptions make it hard to applaud.

Title: *The Song Remembers When* (1993)
Label: MCA
Genre: Country
Pro-Social Content: "I Don't Fall in Love So Easy" explains that real love takes time to develop ("Too strong don't mean it's for too long/Too deep

don't mean it's for keeps/Fast doesn't last"), an encouraging message in a world consumed with one-night stands. Striving to remain committed through hard times is the focus of "Hard Promises to Keep." On the up-tempo love song "If I Ain't Got You," Trisha pays tribute to her man by counting the "things" of life that would be worthless without him.

Objectionable Content: "All you'd have to do is touch me and all my resistance would melt away" indicates the lack of sexual self-control exhibited on "Here Comes Temptation." "One in a Row" describes a woman tolerant of her man's chronic unfaithfulness.

Summary/Advisory: With the noted exceptions, this is a pretty positive collection. An even better option for Christian fans of this style is Andy Landis's CCM album, *Stranger*.

Young, Neil

◆ ◆ ◆ ◆ ◆ ◆ ◆ ◆ ◆ ◆ ◆ ◆ ◆ ◆ ◆ ◆ ◆

Neil Young was born November 12, 1945, in Toronto, Canada. In 1970, he added his name to the successful Crosby, Stills and Nash. As a solo act, Young had only one number-1 hit with "Heart of Gold" (1972), but the release of *Mirror Ball* 23 years later—and concert appearances with Pearl Jam—testify to this veteran's enduring appeal.

Title: *Mirror Ball* (1995)
Label: Reprise
Genre: Rock
Pro-Social Content: Several tracks express love and commitment to friends and family. "Peace and Love" seeks to put mistakes in the past and walk on. "Throw Your Hatred Down" refers to man's "sinful plans" as it condemns ill will toward others and selfish insensitivity.

Objectionable Content: "Song X" suggests that priests exist to administer God's judgment. Amid an erratically flowing stream of consciousness, Young describes himself as a "drug that makes you dream" and expresses a need for "random violence" ("I'm the Ocean"). A party-hearty salute to hippiedom, "Downtown" prompts the listener to visit a place filled with temptations.

Summary/Advisory: Most of Young's messages are mired in lyrical ambiguity. Except for the few positive and negative snapshots noted above, *Mirror Ball* spins largely on the momentum of neutral material and energetic guitar playing.

Conclusion

You Can Impact the Music Industry

Does reading about the lyrical sewage being pumped into our culture frustrate you? It's easy to get fighting mad at a music industry willing to profit from leading our kids astray: The "bad guys." Rock stars who attack Christianity while glamorizing satanism. Rappers who promote gang violence. Record producers and promoters eager to sell teens a damaging set of sexual ethics. Have you ever identified with the vengeful fervor David felt when he prayerfully vented his emotions in Psalm 109? If your disdain has reached a fever pitch, it's worth remembering that Marilyn Manson isn't the *real* enemy. Neither is Korn. It's not the people behind MTV. Sure, their agendas are destructive, and we need to oppose them. But none should be perceived as the enemy. Our *enemy* is Satan.

In Ephesians 6:12, the apostle Paul points out that "our struggle is not against flesh and blood, but against the . . . powers of this dark world and against the spiritual forces of evil in the heavenly realms." That being the case, how should we perceive the immoral pied pipers of pop culture? If Trent Reznor isn't our enemy, what *is* he?

A prisoner of war.

In the midst of an eternal, spiritual battle, our earthly opponents in this civil war of values—from Alanis Morissette to Snoop Doggy Dogg—are themselves captives being manipulated by the ultimate enemy. God loves these people (John 3:16). He longs to see them restored (Ezekiel 33:11). And though it may rub us raw at times, God wants us to share His perspective. After all, Christ was born, crucified, and resurrected for *all* of us.

This book has been published as a tool, a handy reference guide for parents trying to maintain a biblical standard for entertainment in their homes. But let us suggest another use for it: as a *prayer list*. Consider systematically praying for the artists featured on these pages. Instead of wasting energy getting upset about the Spice Girls, intercede on their behalf. Before more rappers are slain by rival gunfire, take the opportunity to pray for them. Only when we perceive our earthly adversaries as Jesus did in Luke 23:34 ("Father, forgive them, for they do not know what they are doing") will we effect the deepest change in our "foes," our children . . . and ourselves.

In addition, you can contact record companies responsible for producing offensive music and express your discontent. Respectfully let them know how you feel. Relate *specifics*. Remember, it's not "censorship" to encourage these people to practice good "citizenship." If label representatives make it sound as if they're at the mercy of artists exercising their First Amendment freedoms, politely point out that you don't object to an artist's right to express himself openly—just their company's decision to give that person a platform, a microphone, and a recording contract. There's no shortage of talented musicians vying for a limited number of record deals. They may need to rethink their standards and back artists with healthier social agendas. Challenges should be firm, but even more important, they should also reflect the love of Christ.

Record Labels

Note: Parent companies are in parentheses.

West Coast Office	*East Coast Office*

A&M
1416 N. La Brea Avenue
Hollywood, CA 90028
(213) 469-2411

825 8th Avenue, 27th Floor
New York, NY 10019
(212) 333-1328

Arista
9975 Santa Monica Blvd.
Beverly Hills, CA 90212
(310) 789-3900

6 West 57th St.
New York, NY 10019
(212) 489-7400

Atlantic
9229 Sunset Blvd.
Los Angeles, CA 90069
(310) 205-7450

1290 Ave. of the Americas, 38th Floor
New York, NY 10104
(212) 707-2000

BMG Music (RCA Records)
8750 Wilshire Blvd.
Beverly Hills, CA 90211
(310) 358-4000

1540 Broadway
New York, NY 10036
(212) 930-4000

Capitol
1750 N. Vine St.
Hollywood, CA 90028
(213) 462-6252

304 Park Avenue South
New York, NY 10010
(212) 253-3000

Chrysalis (Capitol Records)
1750 N. Vine St.
Hollywood, CA 90028
(213) 462-6252

1290 Ave. of the Americas, 35th Floor
New York, NY 10104
(212) 492-5300

Columbia (Sony Music)
2100 Colorado Avenue
Santa Monica, CA 90404
(310) 449-2100

550 Madison Avenue
New York, NY 10022-3211
(212) 833-8000

Curb
3907 W. Alameda Avenue
Burbank, CA 91505
(818) 843-2872

47 Music Square East
Nashville, TN 37203
(615) 321-5080

Def Jam
8981 West Sunset Blvd., Suite 309
West Hollywood, CA 90069
(310) 724-7233

160 Varick St., 12th Floor
New York, NY 10013
(212) 229-5200

EastWest (Elektra)
345 N. Maple Drive, Suite 123
Beverly Hills, CA 90210
(310) 288-3800

75 Rockefeller Plaza
New York, NY 10019
(212) 275-4000

Elektra
345 N. Maple Drive, Suite 123
Beverly Hills, CA 90210
(310) 288-3800

75 Rockefeller Plaza
New York, NY 10019
(212) 275-4000

EMI
8730 Sunset Blvd., Penthouse East
Los Angeles, CA 90069
(310) 652-8078

1290 Ave. of the Americas, 42nd Floor
New York, NY 10104
(212) 492-1200

Epic (Sony Music)
2100 Colorado Blvd.
Santa Monica, CA 90404
(310) 449-2100

550 Madison Avenue
New York, NY 10022
(212) 833-8000

Geffen Records
9130 Sunset Blvd.
Los Angeles, CA 90069
(310) 278-9010

1755 Broadway, 6th Floor
New York, NY 10019
(212) 841-8600

Hollywood (Disney)
500 South Buena Vista St.
Burbank, CA 91521
(818) 560-5670

170 5th Avenue, 9th Floor
New York, NY 10010
(212) 645-2722

Interscope
10900 Wilshire Blvd., Suite 1230
Los Angeles, CA 90024
(310) 208-6547

40 West 57th St., 22nd Floor
New York, NY 10019
(212) 328-5900

Island (Polygram)
8920 Sunset Blvd., 2nd Floor
Los Angeles, CA 90069
(310) 276-4500

825 8th Avenue Worldwide Plaza
New York, NY 10019
(212) 333-8000

Jive (Zomba Records)
9000 Sunset Blvd., Suite 300
West Hollywood, CA 90069
(310) 247-8300

137-139 W. 25th St., 11th Floor
New York, NY 10001
(212) 727-0016

LaFace
8750 Wilshire Blvd., 3rd Floor E
Beverly Hills, CA 90211
(310) 358-4980

3350 Peachtree Rd. NE, Ste. 1500
Atlanta, GA 30326
(404) 848-8050

Mercury (Polygram)
11150 Santa Monica Blvd., Ste. 1000
Los Angeles, CA 90025
(310) 996-7200

825 8th Avenue
New York, NY 10019
(212) 333-8000

MCA
70 Universal City Plaza
Universal City, CA 91608
(818) 777-4000

1755 Broadway
New York, NY 10019
(212) 841-8000

Polygram
11150 Santa Monica Blvd., Ste. 1100
Los Angeles, CA 90025
(310) 996-7200

825 8th Avenue
New York, NY 10019
(212) 333-8000

Priority
6430 Sunset Blvd., Suite 900
Hollywood, CA 90028
(213) 467-0151

32 West 18th St., 12th Floor
New York, NY 10011
(212) 627-8000

RCA
8750 Wilshire Blvd.
Beverly Hills, CA 90211-2713
(310) 358-4000

1540 Broadway
New York, NY 10036
(212) 930-4000

Reprise (Warner Bros.)
3300 Warner Blvd.
Burbank, CA 91505
(818) 846-9090

(Elektra)
75 Rockefeller Plaza
New York, NY 10019
(212) 275-4000

Rush (Def Jam)
8981 West Sunset Blvd., Suite 309
West Hollywood, CA 90069
(310) 724-7233

160 Varick St., 12th Floor
New York, NY 10013
(212) 229-5200

Sire
2034 Broadway
Santa Monica, CA 90404
(310) 828-1033

936 Broadway, 5th Floor
New York, NY 10010
(212) 253-3900

Sony
2100 Colorado Avenue
Santa Monica, CA 90404
(310) 449-2100

550 Madison Avenue
New York, NY 10022
(212) 833-8000

Virgin
338 N. Foothill Rd.
Beverly Hills, CA 90210
(310) 278-1181

304 Park Avenue South, 5th Floor
New York, NY 10010
(212) 253-3100

Warner Bros.

3300 Warner Blvd.

Burbank, CA 91505

(818) 846-9090

75 Rockefeller Plaza

New York, NY 10019

(212) 275-4000

Artist Index

Aaliyah 53
Abdul, Paula 53
Above the Law 54
Ace of Base 55
Aerosmith 56
Alice in Chains 57
All-4-One. 59
Amos, Tori 60
Apple, Fiona 61
Aqua 62
Babyface 63
Backstreet Boys 64
Badu, Erykah 65
Baker, Anita 65
Beastie Boys 66
Beatles, The 67
Beck 69
Bell Biv DeVoe 70
Ben Folds Five 71
Better Than Ezra . . . 71
Black, Clint 72
Blackstreet 73
Blessid Union of Souls . 74
Blige, Mary J 75
Blind Melon 76
Blues Traveler 77
Bolton, Michael 78
Bon Jovi 79
Bone Thugs N
   Harmony 80
Boston 82

Boyz II Men 82
Brandt, Paul 84
Brandy 84
Braxton, Toni 85
Brooks, Garth 86
Brooks & Dunn 88
Brown, Foxy 89
Browne, Jackson . . . 90
Bush 91
Butthole Surfers 92
Cake 93
Campbell, Tevin 93
Candlebox 94
Cardigans, The 95
Carey, Mariah 95
Carlisle, Bob 97
Carpenter, Mary
   Chapin 98
Carter, Deana 99
Chapman, Tracy . . . 100
Chemical Brothers,
   The 101
Chumbawamba . . . 101
Clapton, Eric 102
Cohn, Marc 104
Cole, Natalie 105
Cole, Paula 106
Collective Soul 106
Collins, Phil 108
Colvin, Shawn 109
Connick, Harry Jr. . . 110

Coolio 111
Cooper, Alice 112
Counting Crows . . . 113
Cranberries, The . . 114
Crash Test
   Dummies 116
Creed 117
Crow, Sheryl 118
Cypress Hill 119
Cyrus, Billy Ray . . . 120
Danzig 121
Dave Matthews
   Band 122
Depeche Mode 124
Des'ree 124
Diamond Rio 125
Diffie, Joe 126
Dion, Celine 126
Dogg Pound, Tha . . 128
Dr. Dre 129
Dylan, Bob 130
Eazy-E 131
Enigma 132
Enya 133
Estefan, Gloria 133
Etheridge, Melissa . . 134
Everclear 135
Ewing, Skip 136
Fagen, Donald 136
Foo Fighters 137
Foxworthy, Jeff 138

Fugees 139
Galactic Cowboys . . 140
Garbage 141
Geto Boys 142
Gibson, Debbie . . . 143
Gill, Vince 143
Gin Blossoms 145
Ginuwine 145
God's Property 146
Goo Goo Dolls 147
Grant, Amy 148
Green Day 149
Hammer 150
Hanson 151
Hootie & the
  Blowfish 152
Hornsby, Bruce . . . 153
House of Pain 154
Houston, Whitney . . 155
Howard, Adina 156
H-Town 157
Ice Cube 157
Imbruglia, Natalie . . 158
Indigo Girls 159
Jackson, Alan 160
Jackson, Janet 162
Jagger, Mick 163
Jars of Clay 164
Jewel 164
Jodeci 165
Joel, Billy 166
John, Elton 167
Jordan, Montell . . . 168
Journey 169
Judd, Wynonna . . . 169
K-Ci & JoJo 170
Kelly, R. 171
Kenny G 173
King Missile 173
Kirk Franklin and
  the Family 174

Korn 175
Kriss Kross 176
Lawrence, Tracy . . . 177
Lennox, Annie 178
Lewis, Donna 179
Lil' Kim 180
Live 180
L.L. Cool J 182
Loeb, Lisa 182
Lost Boyz 183
LSG 184
Madonna 185
Manson, Marilyn . . 186
Marcy Playground . . 188
Mase 189
Master P 189
Matchbox 20 190
McBride, Martina . . 191
McCartney, Paul . . 192
McCready, Mindy . . 193
McEntire, Reba . . . 194
McGraw, Tim 195
McKennitt, Loreena. 197
McKnight, Brian . . 197
McLachlan, Sarah . . 198
Meat Loaf 199
Megadeth 200
Mellencamp, John . . 201
Merchant, Natalie . . 202
Metallica 202
Michael, George . . . 204
Mighty Mighty
  Bosstones, The . . 204
Montgomery, John
  Michael 205
Morissette, Alanis . 206
Morrison, Van 207
Nas 208
Naughty By Nature . . 209
Neil, Vince 210
Neville, Aaron 210

New Edition 211
Next 212
Nine Inch Nails . . . 213
Nirvana 214
No Doubt 215
Notorious B.I.G 216
Oasis 217
Offspring, The 218
O'Neal, Shaquille . . 220
Osborne, Joan 220
Overstreet, Paul . . . 221
Pantera 222
Pearl Jam 223
Perry, Steve 225
Petty, Tom 226
Phair, Liz 227
Phish 228
Pink Floyd 228
P.M. Dawn 229
Poison 230
Porno for Pyros 231
Presidents of
  the U.S.A 232
Prince 234
Prodigy 234
Puff Daddy & The
  Family 235
Queensrÿche 236
Radiohead 237
Rage Against the
  Machine 237
Raitt, Bonnie 238
Rancid 239
Raye, Collin 239
Real McCoy 241
Red Hot Chili
  Peppers 241
R.E.M 242
Rimes, LeAnn 243
Robyn 245
Rolling Stones, The . 246

Run-D.M.C. 247
Sade 248
Salt-N-Pepa 249
Sandler, Adam 250
Savage Garden 251
Scarface 251
Seal 252
Selena 253
Seven Mary Three . . 254
Shai 255
Shakur, Tupac 255
Silk 258
Silkk the Shocker. . 259
Silverchair 259
Sister Hazel 261
Slayer. 261
Smash Mouth 262
Smashing
    Pumpkins, The . . 263
Smith, Will. 265
Snoop Doggy Dogg. . 266
Snow 267
Soul Asylum. 268
Soundgarden 269
Soundtracks:
    Anastasia. 270
    Apostle, The 271
    Batman & Robin. . 271
    Batman Forever. . 272
    Blues Brothers
        2000. 272
    Bodyguard, The. . 273
    Crow, The: City of
        Angels 274
    Dangerous Minds . 274
    Evita 275
    Friday 275
    Gridlock'd 276
    Hunchback of Notre
        Dame, The 276
    Jerky Boys, The . . 277

Lion King, The. . . 277
Lost Highway. . . . 278
Men in Black. . . . 278
Mighty Morphin
    Power Rangers . . 279
Mortal Kombat . . 280
Philadelphia 280
Pocahontas 281
Preacher's
    Wife, The 281
Pure Country 282
Romeo + Juliet . . 282
Selena 283
Sleepless in
    Seattle 283
Soul Food 284
Space Jam 284
That Thing
    You Do 285
Titanic. 286
Waiting to
    Exhale 286
Spice Girls 287
Spin Doctors 288
Squirrel Nut
    Zippers 290
Stewart, Rod. 290
Sting. 291
Stone Temple Pilots . 292
Strait, George 294
Sublime 296
Sugar Ray 297
Suicidal Tendencies . 298
Sweat, Keith. 298
SWV 299
Take 6 300
Tears for Fears 301
10,000 Maniacs . . . 302
Third Eye Blind . . . 302
311 303
TLC 304

Tonic 305
Tony! Toni! Toné!. . 306
Too Short 307
Tool 308
Tractors, The 308
Travis, Randy. 309
Tribe Called
    Quest, A 310
Twain, Shania 311
UB40 312
Usher 313
U2 314
Vandross, Luther . . 315
Van Halen 316
Veruca Salt 317
Verve, The 318
Verve Pipe, The . . . 319
Walker, Clay 319
Wallflowers, The . . 320
Warren G 321
Weezer. 322
White, Bryan 322
White Zombie 323
Williams, Vanessa . . 324
Willie D 325
Wonder, Stevie. . . . 326
Wreckx-n-Effect . . 326
Wu-Tang Clan 327
Yankovic, Weird Al . 328
Yearwood, Trisha. . 329
Young, Neil 330

Album Index

A Boy Named Goo—
Goo Goo Dolls............... 147
A Few Small Repairs—
Shawn Colvin 109
*A Lot About Livin' (And a Little 'Bout
Love)*—Alan Jackson 161
A Worm's Life—Crash
Test Dummies............... 116
Ænima—Tool................ 308
Alice in Chains—Alice in Chains .. 57
All Eyez on Me—Tupac Shakur... 257
All-4-One—All-4-One 59
All I Want—Tim McGraw....... 196
American Standard—Seven Mary
Three 254
American Thighs—Veruca Salt... 317
Anastasia—Soundtrack........ 270
And Out Come the Wolves—
Rancid 239
And the Music Speaks—
All-4-One 59
Another Level—Blackstreet....... 73
Another Night—Real McCoy 241
Anthology 1—The Beatles 68
Anthology 2—The Beatles 68
Anthology 3—The Beatles 67
Antichrist Superstar—
Marilyn Manson 186
Anytime—Brian McKnight 198
Apostle, The—Soundtrack....... 271
Aquarium—Aqua 62

Art of War, The—Bone Thugs N
Harmony................... 80
Astro-Creep: 2000—White Zombie .. 323
August & Everything After—
Counting Crows............. 114
Bachelor, The—Ginuwine....... 145
Backstreet Boys—Backstreet Boys... 64
Bad Hair Day—Weird
Al Yankovic 328
Baduizm—Erykah Badu......... 65
Balance—Van Halen 317
Bat Out of Hell II: Back Into Hell—
Meat Loaf 200
Batman & Robin—Soundtrack ... 271
Batman Forever—Soundtrack.... 272
Be Here Now—Oasis.......... 217
Beats, Rhymes and Life—A Tribe
Called Quest................ 310
Bedtime Stories—Madonna...... 186
Before These Crowded Streets—
Dave Matthews Band 122
Behind the Eyes—Amy Grant 148
Big Willie Style—Will Smith 265
Billy Breathes—Phish.......... 228
Black Mafia Life—
Above the Law 54
Black Sunday—Cypress Hill 120
Blessid Union of Souls—Blessid
Union of Souls................ 74
Blind Melon—Blind Melon....... 76
Bliss Album, The—P.M. Dawn ... 230

343

Blue—LeAnn Rimes. 245

Blues Brothers 2000—Soundtrack. . 272

Body Mind Soul—Debbie Gibson. . 143

Bodyguard, The—Whitney
Houston/Soundtrack 155, 273

Book of Secrets, The—
Loreena McKennitt. 197

Borderline—Brooks & Dunn. 88

Both Sides—Phil Collins. 108

Boys for Pele—Tori Amos. 61

Brand New—Salt-N-Pepa. 249

Brandy—Brandy. 84

Breathless—Kenny G 173

Bridge, The—Ace of Base. 55

Bridges to Babylon—The Rolling
Stones 246

Bringing Down the Horse—
The Wallflowers 320

Broken—Nine Inch Nails 214

Brothers—Take 6 300

Butterfly—Mariah Carey. 95

Butterfly Kisses: Shades of Grace—
Bob Carlisle 98

Calm Before the Storm—Paul Brandt. . 84

Candlebox—Candlebox. 94

Carrying Your Love with Me—
George Strait. 294

Charge It 2 Da Game—Silkk the
Shocker. 259

Chronic, The—Dr. Dre 129

Cocktails—Too Short 307

Collective Soul—Collective Soul . . 107

Colour and the Shape, The—
Foo Fighters 137

Colour of My Love, The—
Celine Dion. 128

Come on Over—Shania Twain. . . . 311

Congratulations I'm Sorry—
Gin Blossoms 145

Conversation Peace—
Stevie Wonder. 326

Core—Stone Temple Pilots 294

Cracked Rear View—Hootie & the
Blowfish 153

Crash—Dave Matthews Band 122

CrazySexyCool—TLC 304

Creepin On Ah Come Up—Bone Thugs
N Harmony 81

Cross of Changes, The—
Enigma 132

Crow: City of Angels, The—
Soundtrack 274

Da Bomb—Kris Kross 177

Dangerous Minds—Soundtrack. . . 274

Day, The—Babyface. 63

Daydream—Mariah Carey 96

Definitely Maybe—Oasis. 218

Deluxe—Better Than Ezra 71

Destiny—Gloria Estefan 134

Diary of a Mad Band—Jodeci . . . 166

Did I Shave My Legs for This?—
Deana Carter. 99

Dig Your Own Hole—The Chemical
Brothers 101

Dirt—Alice in Chains. 58

Disciplined Breakdown—
Collective Soul 107

Divine Intervention—Slayer. 261

Division Bell, The—Pink Floyd. . . 229

Do You Wanna Ride?—
Adina Howard. 156

Dogg Food—Tha Dogg Pound . . . 128

Doggfather, Tha—
Snoop Doggy Dogg 266

Doggystyle—Snoop Doggy Dogg. . 267

*Don Killuminati: The 7 Day Theory,
The*—Tupac Shakur 256

Dookie—Green Day 150

Down on the Upside—
Soundgarden. 269

Down with the King—
Run-D.M.C. 247

Downward Spiral, The—Nine Inch
  Nails 213
Dreaming of You—Selena 253
E. 1999 Eternal—Bone Thugs N
  Harmony 81
Easy Come, Easy Go—
  George Strait 295
Electriclarryland—Butthole
  Surfers 92
Elemental—Tears for Fears 301
*Everybody Else Is Doing It, So Why
  Can't We?*—The Cranberries . . . 115
Everything I Love—Alan Jackson . . 160
Everywhere—Tim McGraw 195
Evil Empire—Rage Against the
  Machine 237
Evita—Soundtrack 275
Evolution—Boyz II Men 83
Evolution—Martina McBride 191
Exposed—Vince Neil 210
Extremes—Collin Raye 240
Fairweather Johnson—Hootie & the
  Blowfish 152
Falling Into You—Celine Dion . . . 127
Far Beyond Driven—Pantera 223
Fashion Nugget—Cake 93
Fat of the Land, The—Prodigy . . . 235
Fever for da Flavor—H-Town 157
First Band on the Moon—
  The Cardigans 95
Flaming Pie—Paul McCartney . . . 192
Floored—Sugar Ray 297
Foo Fighters—Foo Fighters 138
For the Love of Strange Medicine—
  Steve Perry 225
Four—Blues Traveler 78
14 Shots to the Dome—L.L. Cool J. . 182
Freak Show—Silverchair 259
Fresh Horses—Garth Brooks 87
Friday—Soundtrack 275
Frogstomp—Silverchair 260

From the Choirgirl Hotel—
  Tori Amos 60
From the Cradle—Eric Clapton . . 103
Funky Headhunter, The—Hammer . 150
Fush Yu Mang—Smash Mouth . . . 262
Games Rednecks Play—
  Jeff Foxworthy 138
Gangsta's Paradise—Coolio 111
Garbage—Garbage 141
Get a Grip—Aerosmith 57
Get In Where You Fit In—
  Too Short 307
Ghetto D—Master P 190
God Shuffled His Feet—Crash Test
  Dummies 116
God's Property—God's Property from
  Kirk Franklin's Nu Nation 146
Gold Experience, The—Prince 234
Good as I Been to You—
  Bob Dylan 130
Good God's Urge—Porno for Pyros . 231
Grand Tour, The—Aaron Neville . . 210
Grave Dancers Union—
  Soul Asylum 268
Great Southern Trendkill, The—
  Pantera 222
Gridlock'd—Soundtrack 276
Happy Hour—King Missile 173
Harbor Lights—Bruce Hornsby . . . 153
Hard or Smooth—
  Wreckx-n-Effect 327
Hard Workin' Man—
  Brooks & Dunn 89
Hardcore—Lil' Kim 180
Harlem World—Mase 189
Head Over Heels—Paula Abdul . . . 53
*Hints, Allegations & Things Left
  Unsaid*—Collective Soul 108
Home—Blessid Union of Souls 74
Home Again—New Edition 211
Hootie Mack—Bell Biv DeVoe 70

Hot—Squirrel Nut Zippers 290

House of Love—Amy Grant 148

House of Pain—House of Pain . . . 154

Human Wheels—
John Mellencamp 201

Hunchback of Notre Dame, The—
Soundtrack 276

I Ain't Movin'—Des'ree 124

I Still Believe in You—Vince Gill . . 144

I Think About You—Collin Raye . . 239

I'm Alive—Jackson Browne 90

I'm Goin' Out Like A Soldier—
Willie D 325

I'm Ready—Tevin Campbell 93

If I Ever Fall in Love—Shai 255

Ill Communication—Beastie Boys . . . 66

Ill Na Na—Foxy Brown 89

In Pieces—Garth Brooks 87

In Utero—Nirvana 214

Insomniac—Green Day 149

It Takes a Thief—Coolio 112

It Was Written—Nas 208

It Won't Be the Last—
Billy Ray Cyrus 120

It's About Time—SWV 299

It's On (Dr. Dre) 187UmKilla—
Eazy-E 131

It's Your Call—Reba McEntire . . . 194

Ixnay on the Hombre—
The Offspring 218

Jagged Little Pill—
Alanis Morissette 206

Janet—Janet Jackson 162

Jar of Flies—Aerosmith 58

Jerky Boys, The—Soundtrack 277

Jesus Wept—P.M. Dawn 229

John Michael Montgomery—John
Michael Montgomery 205

Join the Band—Take 6 301

Kamakiriad—Donald Fagen 136

Keep the Faith—Bon Jovi 79

Keith Sweat—Keith Sweat 298

Kickin' It Up—John Michael
Montgomery 206

Kirk Franklin and the Family—Kirk
Franklin and the Family 175

Last Temptation, The—
Alice Cooper 112

Lead On—George Strait 295

Left of the Middle—
Natalie Imbruglia 158

Legal Drug Money—Lost Boyz . . . 183

Lemon Parade—Tonic 305

Let Your Dim Light Shine—
Soul Asylum 268

Let's Face It—The Mighty Mighty
Bosstones 205

Let's Talk About Love—
Celine Dion 126

Levert.Sweat.Gill—LSG 184

Life After Death—
Notorious B.I.G. 216

Life Is Peachy—Korn 175

Lion King, The—Soundtrack 277

Load—Metallica 203

Longing in Their Hearts—
Bonnie Raitt 238

Lose Control—Silk 258

Lost Highway—Soundtrack 278

Love a Little Stronger—
Diamond Rio 125

Love Always—K-Ci & JoJo 171

Love Deluxe—Sade 248

Machine Fish—Galactic Cowboys . . 140

Made in England—Elton John . . . 167

Marcy Playground—
Marcy Playground 188

Me Against the World—
Tupac Shakur 257

Medusa—Annie Lennox 178

Mellon Collie & the Infinite Sadness—
The Smashing Pumpkins 263

Mellow Gold—Beck 69
Memory of Trees, The—Enya 133
Men in Black—Soundtrack 278
Mercury Falling—Sting 291
Merry Christmas—Mariah Carey. . . 96
Middle of Nowhere—Hanson 152
Mighty Morphin Power Rangers:
  The Movie—Soundtrack 279
Mirror Ball—Neil Young 330
Monster—R.E.M. 243
Mortal Kombat—Soundtrack 280
Much Afraid—Jars of Clay 164
Music Box—Mariah Carey 97
My Life—Mary J. Blige 75
My Own Prison—Creed 117
My Way—Usher 313
Native Tongue—Poison. 230
New Adventures in Hi-Fi—
  R.E.M. 242
New Beginning—Tracy Chapman . . 100
Nine Lives—Aerosmith 56
19 Naughty III—
  Naughty By Nature 209
No Code—Pearl Jam. 224
No Need to Argue—
  The Cranberries 115
No Time to Kill—Clint Black 72
No Way Out—Puff Daddy & The
  Family. 235
Not a Moment Too Soon—
  Tim McGraw. 196
Now in a Minute—Donna Lewis . . 179
Odelay—Beck 69
Off the Ground—Paul
  McCartney 192
OK Computer—Radiohead 237
Older—George Michael 204
One Hot Minute—Red Hot Chili
  Peppers. 241
One in a Million—Aaliyah 53
One Thing, The—Michael Bolton . . 78
Our Time in Eden—
  10,000 Maniacs 302
Philadelphia—Soundtrack 280
Pieces of You—Jewel. 164
Pilgrim—Eric Clapton 102
Pisces Iscariot—The Smashing
  Pumpkins 264
Pocahontas—Soundtrack 281
Pocket Full of Kryptonite—
  Spin Doctors 289
Pop—U2. 314
Porno for Pyros—Porno for Pyros . . 232
Poverty's Paradise—
  Naughty By Nature 209
Preacher's Wife, The—Whitney
  Houston/Soundtrack 155, 281
Predator, The—Ice Cube 157
Presidents of the U.S.A., The—
  Presidents of the U.S.A. 233
Promised Land—Queensrÿche . . . 236
Promises and Lies—UB40. 312
Pure Country—George Strait/
  Soundtrack 282, 295
Purple—Stone Temple Pilots 293
R U Still Down? (Remember Me)—
  Tupac Shakur 256
R. Kelly—R. Kelly 171
Rainy Season, The—Marc Cohn . . 104
Rated Next—Next 212
Ray of Light—Madonna 185
Razorblade Suitcase—Bush. 91
Read My Mind—Reba McEntire. . . 194
Recovering the Satellites—
  Counting Crows. 113
Regulate . . . G Funk Era—
  Warren G 321
Relish—Joan Osborne. 220
Reload—Metallica 202
Resurrection, The—Geto Boys. . . . 142
Revelations—Wynonna Judd. 169
Rhythm of Love—Anita Baker. 66

Right Place, The—Bryan White . . 322

River of Dreams—Billy Joel 167

Robyn Is Here—Robyn 245

Romeo + Juliet—Soundtrack. 282

Rumor Has It—Clay Walker. 319

Savage Garden—Savage Garden. . 251

Score, The—Fugees. 139

Seal—Seal 252

Secret Samadhi—Live. 180

Secrets—Toni Braxton. 85

Selena—Selena/Soundtrack . . 253, 283

Sevens—Garth Brooks. 87

Shaming of the Sun—Indigo Girls. . 159

Shaq Diesel—Shaquille O'Neal. . . 220

Share My World—Mary J. Blige . . . 75

She—Harry Connick Jr. 110

Sheryl Crow—Sheryl Crow 118

Show, The After Party, The Hotel,
The—Jodeci 165

Siamese Dream—
The Smashing Pumpkins. 264

Sign, The—Ace of Base 55

Sittin' on Top of the World—
LeAnn Rimes 244

Sixteen Stone—Bush. 91

Sleepless in Seattle—Soundtrack . . 283

Smash—The Offspring 219

Smells Like Children—
Marilyn Manson 187

Somewhere More Familiar—
Sister Hazel. 261

Song Remembers When, The—
Trisha Yearwood. 329

Songs—Luther Vandross 315

Songs of Faith and Devotion—
Depeche Mode 124

Sons of Soul—Tony! Toni! Toné!. . 306

Soul Food—Soundtrack 284

Space in Your Face—
Galactic Cowboys 141

Space Jam—Soundtrack 284

Sparkle and Fade—Everclear. . . . 135

Spice—Spice Girls 288

Spice World—Spice Girls 287

Stones in the Road—Mary Chapin
Carpenter 98

Straight on Till Morning—Blues
Traveler. 77

Sublime—Sublime 296

Suicidal for Life—
Suicidal Tendencies 298

Superunknown—Soundgarden. . . . 269

Surfacing—Sarah McLachlan. . . . 198

Sweetest Days, The—
Vanessa Williams. 324

Tails—Lisa Loeb 182

Take a Look—Natalie Cole 105

Tell Me Why—Wynonna Judd . . . 170

Ten Summoners' Tales—Sting. . . . 292

Ten Thousand Angels—
Mindy McCready. 193

That Thing You Do—Soundtrack . . 285

They're All Gonna Laugh at You—
Adam Sandler. 250

Thinkin' About You—
Trisha Yearwood. 329

Third Eye Blind—
Third Eye Blind 302

Third Rock from the Sun—
Joe Diffie. 126

This Fire—Paula Cole. 106

This Is How We Do It—
Montell Jordan 168

This Is Me—Randy Travis. 309

Thrall-demonsweatlive—
Danzig. 121

III—Van Halen. 316

III (Temples of Boom)—
Cypress Hill 119

3 Car Garage—Hanson 151

311—311 304

Throwing Copper—Live 181

Tidal—Fiona Apple 61
Tigerlily—Natalie Merchant 202
Time—Paul Overstreet 221
Time Marches On—
Tracy Lawrence. 177
Time Out of Mind—Bob Dylan . . . 130
Timeless (The Classics)—
Michael Bolton 79
Tiny Music . . . Songs from the Vatican
Gift Shop—Stone Temple Pilots . . 293
Titanic—Soundtrack. 286
To the Faithful Departed—
The Cranberries 114
Toni Braxton—Toni Braxton. 86
Too Long in Exile—
Van Morrison 207
Tractors, The—The Tractors 308
Tragic Kingdom—No Doubt. 215
Transistor—311 303
Trial by Fire—Journey 169
Tubthumper—Chumbawamba. . . . 101
Tuesday Night Music Club—
Sheryl Crow. 119
Turn It Upside Down—
Spin Doctors 288
12 Inches of Snow—Snow 267
12 Play—R. Kelly 172
25—Harry Connick Jr. 110
II—Boyz II Men 83
II—Presidents of the U.S.A. 232
Under the Table and Dreaming—
Dave Matthews Band 123
Unplugged—Eric Clapton. 103
Unplugged . . . and Seated—
Rod Stewart. 291
Until I Found You—Skip Ewing. . 136
Urban Hymns—The Verve 318

Velvet Rope, The—Janet Jackson. . 162
Very Necessary—Salt-N-Pepa 249
Villains—The Verve Pipe 319
Vitalogy—Pearl Jam. 224
Voodoo Lounge—
The Rolling Stones 247
Vs.—Pearl Jam 225
Waiting to Exhale—Soundtrack . . 286
Walk On—Boston 82
Wandering Spirit—Mick Jagger . . 163
Weezer—Weezer 322
Welcome to the Neighborhood—
Meat Loaf 199
Whatcha Lookin' 4—
Kirk Franklin and the Family . . . 174
Whatever and Ever Amen—
Ben Folds Five 71
(What's the Story) Morning Glory?—
Oasis. 217
When Love Finds You—Vince Gill. . 144
Whip-smart—Liz Phair 227
Who I Am—Alan Jackson 161
Wildflowers—Tom Petty 226
Woman in Me, The—Shania Twain . 311
World Is Yours, The—Scarface . . . 251
Wu-Tang Forever—
Wu-Tang Clan. 327
Yes I Am—Melissa Etheridge 134
Yield—Pearl Jam 223
You Light Up My Life: Inspirational
Songs—LeAnn Rimes. 244
Young, Rich & Dangerous—
Kris Kross 176
Yourself or Someone Like You—
Matchbox 20 190
Youthanasia—Megadeth. 200
Zooropa—U2 315

About the Authors

As editor of *Plugged In*, **Bob Smithouser** knows well the latest trends in pop culture and how to help parents encourage their children to make sound entertainment choices. He also responds to teens' music questions in "High Voltage," a monthly column featured in both *Brio* and *Breakaway*, Focus on the Family's magazines for teens. Bob holds a masters degree in communication studies from the University of Kentucky.

Formerly a youth pastor and associate editor of *Plugged In*, **Bob Waliszewski** is manager of Focus on the Family's Youth Culture department. He writes and speaks regularly to teens and parents on popular culture, and testified before a California Legislature's subcommittee on the subject of violent lyrics in music. He and his wife, Leesa, reside in Colorado Springs, Colorado, with their two children.

◆　◆　◆

Today's youth culture can make even the most "with it" parent's head spin! That's why Focus on the Family created *Plugged In*, a monthly publication filled with news, reviews and commentary on what's being sung on the latest music releases, and what's now show-ing on both the big and small screens. Best of all, it offers parents enter-taining, uplifting alternatives to build up teens, not tear them down. For more information, contact Focus on the Family at 1-800-A-FAMILY (1-800-232-6459).

More Great Resources for Parents & Teens
From Focus on the Family®

LifeTraining

Help your teens (and the rest of the family!) establish a strong, lasting faith in God. This unique devotional from popular author, speaker, and camp director Dr. Joe White equips parents and kids with tools to strengthen their spiritual foundation. There's even a section devoted entirely to memorization and 100 Bible verses no Christian should leave home without! Hardcover.

No Apologies: The Truth About Life, Love + Sex

Teens get the facts about sex—and how to remain pure—in this exciting new video from Focus on the Family Films. Highlighting abstinence as the only true "safe sex," it's a powerful, hope-filled exposé that delivers an unforgettable message about strength and character, the importance of purity and the risks of promiscuity.

Breakaway and Brio

Encourage young people with gift memberships to *Breakaway* (for teen guys) or *Brio* (for teen girls). They provide a "you can do it" every day of the year! Written and designed by a staff who knows, thinks, and speaks "teen," these exciting monthly magazines are filled with intriguing articles, fascinating stories, uplifting features, and sound advice—all from a biblical perspective. Request one or both, and let Focus on the Family boost the spirit of a teen you love!

• • •

The "Life on the Edge Tour"—Coming Soon to a Community Near You!

Does a day and a half with your teens, learning ways to enhance communication, build your faith and strengthen family unity, sound too good to be true? It's not, and it's exactly what you'll experience at Focus on the Family's "Life on the Edge Tour." Featuring such captivating speakers as Dr. Joe White, *Brio* editor Susie Shellenberger, Miles McPherson, and many others, it's the weekend conference your family will never forget!

Tune Your Teens Into "Life on the Edge LIVE"!

Co-hosted by none other than author, family counselor and teen authority Dr. Joe White, this nationally syndicated live call-in radio show gives teens a safe place to talk about the issues on their minds *and* hearts. Listen along with them and spark conversations you never thought possible!

• • •

For more information or to request any of these resources, simply write to Focus on the Family, Colorado Springs, CO 80995, or call 1-800-A-FAMILY (1-800-232-6459). Friends in Canada may write to Focus on the Family, P.O. Box 9800, Stn. Terminal, Vancouver, B.C. V6B 4G3, or call 1-800-661-9800. Visit our Web site—www.family.org—to learn more about the ministry or to find out if there is a Focus on the Family office in your country.